W9-AGJ-765

What It Means to Be Moral

ALSO BY PHIL ZUCKERMAN

Society Without God
Faith No More
Living the Secular Life
The Nonreligious: Understanding Secular People and Society
(with Luke W. Galen and Frank L. Pasquale)
Invitation to the Sociology of Religion
Strife in the Sanctuary

The Oxford Handbook of Secularism (ed.)
The Social Theory of W. E. B. Du Bois (ed.)

WHAT IT MEANS TO BE MORAL

Why Religion Is Not Necessary for Living an Ethical Life

PHIL ZUCKERMAN

COUNTERPOINT
Berkeley, California

What It Means to Be Moral

First hardcover edition: 2019

Library of Congress Cataloging-in-Publication Data
Names: Zuckerman, Phil, author.
Title: What it means to be moral : why religion is not necessary for living an ethical life / Phil Zuckerman.
Description: Berkeley : Counterpoint Press, 2019.
Identifiers: LCCN 2019004152 | ISBN 9781640092747
Subjects: LCSH: Ethics. | Religion—Controversial literature.
Classification: LCC BJ1031 .Z82 2019 | DDC 170—dc23
LC record available at https://lccn.loc.gov/2019004152

Jacket design by Sarah Brody
Book design by Jordan Koluch

COUNTERPOINT
2560 Ninth Street, Suite 318
Berkeley, CA 94710
www.counterpointpress.com

Printed in the United States of America
Distributed by Publishers Group West

10 9 8 7 6 5 4 3 2 1

CONTENTS

PART THREE: CHALLENGES TO SECULAR MORALITY

INTRODUCTION

In the end, it all came down to God.

Christine Blasey Ford, a professor of psychology, had accused President Trump's Supreme Court nominee Brett Kavanaugh of sexually assaulting her when they were teenagers. The allegations were dire enough to result in the convening of a special Senate Judiciary Committee hearing, held publicly on September 27, 2018.

Dr. Ford's testimony was wrenching. Judge Kavanaugh's denials were forceful. And given the recent national consciousness-raising of the #MeToo movement, and the uncertain balance of the Supreme Court in terms of tilting progressive or conservative for the foreseeable future, as well as an impending midterm election that was predicted to possibly flip the House of Representatives from Republican to Democratic control, the political stakes were about as high as they could get.

The senators had to decide if they would believe the testimony of a woman claiming to have suffered a traumatic sexual assault by Judge Kavanaugh—and thus possibly reject him as a candidate for the Supreme Court—or if they would believe his vehement refutations of those accusations and vote to confirm him as a justice in the highest court of the land.

Both the senators and the country were deeply divided; women were more likely to believe Dr. Ford, while men were more likely to believe Judge Kavanaugh;[1] those on the left were more supportive of Dr. Ford, while those on the right were more supportive of Judge Kavanaugh.

Which side, in this fraught case, held the moral high ground? The Democratic senators surely felt that they were in the right by supporting a woman who courageously stepped forward to speak publicly about a sexual assault she had experienced, while the Republican senators undoubtedly felt just as confident that the right thing to do was to support a man facing unsubstantiated accusations of a decades-old crime, sparing him from the derailment of his career and the sullying of his stalwart reputation.

Ultimately—and as is unfortunately often the nature of accusations of sexual assault—it was her word against his. Who was more believable, Dr. Ford or Judge Kavanaugh? Who was more credible? And beyond the credibility of these two individuals, what was the right thing to do for the country? A tense, troubling, and extremely difficult moment for the United States—both politically and morally.

And that's exactly when God was brought to the fore.

At the very end of an arduous day marked by questions, answers, tears, recriminations, declarations, and pontifications, the final moments in determining the fate of Judge Kavanaugh rested in the hands of John Kennedy, the NRA-backed Republican senator from Louisiana. He was the last senator to hold the floor and the last member of the committee to ask any questions of Judge Kavanaugh. And for the senator, it would be the judge's faith in God that would ultimately settle the matter.

Here are the key excerpts from their brief but potent exchange:

"Do you believe in God?" Senator Kennedy asked.

"I do," Judge Kavanagh replied.

"I'm gonna give you a last opportunity, right here, right in front of God and country. I want you to look me in the eye. Are Dr. Ford's allegations true?"

"They are not accurate as to me. I have not questioned that she might have been sexually assaulted at some point in her life by someone, someplace. But as to me, I've never done this. Never. Done this to her, or to anyone else . . ."

And then:

"None of these allegations are true?" the senator asked.

"Correct."

"No doubt in your mind?"

"Zero. One hundred percent certain."

"Not even a scintilla?"

"Not a scintilla. One hundred percent certain, Senator."

"Do you swear to God?"

"I swear to God."

"That's all I have, Judge," concluded the senator.

And that's all he needed.

If Judge Kavanaugh believed in God, then that was that. If he could solemnly swear to a supernatural being, then he simply must be telling the truth.

For Senator Kennedy—and for many millions of Americans—a proclaimed faith in God is eminently significant when it comes to discerning the nature of truth or lies, good or evil, wrong or right. After all, God-believers are more apt to be more truthful, good, and moral than secular nonbelievers, right? As President Trump's first attorney general, Jeff Sessions, has publicly proclaimed, secular people are actually *incapable* of knowing truth, for "without God, there is no truth."[2] Jeff Sessions's replacement, Attorney General William Barr, has gone even further, declaring that social problems such as crime, drugs, and sexually transmitted diseases are the direct result of a "moral crisis" perpetuated by the "secularists of today."[3] For Senator Kennedy, Attorneys General Sessions and Barr, and so many other powerful people occupying key positions within Trump's administration, God is the underlying bedrock of truth, goodness, and decency. Without God, according to their perspective, moral life simply isn't possible.

It's an oddly ironic perspective to be trumpeted by people supporting a president who is among the most morally bankrupt leaders we've ever had. But, nonetheless, it's a perspective that rests on centuries of certitude.

Theistic Morality

The insistence that morality depends upon God remains one of the most widespread, popularly held notions. As Ivan, one of the main characters in Dostoyevsky's *The Brothers Karamazov* declares, if there is no God, then everything—including sexual assault—would be permitted.[4] Or in the words of leading contemporary Christian philosopher Alvin Plantinga, "God himself is the origin of moral constraints. It is his will, his commands or approvals, that determine what is right and wrong, morally acceptable or morally objectionable."[5] Or in the even more definitive words of Donald Trump supporter and top Evangelical apologist William Lane Craig, "the concept of morality loses all meaning in a universe without God. There can be no right and wrong . . . without God, good and evil do not exist."[6]

Despite the fact that such an unequivocal, age-old, God-based view of morality continues to be shared by millions of people, its global popularity provides no cover for its intrinsic erroneousness. The deeply entrenched beliefs that there must be a God in order for morality to exist—and that we must believe in this God in order to be moral—are both problematic and, in many instances, pernicious. And while such a theistic approach to ethical behavior may have served humans well in bygone centuries, today—given our advanced understanding of human evolution, moral psychology, neurology, sociology, etc.—this God-based morality is at best unhelpful, and at worst maladaptive.[7]

Thus, while I can't speak to the veracity of Judge Kavanagh's denials of Dr. Ford's accusations, I can confidently assert that his publicly purported belief in God during a United States Senate Judiciary Committee hearing should not, in any way, be accepted as some sort of ultimate guarantee of his truthfulness, his character, or his moral compass. And the pervasive premise that personal faith in the supernatural rests at the heart of moral living—a premise shared by our most powerful leaders—should not be accepted uncritically.

The brute fact is that morality based on belief in God—theistic morality—rests on untrue premises, limits our capacity for empathy and compassion, stymies our ability to take responsibility for our choices and actions, obfuscates the naturally evolved sources of ethical conduct, and ultimately thwarts moral progress, holding individuals and societies back from confronting the dire problems of the day and attending to the very real suffering they produce.

That said, my critique of theistic morality is not meant to impugn all people of faith. I happily recognize that many worshippers of God are moral and ethical and do a tremendous amount of good in the world. And not all religious people base their morality solely upon God, to be sure. Nor are all religious people irrationally fervent or dangerously dogmatic in their faith; many are humble in their religiosity, don't think that their religion is the only true one, and don't seek to force their religion on others. Such moderately religious people abound. But, unfortunately, other types of religious people—stronger, more fundamentalist—are also aplenty. For them, faith, ritual, and spiritual involvement are central, foundational aspects of their lives and identities. They are strident and vigorous in their religiosity. They are sure that they possess the One True Faith. They want everyone else to adopt their beliefs. They are dubious of other religious traditions, intolerant of other worldviews, and—above all—they are absolutely certain that without God, there can be no morality.

When confronting religion in the modern world, it is these more dogmatic fundamentalists that we must consistently contend with: Evangelical Christians, zealous Muslims, orthodox Jews, nationalistic Hindus, and so on. And it is these religious groups, and their traditional theistic beliefs, that comprise a loud and boisterous presence, an aggressive and antagonistic societal force, and—most importantly—a politically and culturally influential minority. As Chris Hedges explains in his book *American Fascists: The Christian Right and the War on America*, while conservative religious fundamentalists may not constitute a majority of religious people out there, their societal impact is pervasive, demonstrably outweighing their numbers.[8] As such, they continue to have an outsized role in shaping our world for the worse.[9]

After all, it was the resourcefulness and fortitude of people like Senator John Kennedy, Judge Brett Kavanaugh, and Attorney General Jeff Sessions—individuals supremely confident in a Bible-based morality—that brought us President Trump and his decidedly immoral political agenda.[10]

The Regressive Politics of Theistic Morality

In the United States today, conservative, Evangelical, and usually white Christians—and fellow travelers who subscribe to a similar theistic morality—wield a significant amount of influence on our school boards and city councils, in our military and state assemblies, on our radio waves and cable channels, and in our Congress, Supreme Court, and Oval Office.

The most obvious example of the Evangelical ethos and its unholy influence in America is the fact that 81 percent of white Evangelical Christians supported Donald Trump in the 2016 election.[11] That constituted a higher percentage of white Evangelical support than that which went to previous Republican presidential candidates Mitt Romney, John McCain, or George W. Bush. And according to a 2018 analysis conducted by American sociologist Andrew Whitehead, the single greatest predictor of who supports Trump is not their economic standing, not their demographics, not their views on race or gender or immigrants—nor a host of other possibilities. Rather, the most robust predictor is a particularly nationalistic form of Christian identity: those who think that the government should advocate Christian values, those who think that the United States is a Christian nation, and those who see the success of America as part of God's plan, unambiguously constitute Trump's sociopolitical base.[12]

These nationalistic, Evangelical Trump supporters are men and women who attend church more frequently than other Americans, who insist that the Bible is the inerrant word of God, and who claim to be the most devoutly committed to Jesus. And yet the obvious paradoxical contradiction is that they overwhelmingly supported a presidential candidate who—in both word and deed—has violated just about every ethical precept Jesus ever preached.[13] Jesus was quite clear that we can't serve or worship both God and Mammon (wealth), that the meek and the poor are blessed, that we are to be charitable and merciful, that we are to open our hearts and doors to the despised minorities and immigrants in our midst, and that truth sets us free, and the Prince of Peace unambiguously preached that "he who lives by the sword shall die by the sword." And yet the vast majority of those strongly religious Americans who presumably know these things by heart—conservative, Bible-believing Evangelicals—rallied around a Republican presidential candidate who is the very embodiment of Mammon, publicly mocks the meek, is selfish and spiteful, corrupt and militaristic, refers to the poor as "morons," incites racist xenophobia, stirs up nationalism and tribalism, shuts the door on poor refugees, rips immigrant children from their parents, bolsters authoritarianism, derides truth and despises facts, and loves the gun lobby.

It is impossible to not be both disturbed and alarmed by the reality that such Evangelical Christians—who claim to know and love Jesus more than anyone—remain the demographic most eagerly supportive of ongoing political agendas that go against nearly everything Jesus ever taught. These same men and women who claim to most faithfully worship God, and claim that their worshipping of God makes them moral, are simultaneously the ones who condone and support the most immoral leaders, exhibiting the most unethical attitudes. That is, those publicly pious individuals, groups, and movements across this nation who most proudly promulgate a shiny breastplate of moral righteousness are simultaneously the men and women who most vigorously aid, abet, and advocate immoral, unethical social regression.

When it comes to aiding and abetting such Christ-cloaked social regression, we can obviously look to the most popular pious pundits out there, individuals such as Sean Hannity, a staunch Catholic who produces conservative Christian films while simultaneously cheering on President Trump's most repressive and undemocratic policies, or Baptist-turned-Catholic Laura Ingraham, a Trump apologist who mocks the victims of school shootings and justifies taking immigrant toddlers away from their mothers, or Jesus-loving Ann Coulter, who drools hatred and vitriol upon the crucifix always nestled between her clavicles, or Catholic Bill O'Reilly, who delights in fanning racism and militarism with an arrogant gloat, or

Baptist Mike Huckabee, who sends out racist tweets and fights against equal rights with his Gomer Pyle smile, or conservative Christian duck hunter Phil Robertson, whose Christ-based jihadism is mired in homophobia, or Jewish Dennis Prager, who peddles fear and falsehood ever so politely while championing Trump's agenda—and all of them doing so while proudly proclaiming to be people of faith. But these celebrities are merely the most well-known profiteers of a flagrant hypocrisy that runs very deep and wide in this nation, a particular form of holy hypocrisy predicated upon a long-standing contradiction: that those who are the most religious among us—those who claim to be the most devoted to the Lord—generally tend to advocate the most immoral policies and platforms, and are often the most inhumane in their opinions and worldviews.

Pious Politicians

Consider the Christian politicians who constantly claim to be doing the good will of God as they advocate for laws and policies that only serve to cause harm and suffering. For instance, Mike Pompeo, Trump's secretary of state, is a Rapture-ready Evangelical who works to limit the rights of gays and lesbians, actively thwarts attempts to stop global warming, cozies up to murdering dictators, and fights to inundate America with lethal weapons. Evangelical Republican Scott Pruitt, who was Trump's first pick to head the Environmental Protection Agency, packed his office with industry shills and did all he could to undermine regulations that protect our land, water, air, and the ozone layer; Pruitt claimed to take a "biblical view" of our planet's circumstances, publicly arguing that global warming is good for humanity.[14] And former Texas governor Rick Perry—an Evangelical Christian and the current head of the Department of Energy—openly denies the science behind global warming,[15] thereby allowing planetary degradation to proceed unhindered. Tim Walberg, the Christian congressman from Michigan, publicly fights against attempts to stop climate change, insisting that "if" climate change is really a problem—which he denies—then God will surely come in and fix it.[16] North Carolina representative Larry Pittman, a

Christian man who once compared Abraham Lincoln to Adolf Hitler, continues to craft and push legislation that actually *increases* global warming.[17] Additionally, the current governor of Texas, Greg Abbott, is another Evangelical who fights hard to dismantle laws that protect the environment. Of course, no danger is more pressing than climate change, and the Evangelical goal of allowing it to continue will cause unimaginable pain and suffering in the decades ahead.

The Evangelical senator from Oklahoma Jim Inhofe not only disregards climate change as a hoax, but actively fights against gay and lesbian civil rights, fights against even the most minimal gun safety legislation, and strongly supports the Israeli destruction of Palestinian national life because he believes God mandates such oppression. Tennessee congressman Scott DesJarlais, a churchgoing, outspoken Christian, doggedly fights against providing affordable health care to the poor—not to mention the fact that he pressured his girlfriend to have an abortion, even though he claims to be antiabortion.[18] Evangelical Republican Jim Banks, a congressman from Indiana, works hard to stop stem cell research[19] despite the fact that such research could alleviate countless cases of suffering and fight the battle against ailments such as juvenile diabetes, Parkinson's disease, strokes, etc. The Christian governor of South Carolina, Henry McMaster, denigrated students publicly demonstrating for safe schools as "shameful" and offered up "prayer" as the only solution to gun violence;[20] he's also signed legislation allowing foster care agencies to discriminate against non-Christians.[21]

The nation's secretary of education, Betsy DeVos, is a hard-core Evangelical who actively seeks to undermine and underfund public education, using her office's power instead to "advance God's kingdom."[22] Republican and Christian fundamentalist Greg Gianforte, the congressman from Montana arrested for body-slamming a reporter against a wall and then onto the ground, argues against retirement—because if Noah was still working at the age of six hundred, why should older Americans stop working?[23] So much for compassion for our elderly. Republican and born-again Christian Abigail Whelan, a state senator in Minnesota, fights to allow wealthy corporations the opportunity to avoid paying taxes, further increasing the unfair tax burden on working-class people, all in the name of loving Jesus.[24] Congressman Mo Brooks of Alabama has committed himself so strongly to building a giant border wall to separate Mexicans and Americans that, if his plans are not fulfilled, he has promised to filibuster the Senate by reading the King James Bible.[25] Iowa congressman Steve King, a Christian Republican, retweets white supremacist and Nazi posts and openly mocks the student survivors of the Parkland mass shooting and condemns their push for sane gun laws; he also fights against stem cell research, humane animal rights laws, equality for gays and lesbians—he even voted against providing aid to the victims of Hurricane Katrina.

What all of these powerful men and women have in common is that they claim devotion to Jesus and fealty to God and insist that they are moral and proclaim that those who don't believe in Jesus or God are immoral—and yet their political agenda is flagrantly unethical, in that they seek to destroy mother nature, flood our cities and towns with ever more lethal guns, deny individuals the right to marry who they love, seek to imprison more poor people, seek to turn away refugees in need of safe harbor, and so on.

The bizarre reality is that—aside from the notable exception of churchgoing African Americans—most of the people who fight against structural relief for those in poverty, who fight against equality between men and women, who fight against fairness for gays and lesbians and transgender people, who fight against providing a haven to refugee families fleeing violence, who fight against paid family leave and subsidized health care for the poor, who fight against ending cruelty to animals, who fight against efforts to keep our planet healthy, who fight against stem cell research, who fight against effective sex education, who fight against accurate scientific school curricula, who fight against rehabilitative endeavors in our prisons, who undermine Native Americans' ability to protect the little bit of land they have left, who are the quickest to downplay or ignore racial injustice and disparage movements such as Black Lives Matter, and who fight for the proliferation of semiautomatic weapons, for the governmental use of torture, for increased use of the death penalty, and ongoing militarism at home and abroad—these folks tend to be the very same Americans who claim to nurture the closet relationship to God.

These are also the very same people who indignantly claim to be the moral beacons among us.

Hating on Atheists

In their sanctimony, God-believers such as Sean Hannity, Jeff Sessions, Oliver North, and Mike Pence not only support regressive policies, but they do so while simultaneously asserting their moral superiority. They insist that they are the ethical ones. Indeed, their supporters are widely known as "values" voters.

Values voters? Talk about a semantic bamboozle—as if the secular men and women among us who fight for human rights, who support marriage equality and protecting the environment, who seek to limit the proliferation of semiautomatic assault weapons in our society, who are troubled by racism and sexism, who think the death penalty is barbaric, who recognize the prison industrial complex as inhumane, who worry about increasing income inequality, who support a woman's right to control her own body, who advocate peace, who seek universal health care, and who are horrified by the animal-slaughtering industry—have no values?

But you see, such rhetoric shouldn't surprise us. It's an old trope of religion, and one of the most successful falsehoods promulgated by the strongly devout: that values and morals are something that only godly folks can have.

"Unbelief," proclaimed eminent thirteenth-century theologian Saint Thomas Aquinas, "is the greatest of sins."[26]

Got that?

Not murder, not child abuse, not sexual assault, not lying, not destroying nature, not slavery, not torturing animals. Rather: failing to believe in God. That is the height of immorality, or rather, the very wellspring—according to one of Christianity's most brilliant minds.

This idea that one needs faith in God in order to be moral—and that atheism and immorality are thus intertwined—has roots much older than Saint Thomas Aquinas. According to the Bible, as declared in Psalm 14 of the Old Testament, those who don't believe in God are not only fools, they are not only corrupt, but they are *incapable* of doing good. In the Christian scriptures of the New Testament, atheists are explicitly associated with wickedness and darkness (2 Corinthians 6:14). Similar sentiments can be found in that most holy of Hindu texts, the Bhagavad Gita, which links the absence of religious belief with immorality, stating that secularity leads to destructive tendencies, and that those who lack religious belief have no way of knowing good from bad or right from wrong.[27] And according to the Quran of Islam, those who do not believe in Allah have a diseased heart; they are hell-bound liars[28] who are so evil that they deserve to have their heads and fingers cut off.[29]

Fast-forward through the centuries, and Aquinas's viewpoint echoes into our contemporary world. For example, in the twentieth century's first Christian bestseller, *Mere Christianity*, C. S. Lewis argues that the very concept of justice requires belief in God; without God, there can exist no urge to do right and act responsibly. Lewis's better-selling heir, Evangelical pastor Rick Warren, claims in *The Purpose Driven Life* that people lacking Bible-based religious beliefs have no motivation for being good or moral—their lives are characterized by selfishness and a cold indifference to others. According to convicted felon, accused wife-beater, Twitter racist, Trump ally, and leading conservative Christian Dinesh D'Souza, atheism is "cowardly moral escapism"[30] and, as "the opiate of the morally corrupt," constitutes a delusion promulgated and imbibed by the sexually unrestrained, who insist that there is no God so that they can be free to live lives of sin and depravity.[31] Irish American professor of the New Testament John Dominic Crossan suggests that atheists are akin to sociopaths and psychopaths.[32] American professor of philosophy and religion James Spiegel writes that atheism is "the suppression of truth by wickedness, the cognitive consequence of immorality."[33] Leading American rabbi Shmuley Boteach rants through one YouTube video after another that atheism and immorality are one and the same. Former vice presidential candidate Sarah Palin has declared that "the logical result of atheism . . . is severe moral decay."[34] Former Republican presidential candidate and governor of Ohio John Kasich has argued that when people are secular, they have no sense of right and wrong.[35] The Evangelical Christian that Trump briefly replaced Jeff Sessions with in the position of attorney general, Matt Whitaker, has declared that he takes a "Biblical view of justice" and that any judges who take a secular view are inherently problematic.[36] The late Supreme Court justice Antonin Scalia made such a view explicit, stating that atheists favor the "devil's desires."[37] And Newt Gingrich said—oh, hell, you get the idea. Claims made by pundits, politicians, and pastors about atheists having no morals and religion being the only thing capable of providing values are a dime a dozen.

And sadly, most people buy it.[38] As stated earlier, millions of people are convinced that without belief in God, one cannot be a moral person, one cannot know right from wrong, one cannot be ethical. In fact, an international Pew study from 2014 found that most people around the world subscribe to a decidedly theistic morality in which it is accepted that one must believe in God in order to be a good person. For example: 53 percent of Americans, 56 percent of Mexicans, 70 percent of Indians, 74 percent of Tunisians, 79 percent of Kenyans, 80 percent of Venezuelans, 86 percent of Brazilians, 87 percent of Turks, 91 percent of Nigerians, 93 percent of Filipinos, 95 percent of Egyptians, 98 percent of Pakistanis, and 99 percent of Indonesians believe that it is *necessary* to believe in God in order to be moral.[39]

Fortunately, ample social scientific evidence soundly refutes this mistaken belief.

Good Societies Without God

Societies in the world today with the lowest rates of belief in God and church attendance—such as Sweden, Japan, and the Netherlands—are among the best-functioning and most humane societies on Earth. As has been amply documented by contemporary economists, criminologists, and sociologists,[40] the nations with the lowest murder rates, violent crime rates, infant mortality rates, child abuse fatality rates, incarceration rates, etc. are among the most secular, while those nations with the highest rates of corruption, murder, violent crime, inequality, political repression, and violence—such as Colombia, El Salvador, and Jamaica—are among the most God-worshipping and church-attending. Granted, this is merely a correlation, but it is a powerful correlation that handily knocks out the knees of the claim that only God can provide morals and values for humanity.

It's pretty fascinating, actually: in the Pew study cited above, you can see that 93 percent of Filipinos think that it is necessary to believe in God in order to be moral, but that same study found that only *19 percent* of those in the Czech Republic think as much—and yet, according to the United Nations Office on Drugs and Crime, the Philippines' murder rate is nearly ten times higher than the Czech Republic's.[41] If belief in God kept people moral—and given that the Philippines is one of the most God-believing countries in the world, while the Czech Republic is one of the most atheistic—then theses nations' murder rates should be reversed. But they aren't. Granted, the dramatically differing rates of murder in the Czech Republic and the Philippines is not solely a result of the former's atheism and the latter's theism. There are numerous other factors at play. But that's the point: these other factors are all *secular* in nature—economic, cultural, historical, political. What they are not is divine, spiritual, or supernatural.

And the same correlation between secularity and societal well-being is also found when comparing states within the United States. States with the highest levels of belief in God, like Louisiana, Arkansas, and Alabama, have much higher rates of violent crime and other social pathologies than those states with the lowest levels of belief in God, such as Vermont, Massachusetts, and Oregon.[42] If widespread belief in God kept people moral and a widespread lack of belief in God led to immorality, then we should expect to see an opposite correlation; we should find that those states (and nations) wherein God-belief is strong and popular have the lowest levels of violent crime, while those states (and nations) wherein God-belief is weak and marginal have the highest. But we find just the opposite.

So, we can compare nations to one another and see that where God-belief is lower and religiosity is weaker, so too are violent crime and other societal pathologies. And we can also compare states within our country and observe the exact same correlations. And yet still a third way to debunk the "God-belief is necessary in order to have a moral society" canard is simply to look at a single society over the centuries and note that, in many instances, a precipitous drop in religiosity does not result in an increase of day-to-day violent crime—but just the opposite occurs. Consider the Netherlands: the homicide rate in the capital city of Amsterdam has dropped from forty-seven per one hundred thousand people back in the mid–fifteenth century[43]—when religiosity was strong and pervasive—down to around two per one hundred thousand today,[44] a time when there are more atheists than ever before in Dutch history and church attendance has been plummeting for decades to all-time lows.[45] And the homicide rate in medieval England—a deeply pious time—was on average ten times that of twentieth-century England,[46] a time of rapid secularization. That is, contemporary England—now one of most irreligious societies in the history of the world—is 95 percent less violent than it was back in the Middle Ages,[47] when faith in God and religious devotion were deep and wide. And while all societies have experienced a notable decrease in daily violence over the course of the last several centuries, that decrease has been most acute in those societies that have experienced the greatest degrees of secularization.

Good Individuals Without God

All of this information—correlational as it is—does not prove that secularism or atheism, in and of themselves, automatically result in markedly moral societies. But the fact that highly secular nations and states fare so well compared to religious nations and states, and the fact that many nations have seen violent crime and other social pathologies decrease over time as secularity has simultaneously increased, *does* prove that morality clearly doesn't hinge upon the existence of God, or require belief in God. Which is why atheists such as myself, and my wife, and my kids, and hundreds of millions of others all over the world, are not the immoral monsters that the likes of Saint Thomas Aquinas—or Ted Cruz—make us out to be.

As American professor of psychology Ralph Hood has concluded—based on an extensive survey of relevant research—there exists no empirical support for the myth that religious people are more ethical than their secular peers.[48] Claremont Graduate University researcher Justin Didyoung and his colleagues concur, finding that "the longstanding stereotype that non-theists are less moral than theists is not empirically supported."[49] In addition to their own study comparing atheists with theists—which revealed that the former are no less moral than the latter—there is also the work of various other social scientists, such as Catherine Caldwell-Harris, professor of psychology at Boston University, who has found that atheists exhibit robust levels of compassion or empathy.[50] Or the research of American political scientist Matthew Loveland, who found that secular people are actually more trusting of others than religious people.[51]

And then there's the matter of violent crime—perhaps the most overt manifestation of immorality. Not only have various studies found that secular people are, in fact, less likely to commit violent crimes than religious people,[52] but researchers from both the United States and the United Kingdom have reported that atheists are *under*represented in prisons.[53] Indeed, atheists currently make up an infinitesimal 0.1 percent of federal prison inmates in the United States.[54] As University of Haifa psychology professor Benjamin Beit-Hallahmi has observed, "ever since the field of criminology got started and data were collected of the religious affiliation of criminal offenders, the fact that the unaffiliated and the nonreligious had the lowest crime rates has been noted."[55]

Additional studies have shown that atheists and agnostics, on average, exhibit lower levels of racism and prejudice than their more God-believing peers,[56] as well as lower levels of nationalism and militarism,[57] greater levels of honesty,[58] more robust tolerance for those they disagree with,[59] as well as higher acceptance of women's rights.[60] Secular individuals are also much more likely to support death with dignity than religious individuals,[61] as well as the rights of nontraditional couples to have and adopt children.[62] Secular humanists are also significantly less likely to support the use of torture than their religious peers.[63] And while it is true that liberal, moderately religious people tend to share similar moral values along these same lines as atheists and agnostics, this is largely because they themselves have become *secularized* in their tempered, modest religiosity: they don't think scriptures are inerrant or infallible, they don't think that their religion is the only one true faith, they don't believe in a literal heaven or hell, their concept of God is creatively metaphorical, they are dubious of supernaturalism, and they have rejected nearly all traditional religious dogma.[64] Such liberal, moderately religious people have adopted much of a secular, naturalistic orientation—in stark distinction to strongly, fervently, wholeheartedly religious people whose worldviews are theistic and supernatural. And it is these more strongly devout, more fundamentally faithful religious people who prove themselves to be markedly less caring, less altruistic, and less humane on a host of socially relevant moral matters.

Consider, for example, the issue of helping refugees fleeing war and persecution—a humanitarian crisis all the more pressing in recent years given the tragic events in Syria, Afghanistan, Yemen, and Iraq. According to a 2018 Pew study, only 25 percent of white Evangelicals felt that the United States has a responsibility to help refugees in need, only 43 percent of mainline Protestants felt that way, and only 50 percent of Catholics. The percentage ticked up to 63 percent among Black Protestants—but the "religious" group in America most likely to feel a responsibility to help refugees was those without any religion at all: 65 percent of secular Americans expressed such a moral sentiment.[65] Another Pew study, also from 2018, found a similar correlation in Europe: even when controlling for things like educational attainment and occupation, the most religious Europeans were the least in favor of helping immigrants and refugees and the nominally religious were more in favor—but it was the affirmatively secular who were *most* in favor.[66]

Finally, there's social-psychological research specifically illustrating atheist morality in action, such as the recent international study that looked at children and their likelihood of being generous or selfish.[67] In 2015, a team of researchers headed by Dr. Jean Decety of the University of Chicago went to six different countries—China, Canada, Turkey, Jordan, South Africa, and the United States—and did an experiment with children between the ages of five and twelve; some of the kids had been raised Christian, some had been raised Muslim, and some had been raised without religion. Each child met individually with an adult who had a bunch of different stickers. The boy or girl was then told that he or she could choose any ten stickers to keep. However, after picking their favorites stickers, they were told by the adults that the researchers didn't have time to give out the rest of the stickers to other kids in a different (fictitious) class, but if he or she wanted, the boy or girl could put some of his or her ten stickers in an envelope to be given away to other kids. Well, the nonreligious kids were the most generous—giving away, on average, a higher number of their stickers than the Muslim or Christian kids, who tended to be more selfish.

Sure, it was just one study involving kids and stickers. But it effectively points to a much larger and important reality: that the vast majority of atheists the world over are decent and humane. Goodness without God is not only possible but pervasive. And in one of the more optimistic indicators of secularization in our society, more men and women are coming to accept that religion does not have a monopoly on morality: a growing majority of Americans (65 percent) now say that they rely primarily on things like practical experience, common sense, philosophy, or science for guidance regarding right and wrong—not religion.[68] And in Canada, a whopping 82 percent of adults agree that "it is not necessary to believe in God to be moral and have good values."[69]

The Promise of Secular Morality

The fact that so many North Americans currently rely on nontheistic sources in their moral deliberation is really good news—because religious ethics are brittle, and as British philosopher Derek Parfit makes clear, belief in God can actually prevent the free development of moral reasoning.[70] After all, any ethical system that ultimately depends upon faith in a nonexistent, magical deity who issues commands that one must obey for fear of punishment is inherently unsound.[71]

But aren't there admirable moral teachings in the world's leading religions? You bet—but those admirable moral teachings did not originate with those religions. Rather, those religions merely wrote down and codified what was already emergent in human civilization.

But aren't there wise, just, and humane precepts and tenets found within the world's leading religions? Absolutely—but they are wise, just, and humane for natural, secular reasons, not supernatural, theistic reasons.

But don't many religious movements fight the good fight, working on behalf of the betterment of humanity? Yes, but usually it is secular movements that pave the way on these fronts, with religion only joining up later in the game. As leading American skeptic Dr. Michael Shermer has noted, "once moral progress in a particular area is under way, most religions get on board—as in the abolition of slavery . . . women's rights . . . and gay rights . . . but this often happens after a shamefully protracted lag time."[72]

Still, aren't there millions of religious people out there doing good in the world as a result of their faith? Yes, and they should be lauded and abetted in their good works. But more and more people are losing said faith, so alternative understandings of ethics and morals must arise and, ultimately, prevail.[73]

Despite all the good that one can find within certain corners of religious life—and the countless ethical people out there who do believe in God—theistic morality remains inherently problematic, tending to thwart human progress, both at the individual and societal level. Whatever religion's moral attributes or ethical benefits may have been thousands or hundreds of years ago, today they now largely serve to hold humanity back. Thus, we need to look elsewhere as we strive to grapple with questions of wrong and right, good and bad, just and unjust. Not to the clouds, not to the priests, rabbis, or imams—and most importantly—not to imagined deities. Rather, we need to look to ourselves.[74] It is this secular, humanistic approach to morality that we need not to not only embrace but to rely upon and hang our hopes on.

Fortunately, secular, humanistic, and atheistic approaches to and understandings of morality are sound and solid and, on most if not all fronts, intrinsically superior to what God-based morality has had to offer.[75] In the words of British philosopher A. C. Grayling, secular people who don't believe in God are among "the *most* careful moral thinkers, because in the absence of an externally imposed morality they recognize the duty to examine their views, choices, and actions and how they should behave towards others."[76]

While theistic morality forces us to look outside ourselves for ethical guidance, secular morality forces us to look within—consulting our conscience and our reason. Whereas God-based morality is ultimately founded upon obedience, human-based morality is founded upon empathy and compassion. While religious ethics have required ever-contested interpretations of obscure or contradictory formulations of supposedly divine will, humanistic ethics depend squarely upon ongoing debate and forthright argumentation with and among our fellow human beings. Christianity and Islam—the two largest religions in the world—have taught that our time in this world is fleeting and insignificant and that the really important eternal realm awaits us after death. But secularism forces us to live in the here and now, focusing our energies on this world: the only plane of existence we'll ever inhabit. While the world's leading religions—Christianity and Islam—construct ethical life as a juvenile game of heavenly reward and hellish punishment, which infantilizes morality to a matter of self-centered prudence and fear, nonreligious ethics emphasize rationality and understanding as more mature ways to address and minimize malevolence. And rather than terrorize children with the fear of eternal torture, nonreligious orientations cultivate reflective understanding of actions and consequences among children, employing love and explication over scare tactics. Whereas theistic ethics have ultimately been predicated on a principle of "might makes right," secular humanist ethics are predicated on how best to alleviate the suffering of sentient beings. Christocentric ethical systems have hinged upon the notion that we are born sinners who must actively choose to be moral—a willful choice that goes against the grain of our fallen selves—but secularism embraces the growing body of scientific evidence illustrating the degree to which a proclivity toward cooperation and sociability, care and concern, and altruism and love are the observable outgrowth of our evolved natures.

As more and more of us let go of God, so too must we counter and ultimately reject the notion that our morals come from said God. They don't.[77] Morality and ethics grow out of the human experience: our genes, our minds, our emotions, our evolutionary history, our experiences, our communities, our cultures, and our societies.

I should note here that the very terms "morality" and "ethics"—terms that I'll employ throughout this book—are virtually synonymous in everyday usage. As American philosopher Ryan Falcioni notes, "moral" and "ethical" basically mean the same thing,[78] both having to do with how we treat others, whether our actions are helpful or harmful, and the degree to which we reduce or increase suffering. That said, I generally use the term "moral" to refer to personal values and behaviors that increase the well-being of sentient beings, while "ethical" signifies principles and orientations that aim to increase justice and fairness in society. Again, the terms are nearly interchangeable. And both function better when there's no God in the picture.

But how does godless morality work? How can people be moral if they don't believe in God? How does morality even function if there is no Supreme Overlord issuing forth moral edicts and ethical commandments, watching over us all, judging, rewarding, and punishing? Can objective morality exist without God? And what specific moral precepts, ethical imperatives, and cardinal virtues do nonbelievers actually live by?

In the pages that follow, these questions will be answered as thoroughly and as thoughtfully as possible. First, in Part One, the traditional, hegemonic ethical framework for thousands of years—theistic morality of religious faith—will be debunked and deconstructed. Although most people the world over continue to think that morality begins and ends with God, it doesn't. In Part Two, the nonreligious sources of secular morality will be explored and explained, and the core virtues of atheist ethical living—what I call the "secular seven"—will be presented. Part Three will consider challenges to secular morality, along with respective solutions.

"One is often told," British philosopher Bertrand Russell quipped nearly one hundred years ago, "that it is a very wrong thing to attack religion, because religion makes men virtuous. So I am told; I have not noticed it."[79]

In a world where many of those in top positions of power are strongly religious or are supported by the strongly religious—from Donald Trump in Washington, D.C., to Mohammed bin Salman in Saudi Arabia, from Jair Bolsonaro in Brazil to Vladimir Putin in Russia, from Benjamin Netanyahu in Israel to Ali Khamenei in Iran, from Recep Erdoğan in Turkey to Aung San Suu Kyi in Myanmar, from Viktor Orbán in Hungary to Iván Duque Márquez in Colombia, from Mohamed Abdullahi Mohamed in Somalia to Narendra Modi in India, and well beyond—it is not wrong to attack religion, at least not its most destructive and oppressive manifestations. Skeptical criticism, given the power religion wields, is morally obligatory.

And as for Professor Russell's noting that religion doesn't actually seem to make people virtuous, he's spot-on. When the world's largest Christian organization, the Roman Catholic Church, claims to possess a monopoly on morality while at the same time commanding people not to use condoms—and also aiding and abetting thousands of child molesters—the link between religion and morality cries out for suspicion. When Evangelical Christians insist that the Bible is the sole source of moral guidance, while at the same time championing the proliferation of guns, the ripping apart of refugee families at our borders, and the active thwarting of efforts to halt global warming, the relationship between religious faith and ethical living begs for scrutiny. When orthodox Jews insist that God's commandments form the foundation of moral society, while at the same time denying women in abusive relationships the right to divorce, engaging in ritualistic animal cruelty, and championing the violent oppression of the Palestinian people, the insistence that God is necessary for a moral existence necessitates deconstruction. And when Islamic fundamentalists in Saudi Arabia or Iran champion themselves as the divinely mandated arbiters of moral law, while at the same time beheading enemies of the state in public squares, imprisoning homosexuals, and denying democracy, the connection of theism to ethics demands debunking.

While there is much good within religious life—such as supportive community, strengthened family bonds, meaningful rituals, and charity—the stubborn fact remains that supernatural beings do not create morality and the worship of almighty gods is not the source of ethical living. Rather, the alpha and omega of moral life is *us*, warts and all.

Part One

WHY MORALITY CANNOT BE BASED ON FAITH IN GOD

1

Isms

Back in 2010, leading social scientist and professor of public policy at Harvard University Robert Putnam, along with his colleague David Campbell, published a massive empirical analysis of religious life in America. The tome was called *American Grace*, and it was chock-full of findings that shed light upon numerous facets of religious belief, behavior, and belonging.

Putnam and Campbell reported that, on average, religious people are more charitable than their secular peers. When it comes to things like generosity and volunteering, frequent churchgoers give and do more than non-churchgoers. For example, among the most religious segment of their national sample, the average amount of annual donations to charitable causes per household was $3,000, but among the most secular segment, the average amount was $1,000. And among the most religious swath of Americans, only 6 percent said that they had made no charitable contributions in the previous year, but among the most secular swath of their sample, 32 percent reported as much. The secular, it seems, are stingier. And not only are highly religious individuals more likely to donate to both religious *and* nonreligious causes, and not only are they more likely to do volunteer work, but they are also more likely to give blood and donate money to homeless people than their secular peers.[1] In short, Putnam and Campbell's research revealed that "religiously observant Americans are more generous with time and treasure than demographically similar secular Americans."[2]

We've actually known this for quite a while; numerous studies over the years have attested to religious Americans' higher than average charitable tendencies.[3] So doesn't this then mean that God-believers (theists) are more moral than those who lack such a belief (atheists)?

Before such a conclusion can be made, we need to look a bit more closely at what is going on here. A most valuable element of Putnam and Campbell's research was that they were able to discover just *why* it is that religious people donate more in terms of charity and volunteering than secular people—and it actually has nothing to do with God. Rather, it has everything to do with people.

Simply put: charitable giving increases when people actively gather with others in communal, congregational environments. And when people don't gather with others in such ways, their generosity dwindles, in terms of both time and money. Belief in God simply doesn't matter. How do we know? Because Putnam and Campbell found that people who believe in God but are not members of a religious congregation do not donate time and money in higher than average amounts, and conversely, people who don't believe in God but are members of a religious congregation—for whatever reason—do. Put another way: when people are more isolated from others, with fewer friends and fewer moments of social interaction, their proclivity to engage in charitable and voluntary activities decreases. But when they hang out with others on a regular basis at church or synagogue or mosque or temple, their pro-sociality increases, along with their interest and willingness to be more altruistic.

As Putnam and Campbell explain, while "it is tempting to think that religious people are better neighbors because of their fear of God or their hope of salvation . . . we find no evidence for those conjectures."[4] The "secret ingredient" of religious charity, their data reveal, is not faith in God but rather church attendance. It is the getting together with people on a regular basis, the routinized rituals, the singing and announcements, the sharing of cake and coffee after the service, the conversing and schmoozing, the taking field trips and joining groups—and other such social-bonding activities—that actually increase the likelihood of charitable donating and volunteering. Not a fervent faith in God. "When it comes to the religious edge in good neighborliness," Putnam and Campbell conclude, "it is belonging that matters, not believing,"[5] and "although many devoutly religious people might explain their own civic virtues as manifestations of God's will . . . theology is not the core explanation . . . rather, communities of faith seem more important than faith itself."[6]

It bears repeating: community is more important than faith. Belonging is more important than belief. Gathering is more important than God. As the similar findings of American social psychologists Jesse Graham and Jonathan Haidt have confirmed, bonding with other humans is the driving engine of increased charity and generosity, not believing in a deity.[7]

But what all of the above illustrates is an extremely important distinction that we must set forth and fully understand: the difference between *religion* and *theism*.

Theism

"Religion" is a notoriously multifaceted concept encompassing a plethora of ideologies, identities, associations, and activities. "Theism," however, is an extremely narrow term that refers to just one specific thing: belief in God. That's it. A theist is simply someone who believes in God.

What's the difference? Doesn't being religious mean that you believe in God? And doesn't believing in God make you religious? Yes to the latter, but no to the former.

If you believe in God, then you are certainly religious. But many people are religious without believing in God. For example, there are millions of people who attend religious services, engage in religious rituals, and even identify with a religion—but don't believe in God. Then why are they religiously involved? For a host of nontheistic reasons: they like the music at church, or they want to keep a spouse happy, or they think it is good for their kids, or they enjoy the rituals and celebrations, or they like taking time for quiet contemplation, or they want to maintain a tradition, or it links them to their heritage, or it increases ties to their ethnic community, and so on. As my father used to like to joke: "Yaacov goes to synagogue to talk to God. I go to synagogue to talk to Yaacov." The bottom line is that there are many, many reasons that people can be religiously active, and it can have nothing to do with belief in God.

Remember that there are a lot of religions out there that don't even contain a god in their cosmology. Many animistic indigenous religions all over the world lack any concept of a god, but instead are focused on nature spirits, dead ancestors, and/or other supernatural forces.[8] Additionally, some Eastern religions, such as Jainism and Zen Buddhism, do not contain any beliefs in a god at all. But they are still religions. As philosopher André Comte-Sponville notes, "all theisms are religious, but not all religions are theistic."[9]

Again, *religion* and *theism* are not one and the same. And it is theism—rather than religion, in all its varied manifestations—that comprises the true target of this book. For it is theism's relationship to morality that will be deconstructed in the chapters ahead. And at the heart of that deconstruction is theism's obverse: atheism.

Atheism

Atheism refers to the *lack* or *absence* of a belief in God. That's it. An atheist is someone who does not believe in a god; according to the latest tallies, there are over one hundred million atheists in the world today.[10]

Of course, various individuals have defined atheism more grandly and effusively. For example, Madalyn Murray O'Hair, the founder of American Atheists, defined atheism as "the mental attitude which unreservedly accepts the supremacy of reason and aims at establishing a lifestyle and ethical outlook verifiable by experience and the scientific method, independent of all arbitrary assumptions of authority and creeds."[11] While these are strong and impassioned sentiments, they go well beyond the limited confines of the term "atheism." After all, *a-* is a prefix meaning "without" or "lacking," and *theos* is the Greek term for "god"; so again, atheism refers to nothing more than lacking belief in a god.[12] Perhaps this is a god you have heard of or know a lot about, such as the God of Christianity or Allah of Islam, and you have chosen not to believe in this god—an atheism predicated upon dismissal or rejection. Or perhaps it is a god you have never even heard of, such as Perkunas (the Baltic god of thunder) or Mawu (goddess of the Fon people of West Africa) and, given your utter lack of knowledge or even awareness of these gods, you don't believe in them—an atheism predicated on ignorance. But either way, an atheist is someone who doesn't believe in any gods.

Even though the meaning of atheism is quite simple, things get more complex in the real world; while atheism describes an orientation involving belief (or lack thereof), the term "atheist" is quite a bit more loaded at home, at school, at work, and at the grocery store or softball field. That is, in contemporary society, the designation "atheist" can be, for many people, about identity—and a negative, stigmatized identity at that. For example, according to a 2014 Pew study, when Americans were asked about their feelings about people from various religions on a one-hundred-point "feeling thermometer"—with one hundred being the most warm/positive and zero being the most cold/negative—Jews, Catholics, and Evangelical Christians all rated an average of above sixty, Buddhists came in at fifty-three, Mormons at forty-eight, but atheists were down at forty-one, with only Muslims scoring slightly lower at forty.[13] And according to another Pew study from 2014, when Americans were asked how they would feel if a family member were to marry someone with a given trait or identity (would it make them happy, unhappy, or would it not matter?), only 7 percent said that they would be unhappy if a family member married someone who had been born outside of the United States, 9 percent said that they would be unhappy if the marriage was to an Evangelical Christian, 11 percent would be unhappy if the marriage was to someone of a different race, 14 percent would be unhappy if a family member married someone who had not gone to college, 19 percent would be unhappy if the new spouse was a gun owner—but 49 percent of Americans said that they would be unhappy if a family member married someone who did not believe in God, making atheist the worst possibility, by a long shot.[14]

Certainly, many people who lack a belief in God resist identifying as atheists so as to avoid the negative stigma that comes with the identity.

But there is also the dogmatic nature of atheism at play, which many people find off-putting. Atheists can sometimes come off as closed-minded haters of religion, curmudgeonly types who go out of their way to mock and deride other people's beliefs.

For those folks who do not believe in God, or rather doubt God's existence and are simultaneously less staunch in their nontheism, agnosticism is a more comfortable, intellectually sound option.

Agnosticism

Is there a God? *Who knows?*

Why are we here? *Who can say?*

What happens after we die? *Who knows?*

Why does the universe exist? *Who can say?*

Welcome to agnosticism: the secular orientation that replaces the Christian crucifix, the Jewish star of David, and the Islamic crescent with a hallowed question mark. Like their atheist cousins, agnostics today number over one hundred million globally.[15]

In its most common usage, agnosticism asserts that maybe there is God, maybe there isn't, and no one can really say for sure one way or another. Thus, while the theist believes there is a God and the atheist believes there is not, the agnostic isn't completely convinced by either position.[16] As the ancient Greek philosopher Protagoras—perhaps the world's first known agnostic—remarked back in the fifth century B.C.E.: "Concerning the gods, I am unable to discover whether they exist or not . . . for there are many hindrances to knowledge, the obscurity of the subject and the brevity of human life."[17] Or as contemporary philosopher Julian Baggini explains, an agnostic "claims we cannot know whether God exists and so the only rational option is to reserve judgment."[18]

The term "agnostic" was famously coined by English biologist Thomas Henry Huxley back in the 1860s. Huxley offered up the term—which literally means "without knowledge"—to capture an ideological position expressing the limits of knowledge, and the limits of our ability to know, with empirical certainty. This underlying feel for—and steady sentiment of—existential unknowingness pervades agnosticism. As the American orator Robert Ingersoll, known in the ninteenth century as "The Great Agnostic," wrote, "Many people . . . have tried to guess the riddle—tried to know the absolute—to find origin—to know destiny. They have all failed. These things are beyond our intellectual horizon—beyond the 'reaches of our souls.' Our life is a little journey from mystery to mystery."[19] Or as nineteenth-century British scholar Leslie Stephen expressed it: "we are a company of ignorant beings, feeling our way through mists and darkness . . . dimly discerning light enough for our daily needs, but hopelessly differing whenever we attempt to describe ultimate origin . . . [and thus] we shall be content to admit openly . . . that man knows nothing of the Infinite and Absolute."[20]

Embracing mystery, and letting that mystery be, is at the heart of agnosticism. Agnostics are thus happily down with Hamlet, who said to Horatio that there are more things in heaven and earth than are dreamt of in his philosophy—or any and every possible philosophy stemming from human consciousness.

It's a pretty humble position. After all, it's hard to be dogmatic, truculent, or fanatical when you are admitting a lack of knowledge.

Naturalism

Theism, atheism, and agnosticism all revolve around the God question: the first says there is a God, the second says there isn't, and the third says, well, no one can really ever know. But the secular orientation that transcends the God question and attempts to encapsulate all of reality is naturalism. And to understand naturalism, you need go no further than Scooby-Doo.

Scooby-Doo—the TV cartoon that started in 1969 and has never let up—presents the antics of Scooby and his human friends: Shaggy, Fred, Velma, and Daphne. But here's the funny thing about that show: every episode is the exact same. In every single installment, the main characters stumble upon a spooky mystery—a ghost haunting an old mine, a monster terrorizing a popular beach, a witch bewitching a remote hotel, an alien unnerving a summer camp—and in every episode, the four protagonists and their dog Scooby come to reveal that it was all a hoax. Through basic sleuthing and intrepid skepticism, the heroes show that it is all smoke and mirrors—or silly costumes and fancy lighting, or chemical reactions and audio trickery, and so forth. And the message is thus always the same: there is nothing supernatural out there, only natural phenomena.

Naturalism takes this very position to the extreme: that which can't be observed or proven empirically does not exist. Whatever is out there, it is natural. As the Carvaka thinkers of the ancient Indian school of Lokayata philosophy pronounced over twenty-six hundred years ago: "Only the perceived exists; the unperceivable does not exist by reason of its never having been perceived."[21] But who paints the peacocks such delightful colors? Who causes the birds to sing so sweetly? The Carvaka were adamant: "There exists no cause here excepting nature."[22] Or as contemporary naturalist philosopher Kerry Walters affirms, "there is nothing apart from nature, and nature is self-originating, self-explanatory, and without overall purpose."[23]

For theists—and many other religious people of various traditions—there are essentially two realms of existence: the this-worldly and the otherworldly. Or to use terms already employed: the natural and the supernatural. Religious believers accept that there is a natural world, but they also insist that in addition to this natural world, there exist other realms or planes of existence: heavens, hells, purgatories, etc. And they will claim that in addition to the plentiful beings of nature—such as people, plants, animals, etc.—there are other beings out there: angels, demons, gods, ancestral souls, spirits, imps, jinn, ghosts, etc., etc. Naturalism denies the existence of these otherworldly, supernatural places and things. According to Professor Tom Clark, director of the Center for Naturalism, "what science reveals . . . is a vast, interconnected, multilayered, diversely populated, and yet single realm in which all phenomena partake of the same basic constituents. This realm we simply call nature. There seems no reason to suppose, given scientific observations thus far, that there exists another, supernatural realm that operates according to different laws or that contains radically different phenomena."[24]

The scientific method, empiricism, rationalism, materialism, evidence-based beliefs, and accepting what actually *is* true, rather than what we wish were true—these are the smooth, strong pillars of a naturalistic worldview. And while some may find such a naturalistic worldview less enchanting than a world filled with poltergeists, angels, shamans, healing crystals, amazing miracles, and gods and goddesses, others find it replete with endless opportunities to marvel and gaze in awe at the intricate, chaotic, beautiful, terrible wonder of nature, in all of its majesty and vastness. And while some may find a magicless, indifferent cosmos lonely or dull, most secular men and women find such a reality not only *true* but comforting and affirming.

OK, well, then if there is no God (as atheism maintains), or if there might be a God, or perhaps something else out there, but we can't be sure and no one can really know (as agnosticism maintains), and if, ultimately, whatever may be out there is nonetheless natural and not supernatural (as naturalism maintains), then to whom or what are we to look for to help us or guide us as we flail around on this all-too-natural, godless planet? Whom or what are we to rely upon to help us fight injustice, cure disease, and ensure moral progress?

Ourselves.

Humanism

Humanism begins with denial or doubt concerning the existence of God, and the concomitant embracing of naturalism—but then goes well beyond that by positively affirming and valuing the potential of human beings to solve problems and make the world a better, safer, and more just place. Humanism rests firmly upon the recognition that people have the capacity to do great things, to solve problems, and to act ethically. Thus, a humanist is someone who does not believe in the otherworldly tenets of religion—and soundly rejects both theism and supernaturalism—but who does believe in many things of this world, such as family, friendship, cooperation, reason, art, science, humor, love, rational inquiry, ingenuity, democracy, compassion, tolerance, imagination, open debate, human rights—and then some.

According to British humanist philosopher Stephen Law,[25] humanism is a comprehensive worldview that rests upon these key premises: there are no gods or supernatural beings out there, science and reason are the best tools available for discovering what is true, this is the only life we will ever have, moral values and ethical frameworks should be strongly shaped and informed by an empirically grounded understanding of the human condition, every individual is responsible for making his or her own moral decisions and cannot hand over this responsibility to someone or something else, democratic societies with a clear separation of church and state are ideal, and finally, life can be quite meaningful—in fact, can be *more* meaningful—without the existence of God.

According to the American Humanist Association (which has nearly 650,000 likes on Facebook and counting), humanism is "a progressive philosophy of life that, without theism and other supernatural beliefs, affirms our ability and responsibility to lead ethical lives of personal fulfillment that aspire to the greater good of humanity."[26]

Humanism is what makes atheism and agnosticism actively moral.[27] After all, simply lacking a belief in God does not ensure any sort of ethical orientation—the godless butchers Joseph Stalin and Pol Pot and the godless advocate of selfishness Ayn Rand make that perfectly clear. But humanist principles—especially those that emphasize human worth and dignity, the imperative to respect human rights, reverence for life, and the intrinsic ability of humans to be caring and just—provide the foundations of secular moral orientations.

Of course, the secular humanist can often be met with pessimism and doubt. Whenever I find myself discussing religion and humanism with a group of friends, some individual will express strong skepticism concerning humanity's ultimate goodness. And interestingly, one thing I've noticed from such discussions on this topic is that it is almost always a person of faith—a theist—who takes the position that humans are not intrinsically good but rather intrinsically wicked. And this is to be expected, given Christianity's underlying premise that we are all fallen beings, tainted by sin and in need of salvation that can only be attained through God's grace—oh, and the murder of his Son. Such is the message at the traditional heart of the most successful religion ever concocted.

I don't buy it. I do not believe that all children are born with an evil disposition, that sin is some hereditary toxin passed down from one generation to the next, and that the intransigent, default position of humanity is one of malevolence. Rather, like my fellow humanists, I remain convinced that while some humans sometimes do horrible things, most human beings are—most of the time—good. Sure, we are capable of all kinds of unspeakable barbarity, sadism, and savagery. But those are aberrant, atypical, and sporadic expressions of an otherwise—and obviously—overriding moral nature.

Just consider the daily news. CNN. *The New York Times*. Fox News. Whatever news source you prefer. Now, to be sure, someone who doubts the innate goodness of human beings will invariably say something like: "How can you say that humans are good? Just look at the news! It is full of rape and murder! Every single day the news reports on the most horrific things. Clearly, one look at the newspaper must convince you that people are rotten." It's a potent argument. In fact, just to see it through, I'm going to look at the newspaper right now and see what humans are up to. According to my local city paper, a driver hit a bicyclist and then drove off without caring for the victim, who subsequently died; a man was shot in his apartment; a man attempted to kill his wife during a domestic dispute; two college students were stabbed near their fraternity; a mother and her two children were killed by a drunk driver; the owner of a hair-removal clinic was arrested for inappropriately touching female clients; burglaries at local storage unit facilities are on the rise—and so on. There's a lot of badness going on out there, just this morning, as reported in the *Los Angeles Times*.[28]

But guess what? Daily news reports of various crimes actually *affirm* and *support* the humanistic insistence that humans are essentially good. It is, paradoxically, *the fact* that we read of horrific things in the news on a daily basis that bolsters an abiding faith in humanity. Indeed, there is no greater evidence for the veracity of humanism than the daily news. How so? Simple: it is because the news reports on what is rare, what is unusual, what is *out of the ordinary*. That's why murder and rape are headlines: because they are notable exceptions to otherwise decent, everyday human behavior.

If humanity were naturally, intrinsically evil—if people's default position were bad, immoral, unethical—then the newspaper would look very different. It would be replete with shocking, unbelievable headlines such as: "Fifth Grade Class Visits Local Quilt Museum—All Survive!"; "Candy Store Not Robbed for Seventh Straight Year!"; "Couple Takes Morning Walk Every Day Around Their Neighborhood Without Incident!"; "Sorority Organizes a Picnic at Local Park—No One Maimed!"; "Hospital Staff Delivers a Baby!"—and so on.[29] But we don't see such headlines, because they are the mundane, all-too-expected stuff of cooperative, communal, daily human life.

As anthropologist Sarah Blaffer Hrdy points out, about 1.6 billion people get on airplanes every year, flying here and there.[30] They deal with long lines, delayed departures, cramped seats, and tiny bathrooms. And yet, on how many of these flights do people beat up or kill one another? Less than .001 percent. And while the news occasionally reports on a brawl that breaks out on an airplane, the fact that such a brawl makes the news, going viral online, only speaks to its true rarity; if humans were naturally inclined to be nasty and brutish, then the news and viral videos would be about flights that *don't* experience brawls. The bottom line is that when it comes to air travel, people from all walks of life, from all races, ethnicities, and nationalities, people from all different religions and no religions at all, of varying ages and personality types—the vast majority—experience their flights with virtually no violence, aside from perhaps some mild elbow boxing with the stranger sitting next to them. That's some strong evidence that most people can and do behave well, even within less than comfortable conditions. As American social psychologist Jonathan Haidt observes, "our ability to work together, divide labor, help each other, and function as a team is so all-pervasive that we don't even notice it."[31]

Admittedly, there have always been parts of the world wracked by war. There are neighborhoods right now where gunfire is heard on a nightly basis. There are people caught up in an international web of human trafficking. There are millions of people who lie, steal, cheat, rape, and murder. There are periodic genocides. No doubt: human life is perpetually pocked with misery and malfeasance. But for most people, most of the time, this is not the norm; everyday reality in most societies is characterized by people getting along, cooperating, taking care of one another, and living in peace. If this were not the case, our species would have killed itself off a long, long time ago. But we haven't. Our underlying humaneness reigns, and it is never snuffed out, and it persistently prods the majority of us, most of the time, to do and be good.

And that moral goodness has nothing to do with any god. In fact, morality *can't* depend on God, for such a situation simply does not work—which is why a long line of skeptics, doubters, and secularists have been debunking and deconstructing religious morality based on belief in God ever since Greek philosopher Critias, back in the fifth century B.C.E., noted that the gods were purposely invented by rulers to keep people in line through fear.[32]

In the next few chapters, we'll delve into the most basic, fundamental, and intractable problems with God-based religious morality—for it is only after unpacking and revealing the flagrant flaws and fallacies of this traditional religious approach to ethics that we can then move on to the underlying sources and promises of secular morality.

2

Absence of Evidence Is Evidence of Absence

God likes it when you eat at Burger King. Or McDonald's. Or Wendy's. It warms His Holy Heart. But don't you dare be so impiously impertinent as to go to any of these places and order a *salad*. No way! You've got to eat the flesh of a dead animal, because that's what God expects of you.

Or so my wife's former colleague claimed.

Back in the 1990s, Stacy—who was then my girlfriend—was working in a corporate office building in Santa Monica. One day during their lunch break, another employee offered Stacy some pepperoni pizza. Stacy declined. When the woman asked why, Stacy said, "I'm a vegetarian."

This immediately irritated her coworker, who found Stacy's disinterest in eating meat an affront—not just to her, but to something much bigger: God.

"Don't you know that God made this planet for us?" she explained. "He made pigs and chickens and cows for us—to eat!"

According to this woman's Evangelical worldview, Stacy's vegetarianism was not simply rude but somewhat immoral, because it explicitly violated God's cosmic plan: the Lord had created grass for us to lie on, trees to give us shade, water for us to drink and shower with, and many different animals for us to kill and feast upon. So why the hell was Stacy rejecting what God had made for her?

While Stacy's pepperoni-popping colleague was just one random individual, her love of dead animal flesh comingled with a devout theism is actually quite common in the United States. Conservative Evangelical Christians are much more likely to be meat eaters than nonreligious Americans,[1] and many of them see vegetarianism as downright unethical because of what they read in the Bible. Remember, for example, the story of Cain and Abel? They were Adam and Eve's sons. Cain tended to crops, while Abel was a shepherd. Both gave offerings to the Lord. Cain's offering consisted of grains and vegetables, but Abel's consisted of dead animals—and God liked Abel's blood-soaked offerings much better. Given that Abel and his meat were favored by the Lord, Cain felt humiliated and jealous, and he ended up killing Abel. Thus, the first murder in history—at least according to the big book of Jewish and Christian mythology—paints the vegetarian in a negative light: not only is his offering considered paltry by God, but he turns out to be a violent killer. Sheesh.

Granted, there's a lot more to interpret from this ancient Levantine tale—for example, it is a cautionary parable about what happens between siblings if their parent favors one over the other (not good). But for our purposes here, we can readily see the explicit significance of the biblical God preferring meat over maize—a divine preference that extends into the New Testament, where, in Romans 14, Saint Paul refers to those who only eat vegetables as "weak." Thus, Stacy's colleague's antipathy toward vegetarianism was on solid biblical footing: both the Old Testament God and God's number-one New Testament saint don't like vegetarianism. And so neither did she.

The point of this anecdote involving Stacy's eschewal of pepperoni and her coworker's sacred scorn is not to broach the debate over whether or not we ought to eat animals.[2] Rather, it is about something bigger, deeper, and more perennial: the regularity and degree to which people think that God's preferences are relevant in determining what is good or bad, wrong or right, moral or immoral. Or to put it more simply: the widespread notion that how we ethically ought to live is determined by God's will and wishes.

What Does the Lord Require?

While my wife's former colleague's belief that God made the planet for us to exploit is certainly extreme, and not typical of most religious people—especially not the moderate and progressive ones—the fact remains that many social and political aspects of our world today are the way they are because lots of people think God wants them to be that way. Consider the scourge of anti-homosexuality. While fundamentalist Christians, fundamentalist Muslims, and fundamentalist Jews don't agree on much, they do agree that homosexuality is immoral, basing their position on what they find in their respective holy scriptures. For example, in the Old Testament, we read passages like Leviticus 20:13, in which God commands that homosexuals be executed. In the New Testament, homosexuals are derogatorily described as "shameful," "ungodly," "sinful," and "immoral" (1 Timothy 1), and elsewhere they are condemned as depraved, wicked, and "deserving of death" (Romans 1). In Islam, homosexuality is also condemned by God—or in Muslim parlance, Allah. According to the Quran (7:80), which blatantly plagiarizes the Old Testament, there was a city of Lut where the men preferred having sex with other men instead of with women, and as a result, Allah destroyed them all and obliterated the city; Allah clearly hates homosexuality so much that he'll exterminate entire cities as a result. And Allah's hatred of homosexuals is reiterated in the Hadith—the canonical sayings and doings of the all-perfect Prophet, Muhammad. According to one well-known Hadith (Abu Dawud 4462), the Prophet Muhammad declared that if two men have sex with each other, they shall both be murdered.

Thus, according to the holy scriptures of Judaism, Christianity, and Islam—the latter two being the two largest religions in the world—God considers homosexuality an abomination deserving of death. And so, according to those who look to this God or Allah for moral guidance, we ought not allow homosexuals to have any rights. They shouldn't be allowed to get married, raise kids, or love who they want to love. And in more extreme religious contexts, they shouldn't even be allowed to live. Such has been the situation throughout the reign of Christianity and Islam: homosexuals have been stigmatized, brutalized, and murdered, and they have had their human and civil rights curtailed or denied. And such is still the case in many nations to this day. Why? Because that is what the Lord requires.

Beyond homosexuality—or meat eating—there exist so many additional patterns of human behavior, cultural norms, and laws in our world today because of people trying to live in a way that they think is required by their God. Consider, for example, beating, hitting, or spanking your kids. Is it OK? Is it moral? Well, according to the biblical God, not only is it OK, it is actually necessary; the Lord decrees that it is a moral imperative to physically harm your child. "If you spare the rod," we read in Proverbs 13 of the Bible, "you spoil the child." Proverbs 23 makes it even more explicit: "Do not withhold correction from a child . . . you shall beat him with a rod, and deliver his soul from hell." And Bible-believers take appropriate heed to such Lordly exhortations; a study from 2010 found that the more strongly Christian an American is, the more likely he or she is to consider spanking to be a good method of disciplining children; a full 85 percent of Christian fundamentalists believe in spanking their kids, compared to only 57 percent of nonreligious Americans.[3] Another study, from 2012, compared secular parenting literature with Christian parenting literature; the former was critical of corporal punishment, while the latter was much more positive and supportive of it.[4] And given that a solid body of research reveals the extent to which corporal punishment is damaging to children—psychologically, emotionally, and physically[5]—this divergence in secular versus religious views over corporal punishment is no mere matter of opinion; the effects are of explicit moral concern.

The list of things the Lord commands of us is long: what to eat or not eat, who to have sex with and not have sex with, how to dress, how to tend crops, how to trim our facial hair, how many witnesses to procure in order to prove a crime, what day to rest on, what gender ought to be in charge, and so on—and these commands are taken to be imperatively true and ethically binding by billions, thereby significantly shaping the personal morality of countless believers, who then go on to shape so many aspects of our world.

But here's the rub: there is no evidence that this God even exists.[6]

No Proof

My wife's former colleague insists that God wants us to eat meat—and yet she has no rigorous evidence that this God even exists. The Jewish, Christian, and Islamic fundamentalists who deny homosexuals the right to marry, adopt children, or to simply live—depending on what country we're talking about—do so by insisting that it is God's (or Allah's) will that homosexuals be oppressed. And yet they offer no compelling evidence that this supreme deity is actually real. The parent who hits his children because he believes such abuse is what God wants offers no empirical evidence of this magical being's verifiable reality.

And thus we arrive at the first, most basic critique of religiously ensconced theistic morality: it is based on faith in something that has never been positively proven to exist. The manifest failure of God-based morality is that its underlying basis, its central pillar, its muscle, its heart, its engine, its raison d'être—*God*—has never been shown to actually be real. The traditional theological claim that there is an almighty, all-knowing, all-powerful supernatural being who creates everything, gives commands, and performs miracles, has never been proven beyond a reasonable doubt. Or even a pithy smidgeon of doubt.

Now, some may object that this traditional theological description of God is rudimentary or unsophisticated; not everyone who believes in God conceives of God as an almighty, all-knowing, fatherlike being. True enough. Most contemporary theologians will point out that there are much more intellectually sophisticated and dynamic theological explications or descriptions of God out there.

To which I reply: nonsense.

All such so-called "sophisticated" theology is nothing more than psychedelic poetry propped up by pretentious, pseudointellectual gobbledygook signifying absolutely nothing; it is heady, mind-bending verbiage cloaked in a costume of respectable erudition that doesn't actually mean a thing—and certainly cannot be substantiated empirically, let alone logically defended. Consider, for example, prominent theologian Paul Tillich's definition of God as "infinite and inexhaustible depth and ground of being."[7] Hmm. And that means what, exactly? Nothing at all. According to theologian Hans Küng, God is defined as "the infinite in the finite, transcendence in immanence, the absolute in the relative."[8] Nice words. Poetic and ethereal—especially if you are high. But they don't actually mean anything concrete. Deep Christian thinkers such as Alfred North Whitehead—along with his process theology progeny—declare that God is "permanent . . . fluent . . . one . . . many . . . actual eminently . . . immanent . . ."[9] Got that? You sure? Such "sophisticated" theology amounts to little more than what American philosopher Patrick Grim rightly criticizes as "refuge in vagueness,"[10] or what the famous atheist writer Christopher Hitchens simply dismissed as "theo-babble": religious or spiritual words strung together purportedly describing "God" that have no actual meaning or coherence when pondered for more than thirteen seconds.

And so, whether we are talking about the traditional notion of God (the all-powerful, all-knowing creator being who performs magical feats and reads our minds and watches our every move) or the indefinable, theologically "sophisticated" notion of God (e.g., "God is being-itself"[11]—thanks, Professor Tillich!), both score a zero on the proof-o-meter. As Thomas Jefferson wrote in a letter to John Adams in 1820, "To talk of *immaterial* existences is to talk of *nothings*. To say that the human soul, angels, god, are immaterial is to say that they are *nothings* . . ."[12]

Ever since the Polish Lithuanian nobleman Casimir Liszinksi wrote his treatise *De non existentia Dei* (*On the Nonexistence of God*) in the 1670s—for which he was brutally tortured and then burned to death—a vast array of books, essays, and pamphlets have been written effectively pointing out the glaring lack of evidence for the existence of God. I don't plan to restate all their arguments here, but I'll quickly convey the basic highlights.

Below are some of the most typical theistic claims put forth in attempting to prove God's existence, with the standard skeptical rebuttals.

The Creation of the World

Theistic Claim: Just look at the world! Look at the universe! Look at aardvarks, birch trees, zinc, stalactites, onions, smallpox, and Jupiter! How did all these wondrous things get here if there is no God to create them?

Skeptical Response: This is no proof at all for the existence of God. It is simply known as the "argument from ignorance" or "appeal to ignorance," which is a typical fallacy of informal logic that tries to establish a claim based on the fact that we actually don't know enough about something, or don't possess enough knowledge about something and—in our ignorance—are then mistakenly expected to accept the claim. But the claim has not been proven.

Let me give a quick example of the appeal to ignorance at work.

Suppose you and a friend decide to fly to Beijing. On the plane, your friend leans over and says to you, "The pilot's name is Rootbeer."

You are skeptical: "Rootbeer? Really? That can't be right."

And then your friend asks, "Well, do *you* know what the pilot's name is?"

"No," you admit.

"Aha, so then it must be Rootbeer!"

Pretty ridiculous, right? I mean, your friend hasn't proven anything. Just because you don't know the pilot's name doesn't mean that your friend does. And your admitted ignorance of what the pilot's name is doesn't mean that your friend's unusual claim is then automatically correct. What you would need in order to believe that the pilot's name is in fact Rootbeer is some compelling evidence to convince you. But lacking such evidence, your denial of "Rootbeer" as the pilot's name is fully justified.

Now let's try the same conversation, only this time about God.

You're flying on a plane to Beijing, and your friend leans over and says to you: "Whoa, look at the sun beams coursing through those clouds out there. Check out that vast sky. It must have all been created by God."

You are skeptical. "God? Really? A magic deity created all this? That can't be right."

And then your friend asks, "Well, then, do *you* know who or what created it all?"

"No," you admit.

"Aha, so then it must be God!"

Your friend's claim has not been proven. Not even close. He's just basing an entire argument on ignorance. And as atheist writer B. C. Johnson states, "our ignorance of alternative explanations does not justify acceptance of the theistic explanation, because ignorance does not justify explanations—only knowledge does."[13]

When it comes to knowledge of how the universe came to be, we are clueless. We remain agnostic. As leading American atheist Sam Harris has so soundly expressed, "no one knows how or why the universe came into being. It is not clear that we can even speak coherently about the creation of the universe, given that such an event can be conceived only with reference to time, and here we are talking about the birth of space-time itself. Any intellectually honest person will admit that he does not know why the universe exists."[14]

But surely we know that everything has a cause, right? Religious philosophers, such as Saint Thomas Aquinas and my recent Uber driver, have long reasoned that the universe couldn't just exist on its own—something had to cause it to come into being. That cause, theists assert, is God. But by the very logic of this assertion—that everything has to have a cause—then God would also need to be caused. If the theists insist that God need not have a cause, then they are being blatantly illogical by their own standards.

To insist that God is somehow the great, single "uncaused cause" is, in the phrasing of American anthropologist David Eller, "word-magic at best and a malignant anti-answer at worst."[15] And besides, if God can in fact be miraculously uncaused, then so too could the universe. Or anything. Again, believing that the universe must have been caused by something else—something supernatural, no less—is not supported by any evidence. It is simply guesswork embedded in magical thinking, peppered with illogical fallacies, and wrapped in the tinfoil of faith. To account for the mystery of the existence of the universe by saying it is all the inexplicable work of an uncaused creator god gets us nowhere. Again from A. C. Grayling: "to explain something by invoking something itself unexplained is to provide no explanation at all."[16]

Thus, the reasonable, rational position to take—when it comes to fathoming the incomprehensible existence and wonder of all of creation—is to remain in ignorance and simply admit that we don't know its origin or cause, or if it even has an origin or cause in any imagined sense of the ways in which we employ such words, and humbly leave it at that. As Charles Darwin wrote concerning the ultimate origins of creation, "I cannot pretend to throw the least light on such abstruse problems. The mystery of the beginning of all things is insoluble by us; and I for one must be content to remain an Agnostic."[17]

Complexity and Design

Theistic Claim: The natural world is full of profound complexity and deep design. Consider the intricate composition of the human eye or the complex components of a cell. Surely these things couldn't just occur accidentally or by chance. Their intricacy and complexity obviously point to the conscious, deliberate handiwork of an intelligent designer. That intelligent designer is God.

Skeptical Response: First off, as Richard Dawkins explains in his book *The Blind Watchmaker*, and as Philip Ball further reveals in his book *The Self-Made Tapestry*, mind-blowing complexity and functional intricacy can and do arise without a designer, and the natural world abounds with patterns and designs that all have natural, undesigned, unwilled causes.[18] Just look at snowflakes. Or evolution by natural selection, in which genetic information encoded in DNA changes and is modified by haphazard mutations.

Secondly, what we've got here is just another appeal to ignorance: because the world is full of complex organisms, it is claimed that this must be evidence for an intelligent creator god. But that's a fallacious leap. It is more rational to just humbly scratch our heads at this mind-blowing complexity and accept it as mysterious and as yet hard to explain, rather than lazily accept "God" as the answer.

Third, to explain the apparent inexplicable origin of something deeply mysterious—like the complexity and intricacy of the natural world—by saying it was created by something even more inexplicable and ever more deeply mysterious ("God") is an intellectual dodge. You're just epistemologically punting: substituting one immediate mystery with an even more profound, more deeply unfathomable mystery. That's not an explanation—quite the opposite. Consider, for instance, the profound complexities of the human brain and our very consciousness, which involve hundreds of millions of neurons and synapses working together in a nearly unfathomably intricate system. Science hasn't worked out all the details of this natural, neurological wonder—but as Carl Sagan has pointed out, we don't know any of the details of a magical invisible deity creating it all, either. To simply claim that "God made it" isn't explaining anything at all.[19]

Fourth, theists insist that everything in the universe requires some sort of intelligent designer—except, of course, their God. But if you assert that everything in the universe requires a creator/designer—but that the creator/designer itself doesn't require a creator/designer—then you're just being boldly and blatantly illogical. For if God can exist without having been created or designed, then by the very same logic, so too could anything, including the universe. And also, if there was in fact an intelligent designer God, then who or what designed *it*? Something as amazing and complex as a deity that can create eyeballs and minds couldn't just come out of nothing and nowhere! It must have been created by an even more intelligent designer! In the frank words of American philosopher Daniel Dennett, "If God created and designed all these wonderful things, who created God? Supergod? And who created Supergod? Superdupergod?"[20]

As British poet and pioneering atheist Percy Bysshe Shelley reasoned back in 1811, the natural logic and consequence of this theological argument—that because the universe appears designed, it must be evidence of an intelligent creator god—leads to "an infinity of creative and created

Gods, each more eminently requiring an intelligent author of his being than the foregoing." He continues, "The assumption that the Universe is a design, leads to a conclusion that there are infinity of creative and created Gods, which is absurd."[21] And, I should add, lacking any empirical evidence.

Finally, even if one were to simply admit—yes—that the natural world is so truly full of such irreducible complexity and intricate design that, by all faculties of logic and reason, it *must* be evidence of some nonnatural, out-of-the-universe creator—what evidence is there that this creator is an intelligent god, per se? None. Endless other possibilities abound. As B. C. Johnson once quipped, one could just as easily speculate that the universe "was co-operatively constructed by several generations of billions of minor ghostly beings . . . all of them working together"—and thus—"the design argument, even if successful, does not come close to implying the existence of a God."[22] Or how about this one: all the wondrous design and complexity of the natural world is the result of a small, humble alien being from a mysterious other dimension—a being who is so humble that he didn't want anyone to ever know that he was the superintelligent, superpowerful source of our entire universe, so he specifically planted the idea of a God in the early minds of those who would eventually create the world's religions, just to throw humanity off his humble, alien scent.

Like I said, possibilities abound—both imaginable and unimaginable. And none of them should be embraced without any confirming evidence. Including belief in God.

Do I find it incredibly hard to fathom that the universe, with all its complexity, just "came to be" on its own, without any cause or source? You bet. But the only rational, reasonable conclusion to the intricacy of nature is agnosticism: we don't know its cause or source, and maybe we never will. Deal with it. Accept it. Own it. Embrace it. And definitely don't accept an irrational, unproven explanation as a suitable answer—especially if it involves the supernatural. As Albert Einstein wrote, in explication of his atheism, "we have to admire in humility the beautiful harmony of the structure of this world as far as we can grasp it. And that is all."[23]

Living on a Prayer—or Not

Theistic Claim: God exists because He answers prayers.

Skeptical Response: All stories of answered prayers are merely anecdotal. The actual answering of prayers has never been proven in any sort of controlled, unbiased setting or objective experimental design.[24]

Oh, wait just a minute. That's not quite true. There was that big Templeton study back in 2006.

Led by Dr. Herbert Benson and funded by the Templeton Foundation to the tune of $2.4 million, this was the most rigorous, empirically sound study of the possible positive effects of prayer ever conducted in the history of science. The study was double-blind and involved a control group and an experimental group—just the right conditions to objectively measure the relationship between an independent variable (in this case, being prayed for or not) and a dependent variable (improved health). Here's what Dr. Benson's team did: they randomly divided up over 1,800 coronary bypass heart surgery patients from six different hospitals into three groups: the first group had Christians praying for them—the Christians prayed that the selected heart patients would have "a successful surgery with a quick, healthy recovery and no complications"—and the patients in this group were told that people might or might not be praying for them. The second group of heart patients was *not* prayed for, but they were also told that they might or might not have people praying for them. The third group was prayed for, and these patients were told that they were definitely being prayed for. The Christians that were doing all the praying were given the first name and last initial of the specific patients they were to pray for. The result: there was virtually no difference in the recovery trajectories of each group, with all three groups experiencing more or less the same rates and levels of complications. The only minor differences that did arise actually worked *against* the prayers; for example, 18 percent of the patients who had been prayed for suffered major complications such as strokes or heart attacks, compared to only 13 percent of the patients who did not receive any prayers.[25]

There was also that Duke study back in 2003. In this three-year experiment, nearly 750 heart patients in nine different hospitals, all slated for coronary surgery, were prayed for by a variety of religious people, including Christians, Muslims, Buddhists, and Jews. The results of this double-blind experiment were similarly conclusive: there were no significant differences in the recoveries or health outcomes of those patients who were prayed for and those who were not.[26]

The scientific study of the effectiveness of prayer—or rather, the lack of effectiveness—goes back at least 150 years, with the first known formal attempt to empirically discern prayer's efficacy being carried out in 1872 by pioneering British statistician Francis Galton. He reasoned that since the British royal family received far more prayers on its behalf than everyone else—praying for the royal family was a structured part of Sunday services throughout Great Britain—then they should live longer and experience better health than everyone else. Galton statistically tested this hypothesis and (of course) found that the regular prayers of the mass of British people had no such discernible effect on the royal family—they did not, on average, live longer or enjoy better health than anyone else, given all relevant variables considered. Galton also conducted horticultural tests in which he prayed over randomly selected parcels of land; his prayers had no effect on which sections of land bore better, richer, stronger, or more abundant plant life. And thus, between Galton's research in 1872 and Templeton's in 2006, no compelling evidence has ever been brought forth empirically illustrating the power of prayer.[27]

This doesn't mean, of course, that people don't experience wondrous, inexplicable things all the time, or that every now and then someone's prayers appear to have been answered. Such things happen frequently: a wife is told that her dying husband has a zero chance of recovery. Prayers are prayed. And then—*voilà*—the husband suddenly recovers, astonishing the doctors who are left dumbstruck, unable to explain his recovery. It's nothing short of a miracle. While these things do happen, what is far and away more common is that the husband dies—a heap of fervent prayers notwithstanding. And also note that for every person who miraculously recovers, there's another perfectly healthy person who suddenly, for no apparent reason, drops dead of some minor illness, or strange disease, or undetected aneurism, or stroke, or infection. Such is the precarious randomness of the human body and its functioning—people sometimes recover when all odds are against them, but more often than not, they don't.

Think about it: if praying worked, no prayed-for mothers would ever die of breast cancer; no prayed-for teenagers would ever die on the operating table; no prayed-for dogs or cats would ever fail to return home; hundreds of thousands of praying Tutsi families hiding throughout the woods, alleys, attics, and cellars of Rwanda in 1994 would not have been found and hacked to death by Hutu marauders; hundreds of thousands of trains packed with praying Jewish families on the way to the gas chambers of Auschwitz, Sobibór, and Treblinka in the 1940s would have never reached their destinations; and tens of millions of praying people would never die from starvation resulting from a lack of rain. Heck, three hundred million people died from smallpox in the twentieth century alone—clearly, all of their prayers, and their parents' prayers, and their children's prayers, and their spouses' prayers, did not have the hoped-for healing effect.

In the face of prayer's inefficacy, believers will always say: God may not answer your prayer in the way you want—but He has a plan for you nonetheless and knows better. Of course, they offer no tangible evidence for this assertion. But even if it were true—*especially* if it were true—then why bother praying? If you believe that God already has a plan for you and yours, then praying for any given outcome for you and yours makes no sense. It's all so deeply irrational in a way that only religious faith can be: you pray to God to cure your child's leukemia, and your child recovers, and that's evidence that prayer works—or, more likely, you pray to God to cure your child's leukemia, and your child dies, and that's evidence that God answered your prayer but just in a different way than you wanted, because God has a plan and knows better.

Talk about classic "heads I win, tails you lose" balderdash that defies basic rational scrutiny.

And, well, that's because praying is not rational. It is simply—and understandably—what most humans do when there's nothing left for them to do in dire, scary, or painful situations. It is what theists do when they have little or no control over a situation that they'd like to change. It's what religious men and women do when they need to comfort themselves during trying times. And if it does provide them all with even a modicum of comfort and hope during such times, so be it. Such self-consolation can be a good thing. But it doesn't come close to proving the existence of God.

Finally, on this matter of prayer: even if it could actually be proven that prayers to God do in fact work—that an all-powerful deity heeds earnest mental petitions—then that raises the question: What sort of deity would this be, ethically speaking? One that helps suffering or scared humans only when and if they ask/plead/implore? Seems downright malevolent. As American philosopher Georges Rey commented, "the idea of an omni-god that would permit, for example, children to die slowly from leukemia is already pretty puzzling; but to permit this to happen unless someone *prays* to Him to prevent it—this verges on a certain sort of sadism and moral incoherence."[28]

Proving in the Wrong Direction

Theistic Claim: Well, you can't prove that God *doesn't* exist—so there!

Skeptical Response: The fact that I can't prove that God doesn't exist is not an argument that he does. With that kind of fallacious argumentation, just about anything and everything that anyone anywhere has ever claimed to be true could ostensibly be true. Check it out:

- "There are tiny, imperceptible leprechauns running around in space, singing Peruvian folk songs. You can't prove that there aren't!"
- "All plants were created by Plantomina, an all-powerful, supernatural witch who flies around the universe creating plants on various planets. You can't prove that Plantomina isn't real!"
- "Every time I play *The White Album*, a goat in Bolivia feels melancholy. You can't prove that it doesn't!"

And so on, ad infinitum.

It's a wretched way to establish a claim as empirically true. In fact, it's not establishing any truth at all—it's just avoiding having to prove one's assertion by turning the tables and making the skeptical doubter bear the burden of proof. But the skeptical doubter isn't making any claims. She's just doubting the supernatural claim—in this case, the religious claim that God exists. And any time someone makes such a claim, especially an amazing, highly miraculous claim like the existence of a magical deity—he or she bears the burden of proof; it is his or her job to prove it true, not the skeptic's job to prove it false.

And furthermore, when the theist claims that the atheist can't prove that God does not exist, that raises the question: Which God? Are you demanding that Zeus be proven not to exist? Thor? Ra? Hachiman? Amenhotep? Inti? The God of the Jews? The Heavenly Father of Mormonism? Allah, the god of Islam? And are these all distinct gods—each which must be individually disproven not to exist—or are they all the same god? But even if we stick with the, you know, most popular "God" that American Christians claim to believe in—no one can ever offer a clear, objective definition of this most generic of gods. Everyone has their own understanding of Him—some traditional, others personal, some metaphorical, and still others psychedelic. And then, just to shoot more distracting confetti into the court room, the theist will regularly claim that the God she believes in is incomprehensible, indefinable, ineffable, and unknowable! But to say that God is incomprehensible is to frankly acknowledge that any clear definition of God cannot be offered—for how can you define what cannot be comprehended or grasped?

When the atheist is asked to disprove the existence of God, she faces a never-ending shell game, where the target is ever shifting, the subject impossible to pin down, and the matter under question ultimately one big dynamic sleight of hand—or sleight of mind, in this case. But at least in a real shell game, the manipulator knows where the ball is hiding. When it comes to theism, even the religious believer in God is peddling something ultimately unknowable, inscrutable, ineffable, invisible, undetectable, indefinable, imperceptible, indiscernible—or more succinctly: not there.

Ye of Lots of Faith?

There are countless additional ways in which religious people try to prove the existence of God. None work. None hold up to any sort of evidentiary scrutiny. And that's when they inevitably, and conveniently, turn to faith in defense of their claim that God exists. Thus, the final "argument" for belief in God is not based on any verifiable evidence or sound logic but rather faith. And as Mark Twain rightly quipped, "Faith is believing what you know ain't so." Or as Twain's contemporary and fellow wit Ambrose Bierce put it, faith is "Belief without evidence in what is told by one who speaks without knowledge, of things without parallel."[29] Or as the much less humorous German philosopher Friedrich Nietzsche remarked, faith is nothing more than "the will to avoid knowing what is true."[30]

While faith may certainly be comforting, and it may be inspiring, and it clearly holds a place of value in most people's hearts as they navigate the challenges of life, it is, nonetheless, an inherently poor way to establish the truth of anything. For, as American philosopher George Smith asserts, the essence of faith is "to consider an idea true even though it cannot meet the test of truth . . . faith is required only for those beliefs that cannot be defended."[31]

Even Paul, the true founder of Christianity, honestly articulated the meaning of faith nearly two thousand years ago, which he defines in Hebrews 11 of the New Testament as confidence in what is *hoped* for and the conviction of things *not seen*. That is, faith is believing in what one *wishes* and *hopes* to be true (not what *is* true) and being convinced of things even *without evidence of their empirical reality*. And this is exactly what the theist does: hangs the entire corpus of her morality upon *faith* in something that doesn't even exist.

And this will not do.

Morality and ethics are far too important to be based on some fantastical deity that can't even be proven to exist. Morality and ethics are far too immediate and imperative to hinge upon mere wishes, hopes, and illusions. Morality and ethics—the underlying bases for how we treat one another and how we seek to structure society—cannot stand if they are based on the ephemeral, inscrutable claims of religious theism.[32]

The fact that God has never been clearly defined or proven to exist is enough of a reason to dismiss—or at least be highly dubious of—any ethical system based on theism. As American philosopher Michael Martin has argued, "unless the concept of God is shown to be coherent, theism cannot possibly be thought to be an ontological foundation of morality."[33] And yet, as we know, most people do believe that God exists—regardless of the glaring lack of evidence. And many of these theists base their morals on their faith in God, which spurs their love of pepperoni and dismissal of vegetarianism, bolsters their antipathy toward homosexuals and their opposition to gay marriage, and helps them justify the hitting of their children.

But wait—that's not quite fair.

Not all theists share these views or predilections. Many people who believe in God support vegetarianism, are in favor of gay marriage, and oppose corporal punishment. The fact of the matter is that God-believers hold many different views, harboring a wide diversity of values on a variety of matters of ethical importance. No doubt. But while this impressive diversity of viewpoints among theists is perhaps something to be welcomed and celebrated, it is—at root—yet another significant reason as to why morality based on belief and faith in God is so problematic as to be manifestly untenable.

3

The Insidiousness of Interpretation

One night about twenty years ago, I was lying in bed watching TV, clicker in hand, flipping through channels, when I came across an episode of the show *20/20*. John Stossel, one of the lead reporters, was doing an investigative story on polygamous families. He went to some region of Utah where Mormons still practice what they call "the principle of plural marriage," which entails one man having multiple wives. Stossel and his TV crew hung out with these pious, polygamous men and women for a few days, spent time in their homes, attended their church gatherings, and interviewed them. From the television footage, everyone profiled seemed quite content; I got the sense that none of the adults featured in the show were being forced to live in a polygamous situation, but rather they all seemed to enjoy living a life that was spiritually rich and full of communal and (extensive) family ties.

The part of the episode that is most seared into my memory is when Stossel sits down with about five or six of the Mormon men to talk to them about how they manage life with so many wives and children. One man says that it's quite stressful being the head of such households, full of responsibility. But then Stossel politely challenges him, asking what's so stressful about it. After all, the women take care of all the kids' needs, the women do all the cooking and cleaning, and the men get to have sex with three, four, or five different women, as per their desire. But the women don't get to have sex with any other husbands. It seems unfair. It seems like it's all for the men. When Stossel pushes this matter of gender inequality, one of the men offers an earnest rebuttal: "I didn't make the law, God did."

"Amen," the other men resoundingly affirm in confident, almost gleeful support.

And there you have it: men enjoying an unequal, imbalanced domestic situation. But, hey, *they* didn't make the law—*God* did. They're just obediently living in accordance with the Lord's will, and if it happens to benefit them, what can they do? How can they be to blame? They are ethically obliged to follow the laws of their Heavenly Father—end of story.

I am not personally opposed to polygamy. I think consenting adults should be able to live in whatever kind of domestic unions they choose. And I recognize that polygamy can even have potential benefits for some women; Martha Hughes Cannon (1857–1932), a Mormon wife in a polygamous marriage, was the first female state senator ever elected in the United States, and she was able not only to pursue politics but also to get a medical degree largely because she had numerous "sister wives" to help her, support her, and take care of her children in her absence.

But most Mormon men today are not polygamous because of what it can do for their wives' careers. In fact, Mormon women are significantly less likely to work outside the home full-time than non-Mormon women,[1] and Mormon theology is pretty clear that a woman's primary role is that of homemaker and baby-raiser. And they are definitely not to have more than one husband. Why not? Well, as their husbands can readily explain: God said so. Such is the ultimate bottom line as to why these Mormon men don't change diapers, do dishes, cook casseroles, or let their wives sleep with other blokes. How unabashedly convenient for these fellas. How utterly self-serving. And—above all—how deeply typical of traditionally religious approaches to morality and ethics.

One Wife or Fifty-Five?

The polygamous Mormon men profiled on that *20/20* episode are actually on some rock-solid theological footing. They believe that the founder of their religion, Joseph Smith (1805–1844), was a prophet of God and that God directly communicated with Smith, outlining very clearly what he wills for humanity in the sacred, holy text of the Mormon religion, *Doctrines and Covenants*, which is a collection of God's direct messages to Smith concerning various aspects of how life ought to be lived here on Earth. Among the plethora of prescriptions and proscriptions in *Doctrines and Covenants*, we find some very direct words concerning the structure of marriage; in Chapter 132, God declares the following:

> For behold, I reveal unto you a new and everlasting covenant, and if ye abide not that covenant, then ye are damned; for no one can reject this covenant and be permitted to enter into my glory . . . [then lots of stuff about marriage, stuff about Abraham and David, stuff about Joseph Smith's wife, etc.] . . . if any man espouse a virgin, and desire to espouse another, and the first give her consent, and if he espouse the second, and they are virgins . . . then he is justified; he cannot commit adultery for they are given unto him . . . and if he have ten virgins given unto him by this law, he cannot commit adultery, for they belong to him; therefore he is justified. But if one or either of the ten virgins, after she is espoused, shall be with another man, she has committed adultery, and shall be destroyed.[2]

Pretty clear, right? Men can have up to ten wives, so long as they are virgins, but if a woman is with a man other than her husband, she shall be—um—*destroyed*. How brutally murderous, baldly immoral, heinously unethical. Gross inequality is woven into the marital relationship. But again, let's not forget—Joseph Smith didn't make the law, God did. And despite the fact that none of the men on that *20/20* show were filmed advocating for the murderous destruction of any women, they were clear that, in their decision to live in polygamous marriages, they were simply following the moral commandments of God as most plainly revealed.

Or were they?

According to the current leaders of the Mormon religion based in Salt Lake City—officially known as the Church of Jesus Christ of Latter-day Saints—this passage from *Doctrines and Covenants* is actually *not* what the Lord requires of his flock. At least not anymore. Polygamy is no longer divinely supported, and according to the current Mormon president and the Twelve Apostles—God's present spokespeople on planet Earth—monogamy is what the Lord now requires: one man and one woman. Any other marital arrangement is sinful.

The twisting story of polygamy in Mormonism has been well-told elsewhere,[3] but here's a very brief sketch: at the height of his charismatic heyday, back in the late 1830s, Joseph Smith, who was able to convince tens of thousands of people that he was the prophet of God, started taking additional wives. He eventually received holy sanction for this endeavor in the form of God's direct communication, already outlined above. Although his first wife, Emma, was not happy about this new principle of "plural marriage," Smith was undeterred; one historian, Andrew Jenson, records that Smith eventually had twenty-seven wives, Fawn Brodie counts forty-eight, and Stanley S. Ivins put the number at eighty-four.[4] After the murder of Smith, his successor, Brigham Young, continued to champion the practice of polygamy with religious zeal; estimates vary, but it's safe to say that he had between twenty-seven and fifty-five wives.[5] While most Mormon men could not afford to support multiple wives, many could, and somewhere between 20 percent and 45 percent of Mormon adult men and women lived in polygamous marriages in the latter half of the nineteenth century.[6]

All of these married men living with numerous wives in the territory of Utah caused quite an American scandal: salacious stories—peddled by journalists, novelists, and various anti-Mormonists—percolated throughout the country, raising much intrigue and ire.[7] Subsequently, the federal government got involved, passing a series of anti-bigamy laws, such as the Edmunds-Tucker Act of 1887, aimed directly at destroying the Mormon practice of "plural marriage." Such anti-Mormon legislation severely crippled the Mormon community: many leaders were imprisoned, parents' rights over their children were endangered, the Church's land holdings were threatened, and even the movement for the territory of Utah to join the United States was in peril.

And then, in 1890, the Mormon leadership made a spiritual about-face. Wilford Woodruff, the president of the Church of Jesus Christ of Latter-day Saints, spent a prayerful night struggling with the Lord, the result of which was his issuance of a new manifesto declaring that Mormons would no longer engage in plural marriage. Utah was subsequently admitted as a state in 1896. In 1904, the new president of the Church, Joseph F. Smith, further declared that any Mormons who continued to practice plural marriage would be excommunicated, a declaration approved by the Twelve Apostles. And such has been the official position to this day: the website of the Church of Jesus Christ of Latter-day Saints currently proclaims that the "standard doctrine of the Church is monogamy."[8]

Throughout the short history of Mormonism, this thorny matter of polygamy has caused much schismatic strife. It first spurred a split when the Prophet Smith initially instituted it; his wife, Emma, and her sons were so opposed to the practice that they broke off from Smith's new religious movement and formed their own, non-polygamous version of the Mormon faith: the Reorganized Church of Jesus Christ of Latter-day Saints, with its headquarters in Independence, Missouri—where it remains to this day under the name Community of Christ. Next, when polygamy was officially denounced by the heads of the Mormon Church in Salt Lake City in 1890 and 1904, this caused another schism between those who would now only practice monogamy and those who felt it was the Lord's will to continue practicing polygamy. Some members of the Twelve Apostles resigned over the matter, believing that God still wanted the principle of plural marriage to be practiced, and other like-minded Mormons, dubbed "fundamentalist" Mormons, rejected the Church leaders in Salt Lake City, setting up their own breakaway congregations where polygamy could still be practiced. It was just such a community that John Stossel visited for his *20/20* exposé.

So, there you have it: a small, tight-knit, new religion—founded only some 190 years ago—full of fervent adherents who all believe in God, and all agree that Joseph Smith was God's prophet, and all concur that living a moral life means obeying the will of God—and yet they simply can't agree on whether or not God wants them to be in polygamous or monogamous marriages. And the spiritual stakes are pretty high: the fundamentalist Mormons believe that you can't get into the highest level of heaven (the "celestial kingdom") if you don't practice plural marriage,[9] while other Mormons, those remaining members of the Church of Jesus Christ of Latter-day Saints, believe that you can't get into heaven at all if you *do* practice plural marriage.

And, thus, we come to the second major problem with any ethical system based on God: staunch theists claim that morality is based on belief in God and in following God's will, and yet they can't agree on just what God's will is.[10] *Interpretation* of God's will becomes the name of the game. And what a deeply problematic, all-too-human game it is, with everyone interpreting differently, bringing his or her own interests, experiences, cultural lens, political leanings, tribalism, communal needs, and personal proclivities to the process.

Slavery, Anyone?

There are many other instances from throughout history that reveal the depth of this problem of theistic interpretation.

Consider, for example, the matter of slavery. Is it morally acceptable to forcibly enslave another human? Is it ethical to keep other humans in bondage, forcing them to work for your own advantage, and denying them not only the very fruits of their labor, but their basic right of personal liberty?

According to the logic of theistic morality, the first authority—indeed, the *supreme* authority—to consult in trying to decide upon this matter would be God and his commandments. According to God's Ten Commandments, as recorded in the Book of Exodus in the Old Testament, God doesn't say, "Thou shalt not enslave another." There's no such prohibition. He does provide other prohibitions, such as "Thou shalt not have any other gods before me" and "Thou shalt not make any images of anything that exists in heaven or on earth" and "Thou shalt not lie" and "Thou shalt not steal" and "Thou shall not commit adultery." But nothing about slavery.

Well, that's not quite true. There is that one significant commandment that does sort of seem to accept servitude as permissible: in Exodus 20:17, God declares, "Thou shall not covet they neighbor's house, wife, male servant, female servant, ox, donkey, or anything else that belongs to your neighbor." So, what we have here is a list of things that *can* belong to your neighbor: including objects (a house), animals (oxen, donkeys), as well as people (wives and servants). God thus seems here, at least implicitly, to approve of servitude.

And then God's approval of slavery goes from implicit to explicit. In Leviticus 25, God tells the people of Israel that they can in fact purchase other human beings and own them: "You may buy male and female slaves from among the nations that are around you . . . they shall become your property."

Of course, the wording is crucial here. Does God condone *servitude* or *slavery*? Well, the original Hebrew word used in these biblical passages, written thousands of years ago by a culture dramatically different from our own, is *ebed*. And it is beyond difficult to definitively know just what this ancient Hebrew word *ebed* accurately translates to in our modern American verbiage.[11] Does it correctly correspond to our word "servant," or is it better translated as our word "slave"? We can surely appreciate what a world of difference the words "servant" and "slave" make when it comes to their moral meanings and ethical implications in our contemporary society. So, who has the final say on this matter of interpreting the *true* meaning of *ebed*—some balding, bespectacled professor in Boston or Jerusalem? Alas, how troubling that even the very *translating* of God's commanding words must be based on linguistic and historical *interpretation*, and thus can't ever be definitively, objectively agreed upon.

So is owning another person as a slave morally acceptable to God? According to the New Testament of Christianity, it seems like it definitely is. Jesus does not condemn slavery, and in Luke 12:42, he implicitly condones the practice. Paul, the founder of Christianity and its leading authoritative voice—second only to Jesus—definitely did not condemn slavery. Nor did he condemn slave owners. He did *not* say, "Free those you hold in bondage, as Christ has freed you." Rather, in Ephesians 6:5, Paul declares, "Slaves, obey your masters with respect and fear, and with sincerity of heart, just as you would obey Christ." In Titus 2, Paul again teaches that slaves ought to be "subject to their masters in all things." Elsewhere, in Colossians 3:22—just to make the Lord's position on slavery as unambiguous as possible—Paul reasserts the imperative: "Slaves, obey your earthly masters."

Such biblical injunctions are deeply immoral. Just like the deeply immoral injunction from Exodus 21:20, in which God explicitly declares that people can violently beat their male and female slaves, so long as the beating doesn't end in death. It is nigh impossible to even fathom just how much pain and misery, how much violence and degradation, how much abuse and assault has occurred—just how much human enslavement over the centuries has been physically enacted and religiously justified—from such biblical passages. Perhaps this all helps to explain why Frederick Douglass, the great writer, orator, abolitionist, and former slave, experienced the worst cruelty at the hands of the strongly Christian. As he wrote in 1845:

> Were I to be again reduced to the chains of slavery, next to that enslavement, I should regard being the slave of a religious master the greatest calamity that could befall me. For of all slaveholders with whom I have ever met, religious slaveholders are the worst. I have ever found them the meanest and basest, the most cruel and cowardly, of all others.[12]

And yet despite such cruelty, the architect of Christianity, Paul, exhorts the unfortunate who are forced into bondage, through no fault of their own, to obey their earthly masters—with respect and fear, no less! So it goes, if you uncritically accept the New Testament as holy writ.

Or not.

Many Christians who uncritically accept the New Testament as holy writ have been, and are, antislavery. But how can this be? Don't the Ten

Commandments implicitly allow for servitude? Doesn't Paul explicitly exhort slaves to obey their masters? What is ambiguous here?

A lot. Or nothing. Once again, it is all—and I mean *all*—a matter of interpretation.

In the eighteenth and nineteenth centuries, American Christians—ardent and pious to a soul—were deeply divided over the moral question of slavery. A small number of theologians, preachers, and politicians, such as William Wilberforce, George Bourne, Charles Spurgeon, and John Wesley, condemned slavery as a grave sin and injustice. And the small Christian denomination of Quakers came to believe that slavery was immoral, working hard to undermine what they saw as a cruel, inhumane practice that went against the will of God. But the Quakers and their faithful ilk comprised a distinct moral minority; most Christians of the day interpreted God's will quite differently. As American historian Forrest Wood exhaustively documents, "despite the humanitarian efforts of some Christians on behalf of the millions held in bondage, Christian thought and conduct in the first three centuries of American life came down overwhelmingly on the side of human oppression"[13] and "defenders of slavery among men of the cloth were far more numerous than opponents."[14] Here's but one glaring example: when William Lloyd Garrison, the tireless antislavery activist and editor of *The Liberator* first wanted to offer an abolitionist speech in Boston, every single Christian denomination denied him their stage.[15]

The reigning Christian view in the nineteenth century—among whites, of course—was perhaps best expressed by John Henry Hopkins, bishop of the Episcopal Church, who in his 1861 publication *The Bible View of Slavery* explained that "the Almighty" ordained Black people to slavery "because *he judged it to be their fittest condition*." As for God's son's take on slavery, well, Hopkins pointed out that Jesus "uttered not one word against it!"[16] Indeed, the majority of white Bible-believers in the United States, especially in the South, were convinced that God approves of slavery. As historian, sociologist, and civil rights pioneer W. E. B. Du Bois noted, back in 1913, the Christian Church not only aided and abetted the slave trade for centuries, but it "was the bulwark of American slavery."[17] Du Bois documented the fact that "under the aegis and protection of the religion of the Prince of Peace . . . there arose in America one of the most stupendous institutions of human slavery that the world has ever seen. The Christian Church sponsored and defended the institution . . . the Catholic Church approved of and defended slavery; the Episcopal Church defended and protected slavery; the Puritans and Congregationalists recognized and upheld slavery."[18]

Consider one glaring example, the proslavery Christian leader George Whitefield—known by many as the founder of American Evangelicalism. A slave owner himself, Whitefield was a vociferous defender of this "peculiar institution." And he did so as a devout servant of God: when he testified before the British Parliament, in order to advocate for the introduction of slavery into Georgia, he not only relied on the biblical defense of slavery, but he argued that God had specifically created the climate in Georgia to be suitable for enslaved Africans to feel at home in their bondage.[19] His argument won the day and was deemed morally and ethically correct by most of his fellow Christians, especially Southern whites. Heck, you know the Southern Baptists—the largest Protestant denomination in the United States? Did you ever wonder why they are called *Southern* Baptists, as opposed to just Baptists? It's because of their historical support of slavery: once the white Baptists in the North eventually condemned it, the white Baptists in the South broke from their northern coreligionists and formed their own Southern religious denomination in 1845. And Baptists weren't the only Christian denomination to split over the question of whether or not God commands or condemns the enslavement of other human beings: Presbyterians divided over the matter in 1837 and Methodists in 1844.[20]

Irreconcilable Interpretation

So far, we have looked at the historical extent to which Christians have been split over whether or not God approves of slavery, and we've explored the specific instance in which Mormons diverged over what form of marriage God commands. These represent just two distinctly American versions of theism that have been deeply divided at times over fundamental questions of human conduct—divisions based on incompatible interpretations of God's will.

But we haven't even thrown any other religions into the interpretive mix—like, say, Islam. What does Islam say about polygamy? According to a direct reading of the Quran—which is considered by hundreds of millions to be the precise, literal word of God/Allah—Sura 4:3 states that a man may have up to four wives, so long as he can treat them all equally. So Allah clearly approves of polygamy. Or does he? While the majority of Muslims agree that God allows it, some Islamic theologians have interpreted Sura 4:3 differently, claiming that since it is nearly impossible for a man to truly treat multiple wives equally in all aspects, then polygamy is clearly *not* God's ideal. Today, most Muslim-majority nations allow polygamy, but a handful do not.

Where does Judaism stand in all of this? For most of its early history, Jews interpreted God's will as being in favor of polygamy, and it was widely practiced. But then, after Rabbi Gershom ben Judah of the eleventh century proclaimed it against God's will, it steadily petered out. The state of Israel currently outlaws it. However, one of the most powerful contemporary rabbis in Israel, Ovadia Yosef, came out a few years ago in support of polygamy, and many orthodox rabbis in Israel currently perform polygamous weddings on a regular basis—as their interpretation of God's will condones.[21]

Then there is Hinduism, Sikhism, Bahaism, Zoroastrianism—all with their own different interpretations of God's will (or the gods' will) regarding the ideal, approved marital structure for humanity.

And as for the issue of slavery—again, let's consider Islam. Do Muslims believe that Allah approves of slavery? The answer is: yes, no, yes, no, yes, no—or rather, a multitude of interpretations, depending on this or that Islamic theologian's construal of this or that historical epoch and from this or that school of Islam from this or that part of the world.[22]

The obvious point here is that when it comes to what is ethically correct and morally commanded, the major religions of the world interpret God's will differently, resulting in widespread disagreement. But it's not just the different major religions that are characterized by such conflicting interpretations—it is the case that even within the *same* religious tradition, one finds radically conflicting interpretations of basic questions of God's will concerning human conduct. And this has not only been the case throughout history, but it persists today.

For a contemporary example, we see dramatically different interpretations of God's will when it comes to the morality or immorality of gay marriage: the Roman Catholic Church, American Baptist Churches, Assemblies of God, the Church of Jesus Christ of Latter-day Saints, every Islamic denomination, the Orthodox Jewish Movement, the United Methodist Church, the Southern Baptist Convention, the Lutheran Church–Missouri Synod, and the National Baptist Convention *oppose* it, while the Episcopal Church, the Presbyterian Church (U.S.A.), the Conservative Jewish Movement, the Reform Jewish Movement, the United Church of Christ, the Society of Friends (Quakers), the Unitarian Universalist Association of Churches, and the Evangelical Lutheran Church in America *support* it.[23] And both positions are theologically justified by contradictory interpretations of God's will.

This dysfunctional dynamic of conflicting interpretation both between and within every religion is readily observable and perpetually at play. Whether the question is doctor-assisted suicide or vegetarianism, transgender rights or universal health care, the death penalty or abortion, climate change or mass incarceration, fervent God-believers from different religions can't agree, and even fervent God-believers from within the same religion can't agree—and they all continue to interpret God's scriptures and God's laws and God's will differently. Vastly so. Irreconcilably so.

And thus, to say that morality rests upon God—isn't saying much. To insist that we need God's guidance when confronting ethical dilemmas—isn't insisting much. Because at root, everyone interprets God's will differently.

A God of One's Own

And by everyone, I mean just that: every single person. Because in reality, the widespread array of differing theistic interpretations gets even more granulated and diffuse: subjective, self-serving, contradictory, and incompatible interpretations of God's will inevitably manifest themselves at the individual level.

Consider my friend and colleague Stephen Davis.

Stephen Davis, the Russell K. Pitzer Professor of Philosophy at Claremont McKenna College, is one of the world's leading Christian thinkers. With a Master of Divinity from Princeton Theological Seminary and a PhD from Claremont Graduate University, Professor Davis has published over fifty scholarly articles in academic journals, and he is the author of thirteen books, such as *God, Reason and Theistic Proofs* (1997), *Logic and the Nature of God* (1983), and *Faith, Skepticism, and Evidence* (1978). Professor Davis's scholarly expertise is wide-ranging and highly regarded within Christian circles, and he is specifically respected as an expert on Jesus; in books such as *Risen Indeed* (1993), he argues that the New Testament account of Jesus's resurrection is factually, historically accurate.

Beyond his impressive scholarly achievements, he's a warm, kind, and affable man. And regardless of our stark disagreements on matters of religion, and despite the fact that I devote much of my professional life debunking what he spends much of his professional life defending, he has always treated me respectfully. And he regularly agrees to visit my classes and speak to my students, providing them with an alternative take on God, religion, morality, and so forth.

The last time Professor Davis spoke to my class, he revealed something very interesting—and quite relevant to this discussion of the inevitability of theistic interpretation at the individual level.

It was a night class in the spring of 2017. About twenty-five students were present. Professor Davis was lecturing about God's role in establishing morality, explaining to the students that God establishes clear moral rules and obligations that are objectively true, and he argued that without such a God-based, objective morality, ethics is reduced to nothing more than personal preference, subjective notions, relativism. He said that if morals and ethics were merely subjective and relative, then "anything goes" and it becomes impossible to claim that one's own sense of wrong or right is binding on others. Such an approach to morality, he insisted, won't do.

"Some things just *are* immoral," he emphatically declared. "They are fundamentally, *objectively* wrong." His example of such a thing? "Genocide." As he explained, "Genocide just *is* wrong. It *is* immoral. Case closed."

While all of my students were in agreement about genocide being fundamentally immoral, some of them had immediate difficulty understanding how Professor Davis could square his unequivocal stance on the immorality of genocide with his abiding faith in the biblical God. As one student asked: "If morality comes from God, and you claim that genocide is fundamentally, objectively immoral, then why does God actually command his followers to engage in genocide numerous times throughout the Bible?"

The contradiction was true, and just so glaring: here was the erudite Professor Davis saying that genocide is the ultimate example of something that is truly, unquestionably, manifestly immoral, and yet the very God he worships—and thinks establishes objective morality—both commits and commands genocide throughout the pages of the Bible.[24]

Professor Davis's pat response: "Oh, I don't think that those parts of the Bible in which God commands or commits genocide are true. I don't believe them. I think those things were inserted there by people, but God didn't actually command or commit them. They aren't to be taken as historically true, or as literal. God would never command or commit genocide. I just can't believe that."

Here is a man who is a devoted Christian, a most thoughtful theist, who claims that the Bible is holy, and strongly believes that the New Testament's account of Jesus dying and rising from the dead is factually, historically accurate—empirically supported by convincing evidence—and yet when it comes to different pages of the Bible, wherein God commands and commits genocide, he has no problem simply discarding those passages as untrue, historically inaccurate, and not to be believed. Because the God he believes in just wouldn't do things like that. Because the deity that Professor Davis has devoted his life to would never approve of or engage in genocide, anything in the Bible that states the opposite he simply interprets as untrue.

This self-protective, explicitly illogical move by Stephen Davis is perhaps the most common, widespread form of theistic interpretation out there: individual God-believers simply dismiss anything God says or does that doesn't comport with their own personal view of God. Or in a related vein, individual God-believers interpret something God says or does in such a way that it firmly squares with their own individual concept of morality. Or rather, God-believers adamantly insist that the God they believe in does or does not approve of this or that, as their subjective needs dictate. That is, people who think that slavery is a good and moral thing—or gay marriage, or higher taxes, or meat eating, or the death penalty, or recycling, or building a border wall, or corporal punishment, or smoking marijuana, or using condoms, or getting a divorce, or having multiple wives, or banning women from driving, or guns—each and every single one of them interprets God's will in such a way as to snuggly support their own subjective position with regard to these various issues.

As George Bernard Shaw once quipped, "No man ever believes that the Bible means what it says. He is always convinced that it says what he means."[25]

Theistic Morality as Echo Chamber

To prove that people generally interpret God's values so as to nicely fit their own personal, subjective values, a team of researchers led by University of Chicago Professor of Behavioral Science Nicholas Epley conducted a simple experiment. First, they asked people who believe in God to give their own personal views on various controversial issues in America, such as the death penalty and abortion. Next, they asked these people what they thought various prominent Americans' views were on these same issues—people like Bill Gates. And finally, they asked them what they thought God's views were on these issues. As to be expected, peoples' own values on these controversial issues most strongly aligned with those values they also attributed to God.

But here's what the researchers did next: they took a different group of people and had them engage in a variety of tasks specifically intended to influence or challenge their preexisting views and values on various issues. For example, subjects were instructed to do something like write a speech on the death penalty in which they had to take the position opposite their own. And then, after completing such a task, they were asked what they thought the values were on these controversial issues for various prominent Americans and also God. The result? People shifted a bit concerning the values they attributed to God, but not on those that they attributed to other prominent Americans. In other words, when their own social or political values were shaken up a bit and perhaps softened, this was reflected in what they thought God's values were—which also softened a little, continuing to align closely with their own, newly softened values. But there was no change in what they thought various prominent Americans' values were. Those remained the same. Given these findings, Professor Epley observed that "intuiting God's beliefs on important issues may not produce an independent guide, but may instead serve as an echo chamber to validate and justify one's own beliefs."[26]

Then things got even more interesting, neurologically speaking. Professor Epley and his team went on to use fMRI technology to scan the brains of the people volunteering in this study, looking at what parts of their brains were activated when they were thinking about their own values as well as the values of God and those of other Americans. In the first two—thinking about their own values as well as God's values—the same parts of the brain became active. However, when they thought about what other Americans' values might be, a different part of the brain became active—which suggests that theists literally, physically map God's values onto their own.

As Professor Epley and his team concluded:

> People may use religious agents as a moral compass, forming impressions and making decisions based on what they presume God as the ultimate moral authority would believe or want. The central feature of a compass, however, is that it points north no matter what direction a person is facing. This research suggests that, unlike an actual compass, inferences

> about God's beliefs may instead point people further in whatever direction they are already facing.[27]

The grand takeaway: we ought to be very wary of anyone who claims that God-based morality is objective. It is anything but—given that everyone interprets God's will differently, and all too subjectively.

Which brings us back to Stephen Davis. He is certain that genocide is morally wrong. And he is equally certain that the God he believes in would never approve of genocide—even when the Bible clearly says otherwise. So why does Professor Davis interpret God's nature the way he does, as a deity who would never command or commit genocide? Because Professor Davis is a good, ethical person who finds genocide morally abhorrent. In fact, he is so ethical—and is so intrinsically horrified by the very possibility of genocide—that he projects his own internal moral orientation out into the imaginary heavens and up onto the presumed God he worships. Professor Davis dismisses the passages of the Bible in which God both commits and commands genocide because he can't help but construct a deity that fits his own moral outlook—even as he simultaneously insists that his moral outlook comes from God.

Professor Davis thinks that he is good because he believes in a moral God, but it is actually the other way around: the God that Professor Davis believes in is constructed as good because he—Stephen Davis—is moral. As Paul Kurtz explains in his book *Forbidden Fruit*, such a religious person is often engaged in a flagrant form of self-deception, wherein he or she doesn't even see the true source of his or her own morality and mistakenly places it in the hands of an imaginary deity.

My friend Professor Davis does what all God-believers do: interpret their deity in a way that aligns with their own proclivities and orientations. Theists generally believe in exactly the kind of God they *want* to believe in, or have been socialized to believe in, or at least the kind of God others in their community want and expect them to believe in. Which means that interpretations of God's will are always and invariably projections of people's own inner dispositions, or justifications of political goals, or collective communal constructs, or subjectively self-serving—or a combination of all four. And thus, "God" cannot comprise a sound, solid, or objective basis for our morals and ethics, because theism inevitably and invariably involves interpretation to such a high degree as to make it essentially useless.

But let's say—just for the sake of being open to the possible claims of traditional theism—that all of the differing, contradictory, and irreconcilable interpretations of God's will could somehow, some way, be worked out. Hard as it may be, let's imagine that someone, somehow has the indisputably correct interpretation of God's will for humanity—and that this person could somehow convince everyone that her interpretation was indeed exactly correct. That is, let's imagine a situation in which all God-believers were somehow on the same page concerning what the Lord requires. Would this then make theistic morality feasible? No. In fact, even if there was incontrovertible evidence that God existed, and even if everyone could actually agree on his will, this would not enhance or sustain human morality.

If anything, it would denigrate and destroy it.

The next chapter will explain why.

4

You Will Obey

You've only been in Vietnam for a few weeks. It is hot and the air is heavy and you are nineteen years old and it is 1968. And now you're on patrol, in the jungle, with your platoon. You are unfamiliar with the terrain, fearful of booby traps and mines, skittish about getting ambushed, anxious about fulfilling your obligations and not letting your comrades down, and you're scared to die.

Fortunately, there's Sergeant Rex. He's already been in Vietnam for over two years. He's a thick-skulled, chiseled-chested Midwesterner: sturdy, sharp, and seasoned. And he's in charge of your platoon—which is a damn good thing because he knows what he's doing, he handles stress like a boulder, he's deft at making quick decisions, and he's more than familiar with the ins and outs of your platoon's mission. Recognizing that he is smarter than you, stronger than you, and more experienced than you, and given all that you have learned about conformity, teamwork, and duty while in basic training, you are ready and willing to submit to Sergeant Rex's orders. Hell, you eagerly and happily acquiesce to his authority, and you find it deeply comforting to know that he's in charge and that he'll do everything in his power to protect you.

One day, while on patrol just south of Da Nang, Sergeant Rex gathers you and your platoon mates together and makes an announcement: "This afternoon we're going to be going into a small village that needs our help. We're going to deliver food supplies, bottled water, and first aid kits. We're going to repair some huts and fix a well. The people in this village have been hit pretty hard lately, and we're going to go in there and do what we can to help them. Got that?"

"Yes, sir!" you and your fellow soldiers obediently reply. And you subsequently do just what Sergeant Rex instructs: you go into that village and bring much-needed supplies and spend hours helping the people there. It's an altruistic, feel-good day.

Two days later, while on patrol, Sergeant Rex gathers you all together again and declares the following: "This afternoon we're going to be attacking a small village. Our enemies are there, and we must completely destroy them. And we can't take any chances. So we're going to go into that village and kill everything that moves or breathes—men, women, children, animals. Everything. And then we're going to set fire to the place and burn it all down. Got that?"

"Yes, sir!" you and your fellow soldiers obediently reply. And you subsequently do just what Sergeant Rex ordered: you go into that village and kill everything—every man, woman, and child. It's a bloody, murderous day.

This pattern just continues, day after day: whatever Sergeant Rex commands, you do. Whatever orders Sergeant Rex issues, involving this or that act or deed, you carry out. Willingly. Obediently. You do this because you have full faith in his wisdom and judgment, and you have granted him full authority, deciding to follow his orders. When he tells you to slit someone's throat: "Yes, sir!" When he asks you to write a letter home on behalf of a comrade who's been injured: "Yes, sir!" When he orders you to torture a captured villager: "Yes, sir!" When he tells you to clean some boots: "Yes, sir!" Whatever act it is—be it kind or sadistic, pain-relieving or pain-inducing, charitable or harsh—you do it.

Week after week, month after month: you commit violent or benevolent acts. And in doing so, you have proven yourself a reliable soldier, a dependable private of a well-functioning platoon, a dutiful citizen heeding your country's call. You may certainly be all of these things—but there's one thing that you most definitely are not: *a moral agent.*

By deciding to so completely obey Sergeant Rex, by totally resigning yourself to his discretion, by willingly submitting to his every command, you have fully and wholly abdicated your own personal role as an ethical being who makes his own decisions and choices predicated on his own conscience. In purposefully handing over all decision-making to Sergeant Rex, you have given up your role as a moral contemplator: someone who considers the consequences of his actions, who thinks about the pain or pleasure he is causing to others, who ponders and justifies the motivations and intentions prompting his decisions, who is aware of his position, power, and privilege in relation to others, and who wonders if what he is doing is ultimately making the world a worse or better place. You've given all of that ethical work and moral contemplation up. And by doing so, you have become functionally amoral, simply obeying the will of another, causing pain and suffering one day, joy and healing the next—and all through no decision or choice of your own, but merely as one who follows the orders of another. You have willingly opted to take your own inner moral compass and, while perhaps not completely smashing it to pieces, you have plastered a thick portrait of Sergeant Rex across its face, so that you can no longer read its inner needle's ethical calibrations. All you now read is the will of Sergeant Rex. And that is not being moral.

In fact, it's just the opposite.

If children defer to a more powerful and more experienced authority for moral guidance, that is all well and good, at least sometimes. Usually, they have no choice, either because they are too young, too inexperienced, or too vulnerable to do anything else. But as adults, if we simply defer to a higher, more powerful authority—be it a boss, a sergeant, a senator, a teacher, a parent, a judge, etc.—when navigating morally precarious situations, then we are irresponsibly relieving ourselves of doing the difficult work of moral deliberation. Taking such a deferential route is a negligent stymieing and snuffing out of the ethical ability that distinguishes human nature and culture. It's a cowardly flight from figuring out for ourselves what we ought to do. And the consequences of such ethical abdication/moral cowardice can be devastating.

Charlie Company

Hundreds of thousands of nineteen-year-old Americans were in Vietnam in 1968, and some of them ended up in a unit of the Americal Division's 11th Light Infantry Brigade named Charlie Company. And on March 16, 1968, the men of Charlie Company—who comprised a typical cross-section of American youth—attacked a civilian village and, in the course of about four hours, deliberately murdered around five hundred men, women, and children in cold blood. Many of the adults killed were elderly. Many of the victims—both adults and children—were raped before being shot. Many of the victims were maimed and tormented as well. In short, the American soldiers of Charlie Company engaged in the dictionary definition of immoral, unethical behavior: purposefully brutalizing, assaulting, raping, and killing innocent people.[1]

Why did they do this? How could they do this? There were multiple background factors at play, to be sure. For instance, the young men of Charlie Company had been rigorously trained to kill; they had internalized ongoing racist tropes that painted the Vietnamese as less than human, they had heard rumors that the Viet Cong used women and children as booby traps, and they had been taught that Communism was an evil that was their job to eradicate. Additionally, in the weeks prior to March 16, the platoon had come under sporadic enemy fire, which resulted in wounded flesh and unnerved bones, and in the days immediately leading up to March 16, firefights with the Viet Cong had resulted in the death of five members of Charlie Company. So the men were on edge, to say the least.

Whether you wish to regard the above details as rationalizations, excuses, or simply explanatory, contextual information is up to you. But above and beyond such matters, and what is relevant for our discussion here, is the fact that the wanton slaughter at My Lai ensued after *orders were given to kill.* The young men who tortured and massacred entire families were directly ordered to kill by their commanding officer, Captain Ernest Medina. As one member of Charlie Company recalled: "The order we were given was to kill and destroy everything that was in the village . . . it was clearly explained that there were to be no prisoners. The order that was given was to kill everyone in the village . . . it was quite clear that no one was to be spared in that village."[2]

Twenty other members of Charlie Company recounted the same thing: that the night before March 16, Captain Medina had gathered them all together and was unambiguous in his commanded expectation: a full slaughter. As Private James Flynn remembered: "Someone asked, 'Are we supposed to kill women and children?' and Medina replied, 'Kill everything that moves.'"[3]

The following day, the men of Charlie Company complied. They ruthlessly, savagely carried out Medina's orders. Not all of them, however. A handful refused. For example, Michael Bernhardt, George Garza, and Harry Stanley chose not to participate in the killing; as Harry Stanley explained, "We had orders, but . . . ordering me to shoot down innocent people, that's not an order—that's craziness to me, you know. And so I don't feel like I have to obey that."[4] But these men were the notable exceptions. The humane few. The heroically deviant. Most of the soldiers in Charlie Company killed. Or raped and then killed.

One of the hands-on ringleaders of the massacre at My Lai, Lieutenant William Calley, not only aggressively and repeatedly ordered those below him in rank to kill, but he participated in much of the killing himself; at one point during the hours of carnage, a soldier, Paul Meadlo, was guarding a few dozen cowering villagers when Lieutenant Calley approached him and ordered that he kill them all; when Meadlo hesitated, Calley began shooting the people himself, with Meadlo then joining in. Calley killed many more that day: babies, children, women, the elderly. At his trial, in 1970, Calley—who was pardoned for his crimes by President Nixon—put this forth in his defense:

> I was ordered to go in there and destroy the enemy. That was my job that day. That was the mission I was given. I did not sit down and think in terms of men, women, and children. They were all classified as the same, and that's the classification that we dealt with over there, just as the enemy. I felt then and I still do that I acted as I was directed, and I carried out the order that I was given and I do not feel wrong in doing so.[5]

What is so remarkable about Calley's defense is that it stands in direct violation of Nuremberg Principle IV, which states: "The fact that a person acted pursuant to order of his Government or of a superior does not relieve him from responsibility under international law, provided a moral choice was in fact possible to him." This ethical and legal principle—crafted some twenty years prior to the massacre at My Lai, during the post-Holocaust trials of Nazis who had participated in the systematic extermination of millions of Jews—makes clear that "I was just following orders" is not a valid or reasonable defense in the wake of committing any unlawful crime against humanity. These Nuremberg Principles, created by the International Law Commission of the United Nations, were promulgated not only to help define and hopefully prevent war crimes and crimes against humanity, but to clearly declare that as humans, we all have the ability and responsibility to determine what it means to cause unnecessary harm to innocent victims, and we all have the ability and responsibility to desist from such actions. In short, merely obeying the commands of an authority figure is no excuse for committing rape and murder. Not legally, and certainly not ethically.

Moral Outsourcing

It all boils down to the unavoidable reality of choice. When someone tells us to do something, we always have a choice as to whether or not to comply. Existentialist philosopher Jean-Paul Sartre was emphatic on this point: while we generally do not get to choose the contextual circumstances of our lives—that is, the governments, institutions, people, culture, and laws that we must contend with—we all, nonetheless, are perpetually free, as individuals, to choose how we will respond to the immediate impositions of those contextual circumstances.[6] We can say no, we can say yes—whatever our conscience dictates—and then act accordingly. Sure, there will inevitably be consequences to our choices; it's not as if we are free to choose without repercussions. If we choose to disobey our parents, there will be consequences. If we choose to disobey our government, there will be consequences. If we choose to disobey our commanding officer in the jungles of Vietnam, there will be consequences. And some of those consequences can be quite costly, both emotionally and physically. No doubt. But we still have a choice, consequences notwithstanding. And to deny that we, as conscious individuals, always have a choice is to self-delude and self-dupe; it is to live, as Sartre said, in "bad faith."[7]

Exercising our freedom of choice—to perform a given act or not—is what ultimately determines who and what we are. It is at the very heart of our distinctly human capacity for conscious, clear-eyed moral autonomy. And it comprises the underlying basis of our ethical lives: to choose how we will treat others. As British philosopher Mary Midgley asserts, individual conscience is *central* to morality.[8] But deciding *not* to choose—to avowedly abstain from personally deciding how to act in given situations, to ignore one's conscience, and to instead decide to merely follow the commandments of an authority figure—well, as I have argued above, that is a major abdication of ethical responsibility, a pusillanimous eschewal of moral obligation. As such, it is—in effect—a denial of both one's humanity and the humanity of others.

According to Spanish American evolutionary biologist Francisco Ayala, humans are naturally endowed with three necessary conditions for morality: "anticipation of the consequences of one's actions, the ability to make value judgments, and the ability to choose between alternative courses of action."[9] A strictly God-based ethical orientation ignores (at best) or utterly destroys (at worst) human morality—for it requires that we deny and denounce the very thing that makes us free, self-aware, and naturally endowed moral beings: our ability to choose for ourselves, in given situations, how to act; our capacity to choose, based on conscious reflection and inner deliberation, how we ought to treat others; our ability to freely act upon our moral values.

Instead, in a presumed God-ruled universe, we just faithfully take orders from above. And as American philosophers Scott Aikin and Robert Talisse make clear, such theistic morality is actually quite pernicious, since it is "rooted in an abdication of moral autonomy."[10] It is, indeed, the very worst form of moral outsourcing. And it is observably more prominent within religious culture; various social-psychological studies have found that increased religiosity is correlated with a moral orientation based on following rules and obeying authority, rather than one based on empathy, compassion, or reasoned principles.[11]

Obedience Is Not Morality

You will recall that in an earlier chapter I argued that a fundamental flaw of any ethical or moral system based on God is that this supposed God is not only impossible to define, but this inexplicable deity's very existence has never, ever been proven. So, to say "I get my morals from God" is to say nothing more compelling than "I get my morals from some unclear, ineffable, enigmatic entity that doesn't even exist beyond my faith that he does." And that's a very shaky, shallow, and spurious foundation for ethics, to say the least.

But things get even worse for the God-believer. For even if we were to be open to the possibility that God (whatever that means) does exist (despite the lack of any empirical evidence)—*even if we were to make that leap*—moral problems do not recede upon such a possibility. Rather, they compound. Because, as discussed in the previous chapter, everyone interprets God's commands differently, making theistic moral agreement impossible.

But things get worse still: even if we could all agree what God commands—*especially* if we agree—then all our moral deliberating and ethical considering suddenly all boils down to one simple matter: obedience. That is, if there is an all-powerful, all-knowing, all-creating Supreme Deity out there, whose divine will is crystal clear, then our immediate job appears to become that of obeying His grand authority. Which means—given such a traditional religious framework—that morality is suddenly reduced to following the commands of a Supreme Overlord—and nothing else. That's what is meant by moral outsourcing: doing what someone else tells you to do rather than figuring it out for yourself based on your own moral reflection and personal conscience. With moral outsourcing, you hand the job of ethics over to someone else, like Sergeant Rex, or some*thing* else, like an invisible deity commonly referred to as God. And you obey.

Human ethical systems are corroded, not bolstered, by such religious theism.[12] For obedience is most definitely not morality—nor ought we ever mistake it as such. "No one is good," Scott Aikin and Robert Talisse explain, "in virtue of rote obedience to commands, even if those commands come from God."[13] Obedience is merely acting out of fear, or despondency, or weakness, or resignation, or training, or all five combined. What obedience is *not* is morally sound or ethically responsible.[14]

To be a moral agent, according to American philosopher David Brink, is to be responsible, and a responsible moral agent "must be able to distinguish between the intensity and authority of his or her desires, deliberate about the appropriateness of his or her desires, and regulate his or her actions in accordance with his or her deliberations."[15] And yet, pure theistic morality destroys all of that. For if our sole obligation is to dutifully obey God's commands, then we are no longer acting as autonomous moral agents who look inward, using our own hearts and minds as our guides. We are no longer acting as the existentially free human beings that we are, beings who deliberate about the appropriateness of our desires, weigh options, consider alternatives, examine motivations, assess potential harm or flourishing that might result from our actions, ponder our situations and those of others, accept responsibility, learn from mistakes, adhere to principles, seek to embody values, reflect on our own experiences, check our intuitions and gut feelings, contemplate the implications of our choices for ourselves and those around us and the greater social context—no. For the staunchly religious, none of that matters. It is all for naught. Instead, under the demand of dogmatic theistic morality, we crumple up our existential freedom—and the moral obligation it entails—and toss it away. We then look outward and upward, to a supposed Higher Authority, to tell us what to do and how to act. And just like the young American private in the jungles of Vietnam who does whatever Sergeant Rex says, we become bipedal peons, doing whatever God says. We become functionally amoral at best, willfully immoral at worst. And ethically bankrupt, either way.

It is for these reasons that post-Enlightenment visionary John Stuart Mill deemed any attempt to base our ethics on God as "the greatest enemy of morality."[16]

God's Murderous Commands

There's a relevant biblical story worth mentioning here—a story that reveals just how morally crippling obedience to a deity can be.

It's the tale of Abraham dutifully, willingly obeying God's command to murder his own son, Isaac. As you may recall, according to this Mediterranean gem of grim folklore written over twenty-five hundred years ago, Abraham was a Jew—indeed, the presumed *first* Jew—who came to believe in the One True God of the Israelites. In order to test Abraham's fealty to and faith in him, this almighty God commands Abraham to take his son, Isaac, and tie him up and kill him. And what does Abraham do? He faithfully obeys. He takes Isaac up onto a hill, binds him, and goes to murder him. But—alas—just in the nick of time, God sends an angel down to intervene. Isaac is not killed. God then heaps loads of praise upon Abraham for passing the ultimate test: obeying the divine command to slit Isaac's throat.

Despite endless spin and sophistry by centuries of rabbis, priests, and theologians trying their best to squeeze some potentially positive meaning from this dark tale, the underlying message of the narrative is clear: if you really believe in God, you will do whatever He commands—even if He commands cold-blooded murder.[17] Indeed, such was eminent Christian philosopher Søren Kierkegaard's ultimate takeaway from this biblical story: that true faith is based upon "infinite resignation" to God's will. According to

Kierkegaard, Abraham acted correctly in his willingness to kill his son, for he so believed in God and was such a "knight of faith" that by raising the knife to saw into his own son's neck, he was being truly, unabashedly submissive in a way that is exactly what God wants and expects, and such obedient resignation is the highest ideal of human action based on devout theism.[18]

Kierkegaard was right in this respect: obedience is, indeed, the highest ideal based on devout theism. But it is simultaneously the lowest ideal based on human experience and interaction. Such blindly obedient resignation, even to a deity, is a vile denigration of our ethical responsibilities. As American philosopher Edwin Curley writes, concerning the story of God's commandment that Abraham kill his son:

> If there is a God who is liable to command anything, and if our highest loyalty must be to this God, there is no act—save disobedience to God—that we can safely say is out of bounds, no act of a kind that simply must not be done . . . if we believed God had commanded it. If this God exists and we must obey him unconditionally, then anything whatever might turn out to be permissible. This view is destructive of morality.[19]

Put yourself in Abraham's shoes: Would you obediently kill your child if you were *sure* God wanted you to? Would you kill someone else's child? What if God commanded you to smash one hundred babies' heads with a mallet—would you do it? Sorry to broach such a gruesome image, but that's what the biblical story of Abraham and Isaac forces us to confront: the contours and limits of our own personal ability to commit wanton violence—if simply ordered to do so from on high. As Elizabeth Anderson has accurately pointed out, "if we take the evidence for theism with *utmost seriousness*, we will find ourselves committed to the proposition that the most heinous acts are permitted."[20]

"But God would never command us to do any wantonly violent, heinous acts!"

Such is the constant, desperate refrain from every well-meaning theist that I have ever debated these issues with. They always say the same thing: God would never ask us to commit murder.

Really? Are you sure about that?

Only someone who has never actually read the Bible could be so ignorant of the types of immoral, unethical things God has commanded of his followers.[21] In Deuteronomy 20, God commands the people of Israel to lay siege to various cities and commit genocide: "Do not leave alive anything that breathes. Completely destroy them—the Hittites, the Amorites, the Canaanites, the Perizzites, Hivites and Jebusites—as the Lord your God has commanded you." In Numbers 31, God commands his followers to "kill every male among the little ones, and kill every woman that hath not known man by lying with him." In 1 Samuel 15, the Lord Almighty commands to his people to "attack the Amalekites and totally destroy all that belongs to them. Do not spare them; put to death men and women, children and infants, cattle and sheep, camels and donkeys."

Captain Medina of Charlie Company would feel right at home engaging in such military maneuvers, no doubt.

There's even more on the murderous front: in Leviticus 20, God commands us to murder anyone who has sex with someone who isn't their spouse, or any man who has sex with another man, or anyone who fashions him or herself to be a medium or a spiritualist. In Exodus 22, God commands that female sorceresses be murdered. In Deuteronomy 21, God commands that stubborn or rebellious sons shall be put to death. In Deuteronomy 22, God commands that any woman who is not a virgin upon marriage shall be executed. In Leviticus 24, God commands us to murder blasphemers. In Exodus 35, God commands us to murder anyone who works on the Sabbath. In Numbers 15, the Lord makes it clear that such people should be stoned to death.

There are many more instances in the Bible wherein God commands that humans engage in wanton, savage violence—but others have charted these bloody waters,[22] and a detailed account is beyond our discussion here. And the takeaway point should be obvious: when we decide to simply obey an authority, especially a magical, cosmic, all-powerful authority like the God of the Israelites, we immediately snuff out our capacity for moral reflection. We betray our obligation to act ethically.

It is always immoral to needlessly kill innocent people—be it children in a Vietnamese village, or your own child, or every single man, woman, and child of the Jebusite or Hittite nations, and it is always unethical to murder anyone for having sex with someone who isn't their spouse, or for working on the Sabbath, or for being homosexual, and it doesn't matter if anyone or anything here on Earth or up in the heavens orders you to commit such violent, savage acts. It should go without saying that to commit such atrocities is to cause unwanted pain and suffering, and therefore must never, ever be done. Abraham and Kierkegaard got it wrong. The authors of the Nuremberg Principles got it right.

Might Does Not Make Right

But if God is not the source of morality—or more accurately, if God doesn't exist—then doesn't that mean that "anything goes" down here on Earth, morally speaking? If there is no all-powerful deity overhead, then who can ultimately say what is wrong and what is right? It'll just be every man for himself, acting on his own desires, determining his own subjective morality, and this will result in people just being selfish and doing what is in their own immediate interests, and life will thus be nothing more than people doing whatever they want and whatever they can get away with—unless someone more powerful can stop them. And in such a world, might would make right, and human ethics would all be for naught—which is a terrible prospect for human flourishing.

Well, to begin with: might does *not* make right. Ever. In a world where strong thugs and merciless brutes can run amok, taking whatever they want and doing whatever they want to people, simply because they have the power to do so certainly does indicate that they have "might." But it most definitely does not mean that they have "right." The men of Charlie Company had the *might* to murder innocent men, women, and children—but no one, save perhaps the most heartless or savage among us, would ever suggest that they had the *right* to. Might *never* means right.

But here's the deal: it is not the secular, atheist approach to ethics that inevitably results in a "might makes right" situation. Rather, it is the explicitly religious-theistic approach to ethics that does; it is the religious worldview predicated on faith in and obedience to God that immediately turns ethics into nothing more than a "might makes right" reality. For if all morality hinges on God, and we are thus in a situation wherein we must obey God, then whatever God commands is the right thing to do. And that immediately raises the question: *Why?* The only possible answer: because he's God. But that's not a compelling reason to obey his commands, especially when it comes to questions of wrong and right, harm and help, justice and injustice.

After all, what exactly is it about him being God that means we ought to obey his commands? Because he makes rainbows? Because he's so smart? Because he makes solar systems? Because he commands all of heaven and hell? Because he magically created life? Because he is all-powerful? In short—because of how *mighty* he is? That's correct. And *voilà*: might suddenly makes right.

Except—to repeat—that it doesn't.

Shocking Immorality

Think about one of the most famous—or infamous—studies in the history of social science: Stanley Milgram's *Obedience to Authority*.[23] Dr. Milgram was a professor of psychology at Yale University who, in the 1960s, wanted to see just how easily—and to what degree—people would follow the commands of someone in a position of authority, even if such commands meant directly causing an innocent victim to feel extreme pain, or even worse.

Here's what he did: He found individuals from the local community willing to participate as subjects in an experiment. When an individual subject came in to the lab, he or she was greeted by a smart-looking, scientist-type individual—the "experimenter"—and then (falsely) told that the experiment about to be conducted concerned the mechanisms of learning. The individual was then told that another volunteer—who they met upon arrival—had been randomly selected to play the role of "learner" while they themselves had been randomly selected to play the role of "teacher." They then watched as the "learner"—who was actually an accomplice of the study—was taken to an adjacent room, where he was strapped into a seat resembling an electric chair and hooked up to wires and nodes that could deliver an electric shock. The subject ("teacher") was then instructed to go back to the original room and sit in front of a large machine that would produce electrical shocks every time the "learner" got an answer wrong in a test of memorized word patterns. During this entire time, the "experimenter" in charge of the experiment—dressed in a white coat and holding a clipboard—gave out continuous instructions to the "teacher" on how everything was to proceed.

And then the experiment would begin. And every time the "learner" would get an answer wrong, the "teacher" was instructed by the "experimenter" to administer a shock. And with each wrong answer, the voltage of the shock was to increase. Now, after receiving a shock, the "learner" would express feelings of pain and discomfort: he would yell, or groan, or scream, and, as the voltage increased, beg to be let out of the room. The "learner," of course, wasn't really getting such shocks—it was all faked. But the subject in the role of "teacher" didn't know that.

And on it would go: the "experimenter" would sternly insist that the experiment continue, commanding the "teacher" to continue giving shocks with each wrong answer, no matter how loud the "learner" screamed or pleaded to be let free.

How many subjects did as they were told, obeying the authoritative commands of the white-coated "experimenter" by administering ever-increasingly painful shocks to another human being? Most complied. Indeed, 65 percent of subjects (twenty-six individuals out of forty) administered the full dose of a 450-volt shock—repeatedly—even though the "learner" screamed in agony, complained of a heart condition, and eventually went silent, presumably dead or unconscious from the shocks. Why did these subjects do it? Because the man in a position of authority—a Yale professor running an experiment—told them to do so.

Now, here's the thing: most people would agree that it is manifestly wrong to shock an innocent person. Why? Simple: because it causes them unnecessary pain and suffering. End of story. And it does not matter that the command to administer such a shock comes from a person in a position of authority; the command remains immoral because it causes senseless harm. Most God-believers would agree to all of this. And most would agree that to administer painful or deadly shocks to an innocent person is flagrantly immoral, no matter if the command to do so comes from someone in a position of power.

Oh, wait.

Unless it is God.

In that case, the command to cause pain and suffering to an innocent person suddenly becomes moral. Why? Because the command comes from God. And why does that automatically make it moral? Because God is so mighty. And again, there you have it: might makes right. Such is the potential moral paucity of theistic ethics.

From a secular perspective, we know that no matter how strong a person (or deity) is, no matter how creative or powerful, no matter how magnificent or awesome, this incredible might does not automatically translate into moral righteousness. Yet this is exactly what religious theism teaches: that because God created everything, he must know more than us about how to be moral; because God knows and sees everything, we ought to just obey his commands and trust that he knows best. This approach to morality is, in the words of British philosopher Peter Geach, ultimately nothing more than power worship.[24] It is a form of extreme moral outsourcing, as I've argued in this chapter, that is manifestly immoral.

As Elizabeth Anderson explains:

> Far from bolstering the authority of morality, appeals to divine authority can undermine it. For divine command theories of morality may make

> believers feel entitled to look only to their idea of God to determine what they are justified in doing. It is all too easy under such a system to ignore the complaints of those injured by one's actions, since they are not acknowledged as moral authorities in their own right. But to ignore the complaints of others is to deprive oneself of the main source of information one needs to improve one's conduct. Appealing to God rather than those affected by one's actions amounts to an attempt to escape accountability to one's fellow human beings.[25]

And finally, to say that something is moral just because God commands it opens up a whole can of worms regarding the very ontological basis of God's relationship to morality. It's a can of worms that was ripped open in ancient Greece some twenty-four hundred years ago, and no theist has ever successfully managed to get those worms back in the can.

5

Sally, Butch, and Plato's Dilemma

So far, I've argued that theistic morality—the long-standing, traditional religious approach to morals and ethics in which God is necessarily central—is untenable for three reasons: 1) "God" is an indefinable, incomprehensible entity that has never been proven to exist; 2) even if this unfathomable entity referred to as God were somehow proven to exist, theists can't ever agree on what it wants of us or how it expects us to live, so that theistic morality immediately disintegrates into a morass of competing, contradictory, and subjective interpretations; and 3) even if we could prove that God was real and even if we could all agree on exactly what it wants, then this would suddenly mean that our only duty would be to obey God's commands, which directly results in flagrant moral outsourcing, thereby destroying a true human morality based on choice, freedom, consideration, conscience, deliberation, reflection, sympathy, empathy, and compassion.

But there's something even more deeply problematic with morality based on faith in God than these three matters—something so ontologically and epistemologically insurmountable that no theologian has even been able to dull the biting, brilliant edge of its premise. In order to explain just what this something is—and in homage to the classical Socratic tradition of illustrating philosophical insights through didactic dialogue—I'd like to begin this final critique of theistic morality in the form of a conversation between two acquaintances, Butch and Sally.

It was a Monday morning, around seven, in Eastern Kentucky. Butch, age thirty-five, was sitting on a wooden bench in front of the Rowan County Courthouse. No one else was around, and the courthouse wouldn't be open for another hour. But Butch was already there, and his spine was taut and he was eager—he wanted to be sure to be the first in to see the district attorney.

At around seven thirty, a woman the same age as Butch walked up to the entrance of the courthouse. She peered reluctantly into the glass of the two large, locked doors. And then Butch realized that he knew her.

"Sally?"

"Uh, yes . . . and you are . . . ?"

"Butch Sanders. From high school."

"Oh, my goodness—Butch—how are you?"

"I'm just fine. And you?"

"Good, yes—I mean—other than the fact that I've been called in to see the D.A."

Butch scooted over to the right side of the bench and gestured for Sally to sit down.

"So nice to see you," Sally said.

"You, too. Been a long time," Butch acknowledged.

"You look great. I mean, you look—"

"Different? I know. It's true. I was pretty scrappy back then."

"No, I wouldn't say that."

"It's OK," Butch continued. "I was rough. I know it. Heck, I was really struggling back then. School, things at home, drugs. I was getting into a fight just about every other week. Didn't really mind my manners or my appearance much."

"Well, you know, high school's a tough time for everyone," Sally offered.

"I suppose."

"But you left, didn't you? I don't remember you being at graduation."

"That's right. My folks split up at the end of tenth grade and my dad moved way out into the country and then my mom took off for Cincinnati and I ended up staying with my dad, but I dropped out that summer."

"Oh."

"It's all right. It all worked out. I'm doing really well. Married to a wonderful woman. Five kids. Meaningful work."

"Five kids? Holy moly. And what do you do?"

"I'm a pastor. Lighthouse Church, out on Highway 99."

"Seriously? Butch Sanders—a preacher? I can't believe it!"

"Believe it," he said with a smile. "You should come on out sometime and see what we're doing."

"I would have never guessed it."

"Yeah, I'm a different person. Jesus will do that to a man. Things were not so good when I was a teenager. But you know, my dad was patient, and once I found the Lord, that was that. Been sober and steady ever since."

"I'm so glad to hear it."

"And what about you? What have you been up to?" Butch asked.

"Let's see . . . After graduation I went to State and studied history, and then I got my credential and now I teach at Woodland Middle School."

"That's great, Sally. Sounds solid. And family?"

"I'm married—my husband also works at Woodland, and we have a son, Henry. He's six."

"So what're you doing here at the courthouse?" Butch asked.

Sally sighed heavily, and her shoulders sagged.

"I got a summons from Mr. Hardesty, the district attorney. It's a long story."

"That's OK. You don't have to get into it."

"No, that's all right. I guess I don't mind. It looks like we've got a while here anyway, until the courthouse opens. It's just a bit complicated. See, um, I teach history, right? And last year I started a unit on religion—"

"Good for you."

"And the idea was to teach students about the various religions of the world. It is just so crucial for understanding the growth of civilizations, the development of government and various political struggles, and for understanding nationalism and gender relations, and—"

"And for understanding morals."

"Sure . . . um, yeah . . . and there's just so many aspects of history that involve religion. So I wanted to do a unit on various world religions: Shinto, Buddhism, Hinduism, Judaism, Christianity, Islam, Sikhism, Confucianism, and indigenous African religions."

"Sounds interesting."

"Well, some parents didn't think so. They were concerned that if their children learned about other religions it might affect their faith. And then last year when we got to Islam, there was a big uproar. A bunch of parents complained to the school board, saying that Islam was evil and that they didn't want their children being indoctrinated."

"It is a very violent religion," Butch said.

"Well, I'd say that it's a very diverse religion. There are many versions of Islam. And it's the second largest religion in the world. And there's a lot of good in there—"

"Good in Islam?"

"Sure. But that's beside the point. I'm not trying to defend Islam. Or any religion. All I was wanting was for the kids to be exposed to it, to learn a little about it: the history, the life of Muhammad, a bit about the Quran."

"Hmm . . . But what does this have to do with the D.A.?"

"During the unit on Islam, I invited Mr. Zadeh to speak to my students. He's the imam at the new mosque in Morehead."

"I see."

"And then last month, after the terrorist shooting in California, I guess the cops started sniffing around the mosque—I've heard various rumors—and, well, so now Mr. Hardesty said that he wanted me to come in today so that he could ask me some questions about my 'dealings with and knowledge of Mr. Zadeh and the Morehead mosque.' So here I am."

"It's a good thing that Mr. Hardesty is looking into this."

"You think?"

"Yes. It's his job and his duty to protect the people of Rowan County."

Sally suddenly regretted telling Butch about the whole affair. She could plainly see that his opinion of Islam was low and that he was just as suspicious of Mr. Zadeh as the parents of her students were, without ever even having met the man. So she changed the subject.

"And what about you, Butch? What are you doing here at the courthouse on this Monday morning?"

"I've come to assist Mr. Hardesty with his work concerning the prosecution of a murderer."

"A *murderer*?"

"That's right. My father killed a man last night, and I'm here to help do the right thing."

"Wait—your *father*? He killed a man?"

"Correct."

"Last night?"

"Yes."

"And you're . . . turning him in?"

"More like providing all the facts. Mr. Hardesty is already aware that a death occurred at the hands of my father. I'm just here to help him as best I can."

"To help your father?"

"No. To help Mr. Hardesty."

"I'm confused," Sally confessed.

"Murder is murder," Butch declared.

"Sure, but—"

"No 'but' involved. When the Lord said, 'Thou shalt not kill,' there wasn't an 'if' or an 'and' or a 'but' attached."

"Who did your father kill?"

"What does it matter? Like I said, murder is murder."

"Was it your—?"

"It was no one close to me."

"Was it self-defense?"

"No."

"I'm sorry, Butch. I still don't understand."

"Last week my father hired a couple workers to help him with some things around the farm—construction, repairs, irrigation, and whatnot. He had them sleeping in a tent near the barn. One of the fellas, Lem, started causing trouble right away. He got into it with my dad and also with the other worker. He also harassed Mrs. Muller, who lives down the road. Just a real nasty fellow, as far as I can gather. Anyway, last night Lem got drunk and ended up going after the other worker. They started fighting, and Lem smashed this other guy's head so badly—with a brick—that he passed out cold and looked like he might die. My dad put him in the back of the car to take him to the hospital. But you know, my dad's place is pretty far out of town. It's a good thirty-five miles to the nearest hospital in West Liberty, and the road is pretty rough. So before he left, my dad tied Lem to a chair in the cellar. Then he called 911 and told them to come fetch Lem while he left to take the other guy to the hospital. It took the cops over an hour to get to my dad's place, and when they got there, Lem was dead. They say that the rope was tied too tight, which messed with his breathing or his circulation or his heart, and then he had thrown up and I guess choked on his own vomit."

"So it was an accident?"

"It was my father's doing. He tied up that man and left him there. And Lem died a miserable death."

"Yeah, but your father was taking the injured man to the hospital."

"True."

"And it's not like he meant for Lem to die."

"Whatever his intentions were, he killed that man. He was negligent. And he needs to face justice."

Sally was at a loss for words. It was all so horrible. And yet Butch seemed so matter-of-fact about it, so clearheaded and clear-eyed. So steadfast and sure. How could that be? It was his own father, after all. And this guy Lem seemed like he was dangerous. And violent. The whole thing was, in Sally's eyes, anything but clear-cut.

"So you're not here to plead for mercy on your father's behalf?"

"No."

"Why not?"

"Like I said, Sally. Murder is a sin. And I've devoted my life to combatting sin."

"But isn't your duty to your father—"

"My duty is to the Lord, above all else. Jesus said, in the Gospel of Luke—chapter 14, to be exact—that He comes first and foremost and that our duty is to love Him above all, even above our own parents."

"Well, I can't quote scripture like you can. And I'm not one to go against Jesus. But I'm struck by your conviction. You really seem to know what's what here."

"Just following the Bible, Sally. Just doing what is moral."

"Maybe. I guess. But, I mean, isn't it moral to be on your father's side? Don't you love your dad?"

"Of course I do. And that's why I want him to pay for what he's done. There is salvation in atonement. There is redemption in righteousness. There is deliverance in justice."

"Such big words: 'justice,' 'redemption,' 'righteousness.' Doing what is 'moral.' Doing your 'duty.' But you know what? I've often felt like these things aren't always so black-and-white. Sometimes situations can be ambiguous—hard to be sure what the right thing to do is."

"Not for me."

"If that's the case, and since you seem to be so sure about these things, do you mind if I ask you: How can you be so certain about what the right thing to do is?"

"The right thing to do is always the moral thing."

"And what is 'moral,' Butch? I mean, who is to say, ultimately?"

"Now that, Sally, is just the problem with the world today. Right there. You've just nailed it on the head: people who say that 'wrong' and 'right' are unclear, people who say that 'moral' is anything anyone says it is, people saying that it's all relative, all subjective, all open for interpretation—well, I'm sorry, Sally, but I despise that view with all my heart and soul. Wrong and right are not up for interpretation. There *is* morality, Sally. And we, as Christians, can say so."

"Is that right? OK, then, how would you define it? What is 'moral'?"

"You're seriously asking me that?"

"Yes, I am. What is being moral, Butch? Is it being nice?"

"No. It isn't about being nice, because sometimes we have to be hard and cold to do the moral thing. When I spank my son as a punishment, it isn't particularly nice. But it is the right thing to do. As his father, it's the moral thing to do. Being moral means—at root—doing the Lord's will. Yes, that's pretty much it: 'moral' is what the Lord wills, what the Lord approves of, what the Lord commands."

Sally thought about this for a moment, and then, quite quickly, she could see that Butch's answer deserved more probing.

"So let me see if I understand you here: the moral thing to do is whatever God commands us to do—is that right?"

"Absolutely."

"OK, but that then raises the question: Is something moral because the Lord approves of it and commands it, or does the Lord approve of it and command it because it is moral?"

"What's the difference?"

"Lots. For example, when you step onto a newly mown lawn and inhale its smell and you declare to your wife how fragrant the grass smells, is the grass fragrant *because you say it is*? Or is the grass fragrant *in and of itself*, and then you smell it and recognize it as fragrant and then simply remark on that fact?"

"The grass is fragrant on its own, and I'm just noticing and commenting on it."

"Right. So how about this: What's your oldest daughter's name?"

"Grace."

"OK, was she born as 'Grace' and you simply recognized her as such and called her by her born name after the fact—or did you give her the name 'Grace' and that's how she came to have that name?"

"The second one, obviously. I named her."

"Right. OK. So the grass is fragrant on its own—and you simply recognize it as such. But your daughter had no name until you named her. And you chose the name 'Grace,' but you could have easily named her 'Jane.' You can now certainly see the difference: the grass will emit a fragrant smell whether you are there to comment on it or not—but with your daughter's name, you alone are its source."

"What does this have to do with God and morality?" Butch asked.

"Well, here's my question again: Does God approve of something—or will it or command it—because it is moral *in and of itself* and He simply sees that it is moral, recognizes it as moral, observes it as moral? Or is something moral only when and because God wills it or commands it, by fiat?"

"I'm sorry, I still don't see what you're getting at."

"The difference is quite significant, Butch. For if that which is moral is merely what God wills or commands, then morality is purely arbitrary, and there's nothing about 'wrong' or 'right' or 'good' or 'bad' or 'moral' or 'immoral' that is internal, essential, or intrinsic to its quality or nature. It would have nothing to do with justice or fairness or love or pain. It would just be what God says it is. What God decrees. On the other hand, if God wills or commands things as moral because He recognizes that they are moral *in and of themselves*, then morality exists outside of and independently of God. And thus we're back to where we were, trying to define what is moral, and God does not—and need not—have anything to do with it."

"Sally, I'm afraid you've lost me."

Suddenly, the courthouse doors loudly unlocked. Butch and Sally stood up and gathered their belongings. The conversation had gotten awkward at the end, and it was hard to deny it in the polite smiles the two acquaintances exchanged as they perfunctorily agreed how nice it was to see each other and wished each other luck with their business with the district attorney.

The above conversation is my best attempt to update and modernize one of the most important, foundational philosophical conversations ever written concerning the very nature of morality. Known as the *Euthyphro Dialogue*, it was written by Plato approximately twenty-four hundred years ago, in the first decade of the fourth century B.C.E.

The background of the original dialogue is as follows: Socrates—the progenitor of Western philosophy—was in trouble. His skeptical teachings and questions concerning religious and political authority had gotten him in trouble with the religious and political authorities. He was eventually summoned to court and then officially charged with not believing in the gods and concomitantly corrupting the minds of the youth of Athens. Some suspected him of being an atheist.[1] He was eventually found guilty and sentenced to death in the year 399 B.C.E.

But prior to his trial, Socrates was at court awaiting a pretrial hearing, and it was then that he encountered Euthyphro, who was at court for a different pretrial hearing. In the original dialogue by Plato, Euthyphro is there to file manslaughter charges against his own father. Euthyphro's father had hired a worker who then killed a slave, so Euthyphro's father threw the worker into a pit—bound and gagged—and then left for another city to ask the religious authorities there how to proceed. While gone, the worker died in the pit from starvation and exposure to the elements. Socrates is stunned by Euthyphro's confidence in bringing charges against his own father, and the discussion/debate between the two men ensues.

Despite Plato's own personal view of the gods—and he was a believer, to be sure—the dialogue he wrote, featuring Socrates and Euthyphro, provides a remarkable debate containing strong and compelling insights that cut to the very core of God's relationship to morality. Or rather, the lack thereof. In fact, the Euthyphro dialogue presents a piercing, two-pronged skeptical pitchfork challenging the theism-morality relationship with devastating efficacy. Each prong reveals insurmountable flaws in any God-based ethical framework.

The first prong is this: if some action acquires its moral status only as a result of God commanding it, then morality is arbitrary, based upon nothing but the will, whim, or fiat of a deity. And if an act is deemed moral simply because God commands it, then that means *any* act—even the slaughtering of babies—could automatically be viewed as moral if God commands it. And if that is the case, then the very word "moral" loses all meaning as an adjective of any substance.

The second prong is this: if God commands actions because he sees or recognizes that such actions are moral in and of themselves, then clearly morality exists outside and independently of God and/or his will. He is not the source of morality, nor the cause. Such a situation renders God manifestly redundant/unnecessary in the matter of morality and ethics.

Either way, it's deeply problematic for those who—like Butch—seek to hang the hat of morality on a rack made of God stuff—as is nicely articulated by American philosopher Walter Sinnott-Armstrong:

> Assume that God commanded me not to rape. Did God have a reason to command this? If not, then His command was arbitrary, and an arbitrary command can't make anything morally wrong. On the other hand, if God did have a reason to command us not to rape, then that reason is what makes rape morally wrong, and the command itself is superfluous. Hence, divine commands are either arbitrary or superfluous. Either way, morality cannot depend on God's commands.[2]

As Professor Sinnott-Armstrong rightly emphasizes, it's the *reason* that matters when it comes to moral action and ethical intent. Not the source—even if that source is presumed to be mightily supernatural.

To further understand the trenchant deconstruction of theistic morality captured by Plato's dialogue, let's take a specific example: feeding a hungry person. Is this act moral in and of itself, and God then understands or realizes this, and thus commands us to feed the hungry? Or is it rather that feeding the hungry is morally neutral in and of itself—neither good nor bad—but the act *becomes* moral only when and if God commands it? If you think it is the former, then that means that morality clearly exists independently of God and derives it status from something other than God. And if this is indeed the case, then God is essentially irrelevant to the matter, for we can define or recognize the morality in a given action—such as feeding a hungry person—without any need for or reference to a magical deity. However, if you think it is the latter proposal, that feeding the hungry becomes moral only when and insofar as God decrees or commands it, then morality is nothing more than the capricious will or indiscriminate commandment of God. And this is a rather problematic position to accept, because it means that morality is simply whatever a deity says it is. Heck, God could command cruelty, and then by the logic of the argument, cruelty would be moral. And if that is the case, then the very word "moral" signifies nothing. Moral could just as easily be called immoral. And if moral can be immoral and immoral can be moral, then it makes no sense to even use the adjectives "moral" or "immoral" to begin with. We should just say that God commands things—describing them as "moral" is pointless, for the word would no longer signify anything at all.

Now, getting back to our friends Butch and Sally, you may recall that in their conversation, there was no real conclusion: Butch can't seem to understand the underlying point of Sally's questions. He remains confused, and in his confusion, he avoids and evades their implications. And that's exactly what happens in Plato's original dialogue: Euthyphro can't seem to grasp the significance of Socrates's question: Does God command actions because they are moral in and of themselves, or do actions become moral only when and if God commands them? Perhaps it is not that Euthyphro—or Butch—can't understand the biting significance of this question, but rather that he can't or won't *allow* himself to understand it. For to understand it is to accept the truth of the matter: that morality cannot depend on a god for its existence or content.

The razor of philosophical skepticism is rarely as steely and sharp as it is in the questions Plato had Socrates pose to Euthyphro. And for well over two thousand years, no logical or plausible solution has ever been put forth by even the most learned of theists or theologians. As British intellectual historian Kenan Malik succinctly notes, "There is no getting away from the Euthyphro dilemma."[3]

Professor Craig's Best Effort

Of course, pious God-defenders throughout the centuries have tried their best to do so. They have struggled to dull the sharpness of its two-pronged skeptical pitchfork, or duck its thrust altogether. They have all failed. To go through all their various failed attempts, and present their numerous flaws, would take up way too much time and space.

But let's consider at least one significant contemporary effort to outsmart the Euthyphro dilemma. It comes from analytic philosopher, Trump supporter, and America's number one Evangelical apologist, William Lane Craig, who is a professor at Biola University and the author of numerous books and articles. A most formidable public debater, Professor Craig is also featured in numerous well-produced videos permeating the Internet. In one such YouTube video, Professor Craig takes on the Euthyphro dilemma and thinks that he's got a way around its two devastating prongs. His attempt goes like this: Socrates offers Euthyphro only two choices concerning God's relationship to morality, but there is a third option: namely, God commands or wills things because *He* is, in *essence*, moral and good.[4] It is God's very own *nature* that determines what is moral and good.[5] As Professor Craig explains, "God is, *by nature*, essentially compassionate, just, fair, kind, loving, and so forth, and because he is good, his commandments to us reflect necessarily his nature. And therefore, the commandments of God and our moral duties are rooted in God's essence."[6]

This line of reasoning is deeply flawed.

First off, Professor Craig falls head over heels into the very trap that Euthyphro himself fell into at the skeptical hands of Socrates. For in trying to debunk the Euthyphro dilemma, Professor Craig actually just illustrates the very heart of it.[7] How so? He claims that God's *nature* is compassionate and good—but this merely begs the question: Is God's nature compassionate and good because these attributes are essential, fundamental components of God, or is God's nature compassionate and good because compassion and goodness exists independently and outside of God, and God recognizes them, and then chooses to align his nature with them—thereby opting to be compassionate and good? If you pick the first option, then "compassionate" and "good" are just arbitrary designations that simply refer to God's essential nature—whatever that may be. After all, there is no objective yardstick of goodness or compassion existing outside of or beyond God whereby we can measure or determine God as being "good" or "compassionate." As such, they become meaningless as adjectives, not actually signifying anything we might think of as "compassionate" or "good." Not to mention fallaciously tautological. And if you pick the second option, that God actively *aligns* his nature with goodness and compassion, then goodness and compassion clearly exist independently and outside of God, and thus God being good or compassionate isn't really all that impressive or meaningful; compassion and goodness are again the supreme phenomena, not God, who merely chooses to calibrate his nature in accordance with them.

Secondly, there's the all-important matter of methods—or rather, a flagrant lack thereof. Professor Craig makes a claim about the *nature* of God—but based on what facts, research, or practical expertise? How does Professor Craig know what God's nature is? What's his specific method of data collection? If a primatologist wants to comment on the nature of chimpanzees, she generally spends years in the field observing them, and only after such extensive observational research can she make an informed assessment concerning the nature of chimpanzees. And any other primatologist is free to challenge her conclusions—but they must do so based on extensive research and observations of their own. If a child psychologist wants to make an assertion about the nature of children, he does so only after years of working with and observing them. And that's how it works for anyone who makes any claims about the "nature" of anything that exists: if their claim is to hold any water, it must be based on some observation or experimentation or research. And yet here we have Professor Craig pronouncing on the very nature and essence of God—but how does he possibly know of such things? Has he spent years observing various deities in their natural habitat, and then, based on such extensive fieldwork, is able to conclude something about the nature of the God he believes in? If there are no other gods that exist save his own, has he analyzed or interviewed or observed this God in any unbiased, objective way that would result in his ability to make an informed, data-driven conclusion about this God's very nature? Of course not. He's just subjectively pontificating without a shred of objective evidence to back his claim. Such pseudo "methodology" constitutes the very heart and soul of theology—for as Bertrand Russell observed back in 1943, "in theology there is only opinion."[8]

Furthermore, it manifestly makes no sense to say that something ineffable, inconceivable, unfathomable, and utterly unlike anything we can ever comprehend can have a "nature" that can be grasped and described. What would it even mean to say that God has a "nature"? Does this refer to God's personality? God's genetic makeup? God's proclivities? God's motivations? God's mood? God's overall vibe? What could *possibly* constitute God's nature? Nothing. Alack and alas, to speak of God (whatever that is) as having a "nature" is not simply poppycock mixed with rubbish in a huge heap of balderdash—it's theo-babble writ large. Philosopher A. C. Grayling's words are particularly apt here:

> It is common for religious apologists to respond to critiques . . . by claiming that [their] deity is ineffable and incomprehensible, which of course closes down the debate, for by definition there is nothing to be said about what nothing can be said about. The fact that religious apologists find, despite this, a great deal to be said about such a thing after all—that it exists, that it has such and such a nature . . . does not appear to strike them as contradictory, though it is so.[9]

The Opposite of Loving and Compassionate

Finally, recall that Professor Craig insists that God is "essentially compassionate, just, fair, kind, loving."[10] These are words we generally use to describe motivations and behaviors of humans, and they only mean something in the context of human life and human experience. To apply them to God means that they somehow comport with our understanding of what it means to be compassionate, loving, etc. And if these words are to mean anything at all, when applied to Professor Craig's God, then it is hard to square with the following:

- In the twentieth century alone,[11] 300 million people died from smallpox. This is a horrific, brutal illness—the pain and suffering it causes are unimaginable. Simply Google "smallpox" and click on images; it's nearly impossible to consider a deity who would inflict this kind of blight upon his created beings as compassionate or loving.

Also in the twentieth century alone:

- 530 million people died from cancer.
- 194 million died from malaria.
- 100 million died from tuberculosis.
- 97 million died from measles.
- 6 million died from snake bites.
- Every year, 1.5 million children currently die from diarrhea.

And let's not forget all the humans who have suffered throughout the centuries from cholera, ebola, Lou Gehrig's disease, cystic fibrosis, polio, plague, mad cow disease, Spanish flu, diphtheria, diabetes, cleft palates, meningitis, Alzheimer's, dementia, schizophrenia, rabies, Lyme disease, typhus, rubella, dengue fever, yellow fever, leprosy, ectopic pregnancies, etc., etc.

And then there are the millions of people who have suffered and died as a result of the calamities of the natural world. Consider just the past century alone:

- In 1931, between 1 and 4 million people died in China due to floods.
- In 1970, between 250,000 and 500,000 people died in Bangladesh as a result of a cyclone.
- In 1971, 100,000 people died in Vietnam because of a flood/landslide.
- In 1976, between 200,000 and 700,000 people died in China due to an earthquake.

- In 1985, over 20,000 people in Colombia died because of an earthquake.
- In 2003, 70,000 people died in Europe as a result of a heat wave.
- In 2004, between 230,000 and 280,000 people died in Thailand as a result of a tsunami.

"I create evil," declares God in Isaiah 45:7. This creator of evil is the biblical deity that William Lane Craig worships and claims to base his morality upon. Some translate the word "evil" in Isaiah 45:7 as "bad times," "disaster," "woe," or "calamity." Whatever it is—any being who willfully creates things that cause pain and suffering is not loving or compassionate. To paraphrase the seventeenth-century German philosopher and mathematician Gottfried Wilhelm Leibniz, any God who willingly creates disasters and woe—such as tsunamis and cystic fibrosis—is hardly distinguishable from the devil.

And keep in mind that the limited list of diseases and disasters above only refers to human suffering. When we take into account other animals, we find the vast majority are subject to all kinds of "woe" and "bad times," given that they inhabit a world in which one animal must kill another in order to survive. As American columnist Guy P. Harrison writes:

> The daily routine of life on Earth is a continual bloodbath of fear, suffering, and death . . . every moment of every day, it is business as usual for animals to be eaten alive or even have their organs devoured from within by parasites . . . In Africa I saw two lion cubs gnawing on a zebra . . . their victim was still alive, even as they worked to tear open its abdomen to devour the warm guts.[12]

Or consider American author Gary Paulsen's description of wolves eating a doe:

> It is a slow, ripping, terrible death for the prey. Two wolves held the doe by the nose, held her head down to the ice, and the other wolves took turns

> tearing at her rear end, pulling and jerking and tearing, until they were inside of her, pulling out parts of her and all this time she was still on her feet, still alive.[13]

From the humans who have suffered throughout history from disease and natural disasters to the cats in my neighborhood regularly chewed to death by thin coyotes, it is simply impossible to characterize the all-powerful, all-knowing deity such as the one Professor Craig believes in as having a moral, loving, or compassionate nature.[14] It just doesn't compute. For as the great Epicurus argued, way back in the third century B.C.E.: either God wants to get rid of evil and suffering in the world and yet is unable to do so, or God is quite able to get rid of pain and suffering and yet chooses not to. If he wants to get rid of pain and suffering and is unable to, then he's clearly not all-powerful. But if he is all-powerful—as theists insist—then that means he could most easily get rid of the pain and suffering in the world but chooses not to and is thus clearly not loving or compassionate.[15]

And that's just in relation to earthly suffering. God's created misery is truly boundless once we move beyond this mere planet. We're talking *hell*, described in Christian scriptures as a lake of fire, a fiery furnace, a place of everlasting destruction where pain and suffering are extreme and eternal (Matthew 13:49–50; 2 Thessalonians 1). According to Islamic scriptures, hell is a place where people's skin is roasted and then regrown only to be roasted again (Sura 4:56), people are forced to drink scalding water (Sura 6:70), and people's bellies are boiled and their bodies abused by iron hooks (Sura 22:19–22). It is simply impossible to characterize any deity who would cast billions of people into this hell as "compassionate, just, fair, kind, loving."

One of the greatest of post-Enlightenment philosophers, John Stuart Mill, an English freethinker, could make no semblance of sense of "a being who would make a Hell—who would create the human race with the infallible foreknowledge, and therefore the intention, that the great majority of them were to be consigned to horrible and everlasting torment."[16] If the adjectives that we use to describe the nature, character, or actions of anyone or anything are to have any meaning whatsoever, then we would describe such a hell-creating God as wicked and cruel, not compassionate or loving.

But whether or not the God of Christianity or of Islam or of your neighbor Butch is loving or cruel, compassionate or sadistic, it doesn't ultimately matter when it comes to linking this deity to our own morality. Because the whole point of Plato's dialogue between Socrates and Euthyphro is to show that what we humans consider to be moral cannot be based upon the will, wishes, or commands of any deity at all. For if morality and ethics did hinge upon the commands or wishes of any deity, an immediate problem would arise: morality would either become arbitrary and thus meaningless, or the deity would be rendered redundant and thus unnecessary.

And so, we arrive at the prime, foundational launchpad of naturalistic, humanistic, atheistic, secular morality: there is no compelling evidence that God exists, and even if there were, we can't agree on what it wills, and even if we could, then human morality would be reduced to nothing more than docile obedience—which is an abdication of moral responsibility. And even if we freely submitted to such a slave dynamic, there's nothing to prove that what God commands is "moral," per se, other than criteria somehow existing independently of God, thereby rendering God's relation to morality redundant.

The reality is that it is just us on this planet, and we have to come to terms with what it means to live ethically on our own. This existential situation—this reality in which we construct and create morality on our own, among and within communities—is to be warmly and cheerfully celebrated, for it is only within such godless, natural circumstances that morality can actually have any meaning.

What morality means, then, is the topic to which we now turn.

Part Two

THE FUNDAMENTALS OF SECULAR MORALITY

6

What It Means to Be Moral

You might think that saving someone's life would feel great. It doesn't. It actually feels pretty wretched. Granted, I shouldn't be speaking for firefighters, police officers, emergency medical technicians, first responders, surgeons, nurses, or any other people out there who regularly find themselves in the position of saving someone from imminent death. Perhaps for them, lifesaving experiences are exhilarating or affirming or joyous. But for me, it was none of these things. It was frightening, then unnerving, then depressing, and it ultimately left me with an empty feeling.

I'm glad I did it, but sad that I had to.

It was a Saturday night in Los Angeles in 2016. I was driving on the freeway with my family. My wife, Stacy, was in the passenger seat. Our two daughters were in the back seat, and our son was in the way back seat with the dog. We had just spent the day at my parents' house, eating pizza, playing chess, and watching YouTube videos. We left their house at around 8:00 p.m. It was winter, so the night was well dark and cold, at least for Southern California. We were about halfway home, driving eastbound on the 101, near downtown L.A. There were lots of cars in many lanes, but the traffic was flowing steadily. I was in the fastest lane, farthest to the left, closest to the concrete median divider in the middle, going about seventy miles an hour.

Then I heard my daughter say something like, "Is that a blimp?" and we all looked out the right-side windows to see what might be hovering up in the night sky, and just then I noticed a sudden flurry of red brake lights ahead of me and I started slowing down, and as I sensed something amiss, I pushed down harder on my brakes and then saw her: a young woman walking haphazardly across the freeway, right in front of us. I abruptly stopped, without hitting her. Fortunately, the cars behind me also managed to stop. The woman was sauntering in the white beams of my headlights, arms bent in a mock jogging manner, legs taking wide strides, eyes strangely serene, if not somewhat dazed.

We looked on in fearful confusion, unable to fathom how this woman had just been able to traverse four lanes of a Los Angeles freeway on foot without being obliterated. But her journey was not yet over. She continued toward the median, climbed up and over the cement barrier, and made as if to casually waltz into the fast lane of the oncoming traffic. She was about to be killed, and it seemed as if that was what she wanted.

My wife's reaction was immediate. She screamed: "Stop her!"

I hesitated. "What can I do?"

"*Stop her!*"

Stacy's agony was loud, and her urging me to action was visceral.

I got out of the car and stepped toward the concrete divider and tried to engage the young woman.

"Are you OK?" I tentatively asked.

She just looked back at me with eyes that projected something like bewilderment, inebriation, insanity, distance, desperation.

"Do you need any money?" I impulsively inquired, based on years of living in a city with a large homeless population.

She just muttered a bit and sort of smiled forlornly. I didn't want to try to grab her, for fear that such a move would scare her and cause her to take a single deadly step away from me and into the oncoming rush of cars. I was also slightly afraid of her. Was she dangerous? Well, she was small and her face was oddly calm, and there was a bit of kindness in her eyes. No, I decided that she was not a threat: she was not menacing or angry or exhibiting any violent predilections. But there was something unsettling about her, to be sure.

I opened the back door of the car, and my daughters quickly scooted over and made room. I gestured for the young woman to hop back over the concrete divider and get in. My fear of inviting a disturbed and suicidal stranger into my car with my family inside was overridden by my desire not to see her smashed to death.

"Come on. Get in. It's OK."

She mumbled some words about her brother and something about being rude, and then she climbed over and got in our car. I immediately locked all the doors and started driving for the nearest off-ramp while my wife dialed 911. My children were still and silent. My wife tried talking to the young woman, asking her about her situation, but didn't get very far, for her words were oddly chosen and her tone not quite right.

The 911 dispatchers asked my wife where exactly on the freeway the woman was, but when my wife explained that the woman was now in the car with us, they were confused and concerned and said that she shouldn't be in the car with us and now they didn't know quite how to help. It occurred to me that perhaps we should just get her to a hospital, and so with the help of the GPS, I saw that we could be at one in about ten minutes. I began following the directions through the wide streets of downtown L.A. My wife stayed on the line with 911, my kids remained mute, and the young woman kept talking about things that didn't make much sense.

And then we saw two police cars driving beside us and I waved at them to stop and we all pulled over and got the young woman out of the car and then the officers ordered her onto the sidewalk in a tone I found surprisingly harsh and I heard one of the cops say something to her like "I've seen you ten times out here already now" and then the other cop asked to see my ID and told me that I should have never taken her into my car "especially with your family in there" and I said that we couldn't bear to just watch her die and he said, "Well, I guess you were a hero then."

I got back in my car, and we drove off. And we didn't feel like heroes. We felt utterly gutted. I put my hand on my wife's knee and tried to say something about her having such good instincts, but my words fell flat. She was shaken and sickened by what we had just experienced, and what we had almost witnessed, and the painful desperation of that young woman, clearly unstable, waltzing across a crowded Los Angeles freeway at night, now left muttering on a cold sidewalk, being interrogated by cops.

"What will happen to her?" my older daughter asked.

"Was she drunk?" my younger daughter asked.

"That was scary," my son offered.

"But what will happen to her?" my older daughter asked again.

It was not an easy question to answer. The streets of downtown Los Angeles were peppered with homeless people: some in tents, some in sleeping bags, others on bus benches, some walking aimlessly. And it was around forty-five degrees. And that young woman, with no coat, was clearly not able to take care of herself.

"What she needs is to be taken care of," I said. "She needs doctors to figure out what is wrong with her and to get her on some medication that can improve her condition and stabilize her. She needs people who can help her if she has a drug or alcohol addiction. But most of all, she just needs a warm bed and a safe place to spend the night."

"And she probably won't get any of those things," my wife sighed. Unlike societies such as Scandinavia—where my family and I had previously lived for two years—the United States doesn't have a well-functioning welfare system that can adequately take care of sick, poor, addicted, homeless, or suicidal people deeply in need.

"It's so sad," my younger daughter said.

"It's so sad," my wife and I echoed.

We were quiet for a while as we got back onto the freeway, heading home. We were all consumed by a feeling of dread. There was really nothing good about what we had experienced. Yes, we had saved her life—and possibly the lives of many others, for if she had stepped out into that lane of oncoming cars, who knows what kind of chain collision it might have triggered, involving who knows how many cars and victims.

We wondered: What would become of that young woman? Who would ever care for her? How soon might she be back on that freeway again, sauntering among cars going seventy miles an hour? Such were our sad ponderings as we headed home.

To encounter human suffering at such close range is painful indeed. And it is in the aftermath of just such moments that thoughts and reflections about the meaning and nature of morality are most pronounced.

What It Means to Be Moral

Definitions of morality differ greatly over time, and from culture to culture, and from philosophy department to philosophy department, and from mosque to temple to church to synagogue.[1] Some definitions are quite complex, others more succinct. For example, according to American ethicist David Wong, morality is best understood as a form of social technology containing human-invented values that "answer to compelling needs and desires, and are subject to the constraints derived from human nature and the function of facilitating and promoting social cooperation,"[2] whereas Dutch primatologist Frans de Waal neatly boils morality down to the "two H's": *helping* and not *harming*.[3]

To draw both of these definitions out a bit—and acknowledging that there is no single, definitive definition of morality—we can say that in the here and now, for most people, being moral entails some combination of the following actions and intentions:

- Not causing unnecessary pain, harm, or suffering to humans and other animals
- Easing or relieving the pain or suffering of humans and other animals
- Offering various forms of help and assistance to those who need or seek it

- Comforting and tending to those who are vulnerable or weak
- Striving to make those around us feel supported and safe
- Working to increase health, happiness, and well-being in our families, communities, and society at large
- Working to increase fairness and justice, locally and globally
- Being empathetic and compassionate
- Being honest, conscientious, and caring
- Being altruistic
- Treating people the way in which we ourselves would want to be treated

While all of the above constitute parts of a well-rounded ethical orientation, a bit more needs to be said about the last component specifically—treating others the way we would want to be treated, commonly known as the "Golden Rule."[4] It is a fundamental bedrock of morality: we ought not do to others what we ourselves wouldn't want done to us. This manifestly reasonable, self-evident, empathetic maxim is one of the oldest and most global ethical imperatives, with various articulations of it being found in ancient Egyptian papyri and ancient Greek, Israelite, and Chinese philosophy, as well as within all the major religious traditions of the world.[5]

The Golden Rule is, in the words of American scholar Richard Carrier, "the most universally recognized moral standard," largely because it articulates a basic dynamic of human psychology: "if we embody what we already hate, we will hate ourselves, and be hated by others, but if we embody what we love and respect, we will love and respect ourselves, and be loved and respected by others in turn."[6] The Golden Rule is additionally powerful because it is not only empathetic at root, but it is also rational and, as American skeptic Michael Shermer notes, is steeped in "the basic principle of exchange reciprocity and reciprocal altruism." It just makes moral sense. "By asking yourself 'How would I feel if this were done unto me?' you are asking 'How would others feel if I did it unto them?'"[7]

Shermer provides a truly great historical illustration of the Golden Rule's internal logic and humanitarian core: notes that Abraham Lincoln jotted down on a piece of paper in 1854, well before he was president, concerning slavery:

> If A. can prove, however conclusively, that he may, of right, enslave B.—why not may B. snatch the same argument, and prove equally, that he may enslave A.? —You say A. is white, and B. is black. It is *color*, then; the lighter, having the right to enslave the darker? Take care. By this rule, you are to be a slave to the first man you meet, with a fairer skin than your own.
>
> You do not mean *color* exactly?—You mean whites are *intellectually* the superiors of blacks, and, therefore have the right to enslave them? Take care again. By this rule, you are to be slave to the first man you meet, with an intellect superior to your own.
>
> But, you say, it is a question of *interest*; and, if you can make it your *interest*, you have the right to enslave another. Very well. And if he can make it his interest, he has the right to enslave you.[8]

As Rabbi Hillel taught nearly two thousand years before Lincoln's ruminations on slavery, "That which is hateful to you, do not do unto someone else." Yes, it's about as basic and logical a moral philosophy as one can find.

The Golden Rule, of course, is not to be taken in some sort of pedantic, literal, precise way, such as: because I want a specific medical procedure done to me, then I will make sure that the same exact medical procedure is done to you. Rather, the Golden Rule should be understood in a broader, principled way, such as: because I'd like the right to choose whatever medical treatments I do or don't receive, I'll support your right to choose whatever medical treatments you do or don't receive.

When a person lives as best they can by the Golden Rule—and if he or she exhibits or manifests some of the other traits and virtues listed above, such as not causing unwanted pain or suffering, increasing fairness and justice, being compassionate, and so forth—they are acting in ways that we would consider moral or ethical. And conversely, anyone who does the opposite of the above—purposely causing unnecessary pain or suffering in others, vehemently refusing to comfort or care for those in need, working hard to decrease the happiness and well-being of others, actively fighting to make society more unfair and unjust, or being needlessly dishonest—is acting in ways we would consider immoral or unethical.[9]

Moral Spectrum

This conception of what it means to be moral or immoral should not be treated as an either/or configuration. Rather, it is best to think in terms of an imagined continuum of morality and immorality, in which actions, orientations, and endeavors can be seen as leaning more toward pure, ideational notions of moral on the one end and immoral on the other, though rarely or perhaps never fully reaching or embodying them completely. No one is a total and perpetual moral saint[10] in all aspects of his or her life, nor is anyone an absolute and permanent immoral monster in every single moment of his or her existence.

To illustrate this concept of morality not being an either/or thing but rather existing on an imagined continuum, consider that night on the freeway. While most would agree that our actions certainly leaned toward the moral end, the truth is that we didn't act completely moral in all possible regards. For even though we risked our own personal well-being to get that woman off the freeway and out of immediate danger, we didn't do any more than that: we didn't provide her with any long-term care, we didn't make sure she had a safe place to sleep that night, we didn't enroll her in any drug treatment or counseling programs, and we didn't invite her to live with us and share our home, meals, and money. Again, morality and immorality are always matters of degree.

And as for the various items and components of what it means to be moral listed above—it can't be definitively *proven* that those actions constitute the absolute, unadulterated, and universally accepted meaning of morality. That's because "moral" is nothing more than an adjective we humans use, bound by the limits of language and confined within our sociohistorical circumstances, to describe people's motivations and behaviors. And as such, the meaning of "moral"—like that of any adjective—is always dependent on the cultural context, always somewhat in flux, and always impervious to complete agreement by all.

The exact meaning of the term "moral"—again, just like any adjective, such as "mature," "impressive," or "funny"—doesn't actually exist outside of or beyond human conception and usage. No one can scientifically prove that one definition or meaning of moral is more accurate, true, or "real" than another definition or meaning, because the meaning of adjectives is never anything that can be proven in the way one proves a mathematical theorem, chemical composition, financial amount, meteoric measurement, or weight or height or velocity. Simply put, adjectives are not physical entities or properties that test tube–toting experts detect, observe, or discover. Rather, adjectives are unfixed, amorphous, ever-changeable descriptors that only exist and have meaning in ongoing usage by different people living their lives in varying circumstances, employing shared sounds in the shape of words intended to define things they see, experience, feel, or imagine as best they can.

Recognizing such a reality, all we can do is assert that when we, in the here and now, describe someone as "moral" or "ethical," we generally mean some combination of the criteria listed above. The ultimate point of morality, as American philosopher Bernard Gert has explained, "is to lessen the suffering of those harms that all rational persons want to avoid: death, pain, disability, loss of freedom, and loss of pleasure."[11]

And again, most people would agree that my wife's urge to save that woman's life out on that cold freeway was moral. Most people would concur that by bringing her into our car, getting her off the freeway, and calling 911, we acted morally, because we rescued her from imminent danger—even if its lifesaving impact was limited to that moment alone.

The Social Construction of Morality

The words "most people would agree" are key here. For whenever we designate something as moral, or whenever we debate whether this or that law is moral or immoral, we are ultimately dealing with the social construction of morality. By recognizing that something is "socially constructed," we are soberly acknowledging that it ultimately owes its existence to human thought, human will, human understanding, human feeling, human reflection, communal reinforcement, and widespread societal acceptance and collective recognition—and nothing more.

Let me give a concrete example of social construction: Canada.

Does Canada exist? You bet. I've been there. I've passed through Canadian border control, used Canadian dollars, seen Canadian license plates, heard Canadian people pronounce the word "out," read polls showing that nearly a quarter of Canadians are nonreligious,[12] strolled through Kitsilano, had coffee in Magog, gone to the biffy, and savored a hearty smoothie on Salt Spring Island, and then gone to the biffy again.

But here's the deal: Canada only exists because enough people say that it does, and then act accordingly. Canada—like every other country that has ever existed, currently exists, or will exist in the future—is only a real entity to the extent that enough people collectively agree to recognize it as such and live within the confines of such a shared agreement. What we know as "Canada" is merely an assemblage of symbols, institutions, interactions, customs, laws, and lines drawn on a map that enough humans have agreed to accept as real and legitimately Canadian. But people could just as easily refuse to recognize Canada as real or legitimate. And if that happened, Canada would no longer exist. Perhaps some people could invade Canada and declare it "Nordlandia," replacing all the Canadian symbols, institutions, and laws with different ones, and if they were successful in getting enough people to eventually accept their endeavor as legitimate, then Canada would no longer exist, experiencing the fate of numerous former nations that are no longer with us, such as Kurdistan, Sikkim, Champa, the Yeke Kingdom, Ezo, the Bornu Empire, the Jolof Empire, Tibet, the Republic of Cospaia, and the Vermont Republic. Or some people from within Canada could secede and create one (Quebec?) or two or three new countries on the same ground that was once known as Canada. And if enough people collectively recognized these new countries as real, then they'd exist as real countries, alongside a shrunken Canada. But these new countries would only exist because enough people agreed that they do and then behaved in accordance with that agreement. As pioneering sociologists William and Dorothy Thomas declared back in 1928, if people define situations as real, then they are real in their consequences.

In short, Canada is socially constructed: its existence hinges solely upon the shared beliefs and concomitant actions of people—and nothing more. And all countries are similar social constructions. But not just countries. Many ostensibly "real" elements of our social world owe their existence to nothing more than the same social underpinnings. For example: baseball. It is a human invention and only exists because we say it does and act accordingly. It is not just baseball that is socially constructed, but all sports. And not just all sports—but the very idea of "sport" itself is a social construction. And that's one reason as to why there is no airtight, absolute definitions of the word "sport." People disagree about its meaning, and even disagree as to what activities can rightly be classified as sports. So just what exactly is a "sport"? Whatever enough people say and agree that it is, and then act accordingly—and nothing more.

What Is Crime?

To fully understand the implications of social construction, and to bring us closer to the matter of morality, let's consider the social construction of crime.

What exactly is a "crime"? What thoughts, actions, or behaviors constitute "crime"? Well, that depends entirely on the social and historical context. For example, women taking a Zumba class is not a crime in Indiana, but it is in Iran.[13] Writing this book, which contains criticisms of religion and advocates atheistic approaches to morality, is not a crime in California, but it is in Pakistan—punishable by death.[14] Today, owning another human being as personal property is a crime in South Carolina, but it wasn't a crime there until the North won the Civil War in 1865. The reality is that there exists no definitive, empirical, universally accepted, scientifically provable meaning of what actually or truly constitutes a "crime."

Sure, we can readily agree that a crime is "law violation," but that doesn't help us much because laws change constantly throughout history and are markedly different in various societies today. And while the "causing of harm" might seem like a good guideline for identifying or defining a crime, the reality is that many activities deemed crimes don't cause any obvious harm to anyone or anything. Such so-called "victimless crimes," where there is no aggrieved party or complaining victim, abound. And furthermore, what constitutes "harm" is rarely clear-cut. No two people, or two cultures, can readily agree. Obvious examples of things that some folks currently find downright harmful while others don't in the least include men and women dancing together, circumcision, driving an SUV, immunizations, rock music, gambling, masturbation, hunting, drinking alcohol, polygamy, tax-subsidized universal health care, owning semiautomatic weapons, watching pornography, eating meat, doctor-assisted suicide, spending hours playing certain video games, teaching children that if they sin they will go to hell, not teaching children that if they sin they will go to hell, and so on.

Thus, at root, crime is nothing more than whatever enough people say it is and then act accordingly, and little else. How do we know? Well, one good indication is the fact—already broached above—that the specific acts or behaviors that constitute a crime are different from one society to another, and whatever acts or behaviors—or even thoughts!—constitute a crime change within the same society over time. Furthermore, what constitutes a crime is regularly debated even within the same society at the same time. For yet more examples: smoking marijuana. Is it a crime? Yes in Indonesia. No in the Netherlands. Yes in Malawi. No in Uruguay. Yes in Seattle in 1997, no in Seattle in 2017. Yes right now in Oklahoma, but not right now in Oregon. How about converting to Christianity—is it a crime? No in Norway, but yes in Saudi Arabia. How about not believing in God? No in Scotland today, but yes in Scotland in the 1600s. And so it goes for a nearly infinite number of activities, behaviors, or beliefs—from breastfeeding in public to worshipping certain goddesses, from eating specific foods to marrying certain people, and from enslaving others or helping enslaved people escape to freedom—both of which have been considered crimes at different times and in different places.

As Émile Durkheim, the founding father of sociology and a secular French Jew, rightly observed back in 1893, the only thing that all crimes have in common is nothing more than that they are acts widely condemned by members of a given society.[15] But what such acts may actually *be* varies wildly from culture to culture and era to era.

And we should also be sure to vigilantly note that what acts get designated as criminal is sometimes the result of certain people or groups in power unjustly defining certain acts as criminal—and not others—to their own direct benefit.

But surely all societies condemn murder as a crime, right? Well, not so fast. While there is some strong evidence that all societies condemn the unjustified taking of a life, there exists a vast array of differences as to what people consider "unjustified." For example, various societies throughout history have allowed for the lawful, justified killing of people with certain physical blemishes or anomalies, people of different religions, people of certain ages, people of certain tribes, people of certain sexual orientations, people who break certain laws or taboos, people deemed possessed, people considered traitors, people considered a burden, people considered a threat, people who are born at the wrong time, people who married the wrong person, people designated to serve as sacrificial offerings to the gods, people who were considered witches, people who wrote certain books, people who challenged the authorities, people who shamed their parents, etc., etc. As American philosopher Owen Flanagan has noted, "The commandment 'Thou shall not kill innocents' is widely shared across cultures. But obeying it depends on complex, ever-changing beliefs about who is and who is not innocent."[16]

Just look at the current debate over abortion in the United States. For some, when a woman becomes pregnant, the developing fetus in her womb is a growing life in and of itself, an unborn baby, and the termination of such a growing life is equivalent to murder. For others, the developing fetus is but a collection of tissue, a mere potential life, and not a fully realized living human being, and the ability of a woman to decide whether or not to terminate her pregnancy is a fundamental right, not a crime. Clearly, what constitutes the "unjustified taking of life" is subject to extreme disagreement and seemingly incompatible moral interpretation—even by neighbors who live on the same street in Anywhere, USA, in 2019.[17]

"Oughtness"

Such widespread disagreement—among people, between cultures, and over time—about what constitutes a crime, or about the meaning of countless other terms, concepts, or entities, is a very strong indicator of social construction. But it is only that—an indicator. Disagreement need not exist for something to be socially constructed; many elements of our world that are widely or even *universally* agreed upon are nonetheless socially constructed. After all, everyone agrees that Canada is a country. But it is still, as we have seen, a social construction—despite widespread, near-unanimous acceptance of its existence. And even if everyone in the world were to fully agree about other things—for instance, that failing to bow to the morning sun is a crime punishable by death, or that pigs ought to be pets but not cats, or that every twenty-sixth day of June everyone should wear purple, or that Thor's hammer creates thunder—such things would *still* be socially constructed, despite universal agreement, because their facticity, manifestation, and existence would still reside solely in the hearts, minds, and actions of people living in a social context, and nowhere else. So it goes for morality: its meaning is whatever we collectively say it is, and act accordingly, and nothing more.

But what makes morality special is that the meanings we ascribe to it—being kind, honest, altruistic, and caring, helping out when possible and not causing needless suffering—are all characteristics and behaviors that we think people *ought* to strive for.[18] There is a sense that we *should* be kind and honest—and *everyone* should, not just ourselves. Everyone should help out when and if they can. Everyone ought to be empathetic and compassionate. It is this embedded, implicit imperativeness and universalistic, prescriptive, generalizable "oughtness" that gives morality and ethics their unique status as being something other than, or more than, mere personal preference.

After all, when thinking about how my wife and I helped that vulnerable woman out on the freeway that night, it's not as if my attitude was something like "Well, I personally prefer to save this woman about to be smashed by a car. But, hey, that's just my own thing. If you wouldn't feel like doing anything to save her, that's cool." No, it wouldn't be cool. Nearly everyone would agree that a woman in such a precarious situation *ought* to be helped, if possible. It is what people *should* do.

Morality, then, contains a distinctively compelling core that normatively indicates how others should be—not just how you or I alone should be. As New Zealand–based philosopher Richard Joyce observes, moral assertions possess a distinguishable "practical clout,"[19] or as American philosopher Charles Stevenson puts it, morals contain a "magnetic" quality that pulls or compels us—presumably, all of us—to feel or act in certain ways.[20]

Again, it's qualitatively different from individual taste: while I may personally like listening to the album *One Nation Underground* by Pearls Before Swine and prefer it over most other albums in the world, I don't simultaneously think that you or anyone else needs to listen to it. If other people don't like it, so be it. But morality is different. It's not simply that I happen to prefer honesty over deception or lifesaving over life-destroying or helping others over harming others. Yes, I do prefer these things, but I am additionally convinced that others should as well—in fact, *everyone* should—and I believe that such compelling predilections will have far-reaching consequences on the lives of others, on how society functions, and on the degree of pain/suffering or flourishing/happiness that will result.

Thus, as British writer Iain King reasons, morality occupies its own unique domain, "somewhere between tastes that are personal to each of us and facts outside the world."[21] As such, any attempt to pigeonhole or reduce morality to either of these two things—reflecting mere personal preference or somehow embodying independent, objective factualities—fails to grasp the special meaning of morality and the unique, unparalleled position it occupies in social life. Morality, as American philosopher Michael Ruse succinctly expresses, "has its own being."[22]

"Back in Black"

As a social construction sui generis that entails a heart of "oughtness," morality is something that resides only in the heads, feelings, minds, beliefs, opinions, reactions, judgments, theories, guts, and agreements of people.[23]

Morality, thus, is not—nor could it ever be—objective, if by "objective" we mean things that are the way they are regardless of, or in spite of, people's feelings, thoughts, or opinions. Things that are objective, in this regard, exist whether we want them to or not: their reality is independent of human desire or emotion. Such things are objectively real because they can be proven to exist by appealing to empirically observable aspects within physical reality or logical proof. And objective entities cannot be wished away, imagined away, or hoped away. Again, they exist independent of and impervious to human sentiment, intuition, will, or belief.

The term "subjective," on other hand, refers to things that *only* reside within the realm of human sentiment, opinion, and reflection. "Subjective" refers to people's preferences, predilections, and feelings—and nothing more. Something subjective can never, ever be proven as wrong or right, true or false, correct or incorrect outside of the limited contours of people's reactions, feelings, opinions, tastes, and responses.

Consider my seventh grade crush, Robin Heckle, and her love of AC/DC. The summer before I started junior high, I went to sleepaway camp in a canyon in Malibu. My counselor, a thoughtful UCLA student, was a music aficionado; he had a huge record collection, and he lectured to us constantly about which piece of jazz was superior to another. I had never met anyone in my life up to that point who seemed to know so much about music. Now, it just so happened that AC/DC's album *Back in Black* was topping the charts that summer. So one afternoon, in our cabin, I asked him if he liked the song "Back in Black." He immediately let out a negative and condescending chortle, shook his head in disgust, and explained: "That's garbage. Trash. The whole entire song only has three chords." I took that in. He seemed to have somehow proven to me that no song could be any good with such a small number of chords. A month later, come September, I found myself in seventh grade woodshop, sitting next to Robin Heckle. I noticed that she had "AC/DC" written in bold letters across her notebook. "You know," I explained to her, "that song 'Back in Black' isn't very good. It only has three chords."

"Well," she confidently replied, "I love it."

And that was all I ever needed to learn about the difference between objective and subjective.

The number of chords in the song "Back in Black" is an objective matter. And I don't actually think it is only three, by the way. But however many chords make up that song—be it three or thirteen—it is an empirical, provable matter: the number of chords can be counted. The number of chords is what it is, regardless of anyone's feelings or opinions. And the actual length of the song is also an objective fact. The vibrating sound waves exist for a specific duration of time, whether or not we wish or hope it to be otherwise. So, if I think the song "Back in Black" lasts a certain amount of time, but you think it lasts longer, and we thus disagree, there is an objective way to settle our dispute: measurement. The amount of time the song exists is an empirical, provable reality. But as for hating the song (as my counselor did) or loving it (as Robin Heckle did), that's a purely subjective matter. The song made my counselor feel bad, but it made Robin Heckle feel good. And there's no wrong or right there, just subjective experience. There is no outside source to settle this disagreement. And how *could* there be? What sort of entity could ever exist that would somehow compel a person to like a song they don't like? Sure, one can perhaps learn about a given song, and thus come to appreciate the complexity of it or the technical virtuosity that goes into playing it. But appreciating complexity or recognizing virtuosity is not the same thing as *liking* it. I can muster some appreciation for the complexity and virtuosity of certain operas—but I still can't stand them and I would never choose to listen to them for pleasure. In fact, I would find such an experience distinctly unpleasant. You simply can't empirically *prove* anything when it comes to what people like or don't like in a song, or anything else in the realm of aesthetics.

Should We Eat My Dog?

Such is the case for morality. While it isn't about personal aesthetics, but rather how we all ought to treat one another, no one can *prove* in some sort of empirical, objective manner that we ought or should behave a certain way.

Consider my dog. She is in my office right now. She is black, and her name is Eli. Now, I can *prove* that she is in fact right now in my office: it's an objective aspect of reality because there are empirical means whereby we can establish her presence. We can detect the heat her body is emitting, measure her weight, assess the space she occupies, touch her fur, smell her breath, see her paws.

But now let's ponder how we ought to behave in relation to my dog's existence. Should we pet her? Kick her? Feed her? Eat her? Worship her? Skin her? Alas, there exists no objective, nonhuman source here for guidance or answers. There is no God telling us how we ought to treat the dog in my office, and even if there were, following God's dictates would simply be an act of obedience and submission, not morality. And there are no small, hard-to-detect ethical elves hovering just above my dog that, if we simply squinted hard enough or used infrared goggles, we could see and then read their hand gestures instructing us whether to pet her or beat her. And even if such ethical elves existed—and their guidance were discernable through scientific means—it still doesn't *prove* that their guidance would be *moral*, per se, as a generalized application of the Euthyphro dilemma reveals. Nor is morality swirling around in the form of some strange, proton-like particles; as American philosopher Ronald Dworkin quipped, there are no "morons" whose "energy and momentum establish fields that at once constitute the morality or immorality, or virtue or vice, of particular human acts."[24]

Thus, as Enlightenment titan David Hume so rightly surmised in his short but brilliant comments about the unbridgeable gulf between "is" and "ought," nothing can empirically, indisputably tell us how to go from what objectively exists in the world to how we ought to morally act in relation to its existence. How we are to behave is painfully—or rather inspiringly—up to us: our sentiments, our feelings, our needs, our opinions, our values, our judgments, our goals, our consciences, our culture, our society—all working in combination to manifest as our human-based, socially constructed morality.

And as for those who staunchly insist that morality is an objective affair—they never seem to notice or acknowledge that they always believe that the dictates of this supposed objective morality always aligns perfectly with their own personal moral opinions. How convenient! Oh well, it's just another illustration of the unavoidable, underlying subjectivity of morality—and its socially constructed nature.

Shared, Collective, and Improving

Rest assured, this is all very good news. The social construction of morality is not to be feared or lamented, but rather accepted and embraced. As former Bishop of Edinburgh Richard Holloway puts it, "the creation of morality is our business," and given that it is a central pillar of what defines us as humans, "we should be exhilarated rather than depressed by the prospect."[25]

However, before getting to that, let's keep in mind just a few additional matters concerning morality's social construction.[26]

First off, the *social* is key. The meaning of morality manifests at the collective level—not the individual level. No single person can dictate the meaning of morality by fiat. My neighbor, Chris, can stand on his doorstep and proclaim that drinking RC Cola is moral or that eating corn is immoral—but his proclaiming these things doesn't make them so. Others would have to agree and feel and act accordingly. So it goes for all manifestations of social construction: if one single person insists that a certain country exists or that a certain behavior is a crime, but no one else shares this belief, then that person's pronouncements are empty—her version of realty is simply not shared, and as such, has no teeth or impact. It may even border on the delusional. Admittedly, at rare times in history, there emerge specific individuals—certain ethical innovators—who articulate a pointed moral vision contrary to the thoughts of just about everyone else and thereby spark moral progress. W. E. B. Du Bois referred to them as heralding, ethical "agitators,"[27] and Martin Luther King Jr. dubbed them "disciplined nonconformists."[28] But in order for their morally prophetic assertions to take root and manifest as part of our social reality, it requires collective agreement and concomitant action. Again, what it means to be moral—while subjective in the sense that it can't be empirically proven—is simultaneously a shared, collective, cooperative enterprise. Morality and solipsism are, to be sure, intrinsically incompatible.

Secondly, the social construction of morality—indeed, the social construction of any aspect of life—does not occur in real time. Rather, it is a prolonged process, an ongoing historical development. The existence of Canada—and of all countries—is the result of a complex amalgam of evolved beliefs and worldviews and protracted, coordinated actions of various peoples and groups over long stretches of time. So it goes for what constitutes a crime. Or what the term "family" means, or what the concept "race" entails, or what "art" is. These things are sociohistorical phenomena, cobbled together and debated about and agreed upon—and often unduly influenced by those with power and prestige—over the course of years or decades or millennia of people interacting and thinking and doing. So, by saying that morality is socially constructed, that doesn't mean it is done so in the here and now, contemporarily, or democratically. Rather, current meanings of morality are the outcome of long-term human will and sentiment, and struggle and debate, over time. To paraphrase Karl Marx, people construct the meanings of morality, but always in a state confined and determined by preceding history, and seldom, if ever, under conditions that they necessarily choose—and rarely consciously, deliberately, or by consensus.[29]

Finally, at the beating heart of the social construction of morality is ongoing development, movement, change, and improvement. As Scottish philosopher Alasdair MacIntyre observes, "moral concepts change as social life changes."[30] Since morality is not composed of eternal, unbending commandments crafted by a magical being and set in stone, but rather something intrinsically human—up to no one but us—it can and does get better as the conditions and circumstances of human life change and develop. Morality advances and becomes more humane as we advance and become more humane. And as we—as a species—acquire more knowledge and insight about ourselves and the natural world, and as we develop artistically, literarily, technologically, and creatively, and as our communication with each other grows ever more instantaneous, widespread, and global, and as we have new and varied experiences, such development and growth is reflected in the ever-improving meaning of morality.

From 1750 B.C.E. to 1948 C.E.

For example, think about the Code of Hammurabi in relation to the Universal Declaration of Human Rights. The Code of Hammurabi was a list of official laws and moral guidelines written in rock by order of a Mesopotamian King, Hammurabi, sometime around the year 1750 B.C.E. Predating the Bible by many centuries, it is one of the oldest known writings in the world. The code contains over 280 specific laws, including the following:

- If anyone brings an accusation against a man, and the accused go to the river and leap into the river, if he sink in the river his accuser shall take possession of his house. But if the river prove that the accused is not guilty, and he escape unhurt, then he who had brought the accusation shall be put to death, while he who leaped into the river shall take possession of the house that had belonged to his accuser.
- If anyone is committing a robbery and is caught, then he shall be put to death.
- If a man rent his field for tillage for a fixed rental, and receive the rent of his field, but bad weather come and destroy the harvest, the injury falls upon the tiller of the soil.
- If a man betroth a girl to his son, and his son have intercourse with

her, but he (the father) afterward defile her, and be surprised, then he shall be bound and cast into the water (drowned).

- If a son strike his father, his hands shall be hewn off.
- If a man put out the eye of another man, his eye shall be put out.
- If a man strike a freeborn woman so that she lose her unborn child, he shall pay ten shekels for her loss. If the woman die, his daughter shall be put to death.
- If a builder build a house for someone, and does not construct it properly, and the house which he built fall in and kill its owner, then that builder shall be put to death.
- If a slave say to his master: "You are not my master," if they convict him his master shall cut off his ear.

What we can see from this mere handful of excerpts from the ancient Code of Hammurabi are attempts at ensuring societal stability, and even some rudimentary elements of fairness and justice. But we also see blatant barbarity, patriarchal bias, and bald inhumanity: daughters can be put to death for the crimes of their father, a person's ability to sink or swim in a river is somehow indicative of guilt, and slavery is OK.

Now, let's fast-forward some thirty-seven hundred years to the year 1948. In the aftermath of the horrors of World War II, at the behest of the United Nations, and under the stewardship of Eleanor Roosevelt and Canadian legal scholar John Peters Humphrey, a gathering of humanitarians, diplomats, lawyers, and philosophers from various countries drafted a set of thirty articles intended to solidify standards of international law and thereby improve life on planet Earth. Some of the articles include:

- Everyone has the right to life, liberty, and security of person.
- No one shall be held in slavery or servitude; slavery and the slave trade shall be prohibited in all their forms.
- No one shall be subjected to torture or to cruel, inhuman, or degrading treatment or punishment.
- Everyone is entitled in full equality to a fair and public hearing by

an independent and impartial tribunal, in the determination of his rights and obligations and of any criminal charge against him.

- Men and women of full age, without any limitation due to race, nationality, or religion, have the right to marry and to found a family. They are entitled to equal rights as to marriage, during marriage, and at its dissolution. Marriage shall be entered into only with the free and full consent of the intending spouses.
- Everyone has the right to freedom of thought, conscience, and religion; this right includes freedom to change his religion or belief, and freedom, either alone or in community with others and in public or private, to manifest his religion or belief in teaching, practice, worship, and observance.
- Everyone has the right to take part in the government of his country, directly or through freely chosen representatives.
- Everyone, without any discrimination, has the right to equal pay for equal work.
- Everyone has the right to rest and leisure, including reasonable limitation of working hours and periodic holidays with pay.

Surely, all of us find this latter list from 1948 better—more moral—than the first one from 1750 B.C.E. We applaud its values and principles of fairness, justice, tolerance, equality, humanness, and dignity. The fact that we feel this way—coupled with the historical reality that human beings can construct such different sets of moral and legal guidelines—is evidence of not only the social construction of morality but also its obvious improvement over time. And similar evidence of further moral progress is abundant.

Progress

Today, we shudder at the thought of killing people in order to appease various gods, as the ancient Mayans and Aztecs used to do; one estimate suggests that during the fifteenth century, the Aztecs killed up to 250,000 people a year as sacrifices to their gods.[31] We similarly now shudder at the wanton murder of approximately half a million women accused of witchcraft in Christian Europe between the sixteenth and eighteenth centuries.[32] We cringe at the Chinese practice of foot-binding, which forcefully destroyed millions of girls' feet between the eleventh and ninteenth centuries.[33] Also cringeworthy: the sixteenth to eighteenth–century Italian practice of castrating tens of thousands of prepubescent boys so as to render their voices pleasing to officials of the Catholic Church.[34] And we gape in horror at the police-led, mayor-sanctioned, judge-approved, newspaper editor–celebrated, and mob-fueled lynching of thousands of African Americans in the late nineteenth and early twentieth centuries in the United States.

The point here is that our current feelings of outrage over the unethical and inhumane phenomena broached above are strong evidence that socially constructed morality changes, develops, and improves over time. Additionally, we can explain our pained exasperation and righteous indignation about the above instances of inhumanity from the past that we now condemn as immoral as being predicated upon, and rooted in, the shared meanings of morality outlined earlier in this chapter: that is, we now see such practices and behaviors as clearly having caused unnecessary harm, pain, and suffering; we now recognize that they entailed treating people unfairly and unjustly; we can acknowledge that they were not about being kind, caring, or compassionate; it is apparent that they did not help to make the world a better place; to our contemporary sensibilities, they clearly did not consist of treating people the way that we ourselves would want to be treated. And that is why we condemn them today, even though so many humans of the past celebrated and even defended them on moral grounds. And rest assured, there are many things we do today without a thought, care, or slight pang of conscience—or with strong justification, approbation, and defense—that future humans will look back upon as flagrantly immoral, unethical, and even depraved. Such is the inevitable story of evolving, socially constructed human morality.

As Jewish atheist anarchist Emma Goldman said back in 1916, ethical values such as justice and fidelity "are not conditioned in heaven, but . . . are related to and interwoven with the tremendous changes going on in the social and material life of the human race; not fixed and eternal, but fluctuating, even as life itself."[35]

Nothing to Fear

And as I said before, this is really good news.

The social construction of morality should be embraced because it facilitates moral progress and betterment. We should be inspired by the knowledge that morality is not some reified index of rules eternally, cosmically, or physically set in stone—for such a situation would not render us morally free but captive and submissive. We should celebrate the fact that morality is not created and enforced by a mindreading, rainbow-and-cancer-creating, all-power-wielding deity threatening us with hell or enticing us with heaven—for such a situation would not make for a shared moral life but a communal prison of prudence, with each of us seeking to save our own skins from the watchful gaze of a trans-cosmic dictator.

Furthermore, we must heartily accept that morality is not some physical or metaphysical entity, ultimately discerned by empirical means—for such a situation is manifestly illogical and unfathomable. As Australian philosopher J. L. Mackie reasoned, there cannot exist in the universe any natural entities or physical properties so unimaginably bizarre that they contain some uniquely intrinsic force or power of "to-be-pursuedness" or "not-to-be-doneness" built within them, able to automatically convince any who comes across them of their moral rightness or wrongness in the realm of human behavior.[36]

It is because morality is none of the above, but rather a social construction, that we now condemn and outlaw the castration of nine-year-old boys or the sacrificing of ten-year-old girls to made-up gods, as was once justified and defended by the most upstanding members of society. It is why many of us can now accept homosexuality as a natural, normal form of human love and intimacy, rather than condemn, fear, or hate it as sinful and worthy of violent repression, as so many of us used to. It is why most white Americans now experience shameful disbelief at anti-miscegenation laws, on the books well into the 1960s, that made it illegal for people of different races to marry one another—laws considered morally righteous by the white majority for centuries. It is why there is ongoing, vigorous disagreement about numerous moral matters in the here and now, and why in that disagreement, we are able to continually debate and discuss what it means to be moral, offering opinions, reasons, and explications.

It is good news that morality, as something we humans create, is a never-ending process, evolving and changing as we grow and develop, ever expanding in such a way as to limit pain, curtail suffering, bolster well-being, and strengthen equality and justice.

Lingering Concerns

However, despite the observable historical progress facilitated by the social construction of morality, its reality can unnerve or even scare some people—especially the pious. Their fear takes the form of two main worries.

First, if morality is socially constructed, then who or what can ultimately say what is wrong or right? Is the worldview of marauding, machete-wielding Hutu bands equal to that of pacifist Quakers? Or is one clearly more moral than the other? And if so, according to what objective standards or criteria? Were the values of Nazis killing Jews of equal moral merit as those of the French villagers of Le Chambon-sur-Lignon who hid Jewish children from these murderous Germans? And if not, who says so? And based on what authority? And appealing to what unbiased source of arbitration?

Secondly, there is the nagging, stubborn question—which I would say actually borders on psychopathology—that asks: Why be moral if morality is simply what enough people say it is? What is manifestly binding or obligatory about it?

The answer to the first question, concerning how to evaluate one group's morals compared to another group's—i.e., moral relativism, which will be address more fully in chapter 12—is that we humans are ultimately the only ones who can say why Quaker pacifism is morally superior to Hutu genocidal actions; we humans are ultimately the only ones who can decide that Nazism is not moral and resistance to Nazism is.[37] Will we all agree, all the time, about what actions or behaviors are moral or immoral? Of course not. There is always going to be sharp disagreement among peoples and societies. And sometimes violent conflict. And there is no magical umpire or incorporeal law to settle these things for us. That's the reality of the world we live in, whether we like it or not. The meaning of morality is always going to be something that we must struggle over, grapple with, debate about, negotiate, and sometimes even fight about.

As to the second, perniciously nihilistic question—why be moral?—the answer is pretty much as David Hume explained back in the 1700s: because we are disgusted by cruelty, pained by suffering, angered by injustice, saddened by misery, horrified by sadism, stung by lies, hurt by inequality.[38] In short, we can recognize and understand *harm*—and that alone guides the needle of our moral compass. In the straightforward words of American philosopher Walter Sinnott-Armstrong:

> Why is it morally wrong to kill other people? Because it harms them by depriving them of life. Why is it morally wrong to hit, kick, stab, or shoot other people? Because it harms them by causing them pain. Why is it morally wrong to kidnap children? Because it harms them by terrifying them and taking away their freedom to go where they want. Why is it morally wrong to blind people? Because it harms them by taking away their ability to see. Why is it morally wrong to steal money from neighbors? Because it harms them by reducing their ability to buy what they want . . . Why is it morally wrong to lie? Because lies can undermine trust and mislead people into doing what harms them. And so on.[39]

Anyone who can't understand harm, or is unclear on why it is immoral to harm others, or who needs an invisible deity to command them not to cause harm—because otherwise they would—is simply beyond the pale of rational moral philosophy or compassionate ethical reasoning.

In addition to understanding why harm ought to be avoided, we are also naturally appreciative of kindness, warmed by care and comfort, uplifted by compassion, eased by love, and relieved by justice. And we can see, experience, and rationally reflect upon the benefits of honesty, goodwill, and fairness, both for ourselves and for those around us. Indeed, being moral is truly double-barreled—serving both our community as well as ourselves. On the communal altruistic level, when we behave morally, we make life better for those around us, both in our immediate circle but also in the wider society, thereby contributing to a better life for all. And more selfishly, being moral brings direct benefits to us as individuals; as American scholar Richard Carrier has reasoned, "moral people will naturally make more and stronger friendships, win more genuine love from others, have less to fear, and find more in themselves to love and appreciate. They will set up fewer traps for themselves, live less self-destructive and more creative lives, and enjoy greater security."[40]

Well, that's all good and fine, one may curmudgeonly protest. But what about the various people—comprising an unfortunate, distinct minority of our species—who lack all empathy or compassion, who do not cringe at the pain of others, who don't understand harm, who may even delight in the suffering of others, who favor deception over honesty, cruelty over kindness, and who fight to make the world less safe and more unjust? What about those callous, venal individuals who only seek goods and rewards for themselves, even at the expense, or to the detriment, of others? Such individuals exist, to be sure. Some are psychopaths. Some are sociopaths. Some are simply greedy, dishonest, or unkind in fits and starts. And just as surely, no deontological argument about rational ethical duty or utilitarian explication concerning the greatest good for the greatest number—or any such theoretical didacticism—will have any effect on them. Fortunately, their numbers remain relatively small. And the best that we can do in the face of their malevolence is to seek to reduce, limit, or contain the harm that they may inflict to the best of our abilities, as will be discussed in chapter 9.

Invented and Inherited

British scholar Kenan Malik has eloquently described much of world philosophy, both Eastern and Western, as one long, grand "quest for a moral compass"[41]—an earnest, deeply serious hunt to uncover the true, underlying source of human morality. This philosophical quest for a moral compass has been predicated upon the notion, or hope, that there is someone or something above, beyond, or outside of humanity—something supernatural, metaphysical, empirical, or manifestly objective—that can provide the incontestable and eternally binding reasons, instructions, or justifications concerning how and why to be moral. And while this quest has been one of the noblest and most engaging endeavors of human intellectual history—producing deep insight into what it means to be conscience-abiding animals—it is ultimately a misguided if not futile quest.[42]

Why? Because there is no divine, definitive, otherworldly, or metaphysical source of human morality above or outside of human history, society, and culture. Humanity is both its own generator and interpreter of morality. We decide, over time, what it means to be moral. Nothing else can do it for us, not only because nothing of such a nature exists, but because even it did, we'd still have to be the ones to ultimately decide if its imperatives or commandments or logic caused harm and suffering or not; if they entailed honesty, altruism, compassion, and caring; if they increased fairness and justice; and if they, as such, ought to be followed, obeyed, ignored, or resisted.

Simply put: the moral compass is *us*. As J. L. Mackie provocatively argued back in 1977, humans do not discover right and wrong but rather *invent* it. And yet, despite the truth of Mackie's insight, there is still quite a bit more to morality than it simply being a human invention. That is, while the social construction of morality is certainly a huge and compelling part of the story of human morality—as I've endeavored to illustrate in this chapter—it is only a part. For even though morality is something that we humans invent and construct, it is also something that we can't help but engender and manifest as an entrenched part of our evolved social nature.

Beyond its socially constructed nature, then, being moral is something that we are unconsciously, instinctively driven by. Morality is something that we are compelled to express and experience. In other words, although morality is something that we invent, at a much deeper and more powerful level, it is simultaneously something that we *inherit*: not only from our immediate caregivers and the developing history of our culture, but from our very distant, naturally developed origins.[43] In the words of Australian ethicist Peter Singer, "we are endowed with a moral faculty that guides our intuitive judgments of right and wrong. These intuitions reflect the outcome of millions of years in which our ancestors have lived as social mammals, and are part of our common inheritance."[44]

To illustrate this, let's revisit that night on the Los Angeles freeway one last time.

Why did my wife have such an instantaneously compassionate reaction to seeing that woman on the freeway about to be killed? Why did she so desperately want me to step out of the car and save her, even though doing so might put me and her and our children in harm's way? Why was her altruistic urge to save a complete stranger so forceful, instinctive, and visceral? Why was she so quickly filled with horror at the thought of witnessing a young woman's death? What was the source of her empathetic distress?[45] And why was she so relieved when we got the woman into our car and off the freeway?

Well, I can assure you that it wasn't because Stacy believes in God—she's been an atheist for most of her life. And I can confidently tell you that it was not because my wife has read Aristotle's *Nicomachean Ethics* from 348 B.C.E., or Immanuel Kant's *Groundwork of the Metaphysics of Morals* from 1785, or John Stuart Mill's *Utilitarianism* from 1861—or any such classical works of moral philosophy. My wife did not want to so badly save that young woman's life because she was thinking about the dynamics underpinning the social construction of morality and all the collective, ongoing ways in which we, as humans, decide what it means to be ethical.

Rather, what propelled my wife to act morally in that instant were deep forces far more significant and compelling than anything intellectual or philosophical. These inherited, underlying, natural, evolved, and staunchly secular sources of my wife's morality—and indeed, all our morality—will be our next focus.

7

Where Do You Get Your Morals?

When nuns sing in devotional prayer, they tilt their faces and eyes up toward the heavens. When preachers beg for mercy or forgiveness, they always raise their hands skyward, palms open, as if to receive blessing from above. When the spiritually inclined are contending with the pain of past trauma or addiction, it is to a *higher* power that they turn for relief. When faithful soccer players score a goal, they point upward in reverential celebration, publicly acknowledging the deity who—though unable or unwilling to eliminate childhood leukemia—finds the wherewithal to enable them to nimbly kick balls into nets. And where is this deity? Clearly, up there. Way, way up there.

In the biblical fable of the Tower of Babel, when the ancient peoples of the world sought to get nearer to God, they built a giant tower so as to get as close to heaven as possible, which was up high in the firmament. When Moses met with God, he had to go up on a mountain, to be higher, and thereby closer to God. When Jesus was finished on planet Earth, he *ascended* into heaven, to be up there with God. When Muhammad rode the Buraq—a magical, flying steed—from Mecca to Jerusalem, he also flew *up* into heaven to visit God. The classical paintings of Christian Europe—as well as those from various parts of the Muslim world—all invariably depict God as being up there, high over and above humanity.

Up, up, up.

You ever wonder what's up with this religious obsession with up?

After all, it doesn't even make any directional sense: we live on a spherical planet spinning through space in a universe that doesn't have a top or bottom. So there really is no actual "up" in the way that nuns and preachers indicate through their holy gesticulating. And when a soccer player in Chile points up after scoring a goal, and another soccer player in Angola points up at the same time, and another player in Illinois simultaneously does the same, they are all pointing in different directions—none accurately pointing toward a place that is actually "above us." Moreover—with the prominent exception of some Mormons, who believe that God lives on or near a planet called Kolob—most religious people don't think God actually "lives" somewhere that is a discernable, physical place with anything resembling a geographical location that one could point to as being "there."

So why have the world's Abrahamic faiths conceived of their deity as being *up*? What is it about something being above us that denotes power, authority, awe, and majesty?

For starters, we can look to our infancy. In the early years of our lives, we are small and quite low to the ground. Everything else is physically above us. And the powerful beings that keep us alive—the grown-ups who feed us, warm us, protect us, scold us, love us, and do everything else—are literally higher than us. Towering over us. Babies look *up* for most of their waking hours, and especially if other people are present. It is this infantile model of being down low on the ground, with everything else of power and significance being higher up than us, that gets replicated in the religious worldview.

Then there's also the fact that a major source of life is the sun. It is mighty and bright. And it is up there, above us and over us, and thus we perhaps developed the sense that powerful, life-giving deities must be up there, too.

Finally, there is the initial mystery of the sky itself—its deep blue vastness in daytime and its starry psychedelia at night—which seems to have no end. And lots of astounding things seem to happen in the sky, like thunder and lightning, and other miraculous things come down to us from the sky, like rain and snow. Also, despite its life-sustaining beauty, Earth is somewhat mundane, or at least relatively finite and knowable. You can dig in the dirt, trip on the rocks, shit in the woods, bathe in the stream, sleep on the grass. But sky—well—that's something immense, unknowable, and deeply endless.

These are, admittedly, just speculations. Who can say for sure why religious folks are obsessed with up? All we can know is that—for whatever reasons—the humans that created the leading world religions did so by looking to the sky. It is there, up on high, that mighty God dwells.

And so, for the religious, it is ever upward that we must look for our morality. It is from on high that ethical guidelines are crafted and delivered. It is from God who is above us—literally and figuratively—that we receive information about what to do and what not do to. Such has been the direction of our moral gaze for most of recorded human history.

But the locus of human morality couldn't be farther from such distant, celestial altitudes. Human morality does not come from on high. It is not something dropped down to us from above.

Rather, if we're going to stick with directional metaphors, then it is more accurate and empirically supportable to say that human morality comes from way behind us—as in our distant past. It also comes from just below us, underfoot—as in our infant and early childhood experiences. And it comes from beside and around us—as in the other humans who compose our surrounding culture and society. And finally, it comes from within us—not just the tugging of our guts and the wiring of our brains, but our thoughtful reflection and reasoning.

Moral Acquisition

It's the most common question religious folks pose to atheists: "Where do you get your morals?"

Whether at a dinner party or class reunion, a PTA meeting or a pig pickin', whenever God-fearing people find out that we don't believe in the Lord, don't believe in an afterlife, don't attend church, synagogue, mosque, or temple, don't follow a guru, don't obsess over ancient scriptures, and don't care much for preachers or pontiffs, they immediately inquire about the possible source of our morality—which they find hard to fathom.

And the question "Where do you get you morals?" is usually asked with an embedded implication that morality obviously comes from God and religion, so if you don't have either, then you must have *no* source for morality. On top of this problematic implication, there is often an accompanying judgmental, sneering tone; it's as if what they really want to say is "You must be an immoral lout if you aren't religious and don't believe in God."

To be fair, not everyone who asks atheists where they get their morals is implying something unkind. Given that religion has so fervently, forcefully insisted that it is the only source of morality for so many centuries, many people just honestly and naively believe that to be the case. Thus, not having thought too much about it, they are genuinely curious about where a person gets his or her morals, if not from religion.

But even if the question is asked in total unprejudiced earnestness, it is still a rather odd query. After all, "Where do you get your morals?" suggests that morals are things that people go out and find in order to possess. Like shoes. Or a new set of jumper cables. It implies that people are living their lives, doing this and that, and then at some point, they decide to drive downtown or go online and get ahold of some morals—as if ethical tenets and moral principles were consciously adopted in some sort of deliberate process of acquisition.

Morality, however, doesn't really work that way. While people may deliberately choose to get their donuts from a certain shop or decide to get their dog from a certain pound, when it comes to the core components of our morality—our deep-seated proclivities, predilections, sentiments, values, virtues, and gut feelings in relation to being kind and sympathetic—these things are essentially *within* us.[1] They are an embedded, inherited part of us.[2] We don't go out and "choose" them, per se. Sure, we may change our minds about a certain social issue after learning more about it and critically reflecting upon it; we may develop a love or distaste for something after having had certain new experiences in relation to it; we may start to live our lives differently, with different ethical priorities, after we marry a certain person and cohabitate with them for an extended period of time; we may find our political positions shift when we move to a new state or country and live there for a while.

However, when it comes to our underlying morality, it is not generally something that we "get" in a conscious, deliberate, choosing way. Rather, our deep-seated sense of how to treat other people, our capacity for empathy and compassion, our desire for fairness and justice—these are things that we naturally manifest: our morals have been inherited from our evolutionary past, molded through our early childhood nurturance, enhanced and channeled through cultural socialization, and as such—to paraphrase sociologist Émile Durkheim—they "rule us from within."[3]

What exactly is it that rules us so—morally speaking? And what are the specific foundational sources of our moral proclivities and ethical tendencies? There are four: 1) our long history as social primates, evolving within a group context of necessary cooperation; 2) our earliest experiences as infants and toddlers being cared for by a mother, father, or other immediate caregivers; 3) unavoidable socialization as growing children and teenagers enmeshed within a culture; and 4) ongoing personal experience, increased knowledge, and reasoned, thoughtful reflection.

Our Evolutionary Past

The most basic, fundamental story of humanity is this: for the vast majority of our history—that is, for approximately 95 percent of our time on Earth as a species[4]—we lived in small bands composed of somewhere between twenty and eighty individuals. We foraged, froze, hunted, starved, gathered, picked, scavenged, huddled, copulated, slept, and lived this way for at least some two hundred thousand years, when our kind, *Homo sapiens*, first emerged by evolving off from an older primate species, *Homo erectus*, who also lived in similar such huddled bands for some two million years prior.

During these millions of years, life was precarious for our *Homo erectus* ancestors and our *Homo sapiens* forebears. Food and warmth were often in short supply. Danger always lurked and lingered: inclement weather, parasites, disease, poisonous and predatory animals, and threatening/competing bands of neighboring bipedal primates. And it was out of this multimillion-year situation that significant adaptations for heightened cooperation emerged, adaptations that were advantageous for our ancestors' continued existence. As Charles Darwin reasoned in *The Descent of Man*, those small bands of early humans that could cooperate well did better at surviving and raising their offspring to adulthood than those small bands that did not cooperate well. Thus, cooperation evolved not because it was a "nice" thing but because it conferred a distinct group survival advantage; in the words of American scholar Joshua Greene, "cooperation evolves only if individuals who are prone to cooperation outcompete individuals who are not (or who are less so). Thus, if morality is a set of adaptations for cooperation, we today are moral beings only because our morally minded ancestors outcompeted their less morally minded neighbors."[5]

As for rugged individuals in our ancestral past? Forget it. If you were alone, you did not survive for long. Throughout the millions of years of our evolution, the small group was everything, for it was only within the safety of the protective pack that life was possible. And over the course of millions of years of such group-based existence, various traits that helped with group cooperation and enhanced group cohesion became stronger and more pronounced throughout the course of our evolving development, traits like the ability to communicate well, to surmise what someone else is not just saying but also feeling and thinking, to sense what someone else may be desiring, to respond to the pain or suffering of others, to be altruistic, to take joy and comfort in others' joy and comfort, to feel a sense of shame or guilt at disappointing others, to fear the stigmatization, slander, and possible ostracism of others, to feel good when earning the approval, respect, and trust of others, to care for and defend those unable to care for and defend themselves, to feel safe amidst a sense of group solidarity. And so on.[6]

Selfishness, greed, envy, callous indifference, viciousness, and violent cruelty did not disappear from our primate ancestors—and they certainly remain a part of our repertoire. But such malevolent traits have never been dominant throughout our evolution. Instead, they have always remained atypical and sporadic, rather than daily and normative. And throughout our evolutionary past, such hostile predilections were most consistently directed toward threatening outsiders—other groups—not at one's own kith and kin. Within the group, treating each other well, helping out, caring, and cooperating were the proclivities that fostered individual survival by enhancing group resilience over hundreds of thousands of years. And thus, such proclivities are the underlying, predominant components of our human nature today.

Bonobos and Chimps

Evidence for the naturally inherited, evolutionarily developed core of much of our contemporary morality is abundant. And perhaps the first place to observe it is by simply looking at our closest genetic relatives, bonobos, with whom we share up to 98.8 percent of our DNA.[7]

What do we see when we closely observe bonobos in their natural habitat in Central Africa? Many important differences and distinctions from humans, to be sure. But what is significant here, for our understanding of morality, is that bonobos—our closest primate cousins with whom we share a distant primate ancestor from millions of years ago—live together in small bands quite peacefully. Conflict, tension, and random spates of violence do occur, but they are limited and rare. And no instance of a bonobo killing another bonobo has ever been observed. What predominates, day after day, are perennial prosocial behaviors that foster cooperation and communal living: concern for others, empathy, kindness, nurturance.

Dr. Frans de Waal, the eminent Dutch primatologist, has spent many years observing bonobos, and he has documented numerous instances of bonobos acting in ways that we could describe, at least in human terms, as being prototypically moral. For example, "as soon as one bonobo has even the smallest injury, he or she will be surrounded by others who come to inspect, lick, or groom."[8] Bonobos will not only comfort and tend to those who have been injured, but individual bonobos will even comfort and tend to the small wounds of the very victim of their own personal belligerence. Additionally, whenever there is any kind of struggle, tension, or anxiety within the group, a variety of methods are employed to soothe, reassure, and comfort those involved, as well as those watching—such as hugging, stroking, and various forms of sexual contact. Other researchers have observed bonobos tending to and taking care of deathly ill companions.[9]

As for our other closest primate cousins, chimpanzees, while they exhibit greater degrees of aggression and violence relative to bonobos, they also possess an easily observed, predominating predisposition toward group cohesion, sociability, and empathetic response to the suffering of others. For example, chimpanzees will console and comfort distressed members of their group; they will aid and assist those who happen to be suffering from arthritis or other physical ailments; they will give food and water to those who can't procure it for themselves; they will comfort—physically and emotionally—other chimps who are dying. In short, decades of observation have proven that our closest primate relatives have, in the words of Dr. de Waal, an "altruistic impulse" in that "they respond to signs of distress in others and feel an urge to improve their situation."[10]

What this tells us is that our immediate primate cousins—although quite different from us in many important ways—cooperate and get along, despite periodic conflict and tension. And they routinely employ a variety of methods to care for one another, tend to one another, and comfort one another. They are able to express both sympathy and empathy—traits and capabilities that undergird their sociability. And they do all of this—

nurture their young, share food, protect one another, and foster group cohesion—even though they don't believe in God, don't go to Sunday school, don't listen to sermons, and don't hear Bible stories. They aren't taught that God impregnated one of their bonobo or chimpanzee ancestors, who gave birth to a bonobo or chimpanzee son without having had sex, who then grew up only to die for the sins of all bonobos or chimpanzees. They aren't taught that Allah will cast them into a fiery hell if they don't believe in him. And yet despite this lack of theistic religion, they live cooperatively and peacefully, exhibiting what we can describe as rudimentary, protomoral aptitudes.

The fact that our closest primate relatives possess such traits and capabilities required for cooperative social life is strong evidence that our own underlying moral proclivities are rooted in our natural evolutionary past. As de Waal argues, "Empathy, sympathy, reciprocity, fairness, and other basic tendencies were built into humanity's moral order based on our primate psychology. We did not develop this order from scratch, but had a huge helping hand—not God's, but Mother Nature's."[11]

Another site for evidence of our innate, natural predilection to be moral: babies.

Babies

If much of our morality is endowed and inherited—rather than acquired during confirmation class or chosen from a book—then we should find evidence for it within the youngest among us. And that's exactly where Yale University psychology professor Paul Bloom finds it.

The building blocks of morality—a predisposition to favor kindness over cruelty, exhibit empathy and compassion, and a basic sense of fairness and justice—are easily observable among infants and small children. For many years, Professor Bloom and his wife/colleague, Dr. Karen Wynn, have been conducting various experiments with babies and toddlers at their Infant Cognition Center, housed at Yale. Along with their team of graduate students, they concoct all kinds of performances, games, and situations meant to tease out infants' and young children's responses and reactions to various scenarios and dilemmas. And what they find is that children as young as *five months old* show a clear and persistent preference for kindness, helpfulness, and fairness.

Here's just one example of the kinds of experiments Bloom and Wynn run: babies are placed before a small stage upon which a short puppet show is performed. In the puppet show, a stuffed animal struggles to lift the lid of a box. Then another stuffed animal comes along and helps lift the lid, opening it all the way, while in other performances, a stuffed animal jumps on the lid and slams it shut, thwarting the first animal's attempt at lifting it. Various other versions of such "morality plays" have been presented to babies—some involving runaway balls, etc.—and a strong majority of babies, many not even half a year old, consistently show clear and distinct preferences for the nicer "helper" puppets over the meaner "thwarter" puppets.

In his book *Just Babies*—which goes into greater detail about the nature of the experiments and the ways in which infants' preferences are discerned and interpreted—Dr. Bloom explains that "these experiments suggest that babies have a general appreciation of good and bad behavior,"[12] and this is so because "we naturally possess a moral sense" characterized by "a desire to help others in need, compassion for those in pain, anger towards the cruel, and guilt and pride about our own shameful and kind actions."[13]

The world's most successful religion—Christianity—teaches that we are born wicked, that we come into this world as sinners, that our nature is essentially evil. Of course, no evidence or data has ever been presented in defending such a morose view of humanity. That's because such evidence and data do not exist. What does exist is a robust and growing body of research attesting to the fact that we come into this world equipped with an intrinsic moral sense, readily observable among babies and small children.[14] For example, in addition to the work of Bloom and Wynn, Dr. Maayan Davidov, an Israeli psychologist, has conducted studies showing that concern and care for others is evident in babies less than one year old, attesting to young infants' "fundamental social nature."[15] Dr. Ronit Roth-Hanania, another Israeli social scientist, found that children as young as eight months old exhibit signs of empathy when shown videos of mothers and babies in distress.[16] Additional studies have found that toddlers will spontaneously try to help strangers who have dropped their keys, or help them open a door if their arms are full.[17] As Dr. Wynn recounted during an interview with *60 Minutes*, "study after study after study—the results are always consistently [showing] babies feeling positively towards helpful individuals in the world and disapproving, disliking, [and] maybe condemning individuals who are antisocial towards others."[18]

It's not that babies—or bonobos, for that matter—are astutely moral in some deeply philosophical, intellectually reflective sense: making post hoc judgments about themselves and pondering how one's choices and decisions reflect one's character, considering hypothetical consequences of this or that action for the greater good, striving to adhere to some universal principle or duty, debating how people ought to live, or contemplating the very nature of virtue. No. What the evidence—culled from extensive observation of our closest primate cousins as well as our very youngest selves—simply shows is that the fundamental building blocks of what it means to be moral (e.g., not wanting to cause unnecessary harm to others, seeking to ease the suffering of others, being helpful, promoting happiness, wanting the world to be fair and just) are deeply within us, manifested as a result of millions of years of group living that required, and subsequently enhanced, cooperative tendencies and prosocial proclivities.

And when I say "within us," that's not just in some metaphorical sense. Various mechanisms of morality are *literally* within us, among and amidst the folds of our cranial cockpit.

Brains

We are brain-based beings, and any assessment of anything humans do, think, or feel must take into account our neurological physiology. So it goes for our morality: our ethical impulses and moral proclivities are clearly embedded within our brains.[19]

Consider but one prominent example of a brain-based component of our moral faculties: oxytocin.[20] Discovered in 1906 by Henry Dale, oxytocin—an ancient peptide—is a hormone and neurotransmitter produced by the hypothalamus. Sometimes referred to as the "love hormone," the "trust hormone," or the "attachment hormone,"[21] oxytocin is a key neurological player in our evolved sociability, featuring significantly in our experience of compassion, generosity, and affection; when we care for others, or are cared for by others, oxytocin is released in our brains.[22] As Canadian American philosopher and neuroscientist Patricia Churchland explains in her book *Braintrust*, oxytocin is produced at high levels within women when they get pregnant, becoming more abundant just before and during breastfeeding, and it triggers maternal impulses of concern for the general well-being and safety of infants. And when a mother is successful at making an infant happy, safe, and content, oxytocin is released—both in the brain of the successfully caring mother and in the brain of the cared-for baby.[23] Oxytocin has also been observed to increase trustworthiness in people.[24] German neuroeconomist Michael Kosfeld has done controlled experiments on decision-making in which some subjects are given oxytocin via a nasal spray, and those who receive the oxytocin become markedly more trusting and cooperative.[25] Other studies have shown that receiving nasal infusions of oxytocin increases in-group altruism and cooperation[26] and improves people's abilities to accurately perceive what others are thinking and feeling, thereby increasing empathy.[27] Additionally, levels of oxytocin go up when people watch videos of other people suffering, increasing the viewers' desire to help those in need.[28] Finally, oxytocin levels rise when people experience intimate or friendly physical contact with others.[29]

It's not that oxytocin—or other similar hormones—*make* us moral, in and of themselves, in some mechanistic fashion. Rather, the existence of such neurological peptides linked to sociability and cooperation simply reveals the degree to which our moral predilections have clearly observable physiological components that are the result of our evolution. For example, the ligaments in our knees don't "make" us run, but they are clear indicators that such ligaments are part and parcel of how human mobility evolved, and without such ligaments, our ability to run would be impossible. So it goes with many components of our brain—oxytocin, vasopressin, mirror neurons—and their intimate relation to our innate capacity for morality.

In short, empathy, compassion, a desire to help others, a feel for justice and fairness—these ethical proclivities are possible because of the kinds of brains we have, brains that evolved within a group context wherein cooperation and sociability were not simply beneficial, but essential.

So too is another essential feature of our species: the intense, extensive nurturance of newborns.

Caring

If, as stated earlier, the most basic, primary story of humanity is that for tens of thousands of years we lived in small bands, evolving in packs, then the second most fundamental story of humanity is that each of us—to a man and to a woman—was utterly helpless for a long time, totally dependent on another human for our survival. Unlike other animals—even our closest primate relatives—human babies are completely helpless at birth and cannot physically fend for themselves for at least two years after they are born. If human babies are not tended to, they die. Thus, the intimate interactions between helpless infants and their immediate caretakers—which is almost always their mother—are fundamental to their development as human beings. It is the ultimate, foundational relationship wherein we not only get fed, held, warmed, protected, and cleaned, but it is the key relational dynamic wherein we develop nonverbal communication skills, a sense of self and not-self, a conception of others and our relation to them, feelings of safety and security, initial emotional growth, understandings of objects and our relationship to them, and so forth. And this parent-infant relationship is also a crucial arena for the development of moral aptitudes.[30] It is, in effect, our first and most fundamental experience of being *cared for*. And that infantile experience of being cared for serves as a form of priming, imprinting, or prototyping for us as we grow up into children, teenagers, and adults.

As we have seen, our brains—which evolved within a group context—developed capacities for sociability and cooperation that improved and fostered our chances for survival. But it is our direct, personal experiences of being cared for as infants that mold and strengthen those capacities into the actual capability to care. And this capability—or compulsion—to care about others is at the very heart of what it means to be moral. In the words of American philosopher and educator Nel Noddings, "caring and the memory of caring and being cared for . . . form the foundation of ethical response."[31]

In her book *Caring*, Dr. Noddings argues that the mother-infant relationship creates the foundational schema or blueprint for our subsequent ability to be sympathetic—that is, responsive to the needs and suffering of others. It is the nearly universal dyad between the one caring and the one cared for that primes us, ultimately enabling us—as we eventually grow up—to care for others, to be attuned to their happiness or misery, and, when possible, to promote their well-being. This sympathetic impulse is not grounded in any philosophical argumentation or obedience to a god. Rather, it is largely grounded in the good feelings that we experienced as a result of the formative relationship of being cared for when we were young and helpless ourselves. According to Noddings, the experience of being recipients of care—being cared for by those in our immediate circle—replicates itself, as we grow older, into our own ability to care for others in our immediate circle. And that personal experience of caring for those in our immediate circle eventually goes further, maturing into the ability to care about others who we may not be directly connected to or even know.

Noddings's emphasis on moral development being heavily rooted in the experience of parent-child care is borne out by a strong body of research. For example, Grazyna Kochanska, a Polish American professor of developmental psychology, has conducted extensive studies—with hundreds of participants over many years, both in laboratory settings as well as family homes—examining the impact of parent-child relationships on ethical emergence within children. Her findings are unambiguous: "children who grow up in a context of a highly mutually responsive relationship with their mothers develop strong consciences."[32] Such findings—correlating close parenting bonds between parents and children with positive moral development—have been replicated by many others.[33]

And so we can see the building-block process of human morality at play: it is initially rooted in our evolutionary past, wherein cooperative tendencies and altruistic proclivities benefited our individual survival that was intrinsically bound up with group survival, and upon that basic evolutionary platform, we add the mother-infant relationship, wherein care is central. The next block is socialization, wherein the specific details of our morality become honed, guided, and directed.

Socialization

Most aspects of our personal identities—from what we like to eat to what we like to wear, from our feelings about breastfeeding in public to our feelings about brandishing guns in public, from how we tend to our elderly parents to how we discipline our children, and whether or not we worship Vishnu, Allah, Jehovah, or no deity at all—are directly linked to, and often determined by, the people we live among. As Austrian American sociologist Peter Berger once quipped, "one chooses one's gods by choosing one's playmates."[34] What he meant is that those around us shape not only our social habits, but also our beliefs and worldviews. While exceptions to this rule certainly abound, the fact remains that most of us, most of the time, conform to the norms, ideals, and values of our family, peers, and friends and—more often than not—we generally adopt the underlying assumptions and ideologies of our immediate surrounding culture. And all of this takes place for the most part quite unwittingly. It just happens.

This universal, unavoidable process whereby we are shaped and molded by those around us is called socialization. It is the way in which we—often unconsciously—acquire our culture. It is the way in which we learn how to behave, how to dress, how to express ourselves, what is appropriate, and what is of value. It is the process—again from Peter Berger—whereby our very identities are "socially bestowed."[35]

To illustrate socialization at work, let me offer examples from my own kids. The main reason that my nineteen-year-old daughter, Ruby, just spent seven weeks this past summer studying Yiddish—rather than French, Malay, or Setswana—is because her grandfather, who she has had an especially close and loving relationship with, is a native Yiddish speaker and Ruby has grown up in a home where Yiddish has been talked about a lot and positively linked to her ethnic identity and family heritage. Ruby enjoyed her Yiddish-immersion program, is planning on continuing her study of Yiddish, and is even considering it as a future career path. And yet this very personal passion of Ruby's is almost completely the result of the family she happened to have been raised in; you can be sure that had Ruby been born and raised to a Buddhist family in Thailand, or a Jain family in Gujarat, or an ethnically Tatar family in Chechnya, she wouldn't have a passion for Yiddish.

My younger daughter, Flora, age sixteen, just spent two weeks at a summer program at the University of Oregon, where she took classes on film: Russian films, the films of Hitchcock, film noir, film and politics, etc. Why did Flora take film classes at a summer program in Oregon rather than classes in sharpshooting at a summer program in Montana? Or classes in karate at a summer program in San Francisco? The answer isn't too hard to find: both my wife and I graduated from the University of Oregon, we love Eugene, and since we had friends who told us about the program there, we enrolled Flora in it. Furthermore, my wife, Stacy, went to graduate film school at USC, has made several short films, has been working on a feature script in recent years, and is constantly talking about movies in our home and showing Flora various films she loves. And we live in Los Angeles, where the movie business is supreme. Thus, while Flora's love of films is deeply personal and an intrinsic part of her individuality—it is also the direct result of her immediate social circumstances.

Finally, my son, August, who is eleven years old, spent his summer playing lots of soccer. He went to soccer camps, played in various soccer tournaments, played in a soccer league, and several times a week he asks me to go to a nearby field to kick the soccer ball around and practice various soccer skills. Why does my son love soccer so, and not cricket? Or bowling? Or kabaddi—the national sport of Bangladesh? The answer is pretty simple: soccer is the most popular sport at his elementary school, and when he was in fourth grade, all the fifth- and sixth-grade boys that he looked up to played soccer during recess and invited him to join. Additionally, the town we live in is a soccer town, with most kids playing soccer above all other sports. Thus, it's pretty safe to say that had August grown up in a baseball town (as I did), with all of his friends deeply involved in baseball, he'd be loving baseball more than soccer. But because of his social circumstances, soccer it is.

To be sure, socialization doesn't explain everything. For example, why isn't Ruby as into filmmaking as Flora? Why isn't Flora as into Yiddish as Ruby? And not all kids raised in Claremont are as into soccer as my son August is. Clearly, individual preferences, predilections, and personalities are at play, and socialization is never completely and utterly determinant of people's choices. But it does play a significant role in hemming in those choices—and making some look far more attractive than others.

Socialization isn't just about what we like to do over our summer vacations, however. It's a much more intractable process that accounts for so many deeper aspects of our lives. The people and groups that socialize us—parents, older siblings, other family members, babysitters, neighbors, coaches, peers, friends, schools, religious institutions, movies, television shows, advertisements, and Internet content—shape and determine numerous key aspects of our individual identities. For instance, if we are raised in families and communities where monogamy is the norm, then we grow up to think of monogamous marriage as normal and desirable. But if we are raised in families and communities where polygamy is the norm, then we grow up thinking of polygamous marriage as normal and desirable. If we grow up in homes and communities where eating animals is considered disgusting and immoral, then we will most likely grow up with a negative view of eating animals, and probably not do it. But if we grow up in homes and communities where eating animals is considered wonderful and moral, then we will most likely grow up with a positive view of eating animals and probably enjoy doing it. If we are socialized by people who strongly value money, material possessions, and the accumulation of wealth, or rather, if we are socialized by people who strongly value close family ties, respecting one's elders, and bringing honor to one's parents—then either experience will strongly affect and shape what we ourselves come to value as we live our lives. Again, so much of our individual selves—from our likes and dislikes to how we behave—is heavily shaped and contoured by how we have been socialized.

Of course, socialization is not airtight. As I said, exceptions abound. My wife, for instance, was raised in a hunting and meat-eating home—but she has done neither since she was eighteen. And there may, in fact, be a young woman born and raised in a Buddhist home in Thailand who randomly develops a passion for Yiddish similar to that of my daughter Ruby. But such exceptions to socialization are just that—*exceptions*. More often than not, the people who raise us, and those we live among, and the immediate culture we are immersed in, mold so much of how we see the world and how we act within it.

Internalization

We soak up and absorb the values and patterns of behavior exhibited by those around us to such a strong degree—and often unconsciously—that whatever those around us do and believe can't help but become part of our own individual worldview, our own expectations for ourselves, and our personal outlook. This is most readily observed through the process known as "internalization."

Internalization—the successful end point of socialization—occurs when society's values ultimately become the individual's. It is when the norms and beliefs of our surrounding culture end up becoming our own personal norms and beliefs. It is when the various ways of acting, behaving, thinking, and feeling of those around us—the people who compose our immediate social circle as well as the people who populate the media we take in—get under our skin, transforming our own personal proclivities, dispositions, and ideals. In short, internalization is when we as individuals come to want exactly what we have been socialized to want—and yet we don't feel like we are succumbing to anything. We don't feel like we have been socialized. We just feel like we're being ourselves.

Allow another illustration from my own family: Flora and her bloody shins. Several years ago, Flora called me from across the house with an unmistakable tinge of distress in her voice. She was in the bathroom. She was twelve years old. I went in to find her sitting on the shower floor, with blood streaking down her legs, and a shaving razor in her hand. She had tried to shave her legs for the first time, and it hadn't gone well. Why was she trying to shave her legs? Well, she was about to start the seventh grade, and she wanted her legs to look good. After all, having shaved legs is the norm for women in our culture. It's what all her friends do. It's what her mother and grandmothers do. It's what she sees on TV and in the movies. And since Flora has been socialized in this society wherein women shave their legs—and shaved legs on women are considered beautiful, while hairy legs on women are considered unattractive—she has internalized these norms and values. And the result: she personally *wants* shaved legs. She genuinely thinks that shaved legs on a female look better than unshaved legs. That is, she has her own personal feelings about how her own legs ought to be—shaved—and yet, while this feeling is certainly personal to Flora, it is clearly a direct result of her having internalized it. Her personal feelings about shaved legs are thus the direct result of how she was socialized, and nothing more. And we can be sure that if Flora had grown up in a society that dictated young woman should have the tips of their earlobes cut off—and women's cut earlobes were considered appropriate and attractive, while women's uncut earlobes were considered inappropriate and unattractive—Flora would have taken a knife to her earlobes rather than a razor to her shins. And she would have done so *willingly*. She would have *wanted* cut earlobes. Such is the power of internalization: that which feels individual is actually social at root. That which feels personal is inextricably cultural.

Perhaps the most obvious manifestation of internalization is shame, which occurs when we feel guilty or bad about something we have done or said. We experience shame because we have so deeply internalized certain norms and values from our surrounding social circle that when we violate them, we experience an inner chastisement, an inner scolding, an inner embarrassment. And the point here is that while shame is an internal, emotional experience—its source is inextricably sociocultural. As American sociologist Arlene Stein notes, "shame arises from seeing one's self negatively from the imagined point of view of others."[36] Caring what others think and do—to the point of feeling shame when we violate norms and values that we share in common with them—reveals the depths of socialization and the power of internalization. And both of these processes are relevant for our morality.

Socialization, Internalization, and Personal Morality

While we inherit prosocial, cooperative tendencies from our evolutionary past—which gives us an inherent proclivity for empathy and fairness—and while our ability to feel sympathy, compassion, and care for others is a direct result of our own experience being cared for as infants, how we are socialized—and what we subsequently internalize as a result of that socialization—provides yet another source of our moral orientation.[37]

First off, when we grow up, we mostly see and experience people around us interacting cooperatively. We see those around us sharing and caring for one another to varying degrees, communicating in good faith, responding to one another's needs, and reacting positively to those who behave well and negatively to those who misbehave. We see people lining up to buy tickets at the fair. We see people waiting patiently in the dentist's office. We experience the orderliness of a supermarket. We experience the patience of a kindergarten teacher. We experience the dedication of a football coach. We experience the small-town joy of the local Fourth of July parade. We see the pain a wicked character causes in a given television show. We observe the triumph or happiness an honest and virtuous character experiences in a given movie. While watching the news, we see the warm joy experienced by a family reunited after a tsunami. In other words, all the things that we continually observe and experience in the social world around us as we grow up—from daily interactions to bedtime stories—hone and sharpen our moral aptitude. And while many of the things we experience may be unpleasant or even malevolent, for most of us, most of our experiences are not consistently or routinely had within a perpetually chaotic, unrelentingly violent, or completely destructive social context. Rather, such horrific moments are sporadic and limited. Day-to-day life is, for most of us most of the time, an ongoing routine of people following rules, acting nonviolently, and treating people with varying degrees of consideration.

As American writer and counselor Dorothy Nolte so eloquently expressed in her 1954 poem "Children Learn What They Live," if kids are raised in a social environment characterized by acceptance, patience, honesty, generosity, fairness, and friendliness, they develop into human beings who manifest kind, cooperative, tolerant, prosocial attitudes and moral proclivities. And while some may have considered it trite and simplistic, Robert Fulghum's 1986 national bestseller *All I Really Need to Know I Learned in Kindergarten* captured a key aspect of socialization's role in our moral development: as children, we are consistently exposed to routinized prosocial behavior—such as sharing, not hitting, playing fair, cleaning up after oneself, and holding hands while crossing the street—and we internalize such behavior and then grow up wanting to manifest and exhibit it ourselves. We learn that cutting in line is wrong—and we get to a stage in life where we actually don't want to cut in line, for to do so would make us feel bad about ourselves. We see people treating the elderly with patience and respect, and as we grow, we come to personally want to treat the elderly with patience and respect—it just comes to feel right and proper. In short, we live in a society replete with prosocial conduct and cooperative values, and being socialized in such circumstances, we internalize the norms and ethical ideals of our culture.

Social Issues of Moral Significance

But socialization and internalization are not only important for how we learn to treat others well; they are also prominently at play when it comes to our position on specific moral issues. Take, for instance, gay rights. If a child is raised in a family that believes homosexuality is sinful and abhorrent, and if everyone in that child's neighborhood considers homosexuality to be dirty and disgusting, and if all that child hears about homosexuality at church is that it violates God's rules and homosexuals will be eternally punished, and if the laws in that child's society deem homosexuality illegal to the degree that people caught engaging in homosexual acts are arrested, imprisoned, or worse, and if homosexuals are not allowed to be teachers or Scout leaders or foster parents, and if every story that child hears and every show or movie that child sees depicts homosexuality in a negative light, then we can be fairly certain that child will be more likely to harbor antihomosexual feelings than not. Socialized in such a culture, he or she will most likely internalize what he or she soaks up concerning homosexuality, and subsequently come to personally see it as sinful, disgusting, and wrong. And if such a child ends up being homosexual him- or herself, it is highly likely that he or she will experience varying degrees of shame and self-hatred.

Conversely, if a child is raised in a family that accepts homosexuality as just another way to live and love, and if everyone in that child's neighborhood considers homosexuality to be just fine, and if there are even some out gay or lesbian couples living down the street or around the block, and if all that child hears about homosexuality at church is that it is a respectable, common form of human relation and that God would never condemn or punish anyone because of the sexual identity or gender of who they love, and if the laws in that child's society establish homosexuality to be on equal legal footing as heterosexuality, and if homosexuals are allowed to be teachers or Scout leaders or foster parents or anything else they want to be in the same way as heterosexuals, and if every story that child hears and every show or movie that child sees depicts homosexuality in a positive light, then we can be fairly certain that such a child will be much less likely to be homophobic. Socialized in such a culture, he or she will most likely internalize what he or she soaks up concerning homosexuality, and come to see it as normal, acceptable, and just as worthy of praise and celebration as heterosexuality. And if such a child ends up being homosexual him- or herself, it is likely that he or she will not experience much in the way of shame or self-hatred.

Thus, many of the moral positions we hold—positions predicated on empathy, compassion, and concern for the suffering of others, or a desire for fairness and justice—are arrived at through our socialization and the internalization of the norms and values of those around us, from supporting gay rights to condemning religious extremism, from supporting universal suffrage to condemning dictatorships, from supporting euthanasia to condemning the destruction of the rain forest.

Again, exceptions do occur: a child raised in a strongly homophobic environment can still end up not harboring such an orientation, and a child raised in a tolerant, equitable, and actively nonhomophobic environment can certainly end up opposing gay rights. But such outcomes, though possible, are highly unlikely.

Experiences

While our evolutionary past forms the foundation of our morality, and while that foundation is fortified and perpetuated during the initial parent-infant relationship, and while it is additionally honed and shaped through the processes of socialization and internalization, the final component of our morality is our own individual ability to think and reflect upon our experiences, ponder arguments and consider their merits, mull over issues—and grow morally as a result. Our capacity to become more educated and knowledgeable, as well as our tendency to draw our own conclusions based on our own experiences—thereby wedding what we think and know with what we live and observe—is the resplendent icing on the cake of natural, secular human morality.

And so, last but not least, our morals come from our healthy aptitude for reasoning, learning new things about the world, heeding different perspectives, contemplating new arguments, developing new insights, becoming familiar with other people's perceptions, and drawing conclusions from ongoing personal experiences.

Consider the case of John Brown, one of America's most heroic moral innovators.

John Brown was a white man who, in the mid-nineteenth century, devoted his life to trying to end slavery. An ardent Christian who saw the enslavement of Black people as sinful and immoral, Brown led a small band of armed men to the U.S. armory at Harpers Ferry, West Virginia, in October 1859. The goal was to steal the weapons held at the armory and distribute them to slaves who would take Brown's cue in revolting against their white masters, resulting in a massive overthrow of the South's "peculiar institution" and subsequent freedom for millions. While the morality of his violent methods is certainly up for debate, the morality of his mission is not: he sought to alleviate the pain and suffering of his fellow human beings. He wanted to destroy an inhumane legal and social system that exploited, injured, brutalized, and humiliated men, women, and children.

Although John Brown's plan failed—he and his comrades were not able to take control of the armory, and no widespread uprising took pace—and although Brown was arrested, imprisoned, and then hanged on December 2, 1859, historians have rightfully characterized his raid on Harpers Ferry as the courageous spark that led to the Civil War, which did eventually succeed in freeing millions of African Americans.[38]

In pondering John Brown, we must ask: What would cause a white man back in the 1850s to care so much about the enslavement and suffering of Black people that he was willing to give his life for the cause of their freedom? The sources of Brown's moral crusade are many, including his personal interpretation of biblical scriptures, as well as his having been raised by an antislavery father who worked with the Underground Railroad. But in addition to his Christian faith and having been socialized by an abolitionist father, a specific personal experience prodded Brown's moral development on the matter of slavery: when he was twelve years old, he witnessed an enslaved boy being beaten with iron shovels. At the time, young John Brown happened to be staying for a stretch with a man who owned a Black orphan who was roughly the same age as John. The two boys became friends, and John couldn't help but notice that this boy was dressed poorly, fed poorly, and forced to sleep in a dilapidated dwelling during cold weather. The unfairness and inequity of how John was treated in comparison to his enslaved friend were blatant. And then he saw this boy being repeatedly beaten—not only with iron shovels but with "any other thing that came first to hand." It was his witnessing of human suffering that led Brown to first swear "Eternal war with Slavery."[39]

Brown's lifelong selfless dedication to ending slavery was obviously not shared by most other whites of his day, to be sure. But his activism did play a significant part—over time—in changing many of their minds about slavery and eventually helped bring about slavery's downfall. Brown's moral development was spurred, in part, by his own personal experiences and reflections upon those experiences. And his moral outrage and activism concerning the oppression of enslaved African Americans subsequently helped improve the moral outlook of open-minded white people who, by considering Brown's actions and the justifications for his actions, took heed.

Consideration of Well-Reasoned Works

Fast-forward a hundred years to the case of another white individual whose moral sensitivity toward racism was improved: James Carville, former campaign manager of President Bill Clinton, news pundit, and leading strategist of the Democratic Party. When Carville was a teenager living in the segregated South, the oppression of his Black neighbors was all-encompassing. Blacks were legally segregated, systematically denied financial and professional opportunities, unfairly policed, and humiliated by racist slurs and side-glances on a daily basis. But given that young James was white, and thus personally benefited from various forms of white privilege, the white supremacist oppression didn't bother him; like most white people he knew at the time, he thought that Blacks should just be acquiescent and not make such a fuss—not push so hard about civil rights and whatnot. But then, at age sixteen, something happened. Carville read a book. As he recounts, "I read *To Kill a Mockingbird*, and that novel changed everything . . . I couldn't put it down. I stuck it inside another book and read it under my desk during school. When I got to the last page, I closed it and said, 'They're right and we're wrong.' The issue was literally black and white and we were absolutely, positively on the wrong side."[40]

History is full of such books, pamphlets, tracts, plays, movies, documentaries, television shows, and speeches that have served, in their own way, to improve many people's personal morality. As American professor of English Suzanne Keen has discussed, through the articulation of well-reasoned arguments, or vivid illustrations, or moving accounts, or clear presentation of facts—or a masterful combination of all of these—numerous polemical works have influenced how people come to have more empathy or compassion for the suffering of others, or come to more strongly desire a society characterized by justice and goodwill.[41]

Sticking here with the matter of racism, we can look at the influence that both powerful argumentation and moving storytelling have had over the centuries. During the days of slavery, widely read slave narratives such as William W. Brown's *The Narrative of William W. Brown, a Fugitive Slave* (1847) or Harriet Ann Jacobs's *Incidents in the Life of a Slave Girl* (1861) played a role in kindling antislavery sentiment, as well as works such as Harriet Beecher Stowe's *Uncle Tom's Cabin* (1852) and William Lloyd Garrison's abolitionist periodical *The Liberator* (1831–1865). Speeches such as Sojourner Truth's "Ain't I a Woman?" (1851) or Frederick Douglass's "What to the Slave Is the Fourth of July?" (1852) presented hard-hitting, well-reasoned, and moving critiques of injustice. After slavery, and into the twentieth century, literary masterpieces such as W. E. B. Du Bois's *The Souls of Black Folk* (1903), Richard Wright's *Black Boy* (1945), or Lorraine Hansberry's *A Raisin in the Sun* (1959) all played a part in improving the moral consciousness of white Americans. Such works—and many others—served to help change people's hearts and minds toward a more ethical orientation.

Thus, while racism in the United States is still alive and well—from entrenched economic and educational inequality to murderous police violence and an inhumanely racist criminal justice system—more and more white men and women have made relative moral progress over the centuries in recognizing the immorality of both institutional and personal racism. And the trajectory continues.

Whether the issue is racism or sexism, the persecution of apostates or animal cruelty, global warming or genocide—new books, movies, TED

Talks, speeches, and plays continue to serve a similar function: alerting people to injustices that they may not have been aware of, sparking empathy and compassion, and providing compelling reasons and moving stories that give people pause, whereby they become more moral as a result of thoughtful reflection and consideration of sound argumentation, persuasive assertions, and reasonable contentions.[42]

In Short

Despite what hundreds of millions of people continue to be taught in Sunday schools, Bible camps, madrassas, Jewish day schools, confirmation classes, catechism classes, and Mormon seminary classes, we don't get our morals from magical deities who live above us in the sky, telling us what to do and what not to do. Nor do we get our morals from ancient stone tablets handed down to men on mountaintops, or from angels who visit men in caves, or from enchanted golden plates that men discover buried in the woods.

As this chapter has conveyed, we don't actually "get" our morals from any single venue in some process of deliberate acquisition. Rather, the foundations of human morality come from our evolutionary past, when we lived for hundreds of thousands of years in small bands that both required and fostered cooperation and prosocial proclivities. Within such an evolutionary context, our morality became acutely functional given the kinds of brains we have, which allow for us to experience sympathy, empathy, and compassion. Furthermore, our helplessness as infants has always required that someone cared for each and every one of us, and that vital, necessary relationship between infant and caregiver primes us for our own ability to be concerned about and care for others—usually those with whom we are most intimately related, but also beyond that limited network. And as we grow up, we are unavoidably socialized by the people around us, unconsciously internalizing the norms and values they express and exhibit. Finally, as rational creatures, we can grow from personal experiences and develop as a result of things that we read, hear, and see—thereby fine-tuning our moral compasses as we reflect upon what we come across and learn.

Morality is thus nothing more or less than a completely natural human enterprise. Both our propensity to care about the suffering of others and our desire for justice—these things ultimately define and comprise human ethics. And they don't come from the heavens.

For secular individuals who understand all of this—that is, for nonreligious men and women who do not look to imaginary deities for their morality but instead recognize the natural sources, underpinnings, and dynamics of human ethical orientations—the result is generally quite positive. Indeed, among the greatest and most beneficial manifestations of secularism are the prominent secular virtues one finds among atheists, agnostics, and humanists.

Let's check them out.

8

The Seven Secular Virtues

Pop quiz time.

I'm going to describe three significant individuals from the twentieth century who helped make the world a better place, and we'll see if you can correctly guess who they are.

The first was an African American man who lived during a time of extreme segregation and violent prejudice, when white Americans enjoyed social, political, and legal rights denied to Black Americans. He faced this widespread discrimination and institutional racism with steadfast determination and became a pioneer in his lifelong fight against racial injustice. Known as the architect of the civil rights movement, he ultimately paved the way for achieving legal equality for his Black brothers and sisters. This visionary, well-educated, ever-peaceful, and courageous leader for human dignity exhibited the best in human potential and was selected by Harvard Professor Henry Louis Gates Jr. to be named "the Person of the Twentieth Century."

Who was he?

The second person I'd like you to identify was an eloquent Indian man who, through nonviolent means, fought against the British occupation of his country with unflinching determination. Convinced that India deserved her independence, this calm and resolute leader did all that he could to expose the hypocrisy and ugliness of British colonialism and inspire Indians to fight for their national rights—not with force and bloodshed, but with peaceful civil disobedience. He was ultimately successful in leading the defeat of the British and ushering in Indian independence. He became India's first prime minister in 1947.

What was his name?

The third individual I'd like you to identify was an unassuming, bookish, thoughtful girl who had to contend with the heinous reign of Nazism and the deathly persecution of Jews that transpired under the German occupation of Europe during World War II. Enduring as best she could before eventually being murdered in the Holocaust, she kept a diary, in which she gave thoughtful expression to the sadness, fear, and hope that characterized the dire situation of herself and her people. Before her capture, she wrote that "despite everything, I believe the world was created for good."[1]

How did you do? Were you able to identify these important people from the twentieth century? I'm going to assume that you have guessed: 1) Martin Luther King Jr., 2) Gandhi, and 3) Anne Frank.

If so, you're very close. But, unfortunately, not correct.

The first person I described above was W. E. B. Du Bois (1868–1963), the second was Jawaharlal Nehru (1889–1964), and the third was Hannah Senesh (1921–1944).

One last makeup question, for extra credit: What do these three people have in common? They were all secular. Let me tell you a little more about these three moral beacons and the secular values that guided them.

Du Bois, Nehru, and Senesh

Born in Great Barrington, Massachusetts, W. E. B. Du Bois was raised by a single mom who worked as a maid. Despite the disadvantages of his youth, he rose to become the first African American to earn a PhD from Harvard, and he subsequently founded and led the first civil rights group in our nation's history, the Niagara Movement, as well as the second civil rights group in our nation's history, the National Association for the Advancement of Colored People (NAACP). He was also the founding leader of the Pan-African Congress and the American Negro Academy, and one of the supporting pillars of the Harlem Renaissance. An author, editor, historian, and sociologist, he publicly and actively fought against Jim Crow laws, lynching, discrimination, racism, colonial exploitation, and nuclear weapons, and he fought for African American rights, women's rights, Jewish rights, workers' rights, and world peace. As for religion, by the time he was in his early twenties, Du Bois was a self-described freethinker; he eschewed church, he condemned Christianity, he considered the stories of the Bible to be nothing more than fairy tales, he recognized prayer as useless, and he remained an agnostic.[2]

Jawaharlal Nehru was born in Allahabad, Uttar Pradesh, the son of wealthy parents. A graduate of Cambridge, he became a lawyer in England before returning home to India, where he soon got involved in the movement for national independence. In the 1920s, he helped lead the Non-Cooperation Movement, which advocated nonviolent protests against British oppression and the boycotting of British goods. In the 1930s, he became the leader of the Indian National Congress, advocating for complete independence from Great Britain. He simultaneously fought for the rights of peasants who were under the rule of provincial Indian princes; he became the president of the All India States Peoples' Conference, pushing for a united, democratic India free from both British imperialism and princely subjugation. All of this activism resulted in Nehru's arrest and imprisonment many times. But both he and his cause prevailed. As for religion? Nehru wanted none of it. As an agnostic who was staunchly scientific in his naturalistic worldview, he did not believe in an afterlife and he viewed religious piety and spirituality as absurdist forms of escapism. As a secularist, he saw religious dogma as divisive and antithetical to a pluralistic democracy. And as a dedicated humanist, he placed his faith in humanity rather than a nonexistent deity.[3]

Hannah Senesh was born to an upper-middle-class family of Jewish heritage in Budapest, Hungary. She attended a Christian school growing up and had to pay triple the tuition because she was Jewish. Disgusted by Hungarian anti-Semitism and certain that Jews had no future in Europe, she moved to British-ruled Palestine in 1939 and learned how to farm. In 1944, the Nazis—along with their Hungarian sympathizers of the Arrow Cross—began the systematic extermination of Hungary's Jews. Aware that her community was slated for deportation to Auschwitz, Hannah volunteered to join a small military unit of armed paratroopers. She and her handful of comrades were dropped into Nazi-occupied Yugoslavia with the mission of entering Hungary to fight the Germans and rescue as many Jews as possible. While crossing into Hungary, she was captured, imprisoned, tortured, and eventually executed on November 7, 1944. Most of Hungary's Jews were exterminated, but Hannah's heroic endeavor remains a testament of hope, courage, sacrifice, resistance to Nazism, and Jewish determination against the worst of odds. A fervent socialist, Hannah had no interest in religious faith. And although she did occasionally write of God in her diary—here and there—she made it clear that she used the term "God" in a purely symbolic sense, and nothing more.[4]

Counterbalancing the "Mother Teresa Fallacy"

I've selected these three individuals because they strongly embody various core secular values and ideals. In their humanist activism, they are representative of many people the world over who fight for justice, help those who suffer, and seek to make the world a better place, not because they believe in God but for the very opposite reason: because they know that no God is out there to help us and only we can help ourselves.[5]

It is important to highlight the secularity of men and women like Du Bois, Nehru, and Senesh because most people fail to realize or acknowledge that they were in fact nonreligious—along with so many other great fighters for human rights who have also been nonreligious, especially within the last two hundred years. The secularity of such individuals is always given short shrift.

For example, when it comes specifically to the civil rights movement in the United States, everyone thinks of Martin Luther King Jr.—a deeply religious man whose activism was steeped in Christianity. And yet there were so many others who also fought valiantly for racial justice, and all without religious faith—people like W. E. B. Du Bois, James Forman, A. Philip Randolph, Angela Davis, among others. And when it comes to peaceful resistance against colonialism and imperialism, people automatically think of Mahatma Gandhi—a deeply religious man who undoubtedly deserves his fame—but they ignore the many secular individuals who also fought against foreign oppression and occupation with equal tenacity and courage, people like Jawaharlal Nehru, Nelson Mandela, Kemal Atatürk, and Mohammad Mosaddegh. And when it comes to the Holocaust, while Anne Frank is justifiably recalled as the quintessential innocent whose voice of hope and sincerity was cut short by Nazi persecution, there were so many other Jews during the Holocaust who courageously fought against the Nazis in the woods and in the ghettos, organized the escape of children to safe havens, gave their lives to save others, and struggled mightily in many other ways—and all without religious faith—men and women like Hannah Senesh, Marek Edelman, Vladka Meed, Mordechai Anielewicz, Vitka Kempner, Abba Kovner, Szmul Zygielbojm, among others.

I call this the "Mother Teresa Fallacy": the almost automatic association in people's minds of moral courage and altruistic heroism with deep religiosity and spirituality—even though such attributes are similarly abundant among secular individuals, and often notably lacking among the faithful. And yet the ironclad moral-religious association sticks. Just ask people to think of a selfless humanitarian who helped ameliorate the suffering of others, and they'll immediately name Mother Teresa: a nun always pictured with her distinct habit, she's widely considered an icon of selflessness and sacrifice for others. Although some have sharply challenged her altruistic reputation as overblown and undeserving[6]—the point here is that while many religious and spiritual people have worked selflessly for the well-being of others, and continue to do so, they by no means hold a monopoly on altruism or humanitarianism. Far from it. History is, in fact, replete with many atheists, agnostics, freethinkers, and secularists who did as much as the likes of Mother Theresa—indeed, often more—as a result of their secular, humanist values. And while a complete list of such secular humanitarians is well beyond the scope of this chapter—and would necessitate a hefty volume in its own right—let me just, for the sake of argument, mention some prominent examples.

Consider Enlightenment political hero Johann Struensee. In the 1700s, he was among the first leaders of a nation to successfully fight for human rights, thereby improving life and ameliorating suffering for hundreds of thousands of people. As the de facto regent of Denmark from 1770 to 1772, Struensee passed radical laws banning slavery and indentured servitude and abolishing torture, and additional laws that increased freedom of the press and peasants' rights. Executed by his conservative political enemies in 1772, Struensee was an antireligious freethinker whose secular humanist ideals propelled his valiant efforts for social betterment.

Fast-forward a couple centuries ahead, to contemporary Scandinavia, which is now considered—by most measures—among the most just and humane societies the world has ever known.[7] Nearly all of the political architects of modern Scandinavia were secular, either passively nonreligious or overtly antireligious in varying degrees. Prominent among such Nordic humanist reformers was staunchly secular Olaf Palme, who was the prime minister of Sweden from 1969 to 1976 and again from 1982 to 1986. Under Palme's leadership, Sweden increased its democratic institutions, strengthened its national childcare and elder-care services, improved its free and universal health-care coverage and free and universal educational system, widened affordable housing, worked on behalf of the disabled, strengthened services for single parents, beefed up pensions for the retired, created better support for the unemployed—in short, created a better, fairer, and more humane life for millions of men, women, and children. Palme—an atheist—was also an outspoken opponent of the Vietnam War, of Soviet repression, of the Franco regime, of the Pinochet regime, and of apartheid in South Africa; the latter most likely led to his assassination on February 28, 1986.

Or consider a more recent political leader from another part of the world: José Mujica, the president of Uruguay from 2010 to 2015. After having been imprisoned for thirteen years by a military dictatorship—often in solitary confinement—he went on to lead his country as a democratically elected proponent of humanitarian ideals. Not only did he donate nearly 90 percent of his monthly salary to various charities while in office, but he also legalized gay marriage, thereby granting a basic civil right to hundreds of thousands of people; he legalized marijuana, thereby undercutting crime and corruption associated with the illegal drug trade; he improved women's reproductive rights; and he reduced poverty significantly—and all as an atheist.

Then there's the nineteenth- and early-twentieth-century leaders of the suffragette and first-wave women's rights movement in America, such as Susan B. Anthony, Ernestine Rose, Matilda Joslyn Gage, and Elizabeth Cady Stanton—all secular individuals of varying hues who paved the way for millions of women to live better, safer, and more empowered lives. And let's not forget atheist and pioneering feminist Frances Wright, who was arguably the first white woman in American history to publicly fight against slavery.[8]

The catalog of secular men and women who have been moral beacons abounds: from gay rights leader Harvey Milk to Polish hero Irena Sendler, who risked her own life saving thousands of Jewish children from the Nazis, from the cofounder of Doctors Without Borders, Bernard Kouchner, to the founder of the Red Cross, Henri Dunant, and from Palestinian rights activist Edward Said to second-wave women's rights activist Gloria Steinem and LGBTQ human rights activist Candace Gingrich, secular humanitarians permeate our world.

And yet, despite their numbers and significance, their secularity is often left out of the historical or cultural record. It's a strange and damaging conspiracy: when religious heroes are lauded, their religiosity is featured as part and parcel of their heroism, but when secular heroes are lauded, their secularity is downplayed, denied, or simply ignored. But it shouldn't be. Because, at root, secular values are just as strong and motivational as religious values.

The Secular Seven

One of the obvious reasons that people frequently link religious humanitarians with their given religion—but seldom or never link secular humanitarians with their secularity—is that religious individuals identify with a specific tradition that contains a clear history, an overt organizational structure, and a canonized set of doctrines—things lacking in secular culture. While secularism does have a history of its own, it is disparate and disorganized, random and haphazard, and its story is known only to a handful of interested adherents and scholars.[9] And as for specifically secular and humanist organizations—such as American Atheists, Freedom From Religion Foundation, American Humanist Association, Humanist Association of Ghana, the Brazilian Association of Atheists and Agnostics, the Indian Humanist Union, the Human-Etisk Forbund of Norway, among hundreds of others—these are relatively new and comparatively small organizations, and they remain largely unknown to the wider world. And as for formalized doctrines—no, secular people most certainly do not all adhere to some common holy code of inscribed creeds or denominational articles of faith; there is no official secular humanist canon or dogma.

In short, there is no obvious Team Secular—with all the unified creedal, cultural, celebratory, liturgical, symbolic, communal, and sartorial trappings—akin to Team Christian, Team Muslim, Team Buddhist, Team Jewish, Team Sikh, etc.

However, despite this lack of a recognizable and unified associational existence, most secular people do nonetheless cultivate and promulgate core humanist ideals, shared guiding values, and common personal principles. And they are the very principles that bolster secular morality, serving to guide secular men and women as they go about their daily lives—and also inspiring the likes of W. E. B. Du Bois, Jawaharlal Nehru, Hannah Senesh, and so many other secular humanitarians the world over.

I call them the Secular Seven. They are the underlying tenets that both characterize and propel ethical secular life. They are the "cardinal virtues," if you will, of a humanistic worldview.

The Secular Seven include:

- Freethinking
- Living in Reality
- Here-and-Nowness
- Acceptance of Existential Mystery
- Scientific Empiricism
- Cosmopolitanism
- Empathy/Compassion

Please don't get me wrong. It's not that all secular people embody or express these virtues in total or to the same degree. Nor is it the case that secular men and women are the only people who exhibit these orientations and virtues. Of course not. Secular people most definitely do not hold a monopoly on these values and ideals—just as Christians don't hold a monopoly on forgiveness, or Jews a monopoly on study, or Buddhists a monopoly on acceptance, or Jains a monopoly on vegetarianism, or Muslims a monopoly on charity, or Sikhs a monopoly on yoga, or Quakers a monopoly on silence, or Dervishes a monopoly on whirling. But just as various virtues, tenets, or traits are central within—and commonly associated with—their respective religious traditions, the Secular Seven are equally central and significant within humanist culture, positively contributing to and informing atheistic morality. As such, they deserve to be commonly associated with secular life.

Freethinking

I'll never forget my first lesson in the freedom of thought—or rather its absence.

I was fifteen years old. My girlfriend at the time was Michelle, the daughter of fundamentalist Christians. One day, Michelle's mom was driving us somewhere and started asking us questions about school—specifically about the French class we were taking together. "How's the class going?" she asked cheerily.

"We're reading *The Stranger*," Michelle replied.

Michelle's mom paused.

"It's by Albert Camus," I chimed in, trying hard—and failing—to pronounce "Albert" with a proper French accent.

Michelle's mom remained quiet.

"It's about existentialism," I added.

"Well," began Michelle's mom, in a suddenly more serious tone, "that is not good. Existentialism is spiritually dangerous. We don't believe in that. You should not be reading that, Michelle. That is not something I want you reading anymore."

I was stunned. A mother telling her high school daughter *not* to read something? How could a short novel be "spiritually dangerous"? What does that even mean? And what about the value of education? Don't all parents want their children to be exposed to as many ideas as possible? Don't they want them to read as many books as possible? Isn't mind expansion a universally desirable goal? Clearly not.

Many people—or more specifically, many religious people—are actually quite afraid of certain ideas and thoughts. Why? Because such things might cause them to doubt the holy verities of their faith, and such doubt might very well affect the state of their soul, and if their souls are adversely affected, it just might mean that they will end up in hell. At least that's the ultimate fear within doctrinaire, traditional Christianity and fundamentalist Islam.

This fear is surely part of the reason why it is very common for staunchly secular professors teaching classes on religion or secularism at secular colleges and universities to regularly invite religious people to speak to their students; they *want* religious people to come in and share the details of their faith with their students. Many secular professors also encourage their students to visit religious congregations and attend worship services. It's all for the sake of greater knowledge and increased understanding. However, you will almost never find a strongly religious professor employed at a religious institution regularly inviting atheists, agnostics, skeptics, or naturalists into his or her classes to share the details of their worldviews and beliefs. Nor will such pious professors encourage their students to attend talks or lectures by humanists, atheists, or apostates. Why this difference? Because the secular professor is not existentially threatened by what religious people have to share, and the secular professor doesn't feel like his or her students' very souls are at stake and in need of protection from threatening ideas. The secular professor wants his or her students to learn all about religion and to form their own opinions and views about the topic. The religious professor, on the other hand, would be loath to infect the minds of his or her students with atheism, agnosticism, naturalism, and humanism—for such things are far too dangerous to be presented openly.

But ideas are not, in and of themselves, threatening or dangerous. Even wrong or false ideas—such as those that fly in the face of contrary evidence or rabidly pernicious ideas that urge violence and hatred—are, in the end, just ideas. And thus, they can be freely and openly considered and then readily disproven, dismissed, and discarded. And even learning about such wrong or pernicious ideas actually still teaches us something of value, if nothing more than revealing the depths of erroneous propositions and the contours of the hateful notions that occupy the hearts and minds of some of our fellow humans, haunting and harming our world, and needing to be rallied against.

The underlying principle of freethought is simple: people ought to be able to think anything, wonder about anything, question anything, investigate anything, and learn about anything. And while such an orientation may seem obvious today, for much of human history, religion vehemently opposed it. For thousands of years, religion taught—and in many corners of the globe continues to teach—that there is only one truth—*its* truth—and everything else is damaging or dangerous. While there have always been men and woman who secretly chafed at such dogmatic tyranny, freethought only came into its own as a fully viable public orientation in the nineteenth century. It was then, primarily in Britain,[10] that leading freethinkers such as Charles Bradlaugh, George Jacob Holyoake, Annie Besant, and Harriet Law began promulgating the position that the human mind is—and ought to be—free. Free to doubt. Free to reason. And free to roam. And no leader, ruler, cleric, bishop, mufti, or government has the right to curtail skepticism, imprison minds, or limit thought. As leading English freethinker Chapman Cohen explained, over one hundred years ago, "Freethought is that form of thinking that proceeds along lines of its own determining, rather than along lines that are laid down by authority."[11]

Many religious people today most certainly appreciate the virtue of freethinking. But it is, nonetheless, a virtue most strongly pronounced within secular culture—as various studies have found. For instance, numerous studies, from both within the United States and elsewhere, report that strongly secular people score much higher on psychological measures of open-mindedness than strongly religious people.[12] And in a related vein, secular people are much less likely to feel that it is important to be a member of a group of like-minded people.[13] And psychological studies from Canada have found that secular people are more likely to be intellectually engaged than religious people, and are more likely to exhibit greater complexity of thought and "divergent cognition"—that is, being more open to examining matters from multiple perspectives.[14] Additionally, when parents are asked what traits or characteristics they most seek to cultivate in their children, secular parents are much more likely to select "thinking for oneself"—in contrast to religious parents, who are much more likely to select "obedience to authority."[15] For example, in one study, approximately 60 percent of secular parents selected "thinking for oneself" as the top trait they wanted their children to exhibit, while less than 40 percent of Evangelicals and Baptists selected "thinking for oneself" as the top desired trait; conversely, around 30 percent of Evangelicals and Baptists listed "obedience to authority" as the number one trait they'd like to see exhibited by their children, but only 9 percent of secular parents selected this as their top choice.[16] And in yet another study, researchers found that secular parents are much more likely to want their children to "make up their own minds" about what they do or don't believe, whereas religious parents are much more likely to want to pass on and impose their beliefs onto their children.[17] Perhaps this is why strongly religious individuals are much more likely to have an authoritarian orientation than moderately religious or nonreligious individuals.[18]

The bottom line is that being secular is significantly correlated with embracing and championing a freethinking orientation: the intellectual and moral benefits of questioning, doubting, and exploring any and all sources of knowledge, and the responsibility to think for ourselves rather than conforming to groupthink or letting those in positions of authority—be they parents, priests, or presidents—do our thinking for us.

Living in Reality

The drive was long, the load was heavy, and the trailer tires were small. And no amount of wishing or hoping was going to do a damn thing.

When I was in my early twenties, I helped my wife, Stacy—who was then my girlfriend—move to Oregon. And on that trip, the importance of living in reality came into sharp relief.

Stacy had her massive record collection to move, as well as an impressive library, as well as everything else one would expect—clothes, furniture, artwork, and a few plants. Since there was no way that it was all going to fit in the car, we managed to procure a little trailer from a friend of Stacy's dad. It had small tires. As we loaded as much as we could into the trailer, I remember looking at those tires and wondering if they would be able to make the trip from Los Angeles to Eugene—a good nine hundred miles or so.

And then, at around midnight, while driving up I-5, just outside of Buttonwillow—a couple hours north of Los Angeles—we heard a loud pop. We pulled over to find that one of the tires had burst. We called AAA, paid the guy $75, and he replaced the tire. And so we headed back up the freeway—both hoping hard that the tires would hold out for the remainder of the journey.

But a couple of hours later: *Pop!* Another burst tire. This time, we found a mechanic in Kettleman City who was able to replace it.

As we got back onto the freeway, the reality of our situation began to quickly set in: desperately hoping for trailer-tire durability had not worked; two tires had already popped and we hadn't even gotten past Sacramento. Clearly, no amount of hoping—no matter how fervent—was going to keep those tires from bursting. In fact, such hoping was both dangerous and absurd. It was dangerous because bursting a trailer tire while going seventy miles an hour could possibly cause a wreck, and it was absurd because to keep hoping that the trailer tires would hold out as we drove northward was actually to remain in a state of denial about the reality of the situation, which was all too clear: the durability of those small tires simply had nothing to do with our sincere hopes and desires. Rather, it had everything to do with objective weight and stubborn physics; there were simply too many heavy items in the trailer, and the small tires could only take so much. Once we acknowledged this, we got off the freeway, went to a parking lot, and took two hours to do a major rearrangement, moving all the heavy stuff into the car and putting all the lighter stuff out into the trailer. And then we proceeded to drive really slow the rest of the way to up Oregon. And that did it—no more bursting tires.

Hope hadn't helped. Reality-based action had.

That experience serves as a metaphor for much of life: you can face reality, even when it is inconvenient, or you can deny reality, relying instead on hopes and wishes. Secular people are much more likely to lean toward the former, while religious people are much more likely to lean toward the latter.

Admittedly, reality can certainly be harsh—if not downright devastating. And there's no question that hopes and wishes can feel good and uplifting; heck, we all wish for things in life, and we all need heavy doses of hope from time to time. But when it comes to living life responsibly, honestly, and as successfully as possible, nothing can replace seeing and accepting things for how they really are rather than denying facts and living life in a state of magical thinking.

This matter of magical thinking is, surely, one of the great divides between religious and secular worldviews: while the presence of magical thinking characterizes much of religious life, its absence characterizes much of secular life. This has been observed and attested to in various social-psychological studies; for example, atheists have been found to score significantly lower than their religious peers on Magical Ideation Scales and Magical Thinking Scales,[19] and atheists have been found to score significantly higher on measures of rational thinking and rational reasoning ability compared to religious people.[20] Additional studies employing Implicit Association Tests have found that secular people are significantly less superstitious than religious people, and that the former tend to be more analytical in their thinking while the latter tend to rely more on intuition.[21]

Of course, prayer must be specifically called out here. As already discussed in chapter 2, there is no evidence that it works toward achieving its desired ends. It is magical thinking, par excellence. And yet, the great religions of the world continue to insist that praying—which is nothing more than deep hoping and fervent wishing—can have a real-world effect. It doesn't, and it can't. And worse, religious prayer often serves as an empty, illusory substitute for rational thinking, responsible planning, and needed action. Secular people understand this. And thus, while living in reality may not provide the immediate, warm psychological comfort in the way that religion can, it is still more effective and more honest—and the only proven way to possibly achieve various desired ends. As American philosopher Peter Boghossian asserts, "It's important there's some lawful correspondence between what we believe and the actual state of affairs. Only when our beliefs accurately correspond to reality are we able to mold external conditions that enable us to flourish."[22]

A perfect example: approaches to gun violence. In the United States, the highly religious offer "thoughts and prayers" as the best antidote to the extremely high rate of death caused by guns. But thoughts and prayers have never proven effective ways to hinder gun violence. Alternatively, secular approaches, such as sane gun control, have.[23]

Another example: approaches to sex education. Christian conservatives and their strongly religious allies have pushed for "abstinence only" sex education programs throughout America. But as numerous studies show, they don't work.[24] And, in fact, their existence causes direct harm and suffering, as teenagers are denied important information that would help them avoid infection, pregnancy, and assault. Rather than accept the reality that many young people will have sex before they are married, and that accurate sex education has been proven to reduce pain and suffering,[25] the dogmatically religious prefer to shape public policy for the worse based on what they wish or hope were true, not what is.

Here-and-Nowness

As I approach fifty, loss is becoming a more and more prevalent theme in my life. People that I know and love are dying at an increasingly regular rate. It's just what happens. Everything that lives dies, and the longer you stick around, the more people you will lose. As atheist and humanist Kurt Vonnegut lamented, "So it goes."[26]

In addition to the matter of magical thinking discussed above, another key difference between religious people and secular people is that the former think that there is some sort of life after death. Secular people don't. We accept mortality and the finiteness of being. As such, our worldview is much more grounded in understanding and accepting that this world is all there is—as far as we know for now—and that this life is all that we will ever have. No heaven, no hell, no reincarnation. Just this life. Just the here and now. People who harm others will not be punished in some post-life judiciary realm. Rather, they must be confronted and contended with here, by us, in our own world—or not at all. People who are kind, gentle, and loving will not be rewarded in some heavenly hotel of eternity. Rather, their appreciation and affirmation takes place only here, by those around them, in their families and communities—and nowhere else. And anything we wish to see or experience—justice, fairness, equality, joy—must be made manifest by people, struggling and working, individually and collectively, over the course of their limited lives. There are no other options or solutions. As secular labor activist Joe Hill lamented, there is no pie in the sky after you die.[27]

For some, such a reality is too bleak to bear. They therefore turn to the comforting arms of faith, with its garlands of promises of a life after death.[28] Secular people, however, are not drawn in to such fictitious succor. And the acceptance that this life is all there is—which is inherent in the secular orientation—does not cause undue suffering or fear of death. In fact, several studies report that secular people, despite their lack of a belief in immortality, can actually have an easier time coping with and confronting death than religious people.[29] Consider, for example, a study from 2011, led by Israeli sociologist Yaacov Bachner, that compared secular and religious people who were caregivers for loved ones dying of cancer; it was found that the secular caregivers had a much easier time talking to their loved ones openly about their terminal situation and their approaching death, and when it came to fear of death itself, the religious caregivers experienced significantly higher levels than the secular caregivers.[30] Or consider studies that show increased religiosity is correlated with a preference for more aggressive end-of-life care.[31] The more strongly religious people are, the more likely they are to want intensive or heroic life-prolonging medical care as they face death—suggesting a greater lack of acceptance of their impending death compared to secular people.

Clearly, secular men and women accept that death is a natural part of life. And this does not increase our fear of, or uncomfortableness with, death. Nor does a here-and-now orientation render life pointless or meaningless. Quite the opposite. For instance, countries in which a significant proportion of people—even the majority of the people—do not believe in life after death are characterized by creative, innovative, hardworking, engaged, peaceful, and successful cultures, replete with purpose-driven and meaning-making citizens.[32] Additionally, studies of apostates—people who were religious but are no longer—report that their loss of belief in life after death does not result in paralyzing depression, despondent indifference, or dispiriting ennui.[33] Rather, love of and appreciation for life markedly increases, as does the recognition that one ought to make as much out of life as one can while one can.[34]

Acceptance of Existential Mystery

"We simply don't know."

I uttered that agnostic mantra a lot while putting my kids to bed at night when they were younger. Here's how it would typically occur:

"Papa, did we really evolve from monkeys?"

"Not exactly. It's more that we humans and modern-day monkeys share a common genetic ancestor—a primate species that lived millions of years ago, but no longer exists. We both evolved from that apelike species."

"Where did that species come from?"

"It evolved from an earlier animal species."

"Where did that earlier animal species come from?"

"Well, all life evolved from preexisting forms of life."

"But how did life start?"

"I'm not sure. I don't know if anyone really knows. At least, not yet."

"But where did the Earth come from? And the universe?"

"It all started with the Big Bang."

"But what caused the Big Bang?"

"We simply don't know."

And then, a few moments of silence. Followed by the cracking open of *Harry Potter* or *Little Women* or *Charlotte's Web*.

But it is within those few moments of silence that the abiding soul of agnosticism dwells: accepting and acknowledging the limits of our knowledge, and sitting—comfortably—within a place of existential wonder, unrequited awe, and open mystery.

Secular people—guided by the imperatives of freethought—believe in questioning anything and everything, and using whatever tools are available to find answers, then testing and scrutinizing those answers, then revising our answers based on new information, then revisiting our initial questions, and always considering alternative theories, and generating new insights, and seeking out more data, and always looking for unbiased confirmation of our hypotheses—and on and on and on, in rigorous, ruthless pursuit of true and valid answers and solutions.

However, at the end of the day—both literally and figuratively—we recline, preferably under twinkling stars, and sigh at the ultimate unfathomability of it all. We lie quietly and comfortably with existential mystery. There are just some things that we may never fully comprehend. As British scientist J. B. S. Haldane quipped, "the universe is not only queerer than we suppose, but queerer than we *can* suppose."[35]

It seems that some humans can accept such existential mystery while others can't. The former tend to be secular while the latter tend to be religious. Perhaps this is why recent studies have found that increased religiosity is observably correlated with increased intolerance of ambiguity while increased secularity is correlated with greater tolerance of ambiguity.[36] Of particular note here is the work of American social psychologist Richard Sorrentino, who, in his book *The Uncertain Mind: Individual Differences in Facing the Unknown*, presents empirical research indicating that religious people, on average, are more likely than secular people to need a sense of certainty—and find uncertainty distinctly unpleasant.[37]

Given their discomfort with uncertainty and with ambiguity, many religious folks turn specifically to their faith for answers to the deep questions of being and existing: Why are we here? Why is there a universe? Why is there something instead of nothing? And so on. But the problem is that by favoring faith over reason, they'll accept any answers, even if they are nothing but ancient guesswork or imaginative fantasies devoid of empirical support. As Pakistani-born Canadian writer Ali Rizvi astutely observes, "religion doesn't *provide* answers; it makes them up."[38]

But secular people tend to get it: better to admit and accept the current limits of our knowledge than to faithfully accept answers that are devoid of evidentiary support. Such an orientation dictates that—when confronted with deep existential questions—one be comfortable with saying that we just don't know. Let those mysteries be. And then—in the secular spirit of here-and-nowness—focus on what we can and do know.

And there's no better method for doing that than science.

Scientific Empiricism

Dr. Ignaz Semmelweis was clearly crazy.[39] He had these weird, obsessive ideas that didn't make sense. Worse, his persistence and vehemence offended the reigning professional authorities of his day. And so, in 1865, Semmelweis was committed to an insane asylum. Two weeks into his stay, guards beat him to death.

The root of Dr. Semmelweis's troubles had to do with the simple act of handwashing. He observed—after many years of working in Hungarian hospitals and clinics—that if doctors washed their hands after doing autopsies, as well as after dealing with patients, the likelihood of the doctors getting sick, and of their patients getting sick, was dramatically reduced. For example, a common illness in the hospitals of Europe in the mid-1800s was puerperal fever; it affected women who had just given birth, and it was often fatal. But Dr. Semmelweis started to notice that if he and his medical staff washed their hands regularly while at work, contagion rates plummeted. He decided to test his observations, with control groups and experimental groups, and the results unambiguously confirmed his hunch: handwashing prevented the spread of puerperal fever and other illnesses. Handwashing saved lives. He published his findings and enthusiastically communicated his discovery to doctors—especially obstetricians—throughout Europe.

Unfortunately, no one believed him. The fact was, he couldn't explain *why* handwashing had such a lifesaving effect. Because he had made his observations and done his empirical testing before the germ theory of illness was known, the dynamics of bacterial infection were not understood. So, other doctors dismissed his findings, took offense at his insistence that they wash their hands regularly while working, became annoyed by his obsessive persistence, and eventually considered him nuts. And the more they resisted and even mocked his handwashing theory, the more incensed and obsessed he became. It got to the point where all he could talk about was the curing potential of handwashing, and the flagrant immorality of his colleagues who wouldn't take heed. Eventually, he was committed to an asylum and then beaten to death.

A sad, tragic ending. But a worthy, brilliant life. Dr. Semmelweis was the pioneer of basic antiseptic procedures that today are universally accepted and have saved hundreds of millions of lives. And it was all largely due to his diligent practice of the scientific method: he began with a question related to the spreading of illness, he developed a hypothesis about handwashing based on keen observation, he tested his hypothesis with control groups and experimental groups, he collected data, and, after analyzing the results, he communicated his findings to others. It's pretty basic. And it is the best way to understand the workings of the natural world.

Scientific empiricism—the reliance upon observation, testing, and generating evidence through methods that guard against bias or false conclusions—is responsible for every single advancement that has improved human and animal health, improved communication and transportation, improved building and construction, and then some.

And again: secular people get it. Secular men and women are much more likely to understand and value science, while religious people are much more likely to misunderstand or even deride science. For example, recent results from the General Social Survey show that: 1) strongly religious people are the most likely to be critical or suspicious of science, while secular people are the least likely to exhibit such an orientation; and 2) secular people are more scientifically literate, possessing significantly more knowledge and understanding about well-established scientific facts.[40] Additionally, those who practice science themselves are much more likely to be secular; a Pew survey of scientists who are members of the American Association for the Advancement of Science found that only 33 percent believe in a God, 12 percent believe in some sort of spirit or power, and the remainder—over 40 percent—are atheists and agnostics.[41] And international studies, looking at scientists all over the world, have found them to be significantly more secular than the general population of their respective countries.[42]

Are scientists sometimes wrong? Of course. But they can only be shown to be wrong through—you guessed it—better science. Such was the case for Dr. Semmelweis: the leading scientists of his day thought he was crazy. But they were mistaken—something which only the scientific method allows us to conclude.

Can science explain everything? Of course not; see above, regarding existential mystery. But as for curing deafness, blindness, or cancer, or aiding amputees, or increasing our ability to travel faster and safer, or fighting climate change, or disseminating knowledge, or finding better ways of decreasing crime—all the prayers in the world don't hold a candle to the scientific method.

And the rigor of scientific empiricism also directly helps us when it comes to understanding the brotherhood and sisterhood of humanity.

Cosmopolitanism

Both religion and science tell a story about the intrinsic oneness of all people. But while religion's narrative is a myth based on pure imagination, science's version is fact based on observable evidence.

Both Christianity and Islam, the two largest religions in the world, teach that there is a magical deity who, one day long ago, created humans. Given that we are all the descendants of these first humans, we subsequently constitute one human family. God is our spouseless Father, and we His motherless children—or so the leading religions of the world claim. Of course, no evidence is provided for this story; it has simply been asserted since ancient times, when people thought the Sun revolved around the Earth.

Science, on the other hand, has revealed the true facts underlying human unity: we all constitute one species. And this is not the result of some magical deity's snapping of fingers, but rather it is the result of evolution through natural selection. All humans who have ever lived share a common primate ancestor; we constitute one biological family. And the unity and common origin of the species *Homo sapiens* can be readily proven through various methods of observation and the clear-eyed assessment of numerous evidentiary sources, with genetic analysis being the most obvious.[43]

But the fact that there is a mythological version of the oneness of humanity espoused by the faithful and a scientific version of the oneness of humanity based on evidence is not the real kicker. What's important is how these two versions play out in the real world, in modern society. That is, which narrative actually translates into a more universal or tribal disposition? What we find is that secular people—who understand the evolutionary oneness of humanity—are much more likely to accept and appreciate the unity of all people, while religious people—who have faith in a creation myth—are much more likely to be tribal in orientation, favoring their own over others, and problematically dividing up the world between "us" and "them." In short, secular people are much more likely to be cosmopolitan in orientation than their religious peers.

Cosmopolitanism stresses the essential unity of humanity. Cosmopolitanism recognizes that, at root, we all compose one global society and that we are all brother and sister citizens on the same rotating planet and must treat one another accordingly.[44] Cosmopolitanism teaches us, in the words of American secular humanist Paul Kurtz, that "our highest ethical obligation is toward the world community."[45] Or as British-born Ghanaian American philosopher Kwame Anthony Appiah explains, cosmopolitanism insists that "no loyalty can ever justify forgetting that each human being has responsibilities to every other."[46]

Studies showing that secular people are much more likely to manifest a cosmopolitan orientation than religious people abound.[47] For example, secular men and women are more likely, on average, to espouse a universalistic moral orientation than their more religious peers and are significantly less likely to believe that our moral considerations should be based on in-group loyalty or arbitrary shared group identity.[48]

Consider nationalism, ethnocentrism, and patriotism; they tend to be strongest among the most religious and weakest among the most secular.[49] For instance, a 2018 Pew study found that religious Europeans are significantly more nationalistic, more anti-immigrant, more ethnocentric, and more wary of Jews and Muslims than secular Europeans,[50] while a 2011 Pew Study found that Evangelical Americans are twice as likely as secular Americans to agree that the United States is "the greatest country in the world."[51] A Religion News Service study found that while 68 percent of Evangelicals said they were "extremely proud" to be Americans, and 56 percent of mainline Protestants said as much, as well as 48 percent of Catholics, only 39 percent of secular Americans expressed such a nationalistic sentiment.[52] And this strong and significant correlation between increased religiosity and fervent nationalism/patriotism/ethnocentrism goes well beyond the United States; we see it in abundance in contemporary India, Myanmar, Israel, Russia, Iran, Nepal, the former Yugoslavia, Japan, Turkey, Greece, Pakistan, and elsewhere.[53]

Although the relationship between religiosity and nationalism can be complex,[54] and while there are certainly many secular versions of nationalism, as a general social-psychological rule, those who are more secular tend to have a more universalist conception of humanity that tempers strong nationalism and ethnocentrism, while the more religious tend to more easily fall prey to jingoistic currents, in-group favoritism, and ethnocentric predilections.[55]

For a related correlation, consider prejudice and racism—two malevolent tendencies in direct opposition to cosmopolitanism. Yet again, the research shows that the more religious people are, the more likely they are to manifest such "us versus them" orientations.[56] As leading Canadian social psychologist Bob Altemeyer observes, most relevant studies illustrate a plain and linear finding: "the more one goes to church, the more likely one will be prejudiced against a variety of others."[57] Or as American psychologist of religion Ralph Wood echoes, based on his assessment of existing research, "as a broad generalization, the more religious an individual is, the more prejudiced that person is."[58] Consider, for example, a 2018 Public Religion Research Institute study that looked at how Americans feel about projected demographic trends indicating that by the year 2043 people of color will outnumber whites in the United States. Over half of white Evangelicals said this would be a negative development, along with 39 percent of mainline Protestants and 32 percent of Catholics—but among secular Americans, only 23 percent saw such a demographic shift as being a negative thing, making nonreligious people the least xenophobic of the lot.[59] Or consider a massive meta-analysis conducted in 2009 by Duke University professor Deborah Hall, who analyzed fifty-five separate studies teasing out the relationship between religion and racism. Her conclusion: strongly religious Americans exhibit the highest levels of racism, while atheist and agnostics exhibit the lowest levels.[60] Does this mean that all religious people are racist and all secular people aren't? Of course not. It simply indicates that, on average—even when taking other demographic variables into account—we see clear tendencies within religious and secular culture, with the former tending to be significantly less cosmopolitan and more tribal than the latter.

Indeed, tribalism is often an overt hallmark of religion—especially strong religion. For example, among the most devoutly orthodox Jewish sects, interaction with nonmembers is strictly limited, non-Jews maintain a lesser spiritual status, and marriage to non-Jews is forbidden. The same goes for fundamentalist Christian sects, like the Amish. Such a problematic division of humanity is also deeply ingrained within Catholicism, where marriage between Catholics and non-Catholics is forbidden. Among strongly religious Protestants, the world is perniciously divided between the "saved" and the "not saved," with the former constituting a more moral, blessed, and favored constituency than the latter. Both Mormonism and Scientology erect numerous boundaries between those who are in and those who are out. In India, divisions between Hindus and non-Hindus are strictly maintained—with a host of cultural and political inequities resulting. And as for Islam—many of its adherents divide up humanity between those who are Muslim, constituting the *ummah*, or global community of believers (read "us"), and those who exist outside of the Islamic community, designated as *kafir* (read "them"). And the *ummah* is certainly held in much higher regard—spiritually, culturally, and often legally—than the *kafir*.

In short, religion—despite its central creation myths about the oneness of all people—is one of the oldest and most potent dividers of humanity, separating would-be couples, wrenching apart family members, dividing neighbors, alienating colleagues, tearing apart communities, and destroying nations. As eminent American expert on peace and violence Ervin Staub notes:

> [Throughout history] religion has been an especially important divider. While all religions advocate love, they believe with varying intensity that their God, and their way of worshipping God, is the only right way. Many religions derogate and often persecute those who worship God in a different way. People who stop following the dictates of their religion are excluded from the group and often persecuted as well . . . all of the religions have texts that exemplify and foster enmity and violence towards outsiders.[61]

Of course, not all religious people reject others who do not share their faith, nor do all religious people forbid their members from marrying those outside of the fold, nor do they all adhere to a divisive "us" versus "them" worldview. But rest assured, such religious people with more universalistic tendencies are nearly always the more liberal, less fervent members within their respective faiths; they are the ones who do not take a literal view of scriptures, do not consider their religion the only true one, are less likely to maintain a host of supernatural beliefs, and are less likely to devote their lives to their religion. They are, in fact, the more *secular* within their respective religious folds. Which proves the point: increased secularity prods us toward cosmopolitanism, while increased religiosity prods us toward tribalism.

Empathy/Compassion

As previously broached in chapter 6, deep within the beating heart of secular morality dwell empathy and compassion. These are what ultimately motivate us to help those in need, to treat others well, and to not harm others. "Empathy," writes American psychologist Martin Hoffman, "is the spark of human concern for others, the glue that makes social life possible."[62] Compassion is what motivates us to act on that concern, based on our understanding and experience of what suffering is like and how we would spare others of it, if and when we can.

Religious people are also motivated by empathy and compassion—no question about it. But they bring along a host of other motivational factors—based on fallacious assumptions—that actually serve to cloud their empathetic tendencies and hamper their compassionate feelings. I'm talking about things like promises of heaven and threats of hell, or deference to religious authority figures, or abiding faith in an all-powerful God who issues binding commandments and a nearly all-powerful Satan who goes around the world getting people to be wicked. All of these things can hinder natural human moral proclivities rather than bolster them. For when morality is conceived of as coming from a God—who will reward you if you follow His rules and punish you if you don't—then obedience inevitably cripples autonomous ethical deliberation. When heaven and hell are taught to children as being real—as is the case with Christianity and Islam—then prudent self-preservation cannot help but muddy, if not dominate, one's moral outlook. And when certain high-status individuals such as clerics, popes, imams, and gurus are regarded as existing on a higher spiritual plane, with clearer access to the Divine, then people become passive followers and worshippers of authority—and thus more susceptible to a docile herd mentality—rather than living as mature, freethinking moral agents, with all of the responsibility that that entails.

Secular individuals are not encumbered by such things. Instead, empathy and compassion remain the unfettered motivators of moral life. And as with all of the seven secular virtues put forward in this chapter, there exists empirical evidence that secular people are, on average, more likely to be motivated by empathy and compassion than religious people. For example, American psychologist Laura Saslow and her associates have run several experiments comparing secular people with religious people, finding that—even when controlling for other variables such as a gender, educational attainment, and political orientation—weakly religious or nonreligious people are more strongly motivated by compassion than strongly religious people.[63] British psychologist Jared Piazza has found that the more religious people are, the more likely they are to exhibit a morality based on following rules rather than on how their behavior might or might not affect someone else's state of suffering or well-being.[64] And survey results show that when parents are asked what characteristics they desire to see their children exhibit, secular parents are much more likely to choose "being considerate of others" than religious parents—especially the strongly religious.[65]

When justifying why one ought to help those in need and not harm others, secular people do not look to the gods for reasons. Nor to holy rulebooks. Nor to figures of authority. Rather, secular people empathize with others, thinking about how it must feel to be in their skin, and then act accordingly. And when they see others suffering, compassion kicks in and serves as the main motivator for moral conduct.

Among secular people, morality is not composed of a set of commandments to be diligently obeyed. Nor does it entail a laundry list of dos and don'ts, with respective rewards and punishments attached. Rather, morality is about the feelings and experiences of others: not wanting them to feel pain or dread and treating them the way we ourselves would like to be treated. This secular ethical orientation is at least one main reason as to why secular people are far more likely than religious people to support full equal rights for gays and lesbians.[66] A Pew national survey from 2017 found that while only 35 percent of white Evangelicals support the right of homosexuals to marry, and 44 percent of Black Protestants support such a right, and 67 percent of Catholics, and 68 percent of white mainline Protestants—a full 85 percent of secular Americans do, and going back decades secular Americans have always been more supportive of this right than their religious peers.[67]

When it comes to the matter of the morality or immorality of homosexuality, the pious Jew, Christian, and Muslim asks: What does God dictate on the matter? What do the holy scriptures instruct? What do our religious leaders declare? And while such questions constitute deeply problematic elements of religious moral deliberation for a host of reasons, we can stick with just this one for now: they ignore and deny the subjectivity, experiences, rights, and feelings of homosexual people.

Now, in a more empathetic and compassionate vein, the secular individual—when deliberating about homosexuality—asks: Who is harmed? Who suffers? Who is being denied certain rights, and how does that denial affect their lives and the lives of their loved ones? How would I feel if I were gay or lesbian, and what sort of rights would I want to enjoy? Am I treating others the way I would like to be treated?

The outcome of these differing approaches—and the different ways in which secular versus religious people deliberate about homosexuality—is clear: when it comes to how society ought to treat homosexuals, strongly theistic, staunchly religious people are much less empathetic and compassionate than those of us who are secular. For such fundamentalist religious people, the suffering of homosexuals in a world that condemns and denies them is of little or no importance compared to what God commands, what scripture states, and what religious authorities pronounce. Not so for the secular, who are much more accepting and affirming—and who favor full and equal rights for homosexuals as an expression of their ethical orientation based on empathy and compassion. And this secular orientation based on empathy and compassion reverberates out to a host of contemporary moral matters, from animal rights to opposing corporal punishment, from immigration to prison reform, from reproductive rights to transgender rights, and from doctor-assisted suicide to the legalization of marijuana. For every issue, empathy and compassion guide us—not deities, divine directives, or dogma.[68]

Morality and the Secular Seven

It is clear how empathy and compassion—as constituents of the secular seven—are related to morality. After all, it was empathy and compassion that motivated Dr. Semmelweis to test his observation and then publish his findings that handwashing lowered rates of infection; he pursued the matter until his death because he wanted to battle puerperal fever and other such deadly infections that caused so many patients to suffer and die. It was empathy and compassion that prodded Johann Struensee to abolish slavery and torture in Northern Europe in the eighteenth century. Or Jawaharlal Nehru to fight for the rights of impoverished peasants in the Indian hinterlands.

As for the remaining secular virtues, they, too, help sustain a healthy, hearty morality in a myriad of ways. The value of freethinking allows us to consider various perspectives on any and all topics, ponder counterarguments, learn about others' experiences, and question everything without fear of cosmic calamity or divine wrath. This orientation improves knowledge of justice, increases understanding of fairness, hones our ability to be rational and reasonable, and ever widens our worldview, all of which are necessary to sustaining a full, rich ethical life. The secular tendency to live in reality helps us to accept things for how they really are—not how we wish or hope them to be. This means that we don't rely on prayer or other such magical thinking to alleviate suffering. We have to take thoughtful and deliberate action—and be attentive to those practices and policies that are actually effective in alleviating suffering. We then base our moral choices on what proves to be effective, not merely what we wish or hope to be the case. This relates to the secular orientation of here-and-nowness; because this time and this life are all there is, if we want to increase well-being and decrease misery, we have to do it ourselves in the here and now.[69] Such is the moral imperative of secular living, for no gods or gurus will save us. Concomitantly, an abiding acceptance of existential mystery allows us to focus on the things we can know and experience, rather than obsess, argue, or ruminate about the deep questions of Being and Existence. Morally, this means that we can more responsively focus on those around us—family, friends, neighbors, colleagues, our fellow human beings around the planet, and other forms of sentient life, as well—in calibrating our actions and intentions so as to be kinder, gentler, and more supportive. And as for scientific empiricism—it is crucial for ethical living. While science, being a mere method, cannot tell us what to value or determine what it ultimately means to be moral, it can help us understand the best ways to achieve certain agreed-upon moral ends. So, for example, if we can agree that curing a painful disease is desirable, or that we ought to eliminate poverty, or that global warming is inimical to the well-being of sentient creatures, science and empiricism are the best avenues to tread for possible solutions.[70] And finally, the secular virtue of cosmopolitanism helps us erode tribalism, racism, nationalism, and any other such horrible "us" versus "them" divisions that create enmity among humans.

It all sounds pretty good, right?

In these last few chapters, we have come to a secular understanding of what it means to be moral. We have uncovered the various natural sources of human morality, and we've just now looked at prominent principles and precepts that bolster secular moral life.

However, secular morality is not so neat and clean. Unfortunately, there are challenges to be confronted when understanding morality from a secular vantage point—harsh and dire challenges. After all, if the secular sources of morality are so clear-cut, then how do we account for immorality? There are a lot of ugly, dark, and nefarious human behaviors out there that we have to contend with—from murder to genocide. In order to be robust, secular approaches to morality must make sense of such flagrant immorality.

Furthermore, if morality is socially constructed, then doesn't that mean it is simply relative to society and culture? And if that's the case, doesn't that make it ultimately meaningless or at the very least nonbinding?

Such challenges—from the practical to the theoretical—will be considered and countered in the chapters ahead.

Part Three

CHALLENGES TO SECULAR MORALITY

9

Accounting for Immorality

About twenty years ago, on a balmy summer day in a rural Southern town, Laura Foss was having some difficulty.[1] She was seven months pregnant, and as she walked across the mostly empty supermarket parking lot, she managed to make it to the car while balancing the grocery bags in her arms. But just as soon as she began placing the bags into the back seat of her car, two men approached her. One had a gun.

The strangers ordered Laura into the driver's seat. While one of them got into the back with the groceries, the man holding the gun sat in the passenger seat and ordered her to drive to the woods on the outskirts of town.

Laura's body was found later that day, facedown, with a bullet hole in the back of her head. There were abrasions on her face, bruises on her breasts, signs of choking on her neck, and evidence of sexual assault.

Just about all we can do upon hearing of such a tragedy is feel shock at the savagery of it. And horror, agony, and grief for the way in which this poor woman was killed. And sadness for her. And pained sympathy and sorrow for her friends and family.

But what about her killers? One of them was a man named Bobby Moore. How are we to feel about him? How are we to make sense of him?

What would compel him to treat another person so horribly? After all, Bobby Moore is a human being—the inheritor of the same bio-evolutionary history as the rest of us. His brain produces oxytocin, just like everybody else's. He, too, was cared for as an infant. Given all that was discussed in the previous chapters about the natural, secular sources of human morality—and given that we can understand the evolutionary, psychological, and sociological processes that foster kindness, empathy, and compassion—then we must also be able to account for the kind of cruelty that Bobby Moore and his accomplice inflicted upon Laura Foss.

And such cruelty is abundant, especially here in the United States, where our murder rate is several times higher than that of other wealthy democracies.[2] I myself—despite having grown up in a relatively affluent, peaceful nook of the world—had two friends from my small hometown who were wantonly murdered: Clinton Heilemann, who I went to summer camp with, was shot by a drifter in a parking lot at the age of fifteen, and Teak Dyer, with whom I shared a circle of teenage friends in high school, was abducted by a private security guard the night of her graduation and shot through the heart as she fought off his sexual attack.

Although abundant, such violence—as mentioned in chapter 1—is not the norm. In fact, it is far less common than it was in previous centuries,[3] and it is markedly rarer in certain societies today, such as Japan (where the homicide rate is 0.3 people murdered per 100,000 people in the population), compared to other societies, such as El Salvador (where the homicide rate is 83 people murdered per 100,000).[4] But whether we are looking at the past or present, or societies with high homicide rates or low homicide rates, and whether were are talking about cold-blooded killings or other forms of personal violence and cruelty, the obvious fact remains that not all people act morally all the time. Flagrant, destructive immorality is a perennial part of human history and society, and any secular account of morality must face it head on.

In this chapter, we will contend with immorality at the individual level, trying to understand people who willfully cause pain and suffering to others. Then we will confront larger-scale manifestations of immorality at the societal level, such as genocide. And the foci throughout will map fairly closely onto the main pillars of the previous chapter, because the various secular sources of morality discussed in chapter 7—our brains, our experiences being cared for as infants, our socialization, our evolutionary past, etc.—are also the very same sources of most manifestations of immorality. It's just that they work in the obverse: while our normally functioning brains enable empathetic responses and foster compassion, if our brains are damaged or dysfunctional, their ability to be empathetic and compassionate can deteriorate significantly.[5] And while our experiences being cared for as infants usually produce individuals with an overriding capacity to care, when that caregiver-child relationship is strained or warped, moral capacities within growing children can become markedly crippled. As for socialization—while it usually produces moral individuals, it can readily produce the opposite. And while our evolutionary past primarily fostered a propensity for cooperation and sociability, it simultaneously produced a potent capability to feel and act hostile and aggressively toward outsiders perceived as threats. All of this—and relevant additional matters—will be unpacked and illustrated as we move forward.

But for now, let's get back to Bobby Moore.

Abused

If you were the presiding judge charged with deciding Bobby Moore's fate, what would you recommend? And let's accept that the facts of his crime are uncontested: he helped abduct Laura Foss at gunpoint, he assaulted her in the woods, and he shot her in the back of the head. That he admitted to, so his guilt in her brutal death is not up for debate. Now then, do you think Bobby Moore deserves the death penalty? Life in prison without the possibility of parole? My hunch is that if you are a red-blooded American, you think that any man who can commit such crimes deserves the maximum punishment allowed by law. And perhaps even more than that. And if you are a strongly religious red-blooded American, then you are probably even more likely to want Bobby Moore to suffer as a result of his crime; research has found that religious fundamentalists are much more likely to support harsh, punitive punishment for criminal offenders than moderately religious or nonreligious people.[6]

But before you send Bobby Moore off to the gallows or the electric chair or the firing squad or the lethal-injection chamber or sixty years in solitary confinement, let me tell you just a little bit more about him.

Bobby Moore—who was in his thirties when he killed Laura Foss—contended for most of his life with certain physical and mental deficits. He suffered from dysarthria, a neurological disorder that comes from brain damage, resulting in a motor speech dysfunction that involves a lack of coordination in the muscles needed to produce clear speech. In addition to not being able to speak clearly as a result of damage to his nervous system, Moore also had difficulty with comprehension; when being interviewed by police, detectives, and psychiatrists, he often had a hard time answering simple questions and keeping track of pronouns, and tended to become unfocused during conversations, going off on tangents that had little to do with the matter at hand.

Does any of this information affect your appraisal or judgment of Bobby Moore? Does it change anything for you?

At the time of the murder, Bobby Moore was unable to read beyond a second-grade level. He could not solve basic mathematical problems. He had observable motor deficiencies on the left side of his body, particularly in his left hand—deficiencies that are symptomatic of certain types of cerebral cortical dysfunction. Additionally, from an early age, Bobby often heard voices and had hallucinatory visions; cranial imaging of the right hemisphere of his brain revealed abnormalities consistent with psychosis and schizophrenia.

Bobby had been one of sixteen children, not all from the same father. Poverty-stricken, they had lived in a dilapidated dwelling. Food was regularly in short supply. Bobby's parents were severe alcoholics, and Bobby's childhood was marked by violence: physical fights between his father and mother sometimes resulted in his mother being beaten or choked until she was unconscious, shotguns and knives were pointed at family members on a regular basis, and there was persistent child abuse. For example, when his mom was in a drunken rage, she would sometimes force one of the kids to strip naked and get into a sack, tied at the neck, which she would then hoist up on a rafter, and then beat the child with pipes, shovels, or whatever she could grab. She once tied one of Bobby's brothers to a tree and lit a fire underneath him (he was rescued by older siblings).

Of all the kids, Bobby got the worst of the abuse. Bobby's mother was provoked by the fact that Bobby often talked to himself, seemed detached, and would spend hours by himself sitting up in a tree. Additionally, the fact that Bobby—as a child—had trouble learning to walk, had trouble enunciating, had trouble keeping up his end of a conversation, could not read or write, wet the bed every night, and did poorly in school only added fuel to the rage his mother directed at him. She starved and beat him regularly, for years. At one point, she granted a neighbor permission to beat Bobby while she (the mother) was not at home—a task the neighbor took on with sadistic relish.

How do you feel about Bobby Moore now? Any stirring of sympathy? Sadness? Such feelings are warranted. After all, according to Dr. Jonathan Pincus—longtime chief of neurology services at the VA Medical Center in Washington, D.C., and former professor of neurology at Georgetown University—who undertook extensive psychological and neurological examinations of Bobby Moore in the wake of Laura Foss's murder, there was little doubt that his brain was physically damaged "prenatally through maternal drinking and postnatally by the constant stress of his abusive home."[7] There was also Bobby's psychosis, which was most likely genetically inherited. According to Dr. Pincus, "it was abuse interacting with brain damage and psychosis that sealed Bobby Moore's fate."[8] And tragically, Laura Foss's fate, as well.

While not all cold-blooded killers share a childhood as poor and as violent as Bobby Moore's or have brain damage similar to his, many do—to varying degrees. We know this because of the several decades of research conducted by Dr. Pincus, who didn't just thoroughly investigate Bobby Moore—examining his brain, his coordination, his motor skills, his medical records, interviewing him extensively, and interviewing his siblings and acquaintances—but over 150 other murderers who killed their victims wantonly. And from such in-depth analyses of so many people who killed for no apparent reason, Dr. Pincus found that the majority of them shared some common features, most notably abusive childhoods and various forms of mental illness and/or brain damage, both of which resulted in angry dispositions, violent tendencies, a lack of empathy, and low impulse control. As Dr. Pincus explains, "abuse generates the violent urge. Neurologic and psychiatric diseases of the brain damage the capacity to check that urge,"[9] and thus "it is the interaction of childhood abuse with neurologic disturbances and psychiatric illnesses" that explains most of the murderers he studied. Indeed, out of the nearly 150 first-degree murderers that Dr. Pincus examined, 94 percent had some combination of abusive childhoods and brain damage/mental illness, and thus, as he concludes, "neurologic damage, abuse, and paranoid thinking are almost always present in adult murderers on death row."[10]

Of course, brain damage and/or mental illness, in and of themselves, do not cause people inevitably to become killers. The overwhelming majority of those who suffer from brain damage or mental illness are not violent—if anything, they are more likely to be the victims of violence rather than the perpetrators. Additionally, not all children who experience extensive abuse grow up to become homicidal.[11] And yet, extensive research from numerous criminological studies does reveal a very strong correlation—a pronounced link—between experiencing violent abuse as a child and subsequently being violent as a teenager/adult.[12] As Dr. Pincus's research shows, such abuse plus brain damage or dysfunction increases the risk of immoral behavior; throw in concomitant experiences of dire poverty, sexual abuse, and systemic oppression linked to race, religion, or any other such social identity, and the inability of various individuals to control their violent urges only compounds.

Based on the above information about Bobby Moore—particularly the extent of his abusive childhood—the judge who presided over his fate decided not to kill him via the state's apparatus for execution, but instead sentenced him to life in prison without the possibility of parole. Perhaps you think this was the right thing for the judge to do. Perhaps not. But our goal here is not to debate what kind of punishment Bobby Moore deserved. Nor is it to condemn Moore as evil or shower sympathy upon him as a victim. Rather, the goal is to better understand—more broadly—the kind of cruel, immoral behavior he committed. That is, Bobby Moore's story serves as but one illustrative example containing many key factors that contribute toward various forms of egregious immorality in general. For starters: the brain. When healthy, it serves as the physiological locus of moral tendencies and deliberations. But when unhealthy, troubles can sometimes result.

Empathy Erosion

Learning about the specific details of various acts of personal cruelty and violence, such as Bobby Moore's killing of Laura Foss—or the killing of my high school friend Teak Dye, or the killing of Polly Klaas, or the killing of Emmett Till, or any of the many individual acts of heinous violence that pepper the local sections of our daily newspapers—one all-too-common response is to write off the perpetrators as, well, *evil.* As a descriptive tool and a commonly employed adjective, the designation of "evil" works just fine. We can readily describe someone as evil if they eagerly inflict pain upon other people, willfully causing them to suffer.[13]

But as an *explanatory* tool, the label "evil" doesn't really help us all that much. After all, people aren't evil in some ontological, existential, or genetic sense; individuals aren't born unalterably evil. Nor is evil some supernatural condition, demonic state, or electromagnetic force that inhabits or possesses people. Such commonly assumed possibilities have never been empirically proven. And keep in mind, if such things *were* proven to be the case, then evil individuals couldn't be blamed for any pain and suffering they caused. After all, they would just be acting out their intrinsic nature, over which they have no control.

Thus, the designation "evil" won't help us here. Rather, a better way to characterize and make sense of flagrant, violent immorality—and to more accurately describe what is really going on when people willfully cause others to suffer—is to consider what Dr. Simon Baron-Cohen, professor of developmental psychopathology at the University of Cambridge, refers to as "empathy erosion."

According to Dr. Baron-Cohen, those who suffer from empathy erosion are unable to feel or care about the feelings of others. They are unable to sense or identify with other people's outlook or state of being. They cannot experience sympathy, compassion, or guilt. And while we are all capable of lacking empathy at certain times—in varying degrees and for limited durations—those individuals who commit extreme cruelty and violence are often characterized by unalterable, acute deficits in feeling, responding to, or caring about the pain and suffering of others. They are, according to Baron-Cohen, "imprisoned in their own self-focus. Imprisoned, because for them it is not a temporary state of mind after which their empathy can recover. For them, a self-focus is *all* that is available to them, as if a chip in their neural computer were missing."[14]

And that is, by and large, what Dr. Baron-Cohen's research reveals: when it comes to many perpetrators of cruel violence, something akin to a "missing chip" in the brain is where it's at. Or rather—given that we're dealing with a lack of empathy—where it's not at. Killers such as Bobby Moore often suffer from observable neurological deficits that hinder their ability to be empathetic.

Empathy, according to Baron-Cohen, exists on a bell curve: some of us are super empathetic, most of us fall somewhere in the middle, while others seem to cluster down at the "zero empathy" end. And it is in the region of the brain that makes up our empathy circuitry—the ventromedial prefrontal cortex, the middle cingulate cortex, and other areas of the temporal lobe—where we see the most obvious abnormalities in individuals characterized by glaring empathy deficits. Such empathy-lacking people—who often suffer from a variety of neurological challenges such as borderline personality disorder and psychopathology—are observably more prone to violence, which partially explains why it is that while about 3 percent of males in the general population can be diagnosed with antisocial personality disorders, 50 percent of all inmates warrant such a diagnosis.[15]

Dr. Baron-Cohen is far from alone in his research on neurological dysfunction's correlation with low empathy; numerous studies within the last two decades have linked a lack of empathy with observable damage to, or abnormalities within, the brain.[16] For example, a team of researchers at the University of New South Wales in Australia found that after people had survived a traumatic brain injury, they became less empathetic and less emotionally responsive to others.[17] Other researchers at the University of Swansea, in Wales, found that many individuals who experienced traumatic brain injuries exhibited a subsequent lack of love or warmth with their friends and family members, and such individuals scored much lower on empathy tests than other uninjured control subjects.[18] A team of researchers at the University of Haifa, in Israel, found that individuals who had limited brain damage in the form of prefrontal lesions—specifically within the ventromedial prefrontal cortex—were significantly impaired in their ability to experience empathy when compared to individuals without such lesions.[19] Another team of researchers from three universities in Germany found that gray matter volume in the bilateral anterior insular cortex and the left amygdala was—when compared to control subjects—significantly lower in adolescents exhibiting aggressive behavior and decreased empathy.[20] Several researchers have found a strong correlative link between violent criminal behavior and serotonin levels in the brain.[21] As Irish biopsychologist Nigel Barber recounts, "this link is so strong, in fact, that if you measure the level of serotonin turnover in a violent criminal's brain . . . you can predict their future criminal violence with greater confidence than by all other methods combined . . . in one study, re-offense was predicted with 84 percent accuracy alone."[22]

The body of research on this front is substantial and growing.

The point here, however, should not be misconstrued: it is not that violent, aggressive immorality is directly or solely the result of neurological deficits. Nor is it that individuals with various neurological deficits all become perpetrators of cruelty; we must always vigilantly resist such neurological reductionism.[23] Rather, the humbler point is this: just as we can look to the evolved human brain as the locus of our physiological capacity for empathy, compassion, and cooperation, so too can we look to the brain when such capacities are markedly diminished or lacking in certain individuals. Evidence shows that—sometimes—if our brains are compromised in certain ways, so too may our capacity to act ethically be compromised. And such an insight is warranted, given the growing body of research showing that in certain aggressive or violent people, a pronounced lack of empathy is at play—and this lack of empathy is often linked to certain forms of neural damage and brain dysfunction.[24]

Of course, neurological deficits—while playing a significant role in empathy erosion and potentially concomitant immoral behavior—aren't the whole story. Far from it. They constitute merely one piece of a much broader explanatory picture concerning the potential for some humans to act cruelly to others. A second component is disrupted attachment between infants and their immediate caregivers.

Attachment, Interrupted

Perhaps it was his time spent working with small British children who, during World War II, had been evacuated from bomb-raided London and placed in unfamiliar abodes in safer Cambridge, away from their parents and nannies. Or perhaps it was his observations of Jewish children who, in order to escape Hitler's gas chambers, had been separated from their parents during the Holocaust and ferried to the United Kingdom. Or maybe it was his extensive interactions, both during and after the war, with maladjusted children in various clinics and psychiatric wards throughout England. Or, most likely, it was a combination of all of these formative experiences that led British psychologist, psychiatrist, and eminent expert in child development John Bowlby to pioneer one of the most dominant areas of research in modern psychology: attachment theory.

At the heart of attachment theory is the basic premise that infants need to bond with their caregivers—usually one of their parents—in order to develop into socially centered, emotionally healthy, and morally adept people. As discussed earlier, human infants are utterly dependent upon the care of others in the roughly two years after birth. But it's not just help with physical survival that they require; social nurturance and emotional support are also needed. And it is to their most immediate caregivers—usually their mothers—that babies turn for such things when they feel scared, anxious, lonely, uncomfortable, or insecure. Or even if they're not feeling such things—just being little and alive, infants are evolutionarily predisposed to connect with their caregivers, to interact with them, to bond with them, to engage with them, to be nurtured, to be held, to be loved.[25] By serving as this most fundamental, necessary source of social and emotional sustenance, loving protection, affection, warmth, and safety, it is primary caregivers to whom the baby automatically becomes emotionally and psychologically attached. And when that attachment between baby and caregiver is steady and sound, the baby tends to develop into a trusting, cooperative individual. As American professor of anthropology Sarah Blaffer Hrdy explains, "a baby confident of a rapid response by a mother committed to his well-being is likely to . . . grow up to feel confident about human relations generally," developing into a person whose orientation to the world and others is characterized by "emotional security."[26]

Embedded within this essential relationship of attachment that takes place between a parent and infant—a relationship needed in order to develop emotionally and morally healthy—is a dynamic of caring. This initial care that we experience as infants and toddlers—ideally marked by strong, loving attachment—preps and readies us to become caring people in turn, as we develop and become adults. But when that experience of care is thwarted or limited, our capacity to care suffers precipitously. And in the worst of outcomes, it can become overshadowed by a capacity for malevolence. As Dr. Pincus explains, "parent rejection can lead to a child growing up to become violent or a psychopath. It may not be the only factor, but it can be an important one." And that's because the rejection and abandonment experienced by the young child in such an unfortunate circumstance can develop into strong feelings of pain, hurt, hate, and rage, feelings that are hard to control and "may build up—like steam in a pressure cooker—just waiting to be vented in adolescence or adulthood. The result can be explosive violence."[27]

Thus, according to the logic of attachment theory, when the bond between infants and their primary caregivers is strong, reliable, and loving, children will generally develop into socially capable, emotionally centered, ethical individuals. However, when that bond is severed or fraught, then the social, emotional, and moral development of children is damaged.

Empirical support for all of this theorizing is more than abundant.[28] In fact, it was John Bowlby's first book that started it all off. In *Forty-four Juvenile Thieves*, published in the mid-1940s, Bowlby analyzed forty-four delinquent adolescents from a London suburb who had a history of stealing and compared them to a control group of forty-four demographically similar adolescents who had had no such trouble with the law. What he found was that seventeen of the forty-four criminally involved youths had experienced extended stints of separation (approximately six months or longer) from their primary caregivers at some time within their first five years of life. However, of the forty-four control adolescents with no history of theft, only two had experienced any similar such spates of separation from their parents within their first five years of life. Furthermore, of the delinquent youths, the notable few who had a history of persistent stealing and were observed as being the most "affectionless" and least emotionally engaged had had the longest and most complete experiences of separation from their primary caregivers before the age of five.

Since that pioneering study, a steady flow of research has documented the significant relationship between weak or broken attachments between young children and their primary caregivers and subsequent antisocial, immoral behavior. Summing up such research was a 2012 meta-analysis of seventy-four relevant scholarly articles, conducted by Dutch clinical psychologist Machteld Hoeve and his colleagues, who concluded that "poor attachment to parents was significantly linked to delinquency in boys and girls."[29]

But it's not just a weak or interrupted attachment in early childhood that can hamper natural moral development. As illustrated in the story of Bobby Moore, flagrant neglect and outright abuse during childhood can be even more toxic.

Harvest of Hurt and Harm

Back in 1957, my great-aunt Susan Kohner starred in a film with Sal Mineo called *Dino*. The plot of the movie revolves around a juvenile delinquent who spends extended periods of time in the office of a social worker trying to help him. As we watch this hardened hoodlum soften through the course of his talk therapy, the root of his violent tendencies and antisocial activities becomes apparent: Dino's dad was a violent man who regularly hit and humiliated Dino as he was growing up. That abuse was the obvious source of Dino's own destructive delinquency. Fast-forward sixty years to 2017, when I went to see the movie *It* with my teenage daughter. In that movie—based on Stephen King's novel—one of the adolescents in the small town of Derry is a particularly cruel and sadistic teenager named Henry Bowers, who harasses, beats up, and even stabs younger children. And what do we eventually learn about this horrible kid? Surprise, surprise: Henry's dad was aggressively abusive, regularly humiliating and hurting Henry at home—which readily explains the latter's sadism.

Yeah, it's just about as cliché as it gets in books, plays, movies, and television shows: an angry, mean, and physically violent individual became that way because, as a child, he had been hurt and harmed by emotionally and physically abusive parents. And it's a cliché that is decidedly steeped in reality; decades of research have shown that children who are abused like Dino and Henry Bowers are much more likely to be violent as teenagers and adults.[30]

Consider:

- A National Institute of Justice study from the 1980s compared over 3,000 children in a large city in the Midwest who were demographically similar in terms of class, race, etc., and checked in on them from the time they were eleven years old until they were in their thirties—some had been abused and neglected, while others had not. And the different outcomes were staggering: being abused or neglected when young increased the likelihood of being arrested as a teenager by 59 percent and increased the likelihood of being arrested for a violent crime as an adult by 30 percent.[31]

- In 1991, in a study that looked at over 3,300 parents with children under the age of eighteen, researchers found that children who experienced verbal and physical abuse showed the highest rates of aggression and delinquency.[32]
- In 1995, a study that looked at approximately 1,000 junior high students and their primary caretakers found similar results: when other factors were held constant (race, socioeconomic status, etc.), abused children in the sample had a substantially higher likelihood of being arrested for a crime than nonabused children, indicating that "maltreatment is a significant predictor of . . . violent delinquency."[33]
- In 2002, a U.S. Department of Justice study of nearly 900 cases—again controlling for race, gender, social class, etc.—found that abused and neglected children were 3.1 times more likely to be arrested for a violent crime as adults than children who had not been abused or neglected while growing up.[34]
- Three separate studies from 2007, one that followed a cohort of over 1,400 children in Chicago, one that followed a cohort of nearly 600 children from both Tennessee and Indiana, and one that looked at over 1,800 children in Ontario, Canada, found that childhood abuse and maltreatment were significantly associated with later involvement in violent criminality.[35] For example, the study in Ontario found that a youth who had experienced three or more forms of childhood maltreatment was 11.2 times more likely to be engaged in violent delinquency as a teenager than a youth who had not experienced such abuse or neglect.
- A study from 2016, using structural equation modeling based on a sample of 337 young adults, found that—when controlling for demographics, family income, etc.—childhood physical abuse was directly predictive of later criminality.[36]

I could go on and on—citing more research along these lines—but you get the idea. Finnish professors of psychology Jaana Haapasalo and Elina Pokela, who conducted a meta-analysis of decades of published research on the relationship between child neglect/abuse and subsequent violence/criminality, have summed it all up, concluding that "harsh punishment in child-rearing appears to increase the risk for maladaptive outcomes, such as aggressive, antisocial, violent, and criminal behavior," and "rejecting or neglecting child-rearing methods and child abuse are related to antisocial behavior, adult violence, and offending."[37] And American psychiatrist James Gilligan similarly sums up his analysis of sixty years of research, declaring that "the most solidly confirmed and consistent finding is that the more severely children are punished, the more violent they become, both during childhood and after they become adults."[38]

Of course, just as not every individual with neurological abnormalities becomes unempathetic and cruel, and just as not every child who experiences weak or interrupted attachment with their caregiver becomes unethical, nor does every boy or girl who experiences neglect or abuse become aggressive, violent, or criminally engaged later in life. Most do not. However, childhood maltreatment clearly increases the likelihood of such an outcome. Thus, certain neurological deficits, attachment disruption between young children and their caregivers, and various degrees of childhood abuse are all to be recognized as significant predictive factors that help contribute to the hampering and hindering of otherwise normal, naturally evolved human moral aptitude. And when they occur in combination, they make for an accumulatively potent threat.[39]

Another factor to add in our explanatory enterprise: socialization and internalization of immoral norms and values.

Socialization and Internalization Revisited

As we can never be reminded enough, the systemic lynching of African Americans was an extremely common activity throughout the southern United

States at the turn of the century.[40] While many lynchings in the late 1800s and early 1900s took place in the dark, with only the victims and the murderous mob present, many others throughout the South were public productions carried out in broad daylight—often as community picnics—replete with specially chartered trains, parades and floats, souvenirs, commemorative photos, and hundreds of families gathering for the spectacle.[41] And the physical remains of the victims—their severed fingers and toes, genitalia, and burned bones—were sought after as valued collectibles.

By American sociologist W. E. B. Du Bois's account, over twenty-seven hundred African American individuals were verifiably lynched by white mobs between the years of 1885 and 1914.[42] Just for a sense of perspective, that averages out to about ninety-three African Americans murdered by white mobs every year during that time period, or around eight per month, or about two per week. Hundreds more were lynched in subsequent years, like in 1935, when Reuben Stacy was falsely accused of threatening a white woman. Without witnesses, evidence, or trial, Reuben was forcefully apprehended and—under the leadership of the local sheriff—given over to a white mob who hung him from a pine tree with a wire clothesline and then shot him numerous times. The aftermath of Reuben's savage murder was recorded by local photographers, and one of the most striking elements of the gruesome images of his lynching are of the many well-dressed white children who can be seen standing just beneath Reuben's body, along with their parents, looking up at Reuben's dangling corpse.

Clearly, given one's particular communal environment and the reigning norms and values of one's historical location—and depending on whom one's parents are and what they believe and do—even murder can be something children are raised to see as normal, mundane, and just. That is, you can take a relatively well-cared-for child who, as a growing infant, experienced close attachment with his or her immediate caregivers, was loved and supported and neither physically nor emotionally abused, and whose neurological capacities are normal and well-functioning—and then socialize that child to harbor hatred or fear of certain groups of people, or to be numb to the suffering of certain specified others, or to see certain harmful or violent acts as necessary, natural, or required, and more often than not, he or she will typically internalize such socialization. The result: the child will develop the capacity to act immorally or unethically.

The things people say, the way people behave, the activities people are engaged in, their routine interactions with each other—all of these things are unavoidably observed by young children as they grow up. But not just observed: taken in. *Absorbed.* And because the specifics of what children observe other people doing and saying—in their day-to-day lives—are unconsciously soaked up and spontaneously absorbed, they have a tremendous amount of determining influence on children's subsequent values, beliefs, and what they think is good or bad, moral or immoral. And the closer their emotional and material attachment, the stronger those people's direct influence on children is, so that parents, grandparents, relatives, teachers, coaches, siblings, neighbors—not to mention the various media they are exposed to—all serve to intimately shape children's worldviews and expectations.

More often than not, the invisible influence of what children soak up from those around them doesn't feel coercive or forced. In fact, most children don't even notice the observing-absorbing process taking place. They simply grow up among certain people, in a certain time and place, and unwittingly come to want the very things their socialization has shaped and molded them to want (such as having shaved legs or a circumcised penis), to like or dislike just what those who socialized them informally taught them to like or dislike (such as liking guns and veal or disliking guns and veal), and to share certain taken-for-granted values and beliefs with those people who raised them (such as the properness of lynching Black people who are perceived as threatening white hegemony). When this happens—when children come to take on as their own personal values and beliefs those originating in their immediate surrounding social world—it's called internalization, as was discussed earlier in chapter 7. It means personally wanting exactly what we've been socialized to want, individually admiring or despising exactly what we have been socialized to admire or despise, and feeling natural doing various things we've been socialized to feel natural doing. It's when our family's or culture's norms and values unconsciously become our own.

As discussed in chapter 7, most of the norms and values we internalize are prosocial, cooperative, kind, conducive to community maintenance, and lean toward the more moral end of the spectrum of human orientations and capabilities. However, when people are socialized to hate or harm—when they internalize immoral norms or values—they can readily act immorally, in turn.

Hating on Homosexuals

Like when I harassed a schoolmate some thirty-five years ago.

The memory always makes me cringe with guilt. It was 1985, and I was in seventh grade at Paul Revere Junior High School, and on this one particular day, I walked stridently down the hall with a pack of about six other boys, following this one kid—let's call him Jerry—shouting: "Jerry is a fa-*ggot*! Jerry is a fa-*ggot*! Jerry is a fa-*ggot*!"

It was cruel.

I had been at a friend's house the previous Saturday, and he told me that he had heard that this boy, Jerry, had given another boy a blowjob. This story, of course, was nothing but a unconfirmed rumor. But whether it was true or not didn't matter, for even the mere suspicion of homosexuality was enough to raise our righteous ire. How disgusting! How vile! How outrageous! Being gay in my neck of the woods back in the early 1980s was just about the worst thing a junior high boy could be; this rumor of what Jerry may or may not have done was an immediate stigma of epic proportions. And so, that following Monday at school, when a bunch of us saw Jerry, we homed in on him, unleashing our adolescent derision. We followed him around campus, hounding him with sadistic abandon.

He was clearly hurt by our taunting. You could see it in his eyes, which betrayed his agony and fear. Though he tried his best to ignore us, I can still recall the pained look on his face as we shouted at him. He wanted to cry. And it looked like it took all his might to hold back the tears.

That look on his face struck me, and I subsequently felt badly about the harassment, and thus only participated in that mob that one day. Other boys, however, continued to harass Jerry throughout the year. It must have been hell for him, no doubt. And no one, including me, ever came to his aid or defense. Who would be an ally to a gay kid at Paul Revere Junior High School in 1985? No way.

In addition to being ugly and regretful, there are two important things to stress about the homophobic hatred that I participated in directing at Jerry back in my old junior high. The first: while cruel, it was far from the worst form of malevolence that homosexuals—or perceived homosexuals—have endured throughout history and continue to endure today in all corners of the world. I'm not trying to minimize the harassment Jerry experienced. I'm simply taking into account the historical and sociological reality that hatred of homosexuals has been one of the deepest, widest, harshest, and most deadly hatreds throughout history.[43] People accused of homosexuality have been—and in many societies, still continue to be—hounded, tortured, traumatized, and murdered for something that causes no harm to anyone or anything.

For but a quick historical sweep, consider that in the seventh century, the Sixteenth Council of Toledo, in Hispania, declared that homosexual acts should be punished by castration of the perpetrators. In Jerusalem in the twelfth century, the Council of Nablus decreed execution by burning for homosexual acts.[44] In medieval France, two men caught making love with one another were sentenced to castration for the first offense, dismemberment for the second, and death by burning for the third, and women caught making love with other women faced mutilation for the first and second offenses, and death by burning for the third.[45] In the fifteenth century, Nezahualcoyotl, the ruler of Texcoco in pre-Columbian Mexico, made homosexuality a capital crime, with perpetrators being killed by hanging.[46] Sixteenth-century British law, under both King Henry VIII and Queen Elizabeth, made homosexuality a capital crime, and in 1776, male homosexuals in all thirteen American colonies faced execution if discovered.[47] Today, homosexuality is still punishable by death in thirteen countries, including

Iran, Saudi Arabia, Pakistan, Qatar, and Yemen, and it is illegal—with various nonlethal punishments potentially meted out—in many more, such as India, Libya, and Angola.[48] And the world's religions have been explicit in their hatred of homosexuals and their desire to inflict harm upon them: Jewish scriptures condemn homosexuals to death (Leviticus 20), Christian scriptures castigate homosexuality as shameful, unnatural, and prohibitive of one's entering heaven (Romans 1; 1 Corinthians 6), and in various Islamic hadith—canonical sayings and doings of the Prophet—Muhammad declares that homosexuals should be put to death. Today, millions of homosexuals are denied equal rights and protections in many nations and can be imprisoned, tortured, or killed with impunity.

The second and perhaps more important point to be stressed is that my junior high hatred of Jerry's homosexuality—and all homophobia in general—is not natural. It is not innate. We are not bio-evolutionarily or genetically hardwired to hate gays and lesbians. Homophobia is largely the result of socialization and internalization. How do we know? First, consider me: I soon grew out of it. Less than a year after junior high, I no longer hated homosexuals, I no longer found homosexuality disgusting, and I went on to have many very close gay and lesbian friends in high school, college, and beyond. And I have worked politically to fight for the rights of homosexuals. In short, I very easily went from a thirteen-year-old kid who was uncomfortable with and even hostile to homosexuality, to a teenager (and adult) who made a 180-degree turn, becoming (and remaining) someone who is way more uncomfortable with and hostile to homophobia. Second, consider my own children: among their peers, homophobia is not cool or tolerated. Rather, the rights of gays and lesbians are championed. In my son's social circle, it is considered right, proper, and progressive to be progay rather than antigay. And in my older daughter's high school, there are openly gay and lesbian couples, and no one seems to care. They are not belittled or harassed. In fact, American society is less homophobic than ever before: according to the latest survey research, 62 percent of Americans now support same-sex marriage—and a full 74 percent of Americans born after 1981 accept it.[49] Homosexual marriage is now fully legal not only in the United States, but also in many nations around the world, including Argentina, Uruguay, Canada, the Netherlands, New Zealand, South Africa, Norway, the United Kingdom, and Spain. The fact that homophobia can reduce so dramatically in but one generation here in Southern California (between my own generation and that of my children's), and the fact that most Americans now accept homosexual marriage when only two or three decades ago such a phenomenon would be legally impossible and culturally unthinkable, and the fact that in many societies around the world homosexuals enjoy the same legal and civil rights as heterosexuals, when their existence would have constituted a capital crime in centuries past, and the additional fact that we have extensive evidence of various forms of homosexuality being accepted by certain cultures throughout history, going back thousands of years—all of this speaks to the ultimately socially constructed nature of homophobia. It is something socially and culturally learned, not inborn.

Homophobia entails hostile or negative feelings toward gays and lesbians, which often result in unjust legal sanctions and violent actions that produce real pain, distress, and death, causing men, women, and children to needlessly suffer. It is thus immoral—and it is largely the result of immoral socialization and internalization.

When considering many immoral orientations and related actions—including racism and homophobia, violence against animals, female genital mutilation, destruction of the environment, and so on—we know that people can be taught to accept such immoralities, to absorb the ethical norms and values of those around them, and to replicate them through their own internalization and subsequent socialization of the next generation.

But no discussion of internalization's relation to immorality would be complete without some discussion of one of its most potently deleterious manifestations: shame.

Shame

Three nations with markedly high rates of gang membership, gang violence, and gang-related murder are Guatemala, El Salvador, and Honduras. And that's exactly why sociologist Robert Brennan spent several years in those countries: to understand the men and women involved in such a violent, precarious life. During numerous trips, and while also working as a Mennonite volunteer, Dr. Brennan got to know hundreds of people involved with or working with gangs—members, ex-members, police officers, social workers, social activists, priests, ministers, etc. He took extensive field notes on what he observed and also conducted in-depth interviews with nearly a hundred men and women, learning about various aspects of gang-related violence in Central America. Many of the people he got to know personally had been involved in all kinds of violent activity, from murder on down. In trying to explain such pervasive violence, he found numerous factors at play: widespread poverty and lack of opportunity, weak/counterproductive governmental policies, poor schools, and dysfunctional families. But one common factor that emerged again and again was shame.

Consider the illustrative case of "Pancho." At twenty-three, with most of his body covered by tattoos, Pancho is now an ex-gang member who works full-time with other people trying to exit gang life. But for many years—starting when he was just fourteen—Pancho was a member of the MS-13 gang, in which he engaged in regular immoral behavior: causing pain, loss, and suffering to numerous victims. And according to Brennan's analysis, internalized shame was the core factor at play. In a nutshell, Pancho, who didn't know anything of his absentee father, was rejected by his mother when he was five and subsequently left to be cared for by his ill grandmother and an alcoholic, abusive uncle. A virtual orphan in a society that prizes the sanctity of the family, and with little to no support educationally, Pancho soon gravitated toward gang life. And the shame that gnawed within him—the shame of being unwanted and unloved, the shame of being uneducated and unskilled—made such a gravitation understandable. As Dr. Brennan extrapolates:

> Reports from ex-gang members share a common element—the profound experience of shame . . . although Pancho uses the term "suffering" to describe his early experiences of abandonment and abuse . . . it is clear that

> shame is at the heart of this suffering. He uses the term "stigma" three times during the course of the interview . . . That Pancho is in fact describing a first-hand experience of shame seems clear among other things from the fact that at multiple points in the interview, always when describing his family experience, he finds himself weeping or pausing in order to control his emotion. Even today Pancho has trouble coming to grips with the pain of being singled out for abandonment by his mother. After all, his siblings were not similarly abandoned. "Maybe I was the ugliest of my mother's children, I don't know, but she was embarrassed by me," he recalled.[50]

Shame, as sociologist Arlene Stein describes, "is a judgement against the self, a feeling that one is bad, defective, incompetent, inadequate, weak, unlovable, or disgusting."[51] And the thing about such shame is that it can sometimes germinate into angry and violent manifestations. As sociologist Thomas Scheff has extensively argued, while experiences of mild shame are a common element within all ongoing human interactions, individuals who experience deep shame—and also happen to be socially disadvantaged—can try to hide or bury the pain of their shame by, in effect, shaming others.[52] That is, people feeling badly about themselves can sometimes try to cope with such negative feelings pathologically by acting out and shaming, hurting, or harming other people. The toxic dangerous dynamic: shame felt inward becomes anger directed outward.[53]

According to American psychiatrist James Gilligan—the former director of the Harvard Institute of Law and Psychiatry who has worked for decades with violent prisoners—shame is the underlying "pathogen" that causes violent behavior. As he explains, "the more a person is shamed by others, from childhood by parents or peers who ridicule or reject him, the more he is likely to feel chronically shamed, and hypersensitive to feelings and experiences of being shamed . . . such people . . . are the rule among the violent."[54]

Again, this dynamic is empirically borne out. And rather than restate a long string of specific studies and their specific methods and findings attesting to shame's relation to immoral feelings and actions, I'll simply summarize the work of June Price Tangney, Jeff Stuewig, and Debra Mashek, professors of psychology from George Mason University and Harvey Mudd College; in their comprehensive analysis "Moral Emotions and Moral Behavior," published in the top-ranked scholarly journal *Annual Review of Psychology*, they cite numerous studies from over the course of four decades showing that:

- Feelings of shame thwart and disrupt individuals' ability to experience empathy and to form and maintain empathetic connections with others.
- The link between feeling shame and experiencing/expressing anger, hostility, and rage is robust.
- Individuals who contend with shame are more likely to express anger in destructive ways, including both verbal and physical aggression.

In short, according to Tangney, Stuewig, and Mashek, "shame and anger go hand in hand. Desperate to escape painful feelings of shame, shamed individuals are apt to turn the tables defensively, externalizing blame and anger outward onto a convenient scapegoat. Blaming others may help individuals regain some sense of control and superiority in their life, but the long-term costs are often steep."[55]

Steep indeed—and obviously not just for the individual experiencing the shame, but for those on the receiving end of their anger and rage, to be sure.

Understanding Is Not Excusing

In the fall of 2017, my wife and I were hiking at a national park just outside of Santa Fe, New Mexico. It was a deeply beautiful day: the sky was clear and blue, the temperature hovered around the midsixties, the landscape was psychedelically stunning. Stacy and I enjoyed easy conversation, and the lunch we packed featured crackers, cheese, and fig jam. And apples.

There were quite a few hikers out that day, all navigating a single thin trail that led up to the lookout point and then back down again. No loop. So you had people coming up and coming down the same narrow path in a fairly steady stream. Most said a friendly hello as they passed us by. Some politely nodded. Others ignored us if they were deep in conversation or dealing with a kid. As we were halfway down our descent, we could hear a young man's voice echoing throughout the valley from down below. He was talking loudly to his friends, guffawing and hooting and using a lot of expletives. He soon came into view: a tall white guy, shirtless, around twenty-two years old. And we noticed that as he trekked upward, he would say obnoxious things to the various hikers that passed by him on their way down. Annoying things. Stupid things. Subtle digs that made his friends smirk. For example, he would comment on people's slowness, appearance, or attire. As he got close to us, he said that my hat looked like a train engineer's hat, and he then proceeded to yell "toot-toot!" really loudly, chuckling derisively as he walked past us. Yeah, really juvenile shit. But because of his age and his stature, it was also a bit menacing. And then we could hear him starting in on the next pair of hikers after us as he proceeded along the trail.

That was the extent of our interaction with this young man. And although it was exceedingly brief, one thing was clear: he felt quite badly about himself, and he was compensating for this by making everyone else on the hiking trail feel badly, too. It was so patently obvious. This was not a comfortable, confident, or happy-go-lucky young man making lighthearted comments on a sunny day. Rather, this was someone wounded, or insecure, or full of shame or bitterness, who couldn't help but blast those inner feelings outward in the shape of caustic comments, boisterous banter, and ever-so-menacing bravado.

His behavior was disruptive and annoying at best, and made others feel uncomfortable or threatened at worst. As such, it was to be condemned. And while his comments and malevolent posturing alone obviously shouldn't warrant any kind of arrest, if he were to take it to the next level—if he were to threaten someone or throw something at someone or punch someone or worse—then, yes, he ought to be stopped. Hindered. Arrested. Whatever it takes to keep him from harming others.

But here's the deal: there's a difference between judging or excusing this young man and trying to explain and understand his behavior. These are two very different enterprises altogether. And this chapter has been primarily concerned with understanding and explaining immorality. Not excusing it.

This difference between excusing versus explaining must be stressed because there is a tendency for some people to assume that any explanation of immorality is an automatic attempt to pardon, accept, or even exculpate it. But that's not the case. While I think I understand what compelled that young man on the hiking trail to behave like an asshole—he felt badly about himself—in recognizing this, I make no excuses for him. Or for the killers of Reuben Stacy. Or for the man who murdered by high school friend Teak. To excuse, forgive, judge, condemn—these are personal responses. And they don't do much in terms of addressing root causes, ameliorating damaging behavior, or decreasing immoral behavior. In order to do that, the only path to take is that of understanding and explaining.

That's why the whole point of this chapter has been to account for immorality in its most concentrated form: the willful harming of others. To try to understand how humans—who evolved in a small group context that required and fostered communal proclivities, who are nurtured by parental figures when helpless infants, who have brains that facilitate prosocial feelings and attitudes, and who are generally socialized by other people to live cooperatively—can still sometimes act in ways so as to volitionally cause others to suffer.

Various explanations have been offered that help to understand manifestations of immorality in certain individuals, such as damaged or compromised neural capacities, childhood abuse and neglect, weak or interrupted parent-child attachment, immoral socialization, and internalized shame. But, of course, no single factor causes all individuals who experience any of them to act immorally. Nor does every individual who experiences any of these factors automatically go on to become immoral. Rather, the point is that each of these factors is highly correlated with certain forms of immorality. They are phenomena that significantly increase the likelihood or probability of an individual's moral compass being damaged. And when occurring together, their effect is compounded.

Admittedly, I have not explained or accounted for immorality in its entirety. Rather, I've offered partial, fragmentary explanations. Abnormalities in the brain do explain some instances of immorality. But only some. Childhood abuse and neglect explain some more, but surely not all. Disrupted child-parent attachment explains but a bit more. Immoral socialization a bit more. Internalized shame a little bit more. And taken together, all of these factors account for many—and perhaps even most—instances of individual immorality. But they are not complete answers. Humans are far too complex, far too diverse, far too malleable, and driven by far too many factors—genetic, hereditary, psychological, cultural, sociological, economic—to allow any broad aspect of their behavior to be accounted for completely, comprehensively, and with absolute surety.

Finally, it must be acknowledged that the factors that increase the likelihood of individual immorality discussed in this chapter most definitely do not constitute all possibilities. Many additional factors surely play their part in deleteriously chipping away at people's ability to be moral: sexual abuse, nutritional deficits, hormonal differences, material scarcity or existential threat, access to firearms, abuse of alcohol and other drugs, and so on.

What has yet to be addressed, however, is perhaps the most dangerous and damaging form of human immorality of all: the group kind. That is, while individuals acting immorally can certainly cause heaps of pain and suffering, when large groups, communities, or entire nations come together to collectively coordinate the willful harming of others, the results are truly catastrophic.

Genocide.

Any secular understanding of morality, or any secular humanist belief in the underlying goodness of people, must confront this worst form of immorality head on.

10

A Genocidal Century

Dovey grew up in a small Armenian community in the city of Diyarbakir, in what is today southeastern Turkey. In July 1915, when Dovey was a teenager, her village was beset by Turkish soldiers who began harassing, arresting, and killing Armenians. One night, her father was brutally murdered by soldiers who nailed horseshoes to his bare feet, drove iron spikes through his hands onto wooden boards, and ripped off his genitals. After that night, Dovey was told to stay indoors. And she diligently did, along with her mother and siblings. But one day, in need of some food and household supplies, she ventured out and headed to a nearby town square. When she got there, the happenings she came upon were truly horrific: about fifteen or twenty Armenian women were standing in a circle, having been herded together by Turkish soldiers. As the people of the town looked on, the soldiers began ordering the women to dance. At the first signs of hesitation, the soldiers took out whips and began whipping the women, shouting louder for them to dance. As the whips began shredding the women's clothes, cutting into their backs, breasts, legs, faces, and heads, they quickly became covered in blood. The women's children stood by, gaping in terror, along with many other children who had been rounded up from a nearby Armenian school to be forced to watch. The soldiers then ordered all the children to clap while their mothers danced under the blows of the whips. Children who didn't clap—or didn't clap fast enough—were whipped. And then, as Dovey recalls:

> Two soldiers pushed through the crowd swinging wooden buckets and began to douse the women with the fluid in the buckets, and, in a second, I could smell that it was kerosene. And the women screamed because the kerosene was burning their lacerations and cuts. Another soldier came forward with a torch and lit each woman by the hair . . . I could see the fire growing off the women's bodies, and their screaming became unbearable. The children were being whipped now furiously, as if the sight of the burning mothers had excited the soldiers, and they admonished the children to clap "faster, faster, faster" . . . as the women began to collapse in burning heaps, oozing and black, the smell of burnt flesh made me sick. I fainted . . .[1]

What Dovey witnessed constitutes merely one horrific atrocity—among thousands of similar atrocities—that was part of the twentieth century's first genocide: the systematic killing, starting in 1915, of between one and one and a half million Armenians at the hands of the Turks. The slaughter was premeditated, well-planned, ordered by those in power, and carried out by soldiers, police, and others sympathetic to the cause of ridding Muslim Turkey of its Christian Armenian residents.

The genocide occurred in stages. Initially, Armenian clerics, writers, journalists, teachers, jurists, and community leaders were arrested and killed. Anti-Armenian sentiment was stirred up in the press. Then Armenian villagers were forced to relinquish any guns that they possessed. Next, able-bodied Armenian men were drafted into special labor units and sent off to be worked, starved, and beaten to death. Finally, remaining men, women, the elderly, and children were forced to march in groups toward Syria, often over treacherous mountain passes as well as rugged, parched terrain in sweltering temperatures. And along the way, they were beaten, tortured, raped, starved, and eventually slaughtered. Much of this killing in the wilderness was carried out by members of the "Special Organization" established by the Turkish government and led by officers of the Ottoman Military Academy, which consisted of small units of violent convicts who were let out of prison for the sole purpose of annihilating caravans of helpless Armenians.[2]

British, American, and German individuals—ambassadors, missionaries, and journalists—who were in Turkey, Syria, and Armenia during the genocide provided numerous eyewitness accounts of the widespread brutality. They compiled extensive dossiers and reports on what they saw and heard, and the gruesomeness is chilling: piles of bodies of raped and mutilated women, disfigured corpses with their fingernails and toenails ripped out, and roads littered with children's hacked-off hands.[3]

By 1923, nearly half of the Armenian people had been annihilated.[4]

What Jan Karski Witnessed

Less than twenty years later, German soldiers found that forcing Jewish men, women, and children out into the woods and then shooting them wasn't ideal. For one thing, blood, bone, and pieces of brain tended to splatter back onto the German soldiers. For another, it could be unpleasant having to shoot so many families in such close proximity. But such mass shootings were nonetheless frequently employed by the Nazis during the Holocaust; for example, on September 29 and 30, 1941, they shot nearly thirty-four thousand Jewish people in the woods outside of Kiev. Nazi leaders, however, grew increasingly troubled by the psychological distress this type of killing had on their men; such mass shooting occasionally caused them to feel nauseated. So, they tried a different method: vans. The Germans would pack Jewish families inside vans and then fit a tube to redirect the exhaust back into the interior, killing everyone with carbon monoxide. Such vans killed thousands throughout Eastern Europe, but they also had drawbacks: you could only fit so many people into the vans, the process was relatively slow, and the prolonged screaming of the victims could be disturbing.

And so, the Nazis eventually built their industrialized extermination camps, where large numbers of Jews could be delivered by train, unloaded, and efficiently killed in expansive gas chambers. Approximately one million Jews were thus murdered at Auschwitz, between 700,000 and 900,000 at Treblinka, between 400,000 and 500,000 at Bełżec, some 250,000 at Sobibór, and between 150,000 and 200,000 at Chełmno.

As all of this extermination was taking place, the hunted Jews of Europe were desperate for help, and they had a difficult time getting people to even believe what was happening to them. Thus, some leaders within Europe's rapidly dwindling Jewish ghettos had the idea that it would a require a non-Jew's firsthand testimony to convince the wider world about their dire fate. And that's where Jan Karski came in.

Jan Karski was a young Pole who, in the early 1940s, worked as part of the Polish resistance against Germany. Being sympathetic to the suffering of the Jews, he courageously risked his life serving as a witness and reporting what he saw to the Allied leaders.

One day in 1942, after various bribes and machinations, Karski was outfitted with a guard's uniform and joined in with a group of Germans, "helping" them with their work near a transportation center close to the Bełżec extermination camp in southeastern Poland. He watched as Jewish families were being corralled near waiting trains. When a group of Jews started panicking, he witnessed a German officer pull out his gun and fire randomly into the crowd, killing several. Then guards began shoving Jews into train cars. They packed in hundreds of people. And then more. Shouting, beating, and shooting them, they forced even more in. And then they slammed the doors of the train cars shut.

As Karski recounts:

> The floors of the car had been covered with a thick, white powder. It was quicklime. Quicklime is simply unslaked lime or calcium oxide that has been dehydrated. Anyone who has seen cement being mixed knows what occurs when water is poured on lime. The mixture bubbles and steams as the powder combines with the water, generating a large amount of heat.
>
> Here . . . the moist flesh coming in contact with the lime is rapidly de-

> hydrated and burned. The occupants of the cars would be literally burned to death before long, the flesh eaten from their bones . . . it took three hours to fill up the entire train by repetitions of this procedure. It was twilight when all the forty-six (I counted them) cars were packed . . . from one end to the other, the train, with its quivering cargo of flesh, seemed to throb, vibrate, rock, and jump as if bewitched. There would be a strangely uniform momentary lull and then, again, the train would begin to moan and sob, wail and howl . . .
>
> In the now quiet camp the only sounds were the inhuman screams that were echoes from the moving train. Then these, too, ceased. All that was left was the stench of excrement and rotting straw and a queer, sickening acidulous odor that, I thought, may have come from the quantities of blood that had been let, and with which the ground was stained.[5]

After witnessing this and other similar horrifying scenes, Karski set out to tell the world. As he was leaving Germany, he made a stop in Berlin, paying a visit to an old schoolmate of his, a German named Rudolph Strauch. During dinner with Rudolph and his family, talk of the war was dominant. So too was the Strauchs' hatred of Jews.

> Rudolph and his sister gave vent to all the common Nazi remarks on the subject. I made an effort to pierce their thick skins by describing, in an offhand, neutral fashion, the most abominable and revolting of the practices I had witnessed, the death train, the quicklime . . . their reactions were cool and detached, betraying not the slightest trace of physical, let alone moral, repulsion. Rudolph commented:
>
> "Very efficient. The Jewish corpses will not be allowed to spread disease as they did in life."[6]

Between 1939 and 1945, Hitler himself did not kill any Jews. That job was left to his adoring followers, sadistic anti-Semites, and those prone to dutifully following orders. The extermination of nearly six million people requires the willing cooperation and concerted participation of hundreds of thousands of individuals, as well as the supporting hatred of millions more[7]—average men and women, like Rudolph Strauch and his sister, utterly numb to the savage murder of men, women, and children. Actually, even quite happy about it.

Sole Survivor

Thirty years after the Holocaust, Ronnie Yimsut was thirteen years old as the Khmer Rouge took over his country of Cambodia. It was 1975.

Led by nationalist Communist dictator Pol Pot, the Khmer Rouge wanted to "purify" Cambodia, forcibly ridding the nation of any institutions or citizens tainted by foreign culture, non-Cambodian ethnicity, capitalist ideologies, imperialism, religion, science, or higher education. Urbanites were specifically regarded as enemies. Upon their military occupation of Cambodia's capital, Phnom Penh, the Khmer Rouge expelled at gunpoint approximately two million of its residents out of the city and into the countryside, to live as peasants, work in labor camps, and be "reeducated." All other urban centers throughout the country were similarly liquidated. And for the next few years, millions of Cambodians were beaten, starved to death, and executed.

Ronnie Yimsut and his family lived in the town of Siem Reap in the north of the country, above Cambodia's largest lake, Tonle Sap. When the Khmer Rouge arrived, he and all of his relatives were forcibly marched out into the countryside to work on collective farms. They were regularly relocated to different camps, so during the last days of 1977, when they were told that they were being relocated yet again to a new camp near Tonle Sap, in order to catch fish for the government, they did as they were told.

Along with about eighty other people, including many members of his family, Yimsut was ordered to march on a muddy road. As they trudged on for several hours, everyone's fears began to fester: you never knew if you were indeed going off to work, or rather if you were being taken away to be killed.

It was around 7:00 p.m. when the captive men in the group were separated from everyone else and taken away. Women wept at the departure of their husbands, uncles, and brothers. Children cried as a result of their fear, hunger, and the attacking mosquitos. Everyone was then led about three hundred yards off of the muddy road and told to sit down. And then, about fifty people—armed with guns and large clubs—suddenly came out from behind the trees. Everyone began pleading for their lives. To no avail.

As Yimsut recalls:

> I was beyond horrified when I heard the clobbering begin . . . Oum's elderly father was next to me and his upper torso contracted several times before he fell on me. At that moment, I noticed a small boy who I knew well get up and start to call for his mother. Suddenly there was a warm splash on my face and body. I knew it was definitely not mud—it was the little boy's blood, perhaps his brain tissue scattering from the impact . . . everything seemed to happen in slow motion . . . the first blow came when I was lying face down to the ground with a corpse partially covering my lower back . . . the next one hit me just above my neck on the right side of my head. I believe it was the one that knocked me out . . .
>
> The faint light of a new dawn broke through the sky, revealing my shriveled, blood-soaked body in the mud. It must have been about 4 or 5 o'clock in the morning, January 1, 1978 . . .
>
> I wanted to look around for my relatives, but was unable to turn around. My neck was stiff with pain. My head hurt—oh how it hurt so badly. I could only feel around with my two hands. Everywhere I touched was cold flesh . . . I cried my heart out when I recognized a few dead bodies next to me, one of which was Oum and her unborn child . . . her elderly father and her two sisters were all piled on top of each other . . . I could not go on. My cries turned to sobs . . . I passed out on top of the dead bodies. I was totally out cold.[8]

Yimsut was the only survivor of the slaughter. He eventually made his way to a refugee camp near Thailand.

In all, from 1975 to 1978, the Khmer Rouge was responsible for the deaths of between 1.7 and 1.9 million people—approximately 22 percent of Cambodia's total population.[9] And just as in the earlier genocides of Armenians and Jews, the killing of Cambodians was characterized by egregious sadism; eyewitness accounts describe not only frequent rape and mutilation of victims, but mass killings in which babies were held by their feet as their heads were swung against palm trees, their limp bodies then being tossed onto their dying mothers.[10]

In the Marshes

About fifteen years after Vietnamese soldiers invaded Cambodia in December of 1978, putting an end to the Cambodian genocide, Jeannette Ayinkamiye was an eleven-year-old girl living in Rwanda. Her world quickly descended into unimaginable horror when, on April 6, 1994, the plane carrying Rwandan president Juvénal Habyarimana crashed. His death plunged Rwanda into a frenzied, murderous chaos in which ethnic Hutus—using machetes, clubs, and guns—killed approximately eight hundred thousand ethnic Tutsis and moderate Hutus in a matter of months.

For centuries, the minority Tutsis, who traditionally raised cattle, and the majority Hutus, who traditionally tilled the land as field laborers, lived peacefully side by side. Germany first took over the region in the late 1800s, and then, after World War I, Belgium became the occupying colonial power. In a classic divide-and-conquer strategy, the Belgians favored the Tutsis over the Hutus, granting the former higher positions in politics, businesses, churches, and the educational system. Such actions successfully created caste-based tension and envy between the two ethnic groups, which were reified by the dissemination, in the 1930s, of government-issued identification cards that bore each individual's ethic identity.

Violent conflicts periodically erupted between the peoples, both before and after 1962, when Rwanda was granted independence from Belgium. In 1973, Major General Juvénal Habyarimana—a moderate Hutu—became the head of state. With political and military hostilities between Tutsis and Hutus continuing throughout the 1980s, Habyarimana, in 1993, signed an official agreement that would give more political power to the Tutsis. This move toward power-sharing angered the more militant, nationalistic Hutus in the country. And when Habyarimana's plane was shot down on April 6, 1994, many suspected it was the militant Hutus who were responsible.

Prior to the downing of Habyarimana's plane, Hutu nationalists had been planning to murder their Tutsi countrymen for some time. Shipments of machetes had been pouring into the country for months, and Hutu-run radio stations had long been prepared to issue various code words and declarations that gave armed Hutus instructions on when and where to start killing. And thus, it began: within an hour of the downing of Habyarimana's plane, various branches of the Hutu military and their associates, particularly the Interahamwe—which means "those who attack together"—took over. They set up roadblocks and barricades everywhere and conducted house-by-house searches, slaughtering Tutsi men, women, and children, as well as moderate Hutus who were sympathetic to the Tutsis. Those Tutsis who sought safety in churches were unfortunate; such safe havens, once packed with fearful Tutsis, were shot up and set ablaze. In the countryside, Hutu villagers turned on their Tutsi neighbors, killing them without mercy upon the orders of their Hutu leaders.

Rape was systematically employed by the Hutu militants and the Interahamwe as a means to terrorize and humiliate the Tutsis. In fact, hundreds of AIDS-infected Hutu inmates were released from prison by the militant Hutus and grouped into "rape squads," with the mission of raping as many Tutsi women as possible, thereby infecting them with the HIV virus.[11]

Young Jeannette Ayinkamiye survived all of this hell, but just barely. Her father was killed on the first day of the genocide. Her seven brothers were all killed shortly after. She and her two little sisters, along with their mother, managed to evade their Hutu neighbors and flee into the marshes outside of their village. They survived in the marshes together for over a month: during the day, they would lie in thick mud, hiding underneath papyrus fronds. At night, they would wander among abandoned houses in search of food or a place to sleep.

And then, as Jeannette recalls:

> One day the *interahamwe* unearthed Mama beneath the papyrus. She stood up; she offered them money to kill her with a single machete blow. They stripped her to take the money . . . They chopped her arms off first, then her legs . . .
>
> My two little sisters saw everything because they were lying beside her. They were struck too: Vanessa on the ankles, Marie-Claire on the head. The killers did not cut them completely to pieces. Perhaps because they were in a hurry, perhaps they did it on purpose, as with Mama. I myself only heard the noises and screams, because I was concealed in a hole nearby. When the *interahamwe* had gone, I came out and gave Mama a taste of water.
>
> The first evening she could still speak . . . she was suffering greatly from the cuttings . . . I did not dare spend the night with her. I first had to take care of my little sisters, who were badly hurt but not dying . . .
>
> Mama lay in agony for three days before dying at last. On the second day, she could only whisper, "Goodbye, children," and ask for water . . . on the third day, she could no longer swallow, only moan a few little words, and look around. She never closed her eyes again.[12]

Jeannette and her little sisters survived by continuing to hide in the marshes. They were among the approximately 30 percent of Rwandan Tutsis who survived the genocide.

Even More

As painful and unpleasant as this brief journey through the best-known genocides of the twentieth century has been, it does not constitute a comprehensive account of the ghastly pain and suffering inflicted by humans upon other humans in the previous one hundred years. Additional manifestations of large-scale, nationally imposed, state-sanctioned, or societally enacted immorality against civilians during the twentieth century also include:

- The Herero and Nama: Between 1904 and 1907, the German colonizers in Southern Africa occupying what is today Namibia killed tens of thousands of indigenous Africans of the Herero and Nama tribes.[13]

- The Pontic genocide: Between 1914 and 1922, somewhere between 450,000 and 750,000 Christian Greeks in Anatolia were massacred by the Turks.[14]
- Stalin's famine: Between 1930 and 1933, rapid industrialization and the official Soviet policy of collectivization, in which land and livestock were forcibly handed over to the state, caused an estimated 5.7 million people to die from malnutrition and starvation.[15] The Soviet regions most affected included the Ukraine, the Volga region, and Kazakhstan; nearly 40 percent of all Kazakhs died in the famine as a direct result of Soviet policy.[16]
- Japanese massacre of Nanjing: After invading the Chinese city of Nanjing on December 13, 1937, the Imperial Japanese Army spent six weeks raping thousands of women and murdering somewhere between 40,000 and 300,000 people.[17]
- Mao's famine: Between 1959 and 1961, a combination of Mao's communist policies of forced collectivization, governmental mismanagement of the economy, drought, and unfavorable weather conditions caused somewhere between 15 and 30 million Chinese people to die from malnutrition and starvation.[18]
- Bangladesh: Beginning in March of 1971, as the Bengali people began fighting for their independence, the Pakistani military, along with allied Islamic militias, raped between 200,000 and 400,000 women and killed somewhere between 1 and 3 million people.[19]
- Bosnia and Herzegovina: After the death of Yugoslavian leader Josip Tito, the Balkans descended into fighting along long-simmering nationalistic and ethno-religious lines. Bosnian Muslims suffered the worst of the violence: between 1992 and 1995, somewhere between 10,000 and 20,000 Bosnian Muslim women were raped and approximately 100,000 Bosnian Muslim civilians were killed.[20]

And there are still more bouts of murderous inhumanity that occurred in the twentieth century, including the slaughter of hundreds of thousands of indigenous people in Cyrenaica, Libya, by the Italians in the 1920s and 1930s; the killing of hundreds of thousands of Roma by the Nazis during World War II; the forced roundup, deportation, and killing of hundreds of thousands of Chechen and Ingush peoples by the Soviets in 1944; the annihilation of hundreds of thousands of civilians in Hiroshima and Nagasaki by the United States in 1945; the raping, torturing, and killing of hundreds of thousands of people in East Timor at the hands of the Indonesian military during the 1970s; the killing of tens of thousands of Kurds in the late 1980s during the Iran-Iraq War; and the killing of tens of thousands of Mayans in Guatemala in the 1980s.

And still more recently: Darfur, Yemen, Syria, the Yazidis, and the Rohingya.

It's a truly wretched reality. So much brutal inhumanity, barbarism, and savagery. So much pain and suffering en masse. And all in just one century. The mere writing of these past few pages, and the research that went into them, left me queasy and depressed. It's enough to crush anyone's faith in humanity.

So much for progress, right?

In fact, it is just this wretched depravity—approximately sixty million people killed via genocide in the twentieth century[21]—that leads many folks to ardently place their faith in God, given humanity's clear capacity for so much violence and destruction on such a colossal scale.

Responding to the Good Rabbi

And that's exactly the pious position taken by a thoughtful, well-published rabbi who wrote to me a few years ago about my outspoken views on secularism and religion. In a nutshell, the rabbi argued that a secular humanist orientation was not only misguided but potentially dangerous. His reasoning? Look at the genocides of the twentieth century. Clearly, they evidence our deep, intractable inhumanity. Given such wanton savagery, placing hope in humans to do the right thing is wrongheaded. Only God—according to the rabbi—can ensure peace, justice, and goodwill on planet Earth. We cannot rely on ourselves to live morally. We need God.

My response included the following:

First off, a "need" for God does not establish God's existence. Only evidence can do that, and it is sorely lacking.

Second, if humans wantonly causing other humans to suffer and die is a reason to abandon faith in humanity, then God wantonly causing humans to suffer and die should similarly be a cause to abandon faith in Him. That is, even if enough incontrovertible evidence were to emerge proving God's existence, then he would still need to be rejected as a source of morality or justice, given all the wanton torture and death he is responsible for on planet Earth. For example, according to statistics provided by the Wellcome Trust, a British charity devoted to human health, between the years 1900 and 2000, God caused far more unnecessary and painful death than any humans did.[22] Consider:

- Deaths caused by respiratory infection: 485 million
- Deaths caused by smallpox: 400 million
- Deaths caused by diarrhea: 226 million
- Deaths caused by malaria: 194 million
- Deaths caused by tuberculosis: 100 million
- Deaths caused by natural disasters (volcanoes, earthquakes, etc.): 24 million
- Deaths caused by snakes: 6 million.

In other words, God—through his own deliberate creation of things like volcanoes, malaria, smallpox, diarrhea-causing bacteria, and poisonous snakes—intentionally caused way more pain, suffering, and untimely death in the twentieth century than Hitler, Stalin, Mao, Pol Pot, the Interahamwe, and every other genocidal campaign combined and multiplied fivefold. Does humanity really "need" such a deity?

Third, during every genocide in the twentieth century, millions and millions of people—from Armenia to Poland, Guatemala to Rwanda, and the Ukraine to Nanjing—prayed desperately to God for help, protection, deliverance. And yet God didn't help, protect, or deliver them, so he doesn't appear all that efficacious. To "turn to" or "rely" on such an ineffectual, indifferent deity is, at best, futile.

Fourth, religion often made the genocides of the twentieth century worse. For example, with the Turkish killings of Greeks and Armenians, or the Nazi slaughter of Jews, or the Serbian massacre of Bosnian Muslims, religion was a prominently propelling factor in the genocide rather than an ethical counterweight against it. And when it comes to the Nazis specifically, let's not forget that most of the Nazi leaders were raised in Christian homes; most Nazi leaders—including Hitler—made regular references to God in their writings and speeches; Hitler advocated for religious instruction in schools, believing that without it, children couldn't develop virtuous character; Nazi slogans and oaths explicitly included declarations of faith in God; in whichever countries the Nazis invaded, it was the more religious political factions that embraced and supported them; after the war, it was the Catholic Church that aided and abetted the escape of Nazis to South America.[23] No, we cannot simply ignore the role of religion—nor can we blame secularism—when it comes to the genocides of the twentieth century.

The fact is that religion itself is often an underlying historical source of animosity that feeds genocidal tendencies.[24] As American professor of psychology—and genocide expert—James Waller explains, "most religious belief systems are, by their very nature, ethnocentric and, in the extreme, may even foster a devaluing effect on the human life that falls outside the veil of the faithful. They distinguish all too clearly between 'us' and 'them.'"[25]

In sum, while many religions preach an ethic of peace and love, and while many religious people are motivated by their religious faith to act compassionately and altruistically, the tribal nature of religious communal bonding and spiritual group identity often overshadows such positive aspects of religious commitment—for the worse. And while religious faith in God may provide solace and comfort to people while they are in the midst of trying times—even as they frantically squirm in crowded train cars while their children shriek as their small bodies burn against a floor covered in quicklime, or as they lay hidden under papyrus branches as their family members get hacked to pieces by machetes—such faith in God cannot ultimately protect us against the worst manifestations of inhumanity that periodically flare up throughout history.

As the underlying truth of humanism asserts: there is no God to save us from ourselves. No saints, so spirits. It's just us on this planet, and while most of us, most of the time, behave morally, some of us, some of the time, do not. And as large-scale, collective movements of immorality, genocides constitute the very worst that we are capable of visiting upon ourselves.

In order to soberly face immorality on such a massive scale—in order to explain and understand it—we must begin with the knowledge that genocides are not the result of a punitive God being angry with us. Nor are they the unhappy consequences of God granting us "free will," or the result of Satan's wickedness, or witch spells, or bad karma. Such groundless, evidenceless, and downright perverse religious balderdash provides no help, instruction, or insight.

In reality, there's nothing divine or otherworldly about genocide. It is, rather, an unfortunate result of our own natural predilections.

Evolutionary Rub

For the vast majority of our historical existence—approximately 98 percent of our development as a species—we lived in small bands, consisting of about twenty to eighty people, give or take a cousin or two.[26] In these small bands, we foraged, picked, hunted, and fished. And life was seldom secure. As such, we evolved the capacity to cooperate, to understand one another's ideas and emotions, and to respond to each other's worries and fears. To help each other. This is where and how human morality originated.

Over many millennia, those small groups that cooperated well had a much higher chance of survival than those that did not. Greed, deceit, and brutality might help a given individual gain a specific advantage in a specific moment of need, but groups full of cheaters, liars, and thugs didn't do well in the long run.[27] Rather, it was the more moral bands of *Homo sapiens*, characterized by emotional responsiveness to one another, care and concern, sociability and altruism, that lasted longer, fended off predators better, protected their children better, and increased the likelihood of the survival of their offspring, compared to groups lacking beneficial development of such prosocial tendencies.[28]

Because the evolutionary dynamics of humanity fostered and favored small-group cooperation over the course of hundreds of thousands of years, we have an overriding tendency to be moral. It is our evolutionarily derived default setting to care about and respond to the pain and suffering of others, to be helpful, to be empathetic. It is why, right now, the vast majority of people all over the world are not mercilessly harming others, not being willfully immoral.

And yet, the dynamics of our hundreds of thousands of years of evolutionary development that took place within in a small group setting came with a rub.

A raw, nefarious rub.

Simply put: we developed a distinct capacity to favor those within our own group while simultaneously fearing and mistrusting people outside of our group.[29] That is, as we evolved a propensity to be cooperative with those in our own small band, we simultaneously evolved a tendency to suspect and even hate those other small bands of people out there.[30] Especially the ones who might forage or fish where we want to forage or fish. Or the ones that might want our cave or plateau. Or the ones that might possibly rape us or eat us.

Humanity's socioecological reality—for hundreds of thousands of years—was that each small band's greatest threat was not locusts or tigers or piranhas or wolves or hippos but rather other small bands of people. Those other humans just beyond the river or down valley or in the woods or across the savannah were as smart as us, as crafty as us, and their needs were just as dire as ours. And thus, it was other small groups of people that posed the greatest potential dangers. In this long-standing, natural, evolutionary situation, in-group cooperation was essential, and fear, mistrust, and hatred of all out-groups was not merely prudent but often competitively beneficial. As American philosopher Elliott Sober and American biologist David Sloan Wilson explain, our long history of living in small bands "does provide a setting in which helping behavior directed at members of one's own group can evolve; however, it equally provides a context in which hurting individuals in other groups can be selectively advantageous. Group selection favors within-group niceness *and* between-group nastiness."[31] Or as Irish-born American biopsychologist Nigel Barber puts it, the unfortunate flip side of "in-group altruism" is "out-group aggression."[32]

Again, the rub: we evolved an overriding moral orientation, but it was coalitional, strongest among those we considered to be part of our family, our group, our tribe, our people.[33] And thus, our moral orientation has always been shadowed by another evolved part of our nature: fear and distrust of people outside of our circle, strangers seen as threats, or strangers who are merely different—whatever form or shape that difference may take. As American psychology professors Neha Mahajan and Karen Wynn explain, "we engage in acts of great cooperation and support toward those whom we consider to be *like us*, while relations to those we consider to be *other*, or *unlike us* are often characterized by hostility and conflict, including prejudice, political unrest, and even genocide."[34]

This immoral part of our nature is not dominant, but it exists. Even in babies.

Unjust Babies

You may recall from chapter 7 that for many years, Dr. Paul Bloom and his wife/colleague Dr. Karen Wynn have been conducting all kinds of experiments with babies in their Infant Cognition Center at Yale University. By concocting various games and scenarios and then observing babies' subsequent reactions and choices, they have amassed an impressive amount of reliable, replicable evidence showing that babies as young as five months old show a clear and strong preference for fairness, equality, kindness, and helpfulness. They react to moral characters and just behaviors positively, and they react to immoral characters and unjust behaviors negatively.

But that's not the whole story.

There's evidence of a lesser but still pronounced propensity among toddlers: a tendency to favor those perceived as similar and to have less positive feelings for those who are perceived as different. As Professor Bloom explains, "our initial moral sense appears to be biased toward our own kind. There's plenty of research showing that babies have within-group preferences: three-month-olds prefer the faces of the race that is most familiar to them to those of other races; eleven-month-olds prefer individuals who share their own taste in food and expect these individuals to be nicer than those with different tastes; twelve-month-olds prefer to learn from someone who speaks their own language over someone who speaks a foreign language. And studies with young children have found that once they are segregated into different groups—even under the most arbitrary of schemes, like wearing different colored T-shirts—they eagerly favor their own groups in their attitudes and their actions."[35]

One study that Dr. Bloom is referencing here comes from the Infant Cognition Center at Yale in which babies were given a choice between two kinds of cereal. Once their cereal preference was clear, the babies then watched puppets who acted out having to choose between the same two kinds of cereal. Sometimes the puppets picked the kind of cereal that the individual babies liked; sometimes they picked the other cereal option. And then, shortly after, the babies were observed overwhelmingly liking/preferring the puppets that shared their own personal cereal preference. More than that, they seemed to want the puppet with a different cereal preference to be treated worse—less kindly—than the puppet that shared their preferred cereal. Of course, nothing could be more trivial than the kind of cereal a person (or puppet) prefers, and yet in these babies, even such a small thing created an overt bias.[36]

A similar study, also referenced above by Dr. Bloom, comes from American psychology professors Meagan Patterson and Rebecca Bigler, who looked at preschool children and their tendency to show in-group bias.[37] With a sample of eighty-seven children between the ages of three and five, and with the cooperation of a day-care center, they randomly assigned different colored T-shirts (blue or red) to various children, which were to be worn as "work shirts" during various times of the day—during art or outdoor play, for example. In some classes, teachers added additional significance to the colors, like decorating kids' lockers the same color as their randomly assigned T-shirt or verbally labelling some kids as being part of the "red" or "blue" group. In other classrooms, teachers made no additional mention of the colored T-shirts and did nothing to increase their significance. After six weeks, researchers found that—on a host of measures—the children developed notable, significant in-group biases toward children who shared their own T-shirt color. While the biases were stronger when the teachers made the T-shirt colors more significant—indicating how authority figures can increase in-group bias—the bias was still notably present in the classrooms where no additional significance was made of the different colors. This suggests that even small children tend to favor "their own," even when that is based on something as random and trivial as T-shirt color.

In-Group Favoritism, Out-Group Antipathy

This natural proclivity to favor one's own group—and feel or behave negatively toward outsiders—is not something found only in babies or preschoolers. Social psychologists have long observed it in teenagers and adults, as well.

Perhaps the most famous initial study attesting to our in-group favoritism—and concomitant out-group antipathy—is the Robbers Cave Experiment, conducted by Turkish American professor Muzafer Sherif back in the 1950s.[38] Here's what Sherif and his colleagues did: They went to a summer camp for boys in Oklahoma and, posing as camp staff members, randomly divided up twenty-two eleven- and twelve-year-old boys who didn't know each other and were demographically similar. The two groups of boys were initially separated on the two-hundred-acre campsite. Each group—without knowledge of the other group's existence—named themselves and did a bunch of group-strengthening activities. Then, during the next week, the groups were pitted against each other in a series of sports activities and other competitions. Additional situations were created in which one group lost at the expense of the other—like one group arriving late to a picnic to find that the other group had eaten all the food. A clear and present animosity quickly emerged between the two groups, which became more apparent and more toxic each day. It started with taunting and name-calling between the two sets of boys and escalated to the vandalizing of cabins, burning of each other's flags, stealing of each other's belongings, etc.

At this summer camp in Oklahoma, both in-group bonding and out-group antipathy were quick to congeal. Of course, we may be justly critical of such early studies like the Robbers Cave Experiment—or the famous 1971 Stanford Prison Experiment conducted by Philip Zimbardo—because of the manifestly manipulated nature of the setup and the fact that the researchers themselves played such active roles in how things went down. Indeed, at Stanford, it was Dr. Zimbardo himself who played the role of the warden, commanding the undergrads to act sadistically in their role as guards.

But over the course of half a century, numerous studies have been conducted in much less manipulated, more scientifically controlled contexts that all reveal the same thing: we tend to favor those we consider "us," often at the expense of those we consider "them." And again, this in-group/out-group distinction can be based on the most trivial of differences.

My favorite example along these lines comes from the research of Polish British social psychologist Henri Tajfel. In Dr. Tajfel's experiment, demographically similar teenage boys were divided into two groups randomly, by the flip of a coin. They were then shown various slides of modern art and told that some paintings were by the artist Paul Klee and others by the artist Wassily Kandinsky. They were then asked which artist's work they preferred. Next, they were told that all the participating boys had been separated into groups based on which artist's work they liked best. And this was all random, of course: the boys weren't actually arranged as such, and their preferences didn't even actually match to Klee or Kandinsky. But no matter: all that the boys knew was that some boys shared their art preferences and others did not. Keep in mind that all of the boys had no contact with one another—neither with boys who shared their art preferences nor those that did not—during the entire experiment. And what was the result? Clear in-group bias. The boys rated members of their own group as more pleasant and better workers, and then, when the boys were given a chance to allocate small amounts of money to every boy who participated in the study as compensation for their time, they rewarded those who they thought shared their art preferences significantly more than those they thought did not.[39]

Similar findings have been replicated in dozens of similar studies.[40]

What all of this research indicates is that we possess an instinctive predisposition to feel better toward those we think are part of our group and feel worse toward those we think are not. As South African scientist Lyall Watson argues in his book *Dark Nature: A Natural History of Evil*, the proclivity to divide up the world into camps of "us" and "them" is a human universal, and this predisposition influences how we act morally: we tend to be more empathetic and compassionate toward "us" and less so toward "them."[41]

How Genocide Happens

But how do we go from an in-group bias all the way to genocide? How do we go from babies in a lab at Yale preferring puppets who share their taste in cereal, or preschoolers who exhibit more favorable feelings toward those who have the same colored T-shirts, or teenage boys who allocate more money to those who share their presumed taste in art to gassing a million men, women, and children at Auschwitz? Or to the coordinated raping and killing of eight hundred thousand Tutsis? Or the government-orchestrated starving to death of 40 percent of the entire population of Kazakhstan? Isn't this all quite a stretch?

Yes and no.

No, it is not a stretch to argue that manifestations of genocidal immorality are deeply rooted within us—within a dark but persistent part of us—as a direct result of how we evolved.

But, yes, it is a major stretch to go from observed in-group bias/out-group antipathy to the killing fields of Armenia or Cambodia. Even though so many studies over the years have shown that most of us exhibit various degrees of in-group preference/out-group antipathy, the fact remains that the overwhelming majority of us do not participate in genocides. The babies in those Yale labs will most likely not grow up to become Nazis. Nor will those children in the preschool T-shirt study. And let's also remember that despite the fact that there were many genocides in the twentieth century, genocides themselves are still the exception and not the norm throughout human history; genocides are sporadic flare-ups, not persistent constants the world over. Again, it is a stretch indeed to go from a plethora of studies revealing in-group favoritism/out-group antipathy to the relatively rare reality of genocide.

No matter how intractable a part of our nature this darker aspect is, and no matter how often we observe in-group preference/out-group aversion—both in the lab and in our daily lives—none of this, in and of itself, means that we are all determined or fated by our evolved nature to be biased, ethnocentric louts who only act morally toward those within our inner group, designated as "us." It doesn't mean we're all chomping at the bit to exterminate "them."

Rather, this innate orientation is merely a readily observed *tendency*—a tendency that is more or less significant in different individuals, different groups, and at different times in history. And it is a tendency that can be—and almost always is—readily overridden by our more forceful, insistent moral capacities: our naturally evolved feelings of empathy and compassion, our deep desire to live in a just and fair world, and our rational ability to act ethically toward others, even those beyond our inner circle.

Thus, this universal, social-psychological tendency to favor our own, and be biased against outsiders, does not—in and of itself—lead directly or inevitably to genocide. It merely uncovers the deep evolutionary roots of genocidal impulses, the natural seeds of genocidal potentialities. But again, these roots and seeds rarely sprout into genocidal reality. More often than not, they wither and rot, as our stronger moral instincts usually override them.

In order for the collective immoral elements of our nature to grow and bear genocidal fruit—as they did so abundantly in the twentieth century—they need to be fertilized, watered, and fed. And we have a pretty good idea of how that happens.[42] Looking at the genocides of the past hundred years, the typical procedures and common ingredients for harvesting the worst of our human nature are discernible, with the deadly recipe including a potent combination of the following:

- Authoritarian orientation: cultures characterized by a high degree of respect for authority, a high value placed on obedience to authority, and a preference for hierarchical positioning of power are more prone to genocidal tendencies than cultures characterized by lower degrees of such orientations.[43]
- Dictatorships: genocides are far more likely to occur under dictatorships possessing highly concentrated and centralized power than within democracies in which power is more diffuse, civil liberties are more respected, and civilian oversight is more widespread.[44]
- Pernicious "isms": deep-seated racism, ethnocentrism, and/or nationalism are almost always at play in genocide. When certain groups of people imagine themselves to be racially, culturally, linguistically, nationally, religiously, or somehow symbolically related—and superior to another people seen as inferior—genocidal capabilities increase.[45]
- Scapegoating: when a distinct minority or separate category of people is blamed for societal ills, political instability, economic crises, diseases, plagues, or natural catastrophes, genocidal tendencies are strengthened.[46]
- The dehumanization of potential victims: when those in power—or enough people in a given society—characterize a targeted group as being not fully human, as being an inferior subspecies of hu-

manity, and when such a characterization is successfully established through stories, folktales, songs, school curricula, religious tenets, propaganda, government decrees, and all the various arms of modern media, the potential for genocide intensifies.[47] As American expert on genocide David Livingstone Smith explains, "we are innately biased against outsiders. This bias is seized upon and manipulated . . . to motivate men and women to slaughter one another. This is done by inducing men to regard their enemies as subhuman creatures," and thus, "dehumanization has the specific function of unleashing aggression."[48]

- Goal of those in power: when a leader or government wants to carry out mass killings—and has the technical capabilities to do so—it is very hard to stop. As American professor of government Benjamin Valentino observes, genocidal violence "occurs when powerful leaders come to believe it is the most 'practical' way to accomplish certain radical goals, counter powerful threats or solve military problems," and when such a genocidal strategic policy is put in place, "a tiny minority, well armed and well organized, can generate an appalling amount of bloodshed when unleashed upon unarmed and unorganized victims."[49]
- War: during times of war, in-group solidarity and out-group enmity are both strengthened, fear and hatred are heightened, grievances and a desire for revenge are deepened, violence becomes normalized, everyday morality is shaky, and such conditions make genocide more feasible and logistically easier.[50]
- Men: as James Waller explains, "The direct acts of violence in genocide and mass killing are overwhelmingly the work of men."[51] Indeed, a vast body of research shows that men, in all societies and at all historical time periods, are far more likely to be violent—and homicidally so—than women.[52]

Of course, not all of the above conditions need be present in order for a genocide to occur. Furthermore, some—or even all—of the above conditions can be present, and no genocide need occur. But whatever the mix of ingredients that does produce genocide, one thing is certain: our inherent tendencies to favor "our own" at the expense of the "other" is at play. This immoral tendency is not our primary or dominant orientation. But it is still within us all and, given the right mix of troublesome conditions, can sometimes be tapped and triggered—with murderous results.

From "Us" and "Them" to "We"

Looking at the genocides of the twentieth century—really taking in the depth of depravity, the hatred, the rape, the torture, the burning, the gassing, the hacking, the bludgeoning, the shooting, and the piles of disfigured bodies—it's hard to acknowledge that alongside all of this bloodshed, a much deeper, more pronounced, and more humane process has long been unfolding among people for hundreds of thousands of years: we are actually becoming more united. Our innate tribal tendency to favor "us" over "them" has grown less acute and less discriminating. Genocides notwithstanding, our moral impulses have steadily become less tribal and less parochial throughout the millennia.

Thus, even though genocide has happened—and may happen again—the much larger, overarching story of humanity is that we've gone from small bands of families, fearing and hating other small bands of families, to vast societies with a moral sensibility that extends well beyond our own inner circle. As Australian philosopher Peter Singer has discussed, the circle of who comprises "us" has expanded exponentially over time.[53]

We started living in small bands, but as farming and agricultural technologies developed, we eventually moved into villages and towns. And while we still naturally favored our own kin, social and communal bonds between our fellow villagers and townspeople developed. And then these villages and towns grew bigger, and we found ourselves united to people by virtue of shared values, or shared culture, or shared language, or shared rituals, or share beliefs, or shared mythologies, or a sense of shared fate. Or all of these in combination. And these towns and villages eventually became cities, and large societies, and nations, and all the while the scope of who mattered, who we ought not harm, who we ought to help, and who deserved fairness and justice, continued to grow. We eventually got to a place where we felt like complete strangers, utterly unrelated to us, and living tens of thousands of miles away, who we would never know or meet, still deserved respect, dignity, and compassion.

Admittedly, as this process has played out over the centuries, ugly and damaging divisions among people—based on race, ethnicity, culture, religion, resource competition—have stubbornly persisted. And the historical process of an expanding moral circle has been regularly and perniciously interrupted by outbreaks of warfare, violence, enmity, and genocide. Yet these ugly instances of human savagery have been but periodic and limited explosions. Painful and traumatic as they have been, they have not successfully destroyed the ever-expanding canopy of moral inclusiveness, which has seen its breadth and scope continue to include more and more members—indeed, all people everywhere.

The Expanding Circle

For an example of this ethical expansion, let's revisit the Universal Declaration of Human Rights, which was broached earlier, in chapter 6. As you may recall, the declaration was drafted in 1948 by a team of humanitarians under the leadership of Eleanor Roosevelt.

"The inherent dignity and . . . equal and inalienable rights of all members of the human family is the foundation of freedom, justice and peace in the world," declares the Universal Declaration of Human Rights, which goes on to proclaim, in part:

> Article 1
> All human beings are born free and equal in dignity and rights. They are endowed with reason and conscience and should act towards one another in a spirit of brotherhood.

Article 2
Everyone is entitled to all the rights and freedoms set forth in this Declaration, without distinction of any kind, such as race, colour, sex, language, religion, political or other opinion, national or social origin, property, birth or other status. Furthermore, no distinction shall be made on the basis of the political, jurisdictional, or international status of the country or territory to which a person belongs, whether it be independent, trust, non-self-governing or under any other limitation of sovereignty.

Article 3
Everyone has the right to life, liberty and security of person.

Article 4
No one shall be held in slavery or servitude; slavery and the slave trade shall be prohibited in all their forms.

Article 5
No one shall be subjected to torture or to cruel, inhuman or degrading treatment or punishment.

Article 6
Everyone has the right to recognition everywhere as a person before the law.

Article 7
All are equal before the law and are entitled without any discrimination to equal protection of the law. All are entitled to equal protection against any discrimination in violation of this Declaration and against any incitement to such discrimination.

And so on (there are a total of thirty articles).

The Universal Declaration of Human Rights illustrates just how far we have come in recognizing the oneness of humanity. And its secular, humanistic premises were not delivered to us on a hilltop by a god, they were not recited by a holy prophet in a mystic trance, nor were they unearthed by an angel in the woods. They were written by mere human beings: men and women who were cognizant of the painful realities of warfare and genocide, yet equally aware of the evolved ability of humans to see the humanity in one another—men and women motivated by the ethical desire to live in a world where everyone enjoys the same rights that one would want for one's own friends and family.

The Universal Declaration of Human Rights—all that it contains and all that it aspires to achieve—wouldn't have been conceivable one hundred thousand years ago. Or ten thousand years ago. Or one thousand years ago. Or two hundred years ago. But it was conceivable in 1948, and is conceivable today, because our naturally evolved proclivity to favor our own at the expense of others has been tempered by our stronger and ever-enhanced capacity for ethical inclusiveness and moral universalism. The circle of who comprises "us" has grown, the outer realm of who comprises "them" continues to dissolve, and the growing human reality is an ever-expanded "we."

In the words of Peter Singer:

> If I have seen that from an ethical point of view I am just one person among the many in my society, and my interests are no more important, from the point of view of the whole, than the similar interests of others within my society, I am ready to see that, from a still larger point of view, my society is just one among other societies, and the interests of members of my society are no more important, from the larger perspective, than the similar interests of members of others societies. Ethical reasoning, once begun, pushes against our initially limited ethical horizons, leading us always toward a more universal point of view.[54]

This universal ethical perspective clearly hasn't become reality the world over. Far from it. As of this writing, our planet is replete with pockets of ethnically, racially, nationally, and religiously motivated violence. There are wars being fought and others in preparation. Arms abound and remain poised for action—including the nuclear kind. Racism, misogyny, and homophobia fester. Tribalism continues to corrupt political parties. But, simultaneously, the ideal that we are all truly one species, each of us deserving the same moral consideration, has never been more widespread. It is an ethical ideal that is not only increasingly obvious—if not taken for granted—but one that continues to manifest itself on every continent, despite so many bloody setbacks and ongoing intergroup hostilities.[55]

Preventing Genocide

The ever-expanding circle of empathy is manifestly laudable and has done so much—and will continue to do more—toward curbing future genocides. However, given that the pernicious "us" versus "them" element of human nature is deeply rooted—and is all too easily aroused and ignited—the possibility of mass killings in the century ahead remain. What can we do to prevent such atrocities from happening again, or at least keep them to a minimum?

The best we can do is to heed the various insights of historical, political, and social-psychological analyses of the genocides of the twentieth century, which teach us that if we can do the following, it will help considerably: promote democracy over dictatorship; fortify freedom of the press and other basic civil liberties; develop cultural norms and values that are less authoritarian; foster intercultural, interethnic, interracial, and interreligious cooperation, dialogue, and understanding; deepen international trade and economic interdependence; fight against scapegoating and other fallacious methods employed to blame societal problems on various minorities; debunk and deconstruct political propaganda or media messaging that dehumanizes targeted groups; place strong political and institutional checks on those in power so that they cannot use the military for genocidal ends; be vigilant in monitoring and protecting vulnerable populations during times of war; place economic sanctions on regimes intent on becoming perpetrators; get more women into positions of power and authority; and heed early warning signs concerning where and when the possibility of genocide appears to be heating up and deploy peacekeeping troops as needed. And then some.[56]

None of these secular strategies are particularly easy to employ or accomplish; the logistics are hard, the cost is high, and the political will is often lacking. But genocide can be reined in—not through Bible study, faith-based ritual devotion, or prayers to God—but through diligent and determined humans coming together in the here and now to protect the vulnerable, which takes this-worldly, prosocial moral conviction and courage on the part of each and every one of us.

11

Secular Solutions to Immorality

As the previous two chapters have acknowledged, human beings can behave immorally by willfully harming other people. As individuals, they can cause all kinds of emotional and physical suffering to those around them, and collectively, they can carry out genocides. People are clearly capable of every shade and level of cruelty.

But the previous two chapters have also tried to *explain* and *understand* the daunting reality of human immorality. In chapter 9, we saw that many discernible factors correlate with and contribute toward individual immorality, such as certain neurological deficits and abnormalities, disrupted attachment between infants and parents, experiences of childhood neglect and abuse, internalized shame, as well as being socialized into cultures with immoral norms and values. And in chapter 10, we looked at the ways in which genocidal immorality has its roots in our evolved tendency to divide the world between "us" and "them," to favor those we think are like us, and to be antipathetic to those considered outsiders, and that these innate tendencies can be easily tapped, nurtured, and enflamed by a host of societal circumstances, such as murderous dictatorships, noxious propaganda, successful scapegoating/dehumanizing of targeted populations, and long-standing ethnic or religious rifts.

The purpose of this attempt at understanding and explaining is not to excuse. The agenda here isn't exculpatory. Rather, we strive for understanding because it is the only viable path toward figuring out how to best address immorality—with the ultimate goal of ameliorating it as much as possible.

In this chapter, we'll take a look at the various ways in which people have successfully limited or reduced immorality in their midst. And they are all secular endeavors, to be sure. They have nothing to do with any gods, deities, spirits, avatars, or fairies. They don't rely on faith, prayers, crystals, or sacrificial goats. Rather, they are based solely on rational insights, real-world data, reasonable experiments, sane policies, and evidence-based action.

Return to Robbers Cave

As you may recall, back in the 1950s, a team of social psychologists headed by Muzafer Sherif staged an experiment at a boys' summer camp in Oklahoma: they divided up the boys into two groups and, through a series of small but significant manipulations, immediately drove them into states of mutual hostility. Each group of boys quickly developed a very strong sense of in-group loyalty and out-group animosity, which were made manifest in various escalating acts of taunting, theft, and vandalism. Clearly, as the Robbers Cave experiment revealed, it doesn't take much for our naturally evolved "us" versus "them" orientation to be triggered.

But that's not how Sherif's experiment ended. In fact, the ultimate and conclusive finding of the experiment was quite different and, from a moral standpoint, much more positive.

Once the initial hostilities between the two groups of boys were observably strong and abundant, Sherif and his team wanted to see how hard it would be to reduce and even erase the "us" versus "them" enmity. Turns out it wasn't hard at all. By yet again making some small but significant manipulations, the two groups of boys went from being hostile, opposing enemies to a very cooperative, supportive "we."

First, Sherif and his team came up with some basic tasks and goals that required a bit of teamwork. For example, they purposefully "blocked" a water faucet and set the boys from both teams the task of fixing it. Then they offered up the possibility of showing the film *Treasure Island* to both groups together, but a certain amount of money would need to be raised—an amount that would be easily reached if the boys from both groups pooled their meager funds. Next, while out together in the wilderness, the truck bringing them all food "broke down," and it took both sets of boys working together to roll it a certain distance so that it could be successfully started again. And when it was time to pitch tents on an overnight expedition, all the equipment was mixed up, so the boys from both groups had to sort through it all together to make sure everyone had their needed poles and stakes. And so it went: a series of tasks requiring both teams to pitch in toward a common goal, as well as some fun events all enjoyed together like swimming in a lake, and—*voilà*—rapprochement and friendship were readily achieved.[1]

It was just as easy to induce intergroup hostility among the boys as it was to erase it and replace it with mutual cooperation and a sense of oneness.

While life beyond a boys' summer camp in Oklahoma staffed by meddling social psychologists is obviously much more fraught and complex, and while the problems our world faces as the result of immorality are much more egregious and dire, a lesson is nonetheless learned here: we *can* do things to limit aggression, antipathy, and violence, thereby reducing harm, pain, and suffering.

Elmira, Ypsilanti, and Beyond[2]

Consider but one simple experiment from the 1970s that had extremely positive results. A sample of mostly white, poor, young, and unmarried pregnant women in the small rural town of Elmira, New York, was identified by the lead investigator, American professor of psychology David Olds. These women were considered to be living vulnerable, precarious lives that would most likely adversely affect their offspring. This sample of underprivileged mothers was then split into two groups, an experimental group and a control group. The mothers in the experimental group received home visitations by registered nurses during the latter part of their pregnancies. And then, after the babies were born, each mother was visited by a nurse every week for the first six weeks, and then every other week, and then every two weeks, all the way down to every six weeks by the time their children were two years old. During these home visitations, the nurses would offer parenting advice, help the moms access any needed social services, coordinate visits to the doctor, answer any questions about health, medicine, diet, and nutrition, and basically just be there as a supportive person. While the control group of mothers did receive some information about parenting and, in some cases, were provided transportation for needed doctor appointments, they did not experience the two years of home visitations by nurses.

Did the regular visits by a registered nurse have a beneficial effect? Big time.

When compared to the control group, the mothers in the experimental group—the ones who received the home visitations—were far less likely to become pregnant again, they were much more likely to become gainfully employed, they were much less likely to abuse or neglect their kids, and their children were much less likely to need to go to the emergency room.

In a follow-up study over a decade later, the researchers found that the kids of the mothers who had received regular nurse visitations were significantly less likely to be using alcohol or drugs than the kids whose mothers hadn't, and were much less likely to have been arrested.[3]

Behold the profoundly beneficial possibilities of sound social policy motivated by thoughtful social science.

These researchers had a social-psychological theory: that poor, single, vulnerable moms have a higher likelihood of neglecting or abusing their children, who will then be at an increased risk of delinquency and criminal behavior. So they provided a simple, benign intervention—giving these single moms two years of basic support from a registered nurse—and the results were that well-being was significantly increased and subsequent immorality was substantially decreased.

Similar studies have been conducted elsewhere, with equally beneficial results.[4] For example, the Perry Preschool Project was conducted in a poor, mostly African American community in Ypsilanti, Michigan, in the 1960s. A large sample of poor and otherwise demographically similar families with young children was identified. It was divided into two groups, an experimental group and a control group. Unlike the children in the control group, the children in the experimental group were enrolled in a preschool program that they attended for a few hours a day while they were three and four years old. The program had a low student-teacher ratio, and the curriculum was centered around an "active learning" approach inspired by the ideas of child development expert Jean Piaget. Also, the preschool teachers visited the children and their mothers once a week at their homes for about half an hour.

The researchers kept track of the over one hundred children from this neighborhood—the kids in the control group that weren't part of the program, as well as the kids in the experimental group that were. The results? By the time all the children were adults in their late twenties, those that had gone through the Perry Preschool Project were more likely to be off welfare and gainfully employed than those who had not. Furthermore, those who had gone through the program as children were much less likely to have been arrested for drug, property, or violent crimes as teenagers or adults, and they were only one-fifth as likely to have become active criminals.[5] Think about that: only one-fifth as likely. Criminal behavior was not totally done away with. But it was significantly reduced.

Then there's the Quantum program study from the 1990s. Researchers identified at-risk minority teenagers who came from poor families in poor neighborhoods in several cities in Oklahoma, Pennsylvania, Michigan, and Texas. Students were selected for the program randomly—so there was no self-selection at play. Those who joined the program spent four years in a group with other teenagers, led by an adult instructor, during which they received help with school, were given training in various high-tech vocations, spent time doing community work, took visits to the theater and the opera, and were given a regular stipend that they could spend or, if they chose, put into a savings fund for college. Two years after the program ended, the average number of criminal arrests of those teenagers who had participated in the Quantum program was 50 percent lower than a control group of teenagers who had not. And the Quantum teenagers were twice as likely to be going to college compared to the nonparticipants.[6]

One more example: the Family and Neighborhood Services program from the late 1980s and early 1990s in South Carolina. A large sample of adolescent offenders was identified—teens of various races and social classes who had committed a series of violent crimes. The sample was divided in half: The control group received standard disciplinary sanctions, like curfews and threats of being sent to a youth prison. But the experimental group received visits several times a week from well-trained caseworkers who sought to positively address various aspects of the teenagers' lives, such as their school troubles or any health concerns they might have. But the big focus was family: the caseworkers helped the teenagers cope with and navigate often troubling, difficult family situations. The outcome? Two and a half years after the program ended, those who had participated in the program were *half* as likely to have been arrested as those who had not.[7]

There are so many more such programs out there—not just within the United States but around the world—that target vulnerable populations, provide them with aid and support, and thereby decrease overall criminality.[8] Such programs cost money, to be sure. But they are far cheaper and more cost-effective that not having them.

In truth, we have a very good idea of how to reduce crime—and all the harm and suffering that it produces. Dr. Elliott Currie, an American professor of criminology, has been studying the causes of crime—as well as solutions—for over forty years. In his estimation, the answer to lowering crime is fairly straightforward: prevent child abuse and neglect, enhance children's social and intellectual development, provide support and guidance to vulnerable teens, and work closely and therapeutically with juvenile offenders. Do this—as Currie's extensive research shows—and you'll reduce overall crime significantly.[9]

Poverty and Inequality

Of course, we mustn't forget the wider socioeconomic context.

No matter how hard we work with abusive parents, care for vulnerable children, and develop programs for troubled teens, if we want to thoroughly and systemically reduce violent crime, we've got to attack its underlying structural progenitor—poverty—as well as its great institutional incubator—inequality.[10]

One of the most robust correlations in sociology convincingly indicates that where there is harsh poverty and deep inequality, violent crime abounds.[11] Just look at the countries today with the highest homicide rates, such as Honduras, El Salvador, Ivory Coast, Brazil, Guatemala, Jamaica, Zambia, Uganda, Colombia, and Malawi. They are all characterized by high poverty rates and steep inequality. And countries with the lowest homicide rates—such as Singapore, Iceland, Japan, Brunei, Norway, Austria, Switzerland, Oman, Slovenia, and Germany—are almost all characterized by low levels of poverty and inequality.[12] Japan is particularly noteworthy as having one of the lowest murder rates in the world, as well as being one of the most wealthy and prosperous of nations, and also among the most equal, with relatively low rates of poverty.[13]

In the 1990s, criminologists Ching-Chi Hsieh and M. D. Pugh conducted a statistically sophisticated meta-analysis of thirty-four data-rich studies looking at violent crime, inequality, and poverty, and concluded that the latter two are underlying causes of the first. Their ultimate takeaway: "poverty and income inequality are each correlated with violent crime and . . . these correlations are especially robust with respect to assault and homicide."[14] In the early 2000s, several economists at the World Bank conducted an even more extensive meta-analysis of the relationship between poverty, inequality, and violent crime. By looking at countries all over the world over time and at varying stages of development—and taking into account a host of important variables, such as the average adult educational attainment levels of each country, growth rate of GDP, levels of urbanization, the degree of a given nation's ethnolinguistic fractionalization, and availability of police in each country—the two main conclusions were crystal clear: first, "an increase in income inequality has a significant and robust effect of raising crime rates," and second, "poverty alleviation has a crime-reducing effect."[15]

Examining extensive international data, and controlling for a host of relevant variables, the evidence is unambiguous: where inequality runs deep, violent crime is high, and where inequality is low and poverty is addressed, violent crime is reduced.

The detrimental—and ultimately immoral—effects of inequality are abundant. British epidemiologists Richard Wilkinson and Kate Pickett devoted their data-driven bestselling book *The Spirit Level* to showing how inequality within any society is strongly correlated to a host of social maladies, from obesity and anxiety to teen pregnancy and infant mortality. And violent crime is featured prominently in their international analysis, for they note that of all correlations between inequality and various societal ills, the determining link between a society's degree of inequality and its experiencing of violent crime is among the most readily observable and well-established. As their evidence conclusively reveals, "the association between inequality and violence is strong and consistent; it's been demonstrated in many different time periods and settings [and] evidence of the close correlation between ups and downs in inequality and violence show that if inequality is lessened, levels of violence also decline."[16]

It's pretty easy to understand how much of this works: when people are poor and do not have jobs or good job prospects, when vocational training is scarce, when they can't obtain an education, when they can't afford housing, when they don't have access to decent health care, when they feel a deep sense of hopelessness—all of this breeds despair, humiliation, and shame. And this in turn creates unstable homes wracked with frustration, anger, and violence. Add drugs and alcohol into the mix, and it only gets worse. Such homes then churn out children who are much more likely to have experienced abuse and neglect. And they, in turn, are much more likely to become violent and criminally involved as they grow up, causing harm and suffering to others. It's a vicious cycle of economic inequality and poverty that produces miserable, depressed, uneducated people without job skills living precarious lives who vent their fears and pain upon their children, who are then at a much greater risk of stealing, beating, or killing others later in life. No wonder that nearly all of the states in the United States with the highest murder rates—such as Louisiana, Alabama, Missouri, Mississippi, South Carolina, Tennessee, and Arkansas[17]—also tend to have the highest inequality and poverty rates.[18]

If we really want to reduce violent crime—perhaps the most tangible manifestation of immorality—then we have no choice but to reduce poverty and inequality in society.[19] We need to provide health care for all, quality education for all, job training for all, affordable housing for all, and a variety of needed social services for all. Accomplish this, and violent crime will plummet.

It's a daunting task, but it's doable. Just look at Scandinavia.

The Northern Lights

For centuries, the Nordic nations of Norway, Sweden, Denmark, and Finland were extremely poor, save for a tiny sliver of wealthy royals, aristocrats, clergy, and landowners.[20] Up until the twentieth century, for the masses of people there, life was cold, hungry, and brutal. Most men and women were uneducated, had few job prospects, and were lucky to scrape by from week to week. Many lived as serfs. People starved to death. Children begged in the streets. Sometimes children froze to death in the fields. Some women resorted to killing their newborns because they couldn't provide for them. Inequality was extreme. Workers were exploited, raped, and beaten. If you were injured on the job—tough luck. If your husband was injured on the job—tough luck. If your parents died from typhus—tough luck. And there was lots of crime, from the petty to the violent. There was a lot of religion back then in Scandinavia, too. But all the praying, church-attending, and God-fearing did little to alleviate poverty, reduce inequality, or stem criminality.

And then, in a matter of four or five generations, the nations of Denmark, Norway, Sweden, and Finland became not only among the wealthiest countries on Earth but, much more importantly, among the most equal.[21] Indeed, these fair-minded, hardworking, taciturn Lutherans made societal equality the reigning goal of their political institutions and social policy.[22] The contemporary result: everyone in the Nordic world now has access to excellent and free health care, excellent and free education, excellent and free job training, excellent and heavily subsidized childcare, and excellent and heavily subsidized elder care. And one of the most notable results of all this is that they have among the lowest violent crime rates in the world. For example, according to the United Nations Office on Drugs and Crime,[23] the murder rate in Honduras is 64 people murdered per 100,000 people, in Venezuela it is 57 murdered per 100,000, in Jamaica it is 43, in Uganda 12, in Russia 11, in the Philippines 10, in Pakistan 8, in Mongolia 7, in the United States 5, but in Finland it is 1.6, in Sweden and Denmark it is 1, and in Norway it is 0.5. And according to the Global Peace Index, the Nordic nations are among the safest in the world.[24]

Contrary to popular misconceptions, the nations of Scandinavia do not have the highest suicide rates in the world. Far from it. They do, however, have the highest tax rates in the world. But what Scandinavians get for their taxes is invaluable: safe cities, clean streets, excellent schools, green parks, well-functioning social services, efficient public transportation, humane care for the mentally ill, physical therapy for the physically disabled, extensive paid parental leaves, plenty of paid holidays, heavily subsidized arts and culture—no wonder their citizens consistently indicate that they are among the happiest in the world, with Norway and Denmark repeatedly vying for number one happiest nation on Earth year after year.[25]

By fostering the best aspects of capitalism—competition, profit motive, reward for risk and hard work, private investment and consumer choice—and combining it with a vast and well-subsidized social welfare system, the Nordic nations have created not only prosperous and egalitarian nations but highly moral cultures characterized by extremely low levels of violent crime.[26]

Of course, not everything is perfect in Scandinavia. They have their problems, like any modern society will. But as Jeremy Bentham and John Stuart Mill argued, if the ultimate goal of morality is to increase the happiness and well-being of as many humans as possible and simultaneously to reduce harm and suffering, the Nordic nations have achieved much on this front, showing the rest of the world just how morally progressive modern, industrialized, democratic societies can be.

And it must be remembered that this Nordic miracle was in fact no miracle at all. It didn't come about through faith, God-worship, or holy supplication. Quite the opposite. It was created by secular men and women via secular means and methods, prodded on by Enlightenment values.[27] Workers organized themselves into cooperatives and unions, democratically elected politicians sought rational solutions to social problems, and governments made social welfare a priority, paying for it through progressive taxation. And Scandinavians have become among the most secular people in the world over the course of the last century, which shows that creating a moral society with high levels of human flourishing and low levels of violent crime has little or nothing to do with theism or faith in God but rather with sound social policy, economic wisdom, cultural solidarity, and political know-how.[28]

And amidst all of that, at the heart of Nordic culture is empathy: care for the suffering of others. But it is a pragmatic empathy. It is an empathy bolstered by reason and made manifest through rational action. After all, as American philosopher J. D. Trout discusses, empathy in and of itself is just a feeling. Empathy alone doesn't solve major societal problems. What needs to happen is that empathy—the feeling for someone else's suffering—must prod one to compassionately act so as to help the one in need.[29] And yet, even individuals feeling empathetically and acting compassionately can only accomplish so much. If we want to make life better for all—at the societal level—we need what Trout calls "empathetic social policy."[30] That is, we need governmental policies, political structures, and institutional systems that direct feelings of empathy and individual compassion into widespread societal solutions that ensure well-being for as many people as possible.

Curing Criminals

Consider one specific Scandinavian social policy that successfully engages and ameliorates immorality: how they deal with their criminals. When people in Scandinavia engage in crime—intentionally harming others—their government does not respond by turning them into a continuing or even more dangerous threat. Rather, the Nordic penal system tempers their violent tendencies, quells their antisocial aggression, and seeks to put an end to their future criminality—thereby increasing well-being in society for everyone.

The obvious indicator of this process is the recidivism rate, which measures reincarceration.[31] That is, once people are let out of prison, how likely are they to be reincarcerated? It is about as objective a measurement as possible for assessing the quality of a country's criminal justice system, because it shows what becomes of people after they are released from behind bars: Do they go out and continue to engage in immoral activity—thereby causing more pain and suffering to others—or do they stop engaging in such activity and thereby cease to be public threats?

The Scandinavian nations have among the lowest recidivism rates in the world. In Norway, for instance, only 20 percent of released prisoners get rearrested within their first five years of getting out of prison; by comparison, the United States has a recidivism rate nearly three times worse than that, with over 76 percent of American prisoners being rearrested within five years of their release.[32]

How do they do it in Norway? Simple: they provide incarcerated individuals with extensive counseling, therapy, drug treatment, education, and job training.[33] They work hard to improve incarcerated individuals' sense of themselves—to ease their sense of shame and improve their sense of worth, to strengthen their ability to manage anger and weaken their tendencies to be aggressive. That is, rather than humiliate, degrade, or torture them and subject them to harsh conditions rife with violence and hostility, the goal is to actually make them feel better about themselves. To feel more human. To feel more empathetic. That way, when they are released, they don't go out and cause additional harm. Instead, they become productive members of society. And when that happens, everyone benefits. A relevant Canadian study of over five thousand felons offers further illustrative support: those inmates who received rehabilitative treatment while in prison had significantly lower rates of recidivism than those who did not.[34]

The Scandinavian rehabilitative approach to criminals/prisoners is not only one of the most enlightened but also among the most successful.[35] As we've seen, their recidivism rates are among the lowest in the world, as are their rates of violent crime in general. And when the Scandinavian approach to prisoners is contrasted with the far more draconian and less successful American approach, we can see one of the starkest examples of how a rational, secular approach to immorality is much better, more effective, and ultimately more ethical than many a religious approach.

Humanistic Enlightenment vs. Hell and Damnation

Imagine an individual who commits a violent crime; through his willful action, he causes pain and suffering—not only to his immediate victim but, by extension, to the victim's loved ones, as well. And to a lesser but still important degree, the violent crime he commits also causes societal damage to the wider community in that it increases fear and unease among the public.

Now the question becomes: How should we react to the perpetrator of this violent crime? What should we do with him?

One option is to go for revenge. Be punitive. Make him suffer. Make him feel some of the agony and pain that he willfully caused others to feel. In short: *punish* him. And that punishment should degrade him. It should make him feel so bad about what he did that he'll never go out and do it again. And the circumstances of his punishment should be so unpleasant that they will deter others from committing similar crimes for fear of meeting a similar fate. Clearly, from this perspective, this violent criminal should spend a good long time behind bars in a cramped cell. And again, during that time, he should suffer. It shouldn't be pleasant. After all, he committed a violent crime—causing pain and suffering—and so now he should experience some pain and suffering of his own.

Another option is rehabilitation. While we are repulsed by the violent crime he committed, and as we feel sadness for his victim and sympathy for the victim's loved ones, we now want to do whatever we can to make sure no one else is ever harmed by him again. We want to make it so that he never goes out and does what he did to anyone else. And the best way to do that is not to degrade him, humiliate him, and make him suffer. Rather, we actually need to help him. We need to do whatever it takes to lower his aggressive impulses, overcome his shame and self-hatred, handle his inner demons, increase his sense of well-being and self-worth, and develop greater empathy. This is done by creating decent, humane conditions of imprisonment with extensive counseling, therapy, vocational training, farming, recreation, and educational opportunities. Of course, it may not seem fair: Why should this individual be treated to such amenities when he caused someone else to suffer so? Well, frankly, because the ultimate goal is to make it so that he never goes out and harms other people again.

The United States, with its vocal and active population of Evangelical conservatives, is all too keen on the first penal option. We take angry, violent, and often poor and uneducated individuals who commit crimes—many who suffer from drug and alcohol addiction and learning disabilities—and shove them into cramped cells with other angry, violent, uneducated individuals. The result: we churn out ever more angry and violent ex-cons who go out into the world and cause ever more pain and suffering. As Dr. James Gilligan, who has worked in American prisons for decades, observes, "if one were trying to design a system for deliberately making people paranoid and violent, one could hardly have come up with a more successful model,"[36] given that "the more violent people are . . . the more severely we punish them . . . and the more severely we punish them . . . the more violent they become."[37]

It's truly self-defeating.

In fact, many studies have consistently shown that the punishment of harsh imprisonment does little to deter future criminality of those imprisoned but rather actually *increases* the likelihood that incarcerated individuals will go out and commit more crimes upon release.[38] For example, American criminologists Cassia Spohn and David Holleran looked at one thousand individuals in Missouri who had committed felonies and—while controlling for other significant variables—compared those who got probation versus those who were sent to prison; the ones who were sent to prison ended up having higher rearrest rates than those who only got probation.[39] A similar study of over three thousand offenders in the Netherlands found the same thing: those who were sent to prison were subsequently more likely to commit more crimes post-imprisonment than those who were not.[40] Other studies have found the same results.[41] Thus, as American criminologist Stacy Mallicoat has concluded:

> Research . . . tells us that prisons do not deter offenders. Instead, findings indicate that prison can produce a criminogenic effect. This means that prisons can actually encourage offenders to engage in crime, rather than prevent it . . . these results indicate that the "most punitive" punishment may be the least effective.[42]

However, in more enlightened, rational, moral, and secular societies—such as those of Scandinavia—they go for the better penal option: rehabilitation. And thus, they churn out ex-cons who are less violent, less aggressive, and much less likely to ever commit a violent crime again. As a result, their recidivism rates are far lower than ours and their communities and neighborhoods are much safer. Everyone wins.

Why this difference in penal orientations? Why do some societies—such as the United States—favor punishment over rehabilitation, even though the former increases violence in society and the latter decreases violence?

Religion.

Or more specifically: the traditional, fundamentalist religious belief that there is a mighty God who brutally punishes those who break His rules.

Central to both doctrinaire Christianity and doctrinaire Islam is the paramount article of faith that there is an all-powerful deity who watches everything you do, and if you do something He doesn't want you to do, He will punish you in a very fiery hell. He will make you *suffer.*

Jesus teaches that people who act immorally will be consigned to hell's everlasting flames (Matthew 25), which, according to the Gospels, is a dark place full of weeping and gnashing of teeth. The biblical writings of Paul confirm that hell is a place of everlasting destruction and raging fire. And according to the Book of Revelation, hell is a "lake of fire" where the devil and his minions dwell. Throughout the centuries, Christians have interpreted these passages literally; as the Westminster Confession of the Church of England of the seventeenth century declared: "the wicked, who know not God, and obey not the gospel of Jesus Christ, shall be cast into eternal torments, and punished with everlasting destruction."

Within Islam, hell is even more of a prominent threat. It is mentioned nearly five hundred times in the Quran alone, and the hell of Islam is truly horrific: it is described in Islamic scriptures as a very hot place where people wear chains around their necks and clothes made of fire; people are forced to eat fire; scalding water is poured over people's heads; people are whipped with iron; people's skin is burned off then regrown only to be burned off again repeatedly.[43]

In both Christianity and Islam, the reward for obeying God's laws is entrance into heaven, while the punishment for disobeying God's laws is entrance into hell. And thus, there you have it: a holy, cosmic, theistic model for how to understand and deal with immorality. It is a model deeply embedded in the collective cultures of both Christianity and Islam—and it is thus a model that gets institutionalized. People who believe in a God who judges individuals and punishes them by sentencing them to hell are far more likely to be vengeful and to want to punish criminals with a similar brutality here on planet Earth.[44] On the other hand, people who no longer believe in such a God—or heaven and hell, for that matter—approach criminals with a far more empathetic, rational, and humane view. This helps explain why it is that the more strongly religious a person is, the more likely he or she is to support the death penalty, and the more secular one is, the more likely one is to oppose it.[45] It also helps explain why the most secular democracies in the world today tend to have the most humane penal systems that actually rehabilitate criminals, successfully lowering recidivism and overall violence in society, while the most religious democracies today tend to have the most inhumane penal systems that only create more angry, hardened, and violent criminals, thereby increasing pain and suffering in the wider society.

Before continuing, let me acknowledge that there is no question that religious congregations definitely do a lot of good for a lot of people. Many congregations offer an assortment of groups, classes, and programs that help at-risk youth to avoid criminal engagement, aid ex-cons in getting an education and finding jobs, help criminalized drug addicts overcome their addictions, and comfort those who are suffering from abuse. The communal support of such religious institutions is undoubtedly beneficial for many individuals.[46] But the underlying religious message—the theistic model emanating from the dual heartbeats of Christianity and Islam—is that those who commit crimes are wicked sinners who deserve to be punished by a vengeful God, and this does tremendous damage. It obfuscates the real underlying causes of immoral behavior, it stymies empathy, and above all it upholds penal systems motivated by punishment and revenge rather than understanding and rehabilitation.

From Australia to Brazil

Consider the penal systems of Australia and Brazil. In one country: humane prisons that seek to turn criminals into productive citizens, resulting in a safer society for all. In the other: inhumane prisons that treat criminals with abject cruelty, with no societal benefit whatsoever. And it's in the more secular nation, Australia, that the ethical and successful model is employed, not the more religious one, Brazil.

Australia is currently one of the most secular countries in the world. According to the most recent statistics, somewhere between 30 percent and 38 percent of Australians identify as having "no religion"[47]—ironically making "no religion" the largest "religion" in the country.[48] Think that such high rates of secularity make Australian society immoral? Of course not;

Australia is far safer than most highly religious societies on Earth. And the way they treat many of their criminals is ethically advanced. Consider, for example, the Wandoo Reintegration Facility, located in Murdoch, Western Australia.[49] A minimum-security prison that houses males between the ages of eighteen and twenty-four, the goal of the prison is rehabilitation and reintegration into society. It takes young men with extensive histories of drug problems and arrests—prime candidates for future lives of crime—and seeks to help them become healthier, calmer, law-abiding citizens. At Wandoo, they are not referred to as "prisoners," but rather "residents." They are not forced to wear stigmatizing uniforms, but dress in the same type of attire as the employees—so that there is no visual difference between residents and staff. They are not bossed around, ordered, humiliated, and made to feel controlled. Rather, they take on a fair share of the decision-making, planning, and scheduling of their incarcerated experience. They are provided with drug and alcohol treatment programs, educational opportunities, job training, art classes, classes on life skills, intensive individual case management, and personal support in the immediate months after release—all with the ultimate goal of fostering successful reintegration into Australian society. Of course, not all prisons in Australia are like Wandoo—but the underlying rehabilitative ideal that Wandoo embodies is part and parcel of the Australian approach to how to react to immorality. Such an approach works; Australia's homicide rate is currently among the lowest in the world.

Moving to Brazil, we find one of the most religious countries in all of Christendom—and also one of the most violent, with a homicide rate that is twenty-five times higher than Australia's.[50] Penal facilities such as Wandoo don't exist in Brazil, nor does its underlying ideal of rehabilitation. Instead, in this deeply Catholic, extremely religious nation—with among the lowest rates of secularity in Latin America—we find excessively overcrowded, disease-ridden, and shockingly violent prisons where inmates are treated like animals.[51]

Consider prisons like the Penitenciária Federal de Catanduvas in southern Brazil. In this newly built, heavily fortified, and heavily guarded facility—considered one of Brazil's finest prisons—solitary confinement is among the most readily employed methods whereby prisoners are punished for their crimes. Indeed, many of the inmates at Catanduvas spend twenty-two hours a day in solitary confinement year after year.[52] Such imprisonment is nothing less than torture. For when human beings are deprived of social interaction for extended periods of time, they suffer to unfathomable degrees. As a U.S. Supreme Court ruling stated all the way back in 1890, based on observations of those sent to solitary confinement, "a considerable number of the prisoners fell, after even a short confinement, into a semi-fatuous condition, from which it was next to impossible to arouse them, and others became violently insane; other, still, committed suicide; while those who stood the ordeal better were not generally reformed, and in most cases did not recover sufficient mental activity to be of any subsequent service to the community."[53]

Contemporary research has only bolstered such observations. According to Harvard Medical School psychiatrist Stuart Grassian, solitary confinement can cause "severe psychiatric harm,"[54] with many individuals who experience it suffering from various neurological disorders, florid psychotic delirium, psychosis, severe hallucinatory confusion, severe depression, delirium, disorientation, intense agitation, perceptual distortion, panic attacks, rage, self-mutilation, and paranoia.[55]

And of course, the punishment itself simply doesn't work. It doesn't "cure" immorality. It doesn't produce inmates with improved social skills, heightened empathy, or decreased aggression. Just the opposite: solitary confinement often causes permanent neurological and psychological damage; according to American professor of psychology Craig Haney, not only do individuals in solitary confinement experience emotional breakdowns, apathy, uncontrollable anger, hallucinations, chronic depression, despair, and suicidal tendencies, but they often risk losing a grasp on their very own identities and their connection to the larger social world, becoming uncontrollably fearful and incapable of basic social interaction.[56]

It thus comes as no surprise that several criminological studies have shown that inmates who have spent time in solitary confinement are significantly *more* likely to engage in crime upon their release from prison than inmates who haven't.[57] Clearly, Brazil's widespread use of solitary confinement doesn't do society any good. It's just government-enforced cruelty, premised on the Christian, theologically motivated viewpoint that "bad" people ought to be punished. That sinners ought to suffer. And neither basic human empathy nor the clear findings of social science deter those who oversee the penal system in Brazil, where punishment is seen as an end in and of itself, despite the fact that it doesn't lower crime at all.

Secular Solutions in Sum

In her provocative book *Are Prisons Obsolete?* Angela Davis argues for the complete abolition of jails and prisons. While her scathing critique of the American criminal justice system is compelling—especially her emphasis on its inherent racist and classist underpinnings—and while her challenge to the way in which people uncritically accept prisons and jails as necessary institutions is trenchant, her argument that all facilities of incarceration be abolished outright is misguided. The fact is, there *are* dangerous and violent people out there who willfully harm others, and society needs to do all that it can—in the aftermath of their committing harmful crimes—to prevent them from harming additional victims. And that will sometimes necessitate depriving them of their freedom, housing them somewhere that restricts their ability to cause more pain and suffering. The question is: Once we've apprehended and restricted them, what do we do with them? As the above discussion has shown, we need to help them—not harm and humiliate them. Such an approach is the only proven way to stymie criminals' aggressive, violent tendencies. As such, it reduces harm in society. And thus, it is moral.

The terms "stymie" and "reduce" are key here. For we must admit that there is no ultimate panacea—no foolproof program, policy, or ideal penal system that will ever eliminate immorality in society altogether. There will always be people who lie, steal, cheat, hit, and kill. They will do so as individuals, and they will do so in groups. Such behavior is a part of our natural, evolved inheritance. But it is only a part. And the underlying story of human progress has been the degree to which this potential capability for immoral behavior can be successfully controlled and minimized.

Despite all the ongoing pain and suffering in the world that results from human immorality—vicious, depraved, genocidal, and so on—the promising reality is that daily life is actually far safer and less violent in most societies than in centuries past. As people have become less superstitious, less religious, more literate, and better educated, and with advances in science, medicine, communication, transportation, and technology, and as democracies have proliferated and respect for human rights has surged, day-to-day existence in most places around the world has become markedly less brutal, less violent, and less precarious than ever before.

According to the extensive data amassed by Harvard professor of psychology Steven Pinker, in more nations than not, rates of violence have plummeted over the course of history; wars have become less frequent; legal slavery has been abolished; the rights of women have dramatically improved; the rights of children have dramatically improved; the rights of homosexuals have dramatically improved; most forms of torture have been eliminated, with many societies having abolished the death penalty as well; and animals are treated more humanely.[58]

American scholar Michael Shermer's data-rich analysis closely echoes Pinker's. "As a species," Shermer illustrates, "we are becoming increasingly moral."[59] According to Shermer, humanity's capacity for empathy and understanding has grown exponentially over the centuries, so that "we no longer consider the well-being only of our family, extended family, and local community; rather, our consideration now extends to people quite unlike ourselves, with whom we gladly trade goods and ideas and exchange sentiments and genes rather than beating, enslaving, raping, or killing them (as our sorry species was wont to do with reckless abandon not so long ago)."[60] Shermer's meta-analysis reveals that not only are overall crime rates far lower than what they were in centuries past, but the homicide rate specifically is at an all-time low—from approximately one thousand per one hundred thousand per year in prehistoric times, down to around one hundred per one hundred thousand per year during the Middle Ages, down to about ten per one hundred thousand per year in the eighteenth century, and all the way down to single digits per one hundred thousand per year in most industrialized democracies today.[61]

Now that's some serious amelioration of immorality.

No, murder has not vanished from planet Earth. But in most societies, it is far less frequent than it has ever been before. And keep in mind: this reduction of immoral violence over time has occurred as people and nations have become *less* religious. Thus, while personal faith in God may surely help given individuals in need of comfort, or help them overcome addiction, or help them cope with personal trauma, or provide them with ethical rules to obey, religious piety, faith in God, and supplication of the supernatural are not—in and of themselves—reliable solutions to social problems. Rather, it is secular solutions that do a much better job.

When children are wanted, loved, and supported—and when they don't experience periods of detachment from their primary caregivers, or abuse, or neglect, they readily manifest prosocial proclivities and empathetic capacities, with the likelihood of them growing up to be violent, harmful, or otherwise immoral being significantly reduced. But in order for children to experience such optimal conditions, their parents must have access to health care, social services, and affordable housing. They need jobs and educational opportunities. They need to live in a society that not only respects human rights, but democratically institutionalizes empathetic and compassionate civic and governmental policy. And they need to live in a society without poverty or extreme inequality—two sociological factors that always increase crime and violence. As of this writing, the most successful attempt at establishing such a society is the contemporary Scandinavian model, which combines favorable aspects of capitalism—innovation, competition, and profit motive—with a robust, progressively tax-subsidized welfare state that keeps poverty at a minimum, ensures a healthy level of equality, and provides all citizens with their basic human needs.

Secular solutions to immorality are varied and multipronged—from providing nurse home visitations to poor single mothers to offering counseling and therapy to troubled teens, from enacting supportive and rehabilitative strategies in prison to reducing inequality through progressive taxation, and so on. But what all such secular solutions share is a reliance upon evidence and a rational, empirically based approach to solving social problems with the ultimate goal of alleviating suffering and increasing well-being—the very veins and arteries of morality.

Of course, humanity being what it is—replete with enormous cultural diversity—not all of us agree on what constitutes "suffering" or what "well-being" actually entails. Depending on what culture we are raised in, such concepts can refer to radically different things.

And thus, we come to the last great challenge to secular morality: relativism.

12

Moral Relativism

As an undergraduate, you fell in love with anthropology. You were fascinated by the tremendous variety and diversity of human cultures and how people can live so differently in different parts of the world. You were compelled by the profound insight that had you been born and raised in any given culture, its practices, norms, traditions, and values would seem normal and natural to you. And you found undeniable the underlying anthropological insight that your very *worldview* is unavoidably shaped by the culture that you happen to have been raised in.

So you decided to go to graduate school to pursue a PhD in anthropology, where you found yourself working closely with Professor Klog, an expert on the indigenous peoples of the Amazon. One day, Professor Klog calls you into her office to share some big news: a small, isolated, unknown tribe within the depths of the Amazon has been located. Professor Klog would like you to join her to live among and study them for a couple of years. It's an anthropologist's dream come true, and so you excitedly say yes.

Getting to the tribe is tough: long flight to Brazil, bumpy rides in small planes into the heart of the Amazon, then boats, then canoes, and then several days of hiking through thick jungle. But you finally make it. Fortunately, the tribespeople don't kill you upon your arrival. Instead, they peacefully welcome you to their village and show you a spot near a creek where you can set up your camp. Soon you're able to communicate with them, and you steadily acquire a basic understanding of their civilization: their kinship structures, hunting practices, childrearing habits, sacred rituals, and so forth.

One prominent feature of this tribe's culture is a deep-seated belief that everything exists in a sacred state of balance: inhales by exhales, day by night, water by fire, life by death, and so on. For them, living in accordance with the balance of the world is spiritually and materially crucial, for a balanced life fosters peace and abundance. But when the balance of the world is disregarded or disrupted, calamity ensues: enmity and violence arise, and people die from mysterious causes.

After about a year, Dr. Klog receives news that her brother back home in the United States is dying. She has to leave at once. It is decided that you will stay with the tribe, carrying on your research while she is away. A week after Dr. Klog's departure, one of the teenagers you've gotten to know goes into labor. You are there at the birth. She has twins. The first twin is lovingly tended to by the mother, but the second twin is left on the ground, crying and trembling. Several people explain what's going on: since humans have *one* child at a time and only *animals* have litters, the fact that this young woman gave birth to two children is a problematic disruption of the balance of nature. And in order for balance to be restored, this wrong must be righted. The second baby must die, for if it lives, all hell will break loose, and the entire tribe will suffer. Proclaiming various incantations, an older member of the tribe grabs the second baby by the feet, walks it out toward the border of the village, and tosses it just on the other side of the small creek—right near your campsite.

Now it is nighttime. You are alone in your tent. And about twenty feet away, the newborn baby is crying. Its cries become ever more pained, dire, and desperate. Insects are crawling all over it, getting into its ears and eyes. The moist earth is cold. The baby becomes quiet for a while. But then its shrill cries start up again.

You are now confronted with a tough choice: Do you get out of your tent, pick up the baby, wipe off the insects, get it something to drink, comfort it, and save its life? Or do you just plug your ears and try to block out its agonized suffering, hoping that it'll be dead and quiet by morning? If you save the baby's life, the tribe will know what you have done, and they will subsequently have to endure all the suffering that will be unleashed upon their society as a result of this mistaken baby's survival at your hands. If you let the baby die, you will be respecting the culture of the tribe and letting things play out as they naturally would if you had not inserted yourself—uninvited—into the depths of the Amazon. But then the baby's unnecessary death will be, at least partially, a result of your inaction.

What will you do?

Moral Relativism

What is the right course of action? What is the primary moral obligation here? Perhaps it is of utmost importance to save that baby's life—and the misguided, superstitious culture of the Amazonian tribe be damned. Or perhaps it is more important to let that baby die, thereby respecting the tribe's long-held values. And just as we wouldn't want some member of this tribe to show up—uninvited—at a hospital in our community where a mother is about to give birth to twins and then kill one of them in order to "restore balance," we shouldn't insert ourselves into their tribal society and save the life of a twin, thereby "upsetting balance" and thus wreaking havoc on their world.

While such acute dilemmas rarely arise in most people's lives, and although the entire hypothetical scenario that I have written above is a complete work of fiction, the basic contours are not: various indigenous tribes in the Amazon rain forest have killed twins—sometimes one, sometimes both, sometimes the twins and the mother—as part of their religious and cultural systems, for thousands of years, and some continue to do so to this day.[1] And we could do something about it, if we chose to.

The crucial point, however, is this: whatever you think is the right course of action, rest assured that your answer is ultimately the result of the culture in which you were raised. If you were raised in, say, Kalispell, Montana, among Evangelical Christians, the answer would be both obvious and imperative: save the baby. But if you were raised among the isolated Amazonian tribe, the answer would be different but just as obvious and imperative: let the baby die. In essence, your moral outlook on this dilemma makes sense only in relation to the culture in which you were raised. And thus, your morality is *relative* to your culture. And it seems that no one can avoid this dynamic, since *everyone's* morality is related to some cultural standard.

Think of it this way: a yardstick is three feet long. It comprises a measurable proportion amounting to thirty-six inches in length. If you want to describe a pencil as being really long or really short, you can hold it up against a yardstick and measure it. If it is longer than the yardstick, that's one long pencil. If it measures only half an inch, that's one short pencil. And these measurements will all reflect the same objective reality whether you are in Madagascar in 1818 or Mongolia in 2018. But when it comes to morality—when it comes to describing a practice, action, or behavior as "moral" or "immoral"—there exists no objective, non-culture-bound yardstick against which to prove such an assertion. Practicing infanticide may be considered immoral in one culture but moral in another. And there is no objective guide by which to deem one or the other ethically correct.[2]

Which directly leads us to one of the thornier problems of morality when there is no God: moral relativism.[3] It is, according to American philosopher Robert Holmes, "arguably, the central problem in ethics."[4]

Moral relativism contains three basic interconnected components:[5]

First, recognizing the anthropological fact that people do and believe things quite differently in different cultures around the world.

Second, understanding that people generally think that their culture's practices and morals are the right ones, the normal ones, the good ones—and that others are wrong, mistaken, or simply weird. Thus, morality is inextricably tied to a specific cultural context.

Third, acknowledging that when there is a moral disagreement between two cultures, there exists no objective adjudicator or utterly impartial umpire—a being or entity outside and above culture—that can definitively determine who is correct or right.

Joyful Blessing or Savage Abuse?

Let's take one contemporary example: male circumcision, a practice undergone by approximately 30 percent of the world's living men.[6]

Many cultures around the world slice off some of the skin, neurons, muscle tissue, blood vessels, and mucous membrane of the tip of the penises of boys—and they have been doing so for millennia. Some tribes, like Nelson Mandela's Xhosa tribe in South Africa, cut off the foreskin with a razor blade when boys are around the age of sixteen. Among the people of northern Sudan, boys must be circumcised before they start school when they are eight years old, and here's how it is done: a large straw is inserted by a tribal elder into the tip of the boy's penis and is used to push down the boy's glans while his foreskin is pulled forward, and then a cord is tied around the foreskin, which is then cut with a knife.[7] In the Philippines, the cutting off of the foreskin occurs either immediately after birth or when boys are between the ages of ten to fourteen; sometimes it is done by a tribal elder, other times by professional medical staff. Among the Merina of Madagascar, the cutting off of the foreskin happens when boys are between the ages of one and two,[8] while in Morocco and Iraq, boys are circumcised between the ages of five and seven.[9] Deeply religious Jews cut off the foreskin when a baby boy is eight days old, and then engage in the ritual practice of *metitsah*—the oral sucking of the blood of the tip of the penis by the man performing the procedure. And if you think that odd—or nauseating—consider that several Australian aboriginal tribes not only cut off the foreskin of boys once they hit puberty, but they also conduct "subincision," in which a long slit is cut down the underside of the penis, lengthwise.[10]

Here we clearly see the three components of cultural relativism.

First, diversity of practice and value: different peoples do different things to boys' penises. In some cultures, circumcision is not done at all, while in others it is—and both the timing and the way it is done differ widely. And values and beliefs concerning the justice or injustice, beauty or ugliness, and sanctity or barbarity of circumcision also vary widely: some see the practice as a wonderful, joyful blessing, while others see it as an abhorrent, savage instance of child abuse.

Second, we know that the number one predictor of people's views on the morality of cutting boys' penises depends largely on the culture within which they are raised. If people are raised within a certain tribe, ethnic group, or religion, circumcision will be seen as a beautiful tradition, or a proud part of one's heritage, or a noble linkage between ancestors and descendants, or an obligation to God, or a sublime coming-of-age ritual, or a time of deep celebration and true happiness. And it will be seen as moral. However, if people are raised in a culture that does not engage in the cutting of boys' penises, circumcision will be seen as brutal, heinous, or vicious. It will be seen as immoral.

Finally, in deciding whether or not male circumcision ought to be done, there is no nonhuman ruler to appeal to—no impartial arbiter who is above and outside of a given culture. It's just us, socialized and enculturated, doing things differently in different parts of the world and disagreeing on the morality of what is done.

To be sure, there are many good arguments against male circumcision. And there are also many good arguments for male circumcision. But the point here is not to decide which arguments are right. Rather, the point is to understand that what actually constitutes a "good" argument or "right" decision is inextricably culture-bound. As American sociologist Steven Lukes notes, "the standards of rationality—what counts as a reason and what counts as a good reason—vary from society to society, culture to culture . . . group to group."[11] And this is why the earnest assertion that circumcision is commanded by God/Allah will mean nothing to the atheist. And conversely, the empirical finding that circumcision significantly reduces the prevalence of sexually transmitted diseases will mean nothing to the Scott, Swede, or Slovakian—who can find other perfectly good and much less violent ways to practice safe, healthy sex.

Alas, is male circumcision good or bad? Moral or immoral? There is no *ultimate*, non-culture-bound answer. The morality or immorality of male circumcision is part of and conditioned by one's worldview, which is intractably shaped by one's culture. And if one has been socialized to value one's religious imperatives, cultural traditions, ethnic heritage, and/or socially constructed sense of masculinity, then circumcision is absolutely moral. But if one has been socialized to value the inalienable rights of children to be spared unnecessary pain and suffering, and if one believes that there is no valid excuse for such physical violence, then circumcision is absolutely immoral. As American anthropologist Melville Herskovits famously wrote back in the 1950s, "In every case where criteria to evaluate the ways of different peoples have been proposed, the question has at once posed itself: 'Whose standards?' The force of enculturative experience channels all judgements . . . there is no way to play this game of making judgements across cultures except with loaded dice."[12]

Attempts to Resolve the Dilemmas of Moral Relativism

We live in a world where tens of millions of children's genitals are cut. Is there any way to make judgments about this practice without playing with loaded dice—that is, without being biased and prejudiced by our own cultural upbringing? If we are not from a genitalia cutting/slicing culture, do we have a right to condemn such traditional practices? Or conversely, do we in fact have a *moral obligation* to oppose them? And if so, what form should our opposition take—mere rhetorical persuasion, or actually stepping in and stopping the practice by force? And if we think that we have a right to step into a culture different from our own and force its members to cease cutting their children's genitals, does that then mean that people from other cultures also have the same right to enter our culture and force us to start cutting our children's genitals? Why would our use of force trump theirs? Or their use of force trump ours? Why are our values more legitimate? Or, conversely, why are theirs?

Such are the daunting dilemmas inherent in moral relativism. Indeed, they are so daunting that they actually lead some people to embrace theism:

only a mighty, magical deity—such faithfully religious folks believe—can act as moral judge and arbiter, dictating from above what is wrong or right. Of course, this God delusion is a nonsolution. As chapters 1–3 have already explained, there is no compelling evidence that any such God exists, and even if one did, people cannot agree on how to interpret this God's will, and even if everyone could all agree on this God's will, we would still be reduced to a mere state of obedience when it comes to moral deliberation, and even if we all just willingly abdicated our moral consciences and submitted to a God's commands, it doesn't make those commands moral, per se—as Plato's dialogue between Euthyphro and Socrates illustrates. Heck, circumcision as commanded by God/Allah is a perfect case in point: the injunction presumably comes from on high, but what is *moral* about it, exactly? What could possibly be moral about cutting children's genitalia? It causes pain, fear, suffering, infection, and can reduce sexual pleasure in varying degrees. If anything, it is blatantly immoral in that it is unnecessary violence. But for the God-obeying theists, such ethical deliberation is not even possible. Only following orders is. And that's not being moral at all.

Fortunately, more and more humans are recognizing that a staunchly theistic orientation is totally unacceptable when confronting moral matters. So, how then do secular people—atheists and agnostics who don't believe in God—deal with moral relativism? How do they avoid or dull its daunting dilemmas when confronted with clashing practices and irreconcilable values in the real world?

There are several approaches—none perfect, all flawed. But here they are.

Judging Other Cultures Is Unavoidable

First, some will argue that it is perfectly legitimate for members of any culture to critique the practices of any other culture for the simple reason that such a thing has always been done. It is what unavoidably occurs, whether we like it or not. One not need worry about "infringing" or "imposing" on another culture because such intercultural judging has always been the norm. And in reality, there are no singular cultures utterly removed from outside influence or judgment. Completely isolated people such as my imagined Amazon tribe—hidden away in the jungles, separated from all other cultures—don't actually exist. As British philosopher Mary Midgley has argued, the concept of individual, distinctly monolithic cultures is "utterly unreal and unhistorical."[13]

Every culture on planet Earth has always intermingled with other cultures to varying degrees, which means that no group of people has ever constructed its moral system in complete isolation, hermetically sealed off from other values and ethical viewpoints. As such, people need not desist from influencing people in other cultures. Everyone is free to judge and critique other cultures' values, to try to influence them, to try and change them. It is simply how things have always worked on planet Earth. And besides—just to push the paradoxical heart of moral relativism here—the very notion that one ought not criticize or judge the morality of other cultures is itself a universalistic moral rule that is paradoxically embedded within, and thus relative to, some cultural system. So there's simply no escaping the ironic situation here; all of our morals are relative to some cultural standards.

While it is true that cultures have always existed in a state of mutual influence, and thus intercultural criticism has always been the norm, this still doesn't help us resolve moral disagreements between two cultures in the here and now. For example—and sticking with circumcision here—consider that back in 2011, thousands of people in San Francisco signed a proposal supporting a voter initiative to make it illegal to circumcise boys under the age of eighteen; anyone caught doing so would face a misdemeanor charge that could carry up to a year's sentencing in jail or a fine of up to $1,000. People who viewed the practice of male circumcision as violent abuse felt a moral obligation to try to stop it in their midst; they thus saw this voter initiative as deeply moral and just. Of course, for religious Jews and Muslims, such a law was seen as immoral: it would prohibit and punish them for doing what is of great value to their God and their culture. Circumcision—to them—is a highly moral act, and making it illegal would be immoral and unjust.

The initiative never came to a democratic vote; a judge ordered it withdrawn from the ballot on the grounds that California law stipulates that the regulation of medical procedures can only be decided at the state level, not the city level. But here's the point: people from different cultures—even though living among each other, in the same city, within the same neighborhoods, intermingling and influencing each other in many ways and being totally cognizant of each other's viewpoints—*still* vehemently disagree about the morality or immorality of cutting off the tips of boys' penises. And this disagreement is intrinsically culture-bound. And there is no impartial, objective way to resolve it. Anyone who has an opinion on the matter is coming from some distinct cultural framework that has influenced and informed his or her opinion.

Aligning with Allies from Within

A second secular attempt to try to solve dilemmas inherent in moral relativism takes a related but different approach, which goes like this: it is perfectly legitimate to critique and condemn practices and values of other cultures because, in reality, there is often disagreement *within* every given culture concerning its own beliefs or practices. As American philosopher Martha Nussbaum argues, in every culture there are internal power dynamics that privilege some at the expense of others, that render some individuals or class of individuals more free and others less free, and that always leave some members of any given culture skeptical and critical of their own culture's moral truths.[14] In addition to such fissures of inequality that generate internal moral debate, there are always people in every culture who have not fully internalized its norms and values; as American sociologist Steven Lukes notes, in every group "there will always be, whether openly or secretly . . . uncertain identifiers, ambivalent identifiers, intermittent identifiers, quasi-identifiers, semi-identifiers, cross-identifiers, nonidentifiers, ex-identifiers, and anti-identifiers."[15] Thus, an outsider to a given culture can always ally him- or herself with those individuals from inside the culture who are critical of this or that practice. For example, apropos male circumcision, there are some people from within Jewish and Muslim communities who oppose it, and thus someone from outside of those cultures can actively oppose circumcision by simply aligning themselves with those from within the very cultures that practice it.

Sure. This can happen. But it's not a perfect solution. After all, sometimes all the people within an entire culture can be in complete agreement about a given practice, such as the eating of meat. If everyone in a given culture agrees that eating meat is moral, then what is the animal rights activist from outside that culture to do? What if there is no legitimate "minority position" within that culture that they can align with? The fact is, sometimes different cultures will not exhibit any internal debate about a given practice; everyone in that culture will agree to the value and morality of it. And so, if others outside of the culture find the practice immoral, there is a genuine, unadulterated clash of values. And there is no truly objective way to resolve that clash.

We're Right and They're Wrong

A third secular attempt at avoiding the implications of moral relativism: simply taking the position that some cultures are just plain wrong or mistaken about the morality or immorality of their practices and values. It doesn't matter that the members of a given culture have been doing or believing something for generations, or that they are all in agreement. They can still be morally incorrect. On what basis are they incorrect? Relative to what criteria? According to what objective standard? Well, science, of course!

Such is the confident position championed by bestselling American author Sam Harris. As he has argued in *The Moral Landscape*, all morality is reducible to one scientifically verifiable criterion: the well-being of conscious creatures. Since states of well-being can be measured physically and neurologically, then morality is a factual, scientifically observable matter. That is, given that the experiencing of comfort or suffering can be observed in the brains, heartbeats, and other physical platforms of living beings, any cultural practice that causes conscious creatures to needlessly suffer is demonstrably immoral, while any cultural practice that increases well-being is demonstrably moral. And it doesn't matter what people within any given culture think. They can be, according to Harris, "wrong about morality."[16] As he explains, "just as it is possible for individuals and groups to be wrong about how best to maintain their physical health, it is possible for them to be wrong about how to maximize their personal and social well-being."[17]

While appreciating and sharing Harris's emphasis on the well-being of conscious creatures as a solid moral guide, and while understanding that things like brain scans can indicate whether or not a person is in a state of comfort, fear, or suffering, I'm still not sure how we can rest assured that certain values or morals are "right" while others are "wrong" in some sort of purely objective, scientific sense.

Let's continue to stick with male circumcision here.

The practice clearly causes pain and suffering. And that can be empirically measured. But it sometimes results in much pride, honor, and joy—which can also can be empirically measured. So, which manifestation of suffering or pleasure is more important? Which ought to be privileged?

Furthermore, according to recent scientific research as published in the *Journal of the American Medical Association*, men with circumcised penises have significantly lower rates of urinary tract infections, decreased risk of acquiring a sexually transmitted disease (including HIV), and rates of cervical cancer are markedly lower in the female partners of circumcised men.[18] Additional studies of the specific health benefits of male circumcision find that:

> [m]ale circumcision reduces the risk of acquiring genital herpes by 28 percent to 34 percent, and the risk of developing genital ulceration by 47 percent. Additionally . . . male circumcision reduces the risk of oncogenic high-risk human papillomavirus (HR-HPV) by 32 percent to 35 percent. While some consider male circumcision to be primarily a male issue, one trial also reported derivative benefits for female partners of circumcised men; the risk of HR-HPV for female partners was reduced by 28 percent, the risk of bacterial vaginosis was reduced by 40 percent, and the risk of trichomoniasis was reduced by 48 percent.[19]

So, given Harris's perspective, is the cultural practice of male circumcision moral or immoral? It clearly causes immediate pain and suffering, but it can also markedly decrease pain and suffering and increase health and well-being. Which is more important on the presumably objective morality meter: the brief experience of pain the circumcised boy feels or the long-term personal and societal benefits of a reduction of urinary tract infections and sexually transmitted diseases? It's hard to see how science can objectively help us here. After all, science is simply a method for observing the components and processes of the natural world. It can tell us nothing about the morality or immorality of those components or processes. As Canadian philosopher Kai Nielsen succinctly asserts, scientific knowledge is not moral knowledge.[20]

Consider the eating of animals. It causes pain and suffering for the animals but contentedness and well-being for the humans who eat them. Are animals (conscious creatures) of less moral value than humans (also conscious creatures)? How can "science" objectively settle this matter? What objective units or quantifiable data will count and be measured to settle the debate? None.

There is no question, obviously, that once we come to some agreement regarding what is of value or what is moral, science can certainly help us pursue various ends; Harris is correct on that front. But how do we agree on what is of value or what is moral? That will always be a social, culture-bound enterprise, and one that no amount of empirical measurement can determine.

One Human Family

From a secular vantage point, when pondering conflicts over what practices are moral and immoral in various cultures—and noting that such pondering is always relative to some cultural framework—we can nonetheless make judgments and criticisms of other cultures because, as we have seen: 1) it is simply what has always been done, and no culture is, or has ever been, completely isolated from other cultures' viewpoints; 2) there is almost always internal disagreement within any given culture; and 3) if the well-being of conscious creatures is our accepted guide, then science can indeed provide evidence on what activities and practices enhance or degrade such well-being. But, as discussed above, none of these approaches is perfect. They all have their limitations.

There is, however, a fourth secular approach to the dilemma of moral relativism, grounded in cosmopolitanism, which I find the most promising. It goes like this: we are all part of one human family. That's an empirical fact. And given that we are all, as a species, brothers and sisters—biologically, if in no other way—then, as such, we are free to critique, praise, and judge each other. Will our opinions, perspectives, and moral predilections be shaped by—and thus be relative to—our respective cultural background? You bet. But that's the case for everyone. No one living is "acultural." As such, we have no choice but to acknowledge our relative moral positionality—and then proceed to give voice to our views. As Sam Harris puts it, "we simply must stand somewhere."[21]

If we think that people in some other culture are doing something immoral, we are free to express that. Actually, more than free: we are *obligated* to express that, given the imperatives of empathy, compassion, and justice. Of course, in expressing our viewpoint on moral matters cross-culturally, we must provide our reasons and justifications.[22] We must appeal to principles and ideals. We must defend our viewpoint with facts, logic, stories, and examples. And, in turn, we must strive to listen to those who disagree with us, and we must consider their reasons with the same earnestness that we would like them to consider our own. As American philosopher J. David Velleman puts it:

> The rational way to disagree with people who live differently is to articulate our own self-understanding, [and] listen as they articulate theirs . . . the reason for talking with those who live differently is that we and they share at least some common ground, since all of us are trying to figure out how to make better sense of and to ourselves as human beings . . . [and] we have reason to think that it will lead to progress that is recognizably moral, because our need for mutual intelligibility has its source in our sociality.[23]

Again, we are one human family. On a finite orb. And as we designate some actions as moral and some as immoral, we inevitably disagree. Indeed, at the time of this writing, both Iceland and Denmark are considering passing legislation that would make the circumcising of boys a crime. And Muslims and Jews—both within Iceland and Denmark and without—are none too happy about such a possibility; they are charging that xenophobia, Islamophobia, anti-Semitism, and antireligious bigotry are propelling such laws, which would legally infringe on their sacred rituals and cultural heritages. But the advocates of making circumcision a crime insist that the practice constitutes immoral violence against children and should be stopped. A vehement disagreement, to be sure.

The only option in such a situation? Open discussion and democratic debate among Earth-dwelling men and women, the respectful airing of our ethical differences, and the confident sharing of our culture-bound perspectives. For, as Mary Midgley states, ethical deliberation demands a vaster horizon of insights and possibilities than any single society can supply, given that morality's "field of reference is the world."[24]

As ongoing clashes of morality perpetually flare up, we will most likely never fully agree about this or that practice. Such is life. Such is reality. Moral deliberation and ethical development will never be "done" or "finished," but rather will always constitute arenas of ongoing debate and disagreement, so long as there are humans to speak, act, feel, reflect, fear, imagine, and care. And to think that there is some definitive, absolute, universal, objective approach to all moral dilemmas—an ethical holy grail—just waiting to be discovered, that will put an end to debate and disagreement once and for all, is to dwell in a state of childlike fantasy, pining for some magical security blanket that is simply not to be found in this cosmos. As Australian philosopher John Kekes writes, "nothing is always, in all contexts, at all times, for all people more important than something that may conflict with it. To think otherwise, to suppose that a theory could be constructed about an ideal to which we should adhere no matter what emergencies, conflicts, or changes may occur in the future, is . . . [an] illusion."[25]

Given this situation, one of the greatest paradoxical profundities of moral deliberation is that despite the impossibility of any definitive answers, we still can't help but partake in ongoing ethical debate. Given our naturally evolved faculties for compassion, we are compelled to engage in the unavoidable work of moral negotiation, a work that always entails disagreement and conflict. Such is the intercultural, global, ongoing improvisational work of "ethical jazz."[26] And as we participate in this process of moral negotiation, we rely only upon ourselves and our ability to understand—rather than passively and prudently cower in obedience to some magical otherworldly moral authority that doesn't even exist. And as we engage other people from other cultures with whom we vehemently disagree on moral matters, we strive to find at least some points of value convergence, some links of shared ideals—which most certainly exist given our shared humanity and united evolutionary origins. And from those intersecting kernels of mutual understanding, we develop our arguments sensitively and listen attentively, and as we do this, we best engage in moral deliberation with our human siblings. And that, in the absence of some cosmic arbiter, is the best we can do.

Short of violence, it is all we can do.

Conclusion

The Necessity of Secular Morality

The students at Pitzer College, where I have taught for over twenty years, are an impressively idealistic lot. They meander the campus of this small liberal arts college mindfully intent on making the world a better place. Many of them came to Pitzer with varying depths of community-engaged experience, having already participated in some kind of social justice work as teenagers: raising money for a local hospital, designing a website for a nonprofit, fighting to get solar panels installed at their high school, educating people in Botswana about HIV and AIDS prevention, and tutoring children of recent immigrants.

I remain perpetually heartened by their idealism. Although they worry—like all college students in America these days—about getting a good job after graduation, they also want that job to be in a profession that helps them to fight injustice, work for the rights of the oppressed, care for those in need, bridge divides, and reduce inequality.

Unfortunately, there's something else that most of my students share: a sense that the world is rapidly melting. For the last five years or so, climate change has come up consistently in just about every class I've taught, with virtually all the students expressing a uniform pessimism about the near future: they don't expect it to be all that good. In fact, they expect it to be cataclysmic. They are keenly aware of the scientific evidence regarding climate change, such as the landmark report published by the United Nations in 2018,[1] which states that if greenhouse gas emissions remain the same, the Earth will continue to heat up, the polar ice caps will continue to melt, the sea levels will continue to rise, violent storms will continue to worsen, droughts and famines will increase, and life will become increasingly precarious for most of the world's inhabitants. And this will lead to greater degrees of fear, hunger, suffering, violence, and death. It is a grim future for planet Earth, and one that even my most idealistic students can't help but anticipate. So, paradoxically, while they pursue their bachelor's degrees, intent on making the world a better place, they simultaneously don't expect the world to survive for too much longer.

Given this dispirited disposition, they represent the first generation of college students in American history to be fairly certain that the end of the world is nigh—and not because biblical fantasies predict Jesus's immanent return in all his glory, but rather because ever mounting evidence indicates impending planetary disaster.

My students' shared pessimism regarding the bleak future of the planet is, indeed, grounded in a sober understanding of the best scientific evidence available, all of which points toward rapid global warming.[2] For example, as NASA's latest "Global Climate Change" report explains, sixteen of the seventeen warmest years on record have occurred since 2001, the world's oceans are currently the warmest in recorded history, the Greenland and Antarctic ice sheets have rapidly decreased in mass, glaciers all around the world—from Alaska to the Andes to the Alps—are retreating, the snow cover in the northern hemisphere has been steadily decreasing for over fifty years straight, sea levels are rising at unprecedented rates, sea life around the globe is threatened by unprecedented levels of acidification—and 97 percent of climate scientists agree that all of this is largely the result of human activity.[3]

"I was just up in Santa Barbara," one of my students shared during a recent class discussion. "The best beach that I used to go to when I was a kid is now almost completely underwater. The ocean now covers all of the sand and just goes right up to the stone wall by the road."

"It's been that way for a while," another student lamented.

Bang Bang You're Dead

If climate change haunts the near future of today's college students, getting shot in the face or stomach haunts the very present of our nation's high schoolers.

As I write this, yet another mass shooting at a public high school has just occurred. This one was in Santa Fe, Texas, just outside of Houston. Ten people were killed, thirteen injured, and hundreds scarred for life. Just before the Santa Fe tragedy, there was a mass shooting at a high school in Parkland, Florida. Seventeen people were killed, seventeen more injured, and hundreds scarred for life from the trauma of it all. I am sure that by the time you are reading this sentence, several more such school shootings will have taken place.

It is a bloody, horrific epidemic.

Given the ongoing rate of such violence—close to three hundred school shootings in the United States since 2009—American teenagers are now eighty-two times more likely to be shot to death than teenagers living in the rest of the developed world.[4]

As my two older children have gone through their teenage years, there have been numerous threats of shootings at their high school; we get automated calls from the principal several times a year, telling us of this or that received threat, and why we shouldn't be worried, and that everything is under control, and that our children will be safe at school. But such threats gnaw away at your sense of well-being.

And my children have participated in numerous mandatory safety drills, during which they practice what to do and what not to do in the case of a shooter's presence. Such trainings infuse their veins with fear and insecurity. And it doesn't help that they regularly see news of mass shootings beyond the nation's schools: twelve people shot to death at a bar in Thousand Oaks, California, and eleven people shot to death in a synagogue in Pittsburgh in 2018; fifty-eight people shot to death at a country music festival in Las Vegas and twenty-six people shot to death in a church in Southerland Springs, Texas, in 2017; forty-nine people shot to death at a nightclub in Orlando, Florida, in 2016; fourteen people shot to death at a community center in San Bernardino, California, and nine people shot to death at a community college in Roseburg, Oregon, in 2015; six killed in Isla Vista, California, in 2014; twelve killed in a movie theater in Aurora, Colorado, in 2012; twenty-seven people—mostly children—shot to death at an elementary school in Newton, Connecticut, in 2012.

On average, approximately thirteen thousand Americans are killed by guns every year. And every day, approximately seven children are killed by guns.[5] Such endless horror and ongoing grief makes life in American society feel precarious, to say the least.

Just the other day, I overheard my seventeen-year-old daughter talking in her room with her friends about the possibility of a shooting happening on their campus.

"Would you run or hide?" she asked her two best friends. They discussed the pros and cons of each perilous option.

"Who do you think is most likely to do it?" one of her friends wondered aloud. They discussed various loners, weirdos, and seemingly troubled kids at school, speculating on the potential of each for mass murder.

"They say the shots sound like firecrackers," her other friend offered. They paused, their minds envisioning the scene: the sound of firecrackers, kids running and hiding, the boy entering the room, the blood.

As the secular African American writer, director, actor, and rapper Donald Glover has recently lamented: this is America.

More Bad News

Both impending global warming as a result of human-created climate change and systemic gun violence in America are but two prominent examples of the kinds of brutal challenges we humans face in the early part of the twenty-first century.

And there's so much more.

Here in the United States, racial inequality remains doggedly entrenched. Despite some notable gains over the last fifty years—particularly in civil rights and educational attainment—a 2018 report from the Economic Policy Institute has found that the median white family has almost ten times as much wealth as the median African American family, African Americans are 2.5 times as likely to be living in poverty as white Americans, the African American unemployment rate is approximately twice that of the white unemployment rate, the rate of African American home ownership is 30 percent lower than white home ownership, the African American infant mortality rate is 2.3 times higher than the white infant mortality rate, and the African American incarceration rate is more than six times that of the white incarceration rate.[6] This last matter of Black incarceration calls out for particular emphasis; as African American sociologist Michelle Alexander documents in her book *The New Jim Crow*, the war on drugs has been a political and institutional process that purposefully and disproportionately targeted and imprisoned African Americans while treating white Americans involved with drugs with virtual impunity. For instance, even though the majority of illegal drug dealers and users in the United States are white, three-fourths of all people who have been sent to prison for drug violations have been people of color.[7] On top of entrenched, systemic economic disparities and the racism of the war on drugs, African Americans are frequently the victims of civilian violence and hate crimes across the country, and they are disproportionately stopped, harassed, beaten, shot, and killed by the nation's police.[8]

Another matter of pressing moral concern: worldwide gender oppression. While many women—particularly those living in the most secularized societies, it should be noted—have enjoyed significant improvement in recent decades in terms of political status, educational attainment, control of their bodies, and career options, the fact remains that globally women's lives are significantly worse than men's. As American social scientists Lori

Underwood and Dawn Hutchinson detail in their book *The Global Status of Women and Girls*, females are significantly underrepresented in the world's governments, courts, and business executive boards; they experience legally sanctioned oppression in numerous countries; they are consistently the victims of harassment, sexual abuse, and rape; millions have their genitals severely mutilated; they are subject to forced marriages, often as children; they experience unequal access to health care; they are far more likely than their male counterparts to be illiterate; and they are far more likely to live in poverty than men.[9]

Homosexuals also face oppression and persecution all over the world. Despite tremendous strides toward acceptance and equality in many countries—generally among the most secular of nations, of course—hatred of gay men and women remains quite extreme. For example, an Afrobarometer report from 2015, comprising surveys from thirty-three countries, found that around 80 percent of Africans would be upset if their neighbor were homosexual.[10] In the United States in 2016, over one thousand hate crimes against homosexuals were reported to the FBI,[11] and in 2017, more than one hundred anti-homosexual rights bills were introduced by Christian politicians in twenty-nine states.[12] In countries such as Jamaica and Senegal, homosexuals are regularly kicked out of their homes, fired from work, harassed in public, extorted, subject to arbitrary arrest and detention, beaten, and killed—and with no legal recourse for protection.[13] In Russia, it is illegal to publicly talk about homosexuality in any way other than critical, and those who violate this law can be subject to fines of tens of thousands of dollars.[14] In Brazil, the killing of a homosexual specifically because of his or her sexual orientation happens on a daily basis. In Chechnya, governmental authorities raid homosexual gatherings, arresting, starving, and torturing those captured.[15] Homosexuality is currently a prosecutable crime in seventy-two countries,[16] and in a handful of Muslim-majority nations, the punishment is execution.[17] By some estimates, as many as six thousand homosexuals haven been murdered by the Iranian government since 1979.[18]

Religious minorities all over the world face similar and often worse forms of oppression. According a 2017 report of the United States Commission on International Religious Freedom, all religious believers are severely persecuted in North Korea—often sent to prison camps where they are starved and tortured. In Myanmar, thousands of Rohingya Muslims have been slaughtered in recent years; women have been raped, hundreds of villages burned, and nearly a million people have been forced to flee as refugees.[19] In addition to being the occasional victims of mob violence, Muslims in India face all kinds of inequities and humiliations; they often can't rent apartments, can't get loans, and face regular job discrimination.[20] Muslims also face oppression in the Central African Republic; Falun Gong members are persecuted in China; acts of Jew-hatred—from vandalism of cemeteries to terrorist killings—have been on the rise in Europe for several years; Christians are arrested and tortured in Eritrea and Sudan and oppressed to varying degrees in Yemen, Somalia, Egypt, and Libya; Jews, Bahais, Christians, and Zoroastrians are discriminated against in Iran; Christians and Ahmadi are oppressed in Pakistan; and atheists are deemed terrorists—subject to arrest, torture, and even the death penalty—in Saudi Arabia.[21]

Other pressing problems the world faces: Billions of people live in poverty, with twenty-two thousand children dying every day as a result of poor living conditions.[22] Totalitarian dictators in numerous nations curtail freedom and deny human rights to those unfortunate enough to live under their fists; virulent religious fanaticism has erupted into violent movements—such as ISIS, Boko Haram, Al Queda, and the Lord's Resistance Army—that commit horrific acts of terrorism; gender nonconformists and transgender individuals face hatred and repression; inequality within countries and between countries is extreme and increasingly unsustainable; various nations, such as Palestine, Tibet, and Kurdistan, remain occupied and brutalized; teenagers are trafficked; overpopulation depletes resources at an alarming rate; millions of children are regularly abused and sexually assaulted; more animals are becoming extinct, while millions are raised in torturous, industrial conditions for mass slaughter; nuclear bombs remain poised to incinerate much of humanity; and the Amazon rain forest is being steadily destroyed.

It is a gruesome, overwhelming list of social problems that we face—social problems that are ultimately moral problems at root, for they directly affect the health and well-being of hundreds of millions of men, women, children, and other sentient beings.

Thus, given the state of the world, we need ethics and morality devoid of religious faith—now more than ever. We need secular morality, and we need it fast.

Fortunately, the secular approaches to ethical understanding and moral action outlined in this book are on the rise. More and more people are shedding their religiosity, and as they do so, religion's longstanding, problematic, and unjustifiably tight grip on morality is loosening. And as religion's grip on morality loosens, secular morality strengthens and increases. And as secular morality grows and matures, more rational and effective approaches to solving the world's problems strengthen and expand. Thus, amidst the pressing problems riddling this terrestrial home of ours, there is good reason to take heart.

Let's start with the first positive development: rising rates of irreligion. After that, we'll look at how this dramatic secularization will help us to better address the dire challenges we face.

Secularism Surging

A country-by-country tally of how much religion has faded over the last half century is beyond the scope of this concluding chapter. So instead, I will just present some specific global highlights.

While less than 5 percent of Americans identified with no religion back in the 1960s, today, somewhere between 25 percent and 34 percent of Americans claim no religious identification—and among Americans in their twenties, 38 percent claim no religious identification.[23] These are the highest rates of irreligion ever seen in U.S. history.[24] As for God-belief specifically: Gallup polls indicate that about 10 percent of Americans are now atheist or agnostic,[25] but new research employing more sensitive methodologies suggests that as many as 25 percent of Americans may actually lack a belief in God, although they prefer not to say so, given the stigma attached to such a stance.[26]

In Canada, while less than 5 percent of adults claimed to have no religion back in the 1960s, nearly 25 percent are irreligious today—and in the province of British Columbia, a full 45 percent are nonreligious.[27]

In Australia, those claiming to have *no* religion are now, paradoxically, the largest "religious" group in the country,[28] and 26 percent of adults are atheist or agnostic specifically—the highest rate of unbelief ever seen in Australian history.[29]

In New Zealand, over 40 percent of adults claim to have no religion—and among those in their twenties, approximately 55 percent are irreligious.[30] And at least 28 percent of New Zealanders currently don't believe in God.[31]

The total number of nonreligious individuals in Latin America has increased from 8 percent in 2014 to almost 20 percent today.[32] Uruguay and Chile are at the forefront of this advancing secularization, where a historic high of approximately 40 percent of adults in both countries are now nonreligious.[33] Additionally, 33 percent of those in Belize and Argentina, 25 percent in Mexico, and 20 percent in Venezuela currently say that religion is not an important part of their daily life.[34]

In the United Kingdom, back in 1983, about 30 percent of the people said that they were not at all religious, but today it is up to 53 percent of the population—an all-time British high.[35] And one survey from 2017 found the historically unimaginable: over 70 percent of adults in Scotland are now secular.[36]

As for Scandinavia, for the first time in Norwegian history, there are now more atheists (39 percent) than theists (37 percent), with the remainder of the population being agnostic.[37] In Denmark, 64 percent describe themselves as being neither spiritual nor religious, and in Sweden, 76 percent of people are affirmatively secular.[38]

In other European nations, secularity continues to skyrocket,[39] with rates of disaffiliation, apostasy, atheism, and agnosticism at historically unprecedented levels: 66 percent of Czechs and 56 percent of Estonians do not believe in God.[40] Fifty percent of the Dutch are atheists—the highest rates of Dutch nonbelief ever. And approximately 40 percent of the French and Germans now report being atheist or agnostic.[41] Generationally, all signs point to continued European secularization, given that among younger adults—those in their twenties—approximately 90 percent of Czechs, 80 percent of Estonians, 75 percent of Swedes, 67 percent of Hungarians, 65 percent of Belgians, and 55 percent of those in Spain have no religion.[42]

Irreligion is also rising throughout Asia. In Japan, participation in religious activities at shrines and temples, the performance of Buddhist and Shinto rituals, and household ownership of religious altars have all been declining for over six decades, and while about 70 percent of adults claimed to hold personal religious beliefs sixty-five years ago, that figure is now down to only about 20 percent today.[43] And in South Korea, the percentage of individuals with no religion has risen from 47 percent in 2005 up to nearly at least 56 percent today—the highest rate of secularity in the history of the southern Korean Peninsula.[44]

Although free, unfettered social science is not possible in Communist China or Vietnam—where religion is repressed and those involved in religion or expressing religious beliefs can face various forms of political, legal, civil, and economic hardships—most estimates suggest that huge percentages of the populations of these countries are secular to varying degrees.[45] Free, unfettered social science is also impossible in the many Islamic states headed by dictators, where being secular is harshly sanctioned, even to the point of death. However, even in these nations, signs of growing secularism are abundant.[46]

Of course, in many countries, such as India, religious belief and participation remain quite strong and pervasive; this is particularly true in Muslim-majority nations such as Pakistan and Bangladesh, and also nearly all the countries of Africa, where degrees of irreligiosity are minimal. And some societies have even seen an uptick in religiosity in the last half century, such as several former Soviet countries, where religion was previously suppressed for decades by the communist policy of coercive, state-enforced atheism.[47] But such strongly religious societies, where religion has not significantly weakened or has even gained momentum in recent decades, are in the distinct minority. Most countries around the world have seen rates of religious belief, participation, and identification all decline—many dramatically so.[48] The trend has been so significant that in 2016, *National Geographic* declared "No Religion" the World's Newest Major Religion, noting that while "there have long been predictions that religion would fade from relevancy as the world modernizes . . . all the recent surveys are finding that it's happening startlingly fast."[49]

The Godless Good News

This is extremely good news. For as more and more people shed their religious faith, secular approaches to morality will concomitantly advance. Such a shift from obedience-driven, God-based morality to empathy-driven humanistic morality means that an increasing number of humans will calibrate their ethical decision-making based on whether or not a given choice, act, or policy increases or decrease suffering—rather than simply following rules written down thousands of years ago, ostensibly originating from a magical deity, and subsequently interpreted and promulgated by priests, ministers, imams, rabbis, and gurus. It means that more men and women—when pondering how to vote or what social change or political agenda to support—will ask how they themselves would like to be treated, and treat others in kind, rather than make such decisions based on a prudent yearning for heaven or a deep-seated fear of hell. It means that theistic moral outsourcing will diminish, and natural, socially evolved morality will become increasingly understood and appreciated as the responsibility of existentially free individuals exercising their consciences—which is the way morality should work.

As American journalist and historian Mitchell Stephens observes, surging secularism means that "an increasing number of men and women around the world now can think things through and work out their obligations to their fellow humans and to the planet without having to worry about the diktats of some ancient, jealous, vengeful god."[50] Indeed, with more and more societies secularizing, their populations will become increasingly characterized by moral progress that entails a desire to aid and assist those in fear or pain, to comfort the vulnerable and distressed, to make life safer and more secure for as many people as possible, to increase happiness and well-being, to bolster systems of justice, to be empathetic, compassionate, altruistic, honest, and fair, and to avoid causing unnecessary pain or harm to others—and all because such orientations and proclivities can be rationally understood and reasonably proven to make life better for everyone.

As strident religion withers and secularity becomes more mainstream, the virtues and orientations that are prominent among secular, humanist men and women will be fruitfully brought to bear when confronting the world's problems. For example, the secular virtue of scientific empiricism will be more widely embraced as the only way to address pressing challenges like climate change and gun violence. Cosmopolitanism will be increasingly recognized as essential for overcoming racial, ethnic, and religious conflict, and for ending the repressive occupations of one nation by another. Resolutely living in reality—rather than engaging in magical thinking or delusionally relying on prayer—will be a more commonly acknowledged requirement for understanding and addressing the root causes of numerous social problems, from terrorism and dictatorships to overpopulation and poverty. And empathy and compassion will become ever more salient moral imperatives in the fight for the rights of women, homosexuals, gender nonconformists, religious minorities, racial minorities, abused children, and animals.

With advancing secularization, we can expect even more positive outcomes for humanity. For example, fewer children will be scarred by nightmarish fears of devils, demons, and hell; fewer children's genitals will be cut and mutilated; more people will have wider access to an ever-expanding body of knowledge, ideas, and theories; rational freethinking will be celebrated and encouraged by more and more people; freedom of conscience will expand; scientific literacy will improve; honest, accurate, and healthy sex education will become more widespread and informative, thereby decreasing unwanted pregnancies and sexually transmitted diseases; more women will experience improved status, power, and agency; more women will enjoy greater control over their reproductive capacities; more parents will enjoy greater options for childcare; religiously inspired nationalism and tribalism will falter; fewer humans will be racked with guilty self-loathing over harmless, healthy behaviors such as masturbation; democracy will be bolstered, as fewer people will be comfortable obediently submitting to the power of authority; fewer people will be confined by the narrow boxes of traditional gender norms; fewer homosexuals and gender nonconformists will live in fear; criminal justice will be based on rehabilitation rather than retribution; incarceration will become more humane, thereby reducing crime rates overall; fewer politicians will base their decision-making or justify their policies by appealing to supernatural nonentities; money that would have been spent on building churches, mosques, or temples will be used to build schools, hospitals, solar farms, and wind farms; and so on.

Surety

I recognize that advancing secularization, in and of itself, will not solve all the world's problems. Many of the crises we face are not directly related to religion, per se, and they will not somehow magically evaporate as more and more people lose their faith in gods, embrace a naturalistic worldview, and stop going to church or mosque. Racism, misogyny, tribalism, nationalism, violence, fanaticism, inequality, poverty, environmental destruction—these are multifaceted phenomena deeply rooted in complex dynamics of power and privilege, status and competition, greed and fear, all enmeshed within economic structures, political webs, psychological orientations, and bio-evolutionary proclivities operating well beyond the limited spheres of religious faith and secular humanism.

Secularism—in and of itself—is no global panacea. We can be sure of that.

But just as we can be sure that secularism will not solve everything, we can be equally sure that it will, if nothing more, nudge us in the right direction. The moral heart of secularism—characterized by its pillars of empathy, cosmopolitanism, and the desire to alleviate suffering—motivates and supports movements for justice, fairness, human flourishing, and global health.

And we can also be sure that *without* secularism, few problems will be solved. Prayers will not end gun violence; only rational, human-enforced policies will do that. Faith will not protect the ozone layer or the melting polar ice caps; only science-based, empirically demonstrable solutions will do that. Pining for heaven will not end poverty; only realistic, collaborative social action in the here and now will do that. Looking outside ourselves—and up to the heavens—for moral guidance will not provide the insight and inspiration needed to spread democracy or end child abuse; only a reliance upon ourselves and our capacity to do good will accomplish that.

Thus, secularism remains one of the great forces—among many—of human progress. Not because it allows people to sleep in on Sundays, or does away with this or that obscure ritual, or eases the marriage of two people who love one another despite the differing faiths of their grandfathers. No. The greatest value of secularism is its moral heart, which allows us to be just and humane for all the right reasons, and with all the duties and responsibilities a world without God entails. Such a humanist morality—grounded in the evolutionary history of our development as a species, nurtured by the care and concern of parents with each generation anew, molded and secured by socialization, informed and cultivated by culture, guided by reason and reflection, changing and progressing through time, and ever beating with a heart of empathy and compassion—undoubtedly and inevitably must reside, comfortably and closely, alongside any of the various ideologies and movements propelling us toward a future forged by hope and necessity.

ACKNOWLEDGMENTS

Thank you to:

Miriam Altshuler, Dan Smetanka, Stacy Elliott, Flora Elliott Zuckerman, James Warren, David Vinson, Hemant Mehta, Juhem Navarro-Rivera, Patrick Mason, David Moore, Kyle Thompson, Emily Sophia Levine, John Norvell, Coleen Macnamara, Azim Shariff, Zhuo Job Chen, Fount LeRon Shults, Ryan Cragun, Brian Keeley, Frank Pasquale, Emilio Ferrer-Caja, Abrol Fairweather, and Marvin Zuckerman.

NOTES

INTRODUCTION

1. Domenico Montanaro, "Poll: More Believe Ford than Kavanaugh, a Cultural Shift from 1991," NPR, October 3, 2018, www.npr.org/2018/10/03/654054108/poll-more-believe-ford-than-kavanaugh-a-cultural-shift-from-1991.
2. Jay Michaelson, "Jeff Sessions Said 'Secularists' Are Unfit for Government," *The Daily Beast*, January 12, 2017, www.thedailybeast.com/jeff-sessions-said-secularists-are-unfit-for-government; "Jeff Sessions Doesn't Think Secularists Can Know the Truth," *Patheos*, January 12, 2017, www.patheos.com/blogs/dispatches/2017/01/12/jeff-sessions-doesnt-think-secularists-can-know-truth.
3. "Attorney General Bewails 'Moral Decline,'" *Deseret News*, October 7, 1992, www.deseretnews.com/article/251927/ATTORNEY-GENERAL-BEWAILS-MORAL-DECLINE.html.
4. Guenter Lewy, *If God Is Dead, Everything Is Permitted?* (New Brunswick, NJ: Transaction, 2008).
5. Alvin Plantinga, "Comments on 'Satanic Verses: Moral Chaos in Holy Writ,'" in *Divine Evil? The Moral Character of the God of Abraham*, ed. Michael Bergmann, Michael J. Murray, and Michael C. Rea (Oxford: Oxford University Press, 2011), 109–114.
6. William Lane Craig, *Apologetics: An Introduction* (Chicago: Moody Press, 1984), 37–51.
7. Robert Cliquet and Dragana Abramov, *Evolution Science and Ethics in the Third Millennium*, (Cham, Switzerland: Springer, 2018).
8. Chris Hedges, *American Fascists: The Christian Right and the War on America* (New York: Free Press, 2006).
9. Michael Parenti, *God and His Demons* (Amherst, NY: Prometheus Books, 2010).
10. Nina Burleigh, "Evangelical Christians Helped Elect Donald Trump, but Their Time as a

Major Political Force Is Coming to an End," *Newsweek*, December 13, 2018, www.newsweek.com/2018/12/21/evangelicals-republicans-trump-millenials-1255745.html.

11. Gregory A. Smith and Jessica Martínez, "How the faithful voted: A preliminary 2016 analysis," *FactTank* (blog), Pew Research Center, November 9, 2016, www.pewresearch.org/fact-tank/2016/11/09/how-the-faithful-voted-a-preliminary-2016-analysis.
12. Andrew Whitehead, Samuel Perry, and Joseph Baker, "Make America Christian Again: Christian Nationalism and Voting for Donald Trump in the 2016 Presidential Election," *Sociology of Religion*, 2018, 79(2): 147–171.
13. Andrew Fiala, *What Would Jesus Really Do?* (Lanham, MD: Rowman and Littlefield, 2006).
14. Hemant Mehta, "EPA Head Scott Pruitt: God Gave Us This Planet, So We Can Destroy It," *Friendly Atheist* (blog), *Patheos*, February 23, 2018, www.patheos.com/blogs/friendlyatheist/2018/02/23/epa-head-scott-pruitt-god-gave-us-this-planet-so-we-can-destroy-it; Oliver Milman, "EPA head Scott Pruitt says global warming may help 'humans flourish,'" *The Guardian*, February 7, 2018, www.theguardian.com/environment/2018/feb/07/epa-head-scott-pruitt-says-global-warming-may-help-humans-flourish.
15. "Energy Sec. Rick Perry Denies Humans Are Main Cause of Climate Change," *Friendly Atheist* (blog), *Patheos*, June 20, 2017, www.patheos.com/blogs/friendlyatheist/2017/06/20/energy-sec-rick-perry-denies-humans-are-main-cause-of-climate-change.
16. "Sorry, Conservative Christians, But God Won't 'Take Care of' Climate Change," *Friendly Atheist* (blog), *Patheos*, June 1, 2017, www.patheos.com/blogs/friendlyatheist/2017/06/01/sorry-conservative-christians-but-god-wont-take-care-of-climate-change.
17. Abbie Bennett, "'What is Larry's nuanced take on climate change?' John Oliver blasts NC GOP rep," *The News & Observer* (North Carolina), June 6, 2017, www.newsobserver.com/news/politics-government/state-politics/article154423054.html.
18. Chas Sisk, "The Biggest Hypocrite in Congress?" *Politico*, August 14, 2014, www.politico.com/magazine/story/2014/08/scott-desjarlais-reelection-110028.
19. Brian Francisco, "Banks targets embryonic stem cell research funding," *The Journal Gazette* (Indiana), June 16, 2017, www.journalgazette.net/news/local/indiana/20170616/banks-targets-embryonic-stem-cell-research-funding.
20. Noah Feit, "McMaster calls student walkout a 'shameful' political statement," *The State*, March 14, 2018, www.thestate.com/news/politics-government/state-politics/article205240329.html.
21. Jamie Lovegrove, "Gov. Henry McMaster allows foster care agencies in South Carolina to favor certain religions," *The Post and Courier*, March 13, 2018, www.postandcourier.com/politics/gov-henry-mcmaster-allows-foster-care-agencies-in-south-carolina/article_4ec95fd6-2700-11e8-8313-1b06c3f009a9.html.
22. Emily McGarlan Miller, "5 faith facts about Betsy DeVos," *Religion News Service*, February 6, 2017, www.religionnews.com/2017/02/06/5-faith-facts-betsy-devos-trumps-pick-for-secretary-of-education.
23. Jeva Lange, "The Montana Republican running in the special election doesn't believe in retirement because Noah was still working when he was 600," *The Week*, April 21, 2017, theweek.com/speedreads/693863/montana-republican-running-special-election-doesnt-believe-retirement-because-noah-still-working-when-600.
24. Hemant Mehta, "Asked About Offshore Tax Havens, MN State Rep. Tells Every-

one to Accept Jesus," *Friendly Atheist* (blog), *Patheos*, May 25, 2017, www.patheos.com/blogs/friendlyatheist/2017/05/25/asked-about-offshore-tax-havens-mn-state-rep-tells-everyone-to-accept-jesus.

25. Hemant Mehta, "AL Senate Candidate: I'll Filibuster with the Bible Until We Fund a Border Wall," *Friendly Atheist* (blog), *Patheos*, July 11, 2017, www.patheos.com/blogs/friendlyatheist/2017/07/11/al-senate-candidate-ill-filibuster-with-the-bible-until-we-fund-a-border-wall.
26. Quoted in Melanie Brewster, *Atheists in America* (New York: Columbia University Press, 2014), 1.
27. Bhagavad Gita (16.7–9), quoted in Jessica Frazier, "Hinduism" in *The Oxford Handbook of Atheism*, ed. Stephen Bullivant and Michael Ruse (Oxford: Oxford University Press, 2013).
28. Quran 2:6–10: "Verily, those who disbelieve, it is the same to them whether you (O Muhammad Peace be upon him) warn them or do not warn them, they will not believe. Allah has set a seal on their hearts and on their hearings, (i.e., they are closed from accepting Allah's Guidance), and on their eyes there is a covering. Theirs will be a great torment. And of mankind, there are some (hypocrites) who say: 'We believe in Allah and the Last Day' while in fact they believe not. They (think to) deceive Allah and those who believe, while they only deceive themselves, and perceive (it) not! In their hearts is a disease (of doubt and hypocrisy) and Allah has increased their disease. A painful torment is theirs because they used to tell lies."
29. Quran (8:12).
30. Dinesh D'Souza, *What's So Great About Christianity?* (Washington, D.C.: Regnery, 2007), xvii.
31. D'Souza, *What's So Great*, 267, 269, 272.
32. Luis Rodrigues, *Open Questions: Diverse Thinkers Discuss God, Religion, and Faith*, (Santa Barbara, CA: Praeger, 2010), 70.
33. James Spiegel, *The Making of an Atheist: How Immorality Leads to Unbelief* (Moody Publishers, 2012), 18.
34. Palin, quoted in Chris Stedman, "Does Sarah Palin Know Any Atheists?" December 16, 2013, chrisstedman.religionnews.com/2013/12/16/sarah-palin-know-atheists.
35. "John Kasich: Totally Secular Society Woulds Rob the United States of Its Morality," *Patheos*, October 8, 2015, www.patheos.com/blogs/wwjtd/2015/10/john-kasich-totally-secular-society-would-rob-the-united-states-of-its-morals.
36. "'A biblical view of justice': Matt Whitaker once said judges shouldn't have a secular worldview," *Washington Post*, November 8, 2018, www.washingtonpost.com/religion/2018/11/08/biblical-view-justice-matt-whitaker-once-said-judges-shouldnt-have-secular-world-view.
37. "Scalisa Says Atheism 'Favors the Devil's Desires,'" CNN, October 7, 2013, religion.blogs.cnn.com/2013/10/07/scalia-says-satan-is-a-real-person.
38. Maxine Najle and Will Gervais, "Dislike of and Discrimination Against Atheists and Secular People," in Zuckerman, *Religion: Beyond Religion*; W. M. Gervais, A. F. Shariff and A. Norenzayan, "Do You Believe in Atheists? Distrust Is Central to Anti-Atheist Prejudice," *Journal of Personality and Social Psychology*, 2011, 101(6): 1189–1206.
39. "Worldwide, Many See Belief in God as Essential to Morality," Pew Research Center, March

13, 2014, www.pewglobal.org/2014/03/13/worldwide-many-see-belief-in-god-as-essential-to-morality.

40. Gary Jensen, "Religious Cosmologies and Homicide Rates Among Nations: A Closer Look," *Journal of Religion and Society*, 2006, 8: 1–14; Gregory Paul, "Cross-National Correlations of Quantifiable Societal Health with Popular Religiosity and Secularism in the Prosperous Democracies," *Journal of Religion and Society*, 2005, 7: 1–17; Phil Zuckerman, "Atheism and Societal Health," in Bullivant and Ruse, *Handbook of Atheism*.
41. "List of Countries by Inentional Homicide Rate," Wikipedia, accessed February 25, 2019, en.wikipedia.org/wiki/List_of_countries_by_intentional_homicide_rate.
42. See Phil Zuckerman, *Living the Secular Life* (New York: Penguin, 2014), 49–50; see also Zuckerman, 2013.
43. "Historical Study of Homicide and Cities Surprises the Experts," *New York Times*, October 23, 1994, www.nytimes.com/1994/10/23/us/historical-study-of-homicide-and-cities-surprises-the-experts.html.
44. "Dutch homicide rate falls to lowest level in 20 years," July 29, 2016, DutchNews.nl, www.dutchnews.nl/news/archives/2016/07/dutch-homicide-rate-falls-to-lowest-level-on-record.
45. "Survey: The Netherlands Now Has More Atheists Than Believers, But 60 Percent of Respondents Are Unsure," *Friendly Atheist* (blog), *Patheos*, January 17, 2015, www.patheos.com/blogs/friendlyatheist/2015/01/17/survey-the-netherlands-now-has-more-atheists-than-believers-but-60-percent-of-respondents-are-unsure.
46. "Historical Study of Homicide," *New York Times*.
47. Steven Pinker, *The Better Angels of Our Nature: Why Violence Has Declined* (New York: Penguin, 2011), 61.
48. Ralph Hood, Peter Hill, and Bernard Spilka, *The Psychology of Religion: An Empirical Approach* (New York: The Guilford Press, 2009), chapter 12.
49. J. Didyoung, E. Charles, and N. J. Rowland, "Non-Theists Are No Less Moral Than Theists: Some Preliminary Results," *Secularism and Nonreligion*, 2013, 2, 1–20.
50. Catherine Caldwell-Harris, Angela Wilson, Elizabeth LoTempio, and Benjamin Beit-Hallahmi, "Exploring the Atheist Personality: Well-being, Awe, and Magical Thinking in Atheists, Buddhists, and Christians," *Mental Health, Religion and Culture*, 2010, 14(7): 659–672.
51. Matthew Loveland, Alexander Capella, and India Maisonet, "Prosocial Skeptics: Skepticism and Generalized Trust," *Critical Research on Religion*, 2017, 5(3): 251–265.
52. Lee Ellis, "Denominational Differences in Self-Reported Delinquency," *Journal of Offender Rehabilitation*, 2002, 35: 179–192.
53. H. Koenig, "Religion and Older Men in Prison," *International Journal of Geriatric Psychiatry*, 1995, 10: 219–230; Hemant Mehta, "Atheists Now Make Up 0.1% of the Federal Prison Population," *Friendly Athiest* (blog), *Patheos*, August 21, 2015, www.patheos.com/blogs/friendlyatheist/2015/08/21/atheists-now-make-up-0-1-of-the-federal-prison-population; Hemant Mehta, "What Percentage of Prisoners Are Atheists? It's a Lot Smaller Than We Ever Imagined," *Friendly Athiest* (blog), *Patheos*, July 16, 2013, www.patheos.com/blogs/friendlyatheist/2013/07/16/what-percentage-of-prisoners-are-atheists-its-a-lot-smaller-than-we-ever-imagined; for the United States, see "Percentage of Atheists," accessed February 25, 2019, www.freethoughtpedia.com/wiki/Percentage_of_atheists#note-6; see

also "Prison Incarceration and Religious Preference" by Golumbaski, accessed February 25, 2019, www.adherents.com/misc/adh_prison.html#altformat; for the UK, see "UK Prison Population," Wikipedia, accessed February 25, 2019, en.wikipedia.org/wiki/File:UK_Prison_Population_2009.jpg.

54. Mehta, "Athiests Now Make."
55. Benjamin Beit-Hallahmi, "Morality and Immorality Among the Irreligious," in *Atheism and Secularity*, vol. 1, ed. Phil Zuckerman (Santa Barbara, CA: Praeger-ABC-CLIO, 2010), 134; W. A. Bonger, *Race and Crime* (New York: Columbia University Press, 1943).
56. D. L. Hall, D. C. Matz, and W. Wood, "Why Don't We Practice What We Preach? A Meta-Analytic Review of Religious Racism," *Personality and Social Psychology Review*, 2010, 14, 126–139; Lynne Jackson and Bruce Hunsberger, "An Intergroup Perspective on Religion and Prejudice," *Journal for the Scientific Study of Religion*, 1999, 38(4): 509–523; Hood, Hill, and Spilka, *Psychology of Religion*; Darren Sherkat, *Changing Faith: The Dynamics and Consequences of Americans' Shifting Religious Identities* (New York: New York University Press, 2014).
57. Andrew Greeley and Michael Hout, *The Truth About Conservative Christians: What They Think and What They Believe* (Chicago: University of Chicago Press, 2006), 83; Tobin Grant, "Patriotism God Gap: Is the U.S. the Greatest Country in the World?" *Christianity Today*, August 5, 2011, www.christianitytoday.com/news/2011/august/patriotism-god-gap-is-us-greatest-country-in-world.html; Corwin Smidt, "Religion and American Attitudes Toward Islam and an Invasion of Iraq," *Sociology of Religion*, 2005, 66(3): 243–261; James Guth, John Green, Lyman Kellstedt, and Corwin Smidt, "Faith and Foreign Policy: A View from the Pews," *Review of Faith and International Affairs*, 2005, 3: 3–9; R. F. Hamilton, "A Research Note on the Mass Support for 'Tough' Military Initiatives," *American Sociological Review*, 1968, 33: 439–445; J. F. Connors, R. Leonard, and K. Burnham, "Religion and Opposition to War Among College Students," *Sociological Analysis*, 1968, 29: 211–219.
58. Hood et al., *Psychology of Religion*, 387–389; J. Hoffman and A. Miller, "Social and Political Attitudes Among Religious Groups: Convergence and Divergence Over Time," *Journal for the Scientific Study of Religion*, 1997, 36: 52–70.
59. Robert Putnam and David Campbell, *American Grace: How Religion Divides and Unites Us* (New York: Simon and Schuster, 2010), 482–484; see also Paul Froese, Christopher Bader, and Buster Smith, "Political Tolerance and God's Wrath in the United States," *Sociology of Religion*, 2008, 69(1): 29–44; see also D. Gay and C. Ellison, "Religious Subcultures and Political Tolerance: Do Denominations Still Matter?" *Review of Religious Research*, 1993, 34: 311–332.
60. Sherkat, *Changing Faith*; L. Petersen and G. V. Donnennworth, "Religion and Declining Support for Traditional Beliefs About Gender Roles and Homosexual Rights," *Sociology of Religion*, 1998, 59: 353–371; Hoffman and Miller, "Social and Political Attitudes"; M. B. Brinkerhoff and M. M. Mackie, "Casting Off the Bonds of Organized: A Religious-Careers Approach to the Study of Apostasy," *Review of Religious Research*, 1993, 34: 235–258; M. B. Brinkerhoff and M. M. Mackie, "Religion and Gender: A Comparison of Canadian and American Student Attitudes," *Journal of Marriage and the Family*, 1985, 47: 415–429.
61. Jenifer Hamil-Luker and Christian Smith, "Religious Authority and Public Opinion on the Right to Die," *Sociology of Religion*, 1998, 59(4): 373–391.

62. "Most Americans Oppose Restricting Rights for LGBT People," Public Religion Research Institute, September 14, 2017, www.prri.org/research/poll-wedding-vendors-refusing-service-same-sex-couples-transgender-military-ban.
63. "The Religious Dimensions of the Torture Debate," Pew Research Center, April 29, 2009, www.pewforum.org/2009/04/29/the-religious-dimensions-of-the-torture-debate.
64. "Religious Landscape Study," Pew Research Center, www.pewforum.org/religious-landscape-study/political-ideology/liberal.
65. "Republicans turn more negative toward refugees as number admitted to U.S. plummets," Pew Research Center, May 24, 2018, www.pewresearch.org/fact-tank/2018/05/24/republicans-turn-more-negative-toward-refugees-as-number-admitted-to-u-s-plummets.
66. "Being Christian in Western Europe," Pew Research Center, May 29, 2018, www.pewforum.org/2018/05/29/being-christian-in-western-europe.
67. "Nonreligious children are more generous," *Science*, November 5, 2015, www.sciencemag.org/news/2015/11/nonreligious-children-are-more-generous.
68. "Chapter 1: Importance of Religion and Religious Beliefs," Pew Research Center, November 3, 2015, www.pewforum.org/2015/11/03/chapter-1-importance-of-religion-and-religious-beliefs.
69. Reginald Bibby, *Resilient Gods* (Vancouver, BC: UBC Press, 2017), 66.
70. Derek Parfit, *Reasons and Persons* (New York: Oxford University Press, 1984).
71. Kai Nielsen, *Ethics Without God* (Amherst, NY: Prometheus Books, 1990); Thomas Nagel, *What Does It All Mean?* (New York: Oxford University Press, 1987), 59–61.
72. Michael Shermer, *The Moral Arc* (New York: Henry Holt, 2015), 151.
73. Erik Wielenberg, *Robust Ethics: The Metaphysics and Epistemology of Godless Normative Realism* (New York: Oxford University Press, 2014).
74. Kenneth Taylor, "Without the Net of Providence: Atheism and the Human Adventure," in *Philosophers Without Gods*, ed. Louise Antony (New York: Oxford University Press, 2007).
75. Paul Kurtz, *Forbidden Fruit: The Ethics of Secularism* (Amherst, NY: Prometheus Press, 2008); Richard Robinson, *An Atheist's Values* (Oxford: Clarendon Press, 1964).
76. A. C. Grayling, *The God Argument* (New York: Bloomsbury, 2013), 104.
77. Torbjörn Tännsjö, *Understanding Ethics* (Edinburgh, UK: Edinburgh University Press, 2013), chapter 1.
78. Ryan Falcioni, "Secularism and Morality," in Zuckerman, *Religion: Beyond Religion.*
79. Bertrand Russell, *Why I Am Not a Christian* (New York: Touchstone, 1927), 19.

CHAPTER 1

1. Robert Putnam and David Campbell, *American Grace: How Religion Divides and Unites Us* (New York: Simon and Schuster, 2010), chapter 13.
2. Putnam and Campbell, *American Grace*, 453.
3. Elton Jackson et al., "Volunteering and Charitable Giving: Do Religious and Associational Ties Promote Helping Behavior?" *Nonprofit and Voluntary Sector Quarterly*, 1995, vol. 24(1; Spring); Arthur Brooks and James Q. Wilson, *Who Really Cares: The Surprising Truth About Compassionate Conservatism* (New York: Basic Books, 2007); "Religious Americans Give More, New Study Finds," *Chronicle of Philanthropy*, November 25, 2013, www.philanthropy.com/article/Religious-Americans-Give-More/153973.

4. Putnam and Campbell, *American Grace*, 467.
5. Putnam and Campbell, *American Grace*, 473.
6. Putnam and Campbell, *American Grace*, 444.
7. J. Graham and J. Haidt, "Beyond Beliefs: Religions Bind Individuals into Moral Communities." *Personality and Social Psychology Review*, 2010, 14(1): 140–150; Phil Zuckerman, Luke Galen, and Frank Pasquale, *The Nonreligious: Understanding Secular People and Secular Societies* (New York: Oxford University Press, 2016), chapter 8; Luke Galen, "Atheism, Wellbeing, and the Wager: Why Not Believing in God (with Others) Is Good for You," *Science, Religion and Culture*, 2015, 2(3): 54–69.
8. Rebecca Stein and Philip Stein, *The Anthropology of Religion, Magic, and Witchcraft* (New York: Routledge, 2010); Jack David Eller, *Cruel Creeds, Virtuous Violence: Religious Violence Across Culture and History* (Amherst, NY: Prometheus Books, 2010).
9. André Comte-Sponville, *The Little Book of Atheist Spirituality* (New York: Viking, 2006), 3.
10. Ariela Keysar and Juhem Navarro-Rivera, "A World of Atheism: Global Demographics," in Bullivant and Ruse, *Handbook of Atheism*.
11. "Madalyn Murray O'Hair quotes," Goodreads, accessed February 26, 2019, www.goodreads.com/author/quotes/635290.Madalyn_Murray_O_Hair.
12. Ryan Cragun, "Defining That Which Is Other to Religion," in Zuckerman, *Religion: Beyond Religion*.
13. "How Americans Feel About Religious Groups," Pew Research Center, July 16, 2014, www.pewforum.org/2014/07/16/how-americans-feel-about-religious-groups.
14. "Section 3: Political Polarization and Personal Life," Pew Research Center, June 12, 2014, www.people-press.org/2014/06/12/section-3-political-polarization-and-personal-life/#marrying-across-party-lines.
15. Keysar and Navarro-Rivera, "A World of Atheism."
16. Robin Le Poidevin, *Agnosticism: A Very Short Introduction* (New York: Oxford University Press, 2010).
17. Protagoras, quoted in Jan N. Bremmer, "Atheism in Antiquity," in *The Cambridge Companion to Atheism*, ed. Michael Martin (New York: Cambridge University Press, 2007), 12.
18. Julian Baggini, *Atheism: A Very Short Introduction* (New York: Oxford University Press, 2003), 4.
19. Eva Ingersoll Wakefield, ed., *The Letters of Robert Ingersoll* (New York: Philosophical Library 1951), 348.
20. Stephen, quoted in Christopher Hitchens, ed., *The Portable Atheist: Essential Readings for the Nonbeliever* (Cambridge, MA: Da Capo Press, 2007), 110–111.
21. Jennifer Michael Hecht, *Doubt: A History* (San Francisco: Harper Perennial, 2003), 96.
22. Hecht, *Doubt*, 98.
23. Kerry Walters, *Atheism: A Guide for the Perplexed* (London: Continuum, 2010), 37.
24. Thomas Clark, "Naturalism and Well-Being," in Zuckerman, *Religion: Beyond Religion*, 365.
25. Stephen Law, "What Is Humanism?" in Bullivant and Ruse, *Handbook of Atheism*.
26. "Are you Humanist?" American Humanist Association, accessed February 26, 2019, www.americanhumanist.org/Humanism.
27. Greta Christina, "Why Atheism Demands Social Justice," *Free Inquiry*, 2012, 32(3): 12.

28. Looked at on August 23, 2016.
29. Jonathan Haidt, *The Righteous Mind: Why Good People Are Divided by Politics and Religion* (New York: Vintage, 2012), 230.
30. Sarah Blaffer Hrdy, *Mothers and Others: The Evolutionary Origins of Mutual Understanding* (Cambridge, MA: Belknap Harvard Press, 2009).
31. Haidt, *The Righteous Mind*, 229–230.
32. Bremmer (2007).

CHAPTER 2

1. J. DeLeeuw, L. Galen, C. Aebersold, and V. Stanton, "Support for Animal Rights as a Function of Belief in Evolution and Religious Fundamentalism," *Animals and Society*, 2007, 15: 353–363; "Beyond Guns and God: Understanding the Complexities of the White Working Class in America," Public Religion Research Institute, September 20, 2012, www.prri.org/research/race-class-culture-survey-2012; "Why Are So Few Christians Vegan?" Animal Liberation Currents, Feburary 12, 2017, www.animalliberationcurrents.com/why-are-so-few-christians-vegan.
2. For a clear answer to that, see Peter Singer, *Animal Liberation* (San Francisco: HarperCollins, 2009 [1975]).
3. Ryan Cragun, *What You Don't Know About Religion (But Should)* (Durham, NC: Pitchstone Publishing, 2013), 87.
4. Jeff Nall, "Disparate Destinations, Parallel Paths: An Analysis of Contemporary Atheist and Christian Parenting Literature," in *Religion and the New Atheism*, ed. Amarnath Amarasignam (Chicago: Haymarket Books, 2012).
5. Elizabeth Gershoff, "More Harm Than Good: A Summary of Scientific Research on the Intended and Unintended Effects of Corporal Punishment on Children," *Law and Contemporary Problems*, 2010, 73(2): 31–56.
6. Richard Gale, "The Failure of Classical Theistic Arguments," in Martin, *Cambridge Companion to Atheism*; Michael Martin, *Atheism: A Philosophical Justification* (Philadelphia: Temple University Press, 1990); Richard Dawkins, *The God Delusion* (New York: Houghton Mifflin, 2006); Victor Stenger, *God: The Failed Hypothesis* (Amherst, NY: Prometheus Books, 2008).
7. Paul Tillich, *The Shaking of the Foundations* (New York: Charles Scribner's Sons, 1948), 57.
8. Küng, quoted in J. L. Mackie, *The Miracle of Theism: Arguments For and Against the Existence of God* (New York: Oxford University Press, 1983), 241.
9. Alfred North Whitehead, *Process and Reality* (New York: The Free Press, 1978), 347–348, 351.
10. Patrick Grim, "Impossibility Arguments," in Martin, *Cambridge Companion to Atheism*, 199.
11. Paul Tillich, *Systematic Theology*, vol. 1 (Chicago: University of Chicago Press, 1951), 237.
12. Matthew Stewart, *Nature's God: The Heretical Origins of the American Republic* (New York: W. W. Norton, 2014), 99–100.
13. B. C. Johnson, *The Atheist Debater's Handbook* (Amherst, NY: Prometheus Books, 1981), 124.
14. Sam Harris, *Letter to a Christian Nation* (New York: Knopf, 2006), 73–74.
15. David Eller, *Natural Atheism* (Cranford, NJ: American Atheist Press, 2004), 26.
16. Grayling, *The God Argument*, 111.

17. Darwin, quoted in S. T. Joshi, *Atheism: A Reader* (Amherst, NY: Prometheus Books, 2000), 197–198.
18. Richard Dawkins, *The Blind Watchmaker* (New York: W. W. Norton, 2015); Philip Ball, *The Self-Made Tapestry: Pattern Formation in Nature* (New York: Oxford University Press, 2001).
19. Carl Sagan and Ann Druyan, *The Varieties of Scientific Experience: A Personal View of the Search for God* (New York: Penguin, 2007).
20. Daniel Dennett, "Atheism and Evolution," in Martin, *Cambridge Companion to Atheism*, 143.
21. Shelley, quoted in Hitchens, *Portable Atheist*, 51.
22. Johnson, *Atheist Debater*, 59.
23. Einstein, quoted in Hitchens, *Portable Atheist*, 163.
24. Brian Bolton, "Have Christians Accepted the Scientific Conclusion That God Does Not Answer Intercessory Prayer?" *Free Inquiry*, Dec. 2018/Jan. 2019, 39(1): 20–24.
25. "Long-Awaited Medical Study Questions the Power of Prayer," *New York Times*, March 31, 2006, www.nytimes.com/2006/03/31/health/31pray.html.
26. "Power of prayer found wanting in hospital trial," *The Telegraph*, October 15, 2003, www.telegraph.co.uk/news/worldnews/northamerica/usa/1444144/Power-of-prayer-found-wanting-in-hospital-trial.html.
27. R. Sloan, E. Bagiella, and T. Powell, "Religion, Spirituality, and Medicine," *Lancet*, 1999, 353: 664–667.
28. Georges Rey, "Meta-Atheism: Religious Avowal and Self-Deception," in Antony, *Philosophers Without Gods*, 261.
29. Bierce, quoted in S. T. Joshi, *Atheism*, 23.
30. Nietzsche, quoted in S. T. Joshi, *Atheism*, 205.
31. George Smith, *Atheism: The Case Against God* (Amherst, NY: Prometheus Books, 1989), 123–124.
32. Graham Oppy, "Arguments for Atheism," in Bullivant and Ruse, *Handbook of Atheism*.
33. Michael Martin, *Atheism, Morality, and Meaning* (Amherst, NY: Prometheus, 2002), 117.

CHAPTER 3

1. "How Many Mormon Women Work Outside the Home?" Religion News Service, July 19, 2013, www.religionnews.com/2013/07/19/how-many-mormon-women-work-outside-the-home.
2. *Doctrines and Covenants*, 132.
3. Lawrence Foster, *Religion and Sexuality* (Urbana: University of Illinois Press, 1984); Sarah Berringer Gordon, *The Mormon Question: Polygamy and Constitutional Conflict in Nineteenth-Century America* (Chapel Hill: University of North Carolina Press, 2002).
4. Foster, *Religion and Sexuality*, 151.
5. Foster, *Religion and Sexuality*, 198.
6. Foster, *Religion and Sexuality*; Kathleen Flake, *The Politics of American Religious Identity: The Seating of Senator Reed Smoot, Mormon Apostle* (Chapel Hill and London: University of North Carolina Press, 2004); Marie Cornwall, Camela Courtright, and Laga Van Beek, "How Common the Principle? Women as Plural Wives in 1860," *Dialogue: A Journal of Mormon Thought*, 1993, 26 (Summer): 139–153.

7. Patrick Mason, *The Mormon Menace: Violence and Anti-Mormonism in the Postbellum South* (New York: Oxford University Press, 2011).
8. "Polygamy: Latter-day Saints and the Practice of Plural Marriage," The Church of Jesus Christ of Latter-Day Saints, accessed February 27, 2019, www.mormonnewsroom.org/article/polygamy-latter-day-saints-and-the-practice-of-plural-marriage.
9. Janet Bennion, *Women of Principle: Female Networking in Contemporary Mormon Polygyny* (New York: Oxford University Press, 1998).
10. Michael Martin, *The Case Against Christianity* (Philadelphia: Temple University Press, 1991), Appendix: The Divine Command Theory.
11. Forrest Wood, *The Arrogance of Faith: Christianity and Race in America from the Colonial Era to the Twentieth Century* (New York: Knopf, 1990), 44–47.
12. Frederick Douglass, "The Narrative of the Life of Frederick Douglass," 1845, accessed February 27, 2019, www.pagebypagebooks.com/Frederick_Douglass/The_Narrative_of_the_Life_of_Frederick_Douglass/Chapter_X_p7.html.
13. Wood, *Arrogance of Faith*, 36.
14. Wood, *Arrogance of Faith*, 292.
15. Petra Klug, "Anti-Atheism in the United States," doctoral dissertation, University of Bremen, Germany, 2018.
16. Hopkins, quoted in Klug, "Anti-Atheism."
17. Du Bois, quoted in Reiland Rabaka, *Du Bois's Dialectics* (Lanham, MD: Lexington Books, 2008), 141–142.
18. Du Bois, quoted in Rabaka, *Du Bois's Dialectics*, 141–142.
19. Michael Emerson and Christian Smith, *Divided by Faith* (New York: Oxford University Press, 2000), chapter 2.
20. Wood, *Arrogance of Faith*; Emerson and Smith, *Divided by Faith*, chapter 2.
21. "In defiance of Israeli law, polygamy sanctioned by top rabbis," *Times of Israel*, December 27, 2016, www.timesofisrael.com/in-defiance-of-israeli-law-polygamy-sanctioned-by-top-rabbis.
22. William Gervase Clarence-Smith, *Islam and the Abolition of Slavery* (New York: Oxford University Press, 2006).
23. "Where Christian churches, other religions stand on gay marriage," Pew Research Center, December 21, 2015, www.pewresearch.org/fact-tank/2015/12/21/where-christian-churches-stand-on-gay-marriage.
24. Dan Barker, *God: The Most Unpleasant Character in All Fiction* (New York: Sterling, 2016); Ken Smith, *Ken's Guide to the Bible* (New York: Blast Books, 1995); Elizabeth Anderson, "If God Is Dead, Is Everything Permitted?" in Antony, *Philosophers Without Gods*.
25. Shaw, quoted in Victor Stenger, "Do Our Values Come from God? The Evidence Says No," *Free Inquiry*, 2006, 26(5): 42–45.
26. Andy Coghlan, "Dear God, please confirm what I already believe," *New Scientist*, November 30, 2009, www.newscientist.com/article/dn18216-dear-god-please-confirm-what-i-already-believe.
27. Nicholas Epley, Benjamin A. Converse, Alexa Delbosc, George A. Monteleone, and John T. Cacioppo, "Believers' Estimates of God's Beliefs Are More Egocentric Than Estimates of

Other People's Beliefs," *Proceedings of the National Academy of Sciences of the United States of America*, 2009, 106(51): 21533–21538.

CHAPTER 4

1. Michael Bilton and Kevin Sim, *Four Hours in My Lai* (New York: Penguin, 1992).
2. Bilton and Sim, *Four Hours*, 99.
3. Bilton and Sim, *Four Hours*, 99.
4. Bilton and Sim, *Four Hours*, 19.
5. Bilton and Sim, *Four Hours*, 335.
6. Jean-Paul Sartre, *Existentialism Is a Humanism* (New Haven, CT: Yale University Press, 2007 [1945]).
7. Alison Stone, "Existentialism," in Bullivant and Ruse, *Handbook of Atheism*; Sartre, *Existentialism*; see also Peter Berger, *Invitation to Sociology* (New York: Anchor Books, 1963).
8. Mary Midgley, *Can't We Make Moral Judgements?* (New York: St. Martin's Press, 1991), 43.
9. Francisco Ayala, "What the Biological Sciences Can and Cannot Contribute to Ethics," in *Contemporary Debates in Philosophy of Biology*, ed. Francisco Ayala and Robert Arp (Oxford: Wiley-Blackwell, 2009), 1.
10. Scott Aikin and Robert Talisse, *Reasonable Atheism: A Moral Case for Respectful Disbelief* (Amherst, NY: Prometheus Books, 2011), 127.
11. I. Getz, "Moral Judgment and Religion: A Review of the Literature," in *Counseling and Values*, 1984, 28: 94–116; D. Narvaez, I. Getz, J. Rest, and S. Thoma, "Individual Moral Judgment and Cultural Ideologies," *Developmental Psychology*, 1999, 35: 478–488; Thomas Blass, "Understanding Behavior in the Milgram Obedience Experiment: The Role of Personality, Situations, and Their Interactions," *Journal of Personality and Social Psychology*, 1991, 60: 398–413.
12. Edwin Curley, "On Becoming a Heretic," in Antony, *Philosophers Without Gods*.
13. Aikin and Talisse, *Reasonable Atheism*, 117.
14. Paul Cliteur, *The Secular Outlook: In Defense of Moral and Political Secularism* (Chichester, UK: Wiley-Blackwell, 2010).
15. David Brink, "The Autonomy of Ethics," in Martin, *Cambridge Companion to Atheism*, 158.
16. Mill, quoted in Hitchens, *Portable Atheist*, 58.
17. Stewart Shapiro, "Faith and Reason, the Perpetual War: Ruminations of a Fool," in Antony, *Philosophers Without Gods*; Carol Delaney, *Abraham on Trial: The Social Legacy of Biblical Myth* (Princeton, NJ: Princeton University Press, 1998).
18. Søren Kierkegaard, *Fear and Trembling* (New York: Penguin Classics, 1986 [1843]).
19. Curley, "On Becoming a Heretic," 88.
20. Elizabeth Anderson, "If God Is Dead, Is Everything Permitted?" in Antony, *Philosophers Without Gods*.
21. Anderson, "If God Is Dead."
22. Dan Barker, *God: The Most Unpleasant Character in All Fiction* (New York: Sterling, 2016); Michael Parenti, *God and His Demons* (Amherst, NY: Prometheus Books, 2010).
23. Stanley Milgram, *Obedience to Authority: An Experimental View* (New York: Harper Perennial Modern Classics, 2009).

24. Peter Geach, *God and the Soul* (London: Routledge & Kegan Paul, 1969), 117–129.
25. Anderson, "If God Is Dead," 229.

CHAPTER 5

1. Barbara MacKinnon and Andrew Fiala, *Ethics: Theory and Contemporary Issues* (Stamford, CT: Cengage, 2015), 22.
2. Walter Sinnott-Armstrong, *Morality Without God?* (New York: Oxford University Press, 2009), 106.
3. Kenan Malik, *The Quest for a Moral Compass: A Global History of Ethics* (Brooklyn, NY: Melville House, 2014), 340.
4. J. Moreland and William Lane Craig, *Philosophical Foundations for a Christian Worldview* (Downers Grove, IL: InterVarsity Press, 2003), 491.
5. Philip Quinn, "Theological Volunteerism," in *The Oxford Handbook of Ethical Theory*, ed. David Copp (New York: Oxford University Press, 2006).
6. "What is The Euthyphro Dilemma? With William Lane Craig," posted September 13, 2013, www.youtube.com/watch?v=IgGB4Oxs5VU.
7. Ryan Falcioni, "Secularism and Morality," in Zuckerman, *Religion: Beyond Religion.*
8. Russell, quoted in Hitchens, *Portable Atheist*, 202.
9. A. C. Grayling, "Critiques of Theistic Arguments," in Bullivant and Ruse, *Handbook of Atheism*, 39.
10. R. Garcia and N. King, eds., *Is Goodness Without God Good Enough*? (New York: Rowman and Littlefield, 2009), 30.
11. David McCandless et al., "20th Century Death," 2013, www.informationisbeautiful.net/visualizations/20th-century-death.
12. Guy P. Harrison, *50 Reasons People Give for Believing in God* (Amherst, NY: Prometheus Books, 2008), 68.
13. Paulsen, quoted John Loftus, *Why I Became an Atheist* (Amherst, NY: Prometheus Books, 2008), 238.
14. Andrea Weisberger, "The Argument from Evil," in Martin, *Cambridge Companion to Atheism.*
15. For a discussion of Epicurus's characterization of God, see Martin, *Atheism*, chapter 14.
16. Mill quoted in Gavin Hyman, *A Short History of Atheism* (London: Tauris, 2010), 127.

CHAPTER 6

1. Steven Lukes, "The Social Construction of Morality?" in *Handbook of the Sociology of Morality*, ed. Steven Hitlin and Stephen Vaisey (New York: Springer, 2013).
2. David Wong, *Natural Moralities: A Defense of Pluralistic Relativism* (New York: Oxford University Press, 2006), 235.
3. Frans de Waal, *The Bonobo and the Atheist* (New York: W. W. Norton, 2013), 156.
4. Jeffrey Wattles, *The Golden Rule* (New York: Oxford University Press, 1996).
5. Phil Zuckerman, *Living the Secular Life* (New York: Penguin, 2014), chapter 1.
6. Richard Carrier, *Sense and Goodness Without God* (Bloomington, IN: AuthorHouse, 2005), 322.
7. Shermer, *The Moral Arc*, 180–181.

8. Lincoln, quoted in Ronald White, "Notes to Self," *Harper's Magazine*, 2013, 336: 49–52; see also Shermer, *The Moral Arc*, 208.
9. Bernard Gert, *Common Morality: Deciding What to Do* (New York: Oxford University Press, 2004).
10. Susan Wolf, "Moral Saints," *Journal of Philosophy*, 1982, 79: 419–439.
11. Gert, *Common Morality*, 7.
12. "2011 National Household Survey: Immigration, place of birth, citizenship, ethnic origin, visible minorities, language and religion," Statistics Canada, May 8, 2013, www.statcan.gc.ca/daily-quotidien/130508/dq130508b-eng.htm.
13. "Iran bans women's Zumba aerobics classes," *Los Angeles Times*, June 13, 2017, www.latimes.com/world/middleeast/la-fg-iran-zumba-20170613-story.html.
14. "Pakistan's secret atheists," BBC News, July 12, 2017, www.bbc.com/news/magazine-40580196.
15. Émile Durkheim, *The Division of Labor in Society* (New York: Free Press, 1984 [1893]), 39.
16. Owen Flanagan, *The Geography of Morals* (New York: Oxford University Press, 2017), 136.
17. Faye Ginsburg, *Contested Live: The Abortion Debate in an American Community* (Berkeley and Los Angeles: University of California Press, 1989).
18. Gordon Marino, ed., *Ethics: The Essential Writings* (New York: Modern Library, 2010); Steven Hitlin, *Moral Selves, Evil Selves: The Social Psychology of Conscience* (New York: Palgrave Macmillan, 2008).
19. Richard Joyce, *The Evolution of Morality* (Cambridge, MA: MIT Press, 2006), 57–64.
20. Charles Stevenson, "The Emotive Meaning of Ethical Terms," *Mind*, 1963, 46(181): 14–31.
21. Iain King, *How to Make Good Decisions and Be Right All the Time: Solving the Riddle of Right and Wrong* (London: Continuum, 2008), 69.
22. Michael Ruse, *Atheism: What Everyone Needs to Know* (New York: Oxford University Press, 2015), 97.
23. Kevin McCaffree, *What Morality Means: An Interdisciplinary Synthesis for the Social Sciences* (New York: Palgrave Macmillan, 2015).
24. Ronald Dworkin, "Objectivity and Truth: You'd Better Believe It," *Philosophy and Public Affairs*, 1996, 25(2): 87–139; see also James Dreier, "Moral Relativism and Moral Nihilism," in Copp, *Oxford Ethical Theory*, for a discussion of the nonexistence of moral protons dubbed "eudaemons."
25. Richard Holloway, *Godless Morality: Keeping Religion Out of Ethics* (Edinburgh, UK: Canongate, 1999), 32–33.
26. Lukes, "The Social Construction of Morality?" in Hitlin and Vaisey, *Sociology of Morality.*
27. W. E. B. Du Bois, "The Value of Agitation," *The Voice of the Negro* [1907], in *The Social Theory of W. E. B. Du Bois*, ed. Phil Zuckerman (Thousand Oaks, CA: Pine Forge, 2004), 109–110.
28. Martin Luther King, Jr., *Strength to Love* (New York: Harper and Row, 1963), 26.
29. Karl Marx, *The Eighteenth Brumaire of Louis Bonaparte* (New York: International Publishers, 1994 [1852]).
30. Alasdair MacIntyre, *A Short History of Ethics*, (London: Routledge, 1998 [1966]), 1.
31. Ross Hassig, *Aztec Warfare: Imperial Expansion and Political Control*, (Norman: University of Oklahoma Press, 1988).

32. Elliott Currie, "Crimes Without Criminals: Witchcraft and Its Control in Renaissance Europe," *Law and Society Review*, 1968, 3(1): 7–32.
33. Dorothy Ko, *Cinderella's Sisters: A Revisionist History of Footbinding* (Berkeley: University of California Press, 2005).
34. Patrick Barbier, *The World of Castrati* (London: Souvenir Press, 1998).
35. Goldman, quoted in Hitchens, *Portable Atheist,* 133.
36. J. L. Mackie, *Ethics: Inventing Right and Wrong* (New York: Penguin, 1977).
37. Taylor, "Without the Net," in Antony, *Philosophers Without Gods.*
38. David Hume, *A Treatise of Human Nature* (New York: Penguin Books, 1985 [1738]); Michael Slote, "Moral Sentimentalism and Moral Psychology," in Copp, *Oxford Ethical Theory.*
39. Walter Sinnott-Armstrong, *Morality Without God?* (New York: Oxford University Press, 2009), 58.
40. Carrier, *Sense and Goodness*, 318.
41. Kenan Malik, *The Quest for a Moral Compass: A Global History of Ethics* (Brooklyn, NY: Melville House, 2014).
42. H. A. Prichard and Jim MacAdam, *Moral Writings* (Oxford: Clarendon Press, 2002).
43. Matt Riddley, *The Origins of Virtue: Human Instincts and the Evolution of Cooperation* (New York: Penguin, 1996).
44. Peter Singer, *Ethics in the Real World* (Princeton, NJ: Princeton University Press, 2016), 17.
45. Martin Hoffman, *Empathy and Moral Development* (New York: Cambridge University Press, 2000), chapter 3.

CHAPTER 7

1. Marc Hauser, *Moral Minds: The Nature of Right and Wrong* (New York: Harper Perennial, 2006); John Teehan, "Ethics, Secular and Religious: An Evolved-Cognitive Analysis," in *The Oxford Handbook of Secularism*, ed. Phil Zuckerman and John Shook (New York: Oxford University Press, 2017).
2. Hrdy, *Mothers and Others*; Christopher Boehm, *Moral Origins: The Evolution of Virtue, Altruism, and Shame* (New York: Basic Books, 2012).
3. Émile Durkheim, *The Rules of Sociological Method* (New York: Free Press, 1982 [1895]), 130.
4. Robert Sapolsky, *Behave: The Biology of Humans at Our Best and Worst* (New York: Penguin Press, 2017), 315.
5. Joshua Greene, *Moral Tribes: Emotion, Reason, and the Gap Between Us and Them* (New York: Penguin Press, 2013), 24.
6. Jonathan Turner, "Natural Selection and the Evolution of Morality in Human Societies," in Hitlin and Vaisey, *Sociology of Morality.*
7. De Waal, *Bonobo and Atheist.*
8. De Waal, *Bonobo and Atheist*, 80.
9. R. M. Yerkes, *Almost Human* (New York: Century, 1925).
10. De Waal, *Bonobo and Atheist*, 33.
11. De Waal, *Bonobo and Atheist*, 167.
12. Paul Bloom, *Just Babies: The Origins of Good and Evil* (New York: Broadway Books, 2013), 30.
13. Bloom, *Just Babies*, 31.
14. A. Knafo, C. Zahn-Waxler, C. Van Hulle, J. Robinson, and S. Rhee, "The Developmental

Origins of a Disposition Toward Empathy: Genetic and Environmental Contributions," *Emotions*, 2008, 7: 737–752; J. Kiley Hamlin, Karen Wynn, Paul Bloom, and Neja Mahajan, "How Infants and Toddlers React to Antisocial Others," *PNAS*, 2011, 108(50), www.pnas.org/content/108/50/19931.

15. Maayan Davidov, Carolyn Zahn-Waxler, Ronit Roth-Hanania, and Ariel Knafo, "Concern for Others in the First Year of Life: Theory, Evidence, and Avenues for Research," *Child Development Perspectives*, 2013, 7(2): 126–131.
16. Ronit Roth-Hanania, Maayan Davidov, and Carolyn Zahn-Waxler, "Empathy Development from 8 to 16 Months: Early Signs of Concern for Others," *Infant Behavior and Development*, 2011, 34: 447–458.
17. Felix Waraken and Michael Tomasello, "Altruistic Helping in Human Infants and Young Chimpanzees," *Science*, 2006, 311(5765): 1301–1303.
18. "Born good? Babies help unlock the origins of morality," *60 Minutes*, CBS News, posted November 18, 2012, www.youtube.com/watch?v=FRvVFW85IcU.
19. Donald Pfaff, *The Altruistic Brain: How We Are Naturally Good* (New York: Oxford University Press, 2015).
20. Sapolsky, *Behave*, chapter 4.
21. Simon Baron-Cohen, *The Science of Evil* (New York: Basic Books, 2011).
22. Paul Zak, *The Moral Molecule: How Trust Works* (New York: Penguin, 2012).
23. Patricia Churchland, *Braintrust* (Princeton, NJ: Princeton University Press, 2011), 40.
24. J. Decety and M. Svetlova, "Putting Together Phylogenetic and Ontogenetic Perspectives on Empathy," *Developmental Cognitive Neuroscience*, 2012, 2:1–24.
25. Michael Kosfeld, M. Heinrichs, P. J. Zak, U. Fischbacher, and E. Fehr, "Oxytocin Increases Trust in Humans," *Nature*, 2005, 435(7042): 673–676.
26. Carsten de Dreu, Lindred Greer, Michiale Handgraaf, Shaul Shalvi, Gerben Van Kleef, Matthijs Baas, Femke Ten Velden, Eric Van Dijk, and Sander Feith, "The Neuropeptide Oxytocin Regulates Parochial Altruism in Intergroup Conflict Among Humans," *Science*, 2010, 328(5984): 1408–1411.
27. Gregor Domes, "Oxytocin Improves 'Mind-Reading' in Humans," *Biological Psychiatry*, 2007, 61(6): 731–733; R. Ebstein, S. Israel, E. Lerer, F. Uzefosky, I. Shalev, I. Gritsenko, M. Riebold, S. Salomon, and N. Yirmiya, "Arginine, Vasopressin, and Oxytocin Modulate Human Social Behavior," *Annals of the New York Academy of Sciences*, 2009, 1167: 87–102.
28. Paul Zak, "The Physiology of Moral Sentiments," *Journal of Economic Behavior and Organization*, 2011, 77: 53–65.
29. V. Morhenn, J. Park, E. Piper, and P. Zak, "Monetary Sacrifice Among Strangers Is Mediated by Endogenous Oxytocin Release After Physical Contact," *Evolution and Human Behavior*, 2008, 29: 375–383.
30. Joyce, *Evolution of Morality*, chapter 2.
31. Nel Noddings, *Caring* (Berkeley: University of California Press, 2013), 1.
32. Grazyna Kochanska, "Mutually Responsive Orientation Between Mothers and Their Young Children: A Context for the Early Development of Conscience," *Current Directions in Psychological Science*, 2002, 11(6): 191–195.
33. D. J. Laible and R. Thompson, "Mother-Child Discourse Attachment Security, Shared Positive Affect, and Early Conscience Development," *Child Development*, 2000, 71: 1424–1440;

R. N. Emde, Z. Biringen, R. Clyman, and D. Oppenheim, "The Moral Self of Infancy: Affective Core and Procedural Knowledge," *Developmental Review*, 1991, 11: 251–270; E. E. Maccoby, "The Uniqueness of the Parent-Child Relationship," in W. A. Collins and B. Laursen, eds., *Minnesota Symposia on Child Psychology*, vol. 30, *Relationships as Developmental Contexts* (Hillsdale, NJ: Erlbaum, 1999), 157–175.

34. Peter Berger, *Invitation to Sociology* (New York: Anchor Books, 1963), 120.
35. Berger, *Invitation to Sociology*, 100.
36. Arlene Stein, *Shameless: Sexual Dissidence in American Culture* (New York: New York University Press, 2006), 6.
37. Rengin Firat and Chad Michael McPherson, "Toward an Integrated Science of Morality: Linking Mind, Society, and Culture," in Hitlin and Vaisey, *Sociology of Morality*.
38. Tony Horwitz, *Midnight Rising: John Brown and the Raid That Sparked the Civil War* (New York: Picador, Henry Holt and Co., 2011).
39. "Letter from John Brown to Henry Stearns," July 15, 1857, www.digitalhistory.uh.edu/active_learning/explorations/brown/jbrown_words1.cfm.
40. James Carville, *We're Right and They're Wrong* (New York: Random House, 1996), xiv.
41. Suzanne Keen, *Empathy and the Novel* (New York: Oxford University Press, 2007); Steven Pinker, *The Better Angels of Our Nature: Why Violence Has Declined* (New York: Penguin, 2011), 177.
42. Kevin McCaffree, *What Morality Means: An Interdisciplinary Synthesis for the Social Sciences* (New York: Palgrave Macmillan, 2015), chapter 3.

CHAPTER 8

1. Hannah Senesh, *Her Life and Diary* (Nashville, TN: Jewish Lights, 2007 [1941]).
2. Brian Johnson, *W. E. B. Du Bois: Toward Agnosticism, 1868–1934* (Lanham, MD: Rowman and Littlefield, 2008); Phil Zuckerman, "The Irreligiosity of W. E. B. Du Bois," in *The Souls of W. E. B. Du Bois*, ed. Edward Blum and Jason Young (Macon, GA: Mercer University Press, 2009); for a more nuanced view, see Edward Blum, *W. E. B. Du Bois: American Prophet* (Philadelphia: University of Pennsylvania Press, 2007).
3. Jawaharlal Nehru, *Toward Freedom: The Autobiography of Jawaharlal Nehru* (New York: The John Day Company, 1941); Suneera Kapoor and Shrawan Singh, "Gandhi and Nehru on Religion," *The Indian Journal of Political Science*, 2005, 66(3): 503–514; Vidhu Verma, "Secularism in India," in Zuckerman and Shook, *Handbook of Secularism*.
4. Linda Atkinson, *In Kindling Flame: The Story of Hannah Senesh, 1921–1944* (New York: Lothrop, Lee, and Shepard Books, 1985), 82.
5. David Orenstein and Linda Ford Blaikie, *Godless Grace: How Nonbelievers are Making the World Safer, Richer, and Kinder* (Washington, D.C.: Humanist Press, 2015).
6. Christopher Hitchens, *The Missionary Position: Mother Teresa in Theory and Practice* (New York: Twelve, 2012).
7. Anu Partanen, *The Nordic Theory of Everything: In Search of a Better Life* (New York: HarperCollins, 2016).
8. Celia Morris, *Fanny Wright: Rebel in America* (Cambridge, MA: Harvard University Press, 1984).
9. Mitchell Stephens, *Imagine There's No Heaven: How Atheism Helped Create the Modern World* (New York: Palgrave Macmillan, 2014); Hecht, *Doubt*; Susan Jacoby, *Freethinkers: A*

History of American Secularism (New York: Henry Holt, 2004); Tim Whitmarsh, *Battling the Gods: Atheism in the Ancient World* (New York: Alfred Knopf, 2015); James Thrower, *Western Atheism: A Short History* (Amherst, NY: Prometheus Books, 2000).

10. Edward Royle, *Victorian Infidels: The Origins of the British Secularist Movement, 1791–1866* (Manchester, UK: Rowman and Littlefield, 1974); Edward Royle, *Radicals, Secularists and Republicans: Popular Freethought in Britain, 1866–1915* (Manchester, UK: Rowman and Littlefield, 1980); Laura Schwartz, *Infidel Feminism: Secularism, Religion and Women's Emancipation, England 1830–1914* (Manchester, UK: Manchester University Press, 2015).
11. Cohen, quoted in Paul Cliteur, *The Secular Outlook: In Defense of Moral and Political Secularism* (Chichester, UK: Wiley-Blackwell, 2010), 70.
12. P. J. Watson, Z. Chen, N. Ghorbani, and M. Vartanian. "Religious Openness Hypothesis: I. Religious Reflection, Schemas, and Orientations Within Religious Fundamentalist and Biblical Foundationalist Ideological Surrounds," *Journal of Psychology and Christianity*, 2015, 34(2): 99–113; P. J. Watson, Z. Chen, R. Morris, and E. Stephensen, "Religious Openness Hypothesis: III. Defense Against Secularism Within Fundamentalist and Biblical Foundationalist Ideological Surrounds," *Journal of Psychology and Christianity*, 2015, 34(2): 125–140; P. J. Watson, Z. Chen, and R. Morris, "Varieties of Quest and the Religious Openness Hypothesis Within Religious Fundamentalist and Biblical Foundationalist Ideological Surrounds," *Religions*, 2014, 5: 1–20; P. J. Watson, Z. Chen, and R. W. Hood, "Biblical Foundationalism and Religious Reflection: Polarization of Faith and Intellect Oriented Epistemologies Within a Christian Ideological Surround," *Journal of Psychology and Theology*, 2011, 39(2): 111–121; V. Saroglou, "Religion and the Five Factors of Personality: A Meta-analytic Review," *Personality and Individual Difference*, 2002, 32: 15–25; Luke Galen and J. Kloet, "Mental Well-being in the Religious and the Non-religious: Evidence for a Curvilinear Relationship," *Mental Health, Religion, and Culture*, 2011, 14: 673–689; H. Streib, R. Hood, B. Keller, R. Csöff, and C. Silver, *Deconversion: Qualitative and Quantitative Results from Cross-Cultural Research in Germany and the United States of America* (Göttingen, Germany: Vandenhoek and Ruprecht, 2009).
13. "Nones on the Rise: Religion and the Unaffiliated," Pew Research Center, October 9, 2012, www.pewforum.org/2012/10/09/nones-on-the-rise-religion.
14. Bob Altemeyer and Bruce Hunsberger, *Amazing Conversions: Why Some Turn to Faith and Others Abandon Religion* (Amherst, NY: Prometheus Books, 1997); Bruce Hunsberger, B. McKenzie, and M. Pratt, "Religious Doubt: A Social Psychological Analysis," *Research in the Social Scientific Study of Religion*, 1993, 5: 27–51.
15. Brian Starks and Robert Robinson, "Who Values the Obedient Child Now? The Religious Factor in Adult Values for Children, 1986–2002," *Social Forces*, 2005, 84(1): 343–359.
16. Christopher Ellison and Darren Sherkat, "Obedience and Autonomy: Religion and Parental Values Reconsidered," *Journal for the Scientific Study of Religion*, 1993, 32: 313–329.
17. Altemeyer and Hunsberger, *Amazing Conversions*
18. Bob Altemeyer, "Highly Dominating, Highly Authoritarian Personalities," *Journal of Social Psychology*, 2004, 144(4): 421–447.
19. Catherine Caldwell-Harris, Angela Wilson, Elizabeth LoTempio, and Benjamin Beit-Hallahmi, "Exploring the Atheist Personality: Well-being, Awe, and Magical Thinking in Atheists, Buddhists, and Christians," *Mental Health, Religion and Culture*, 2010, 14(7): 659–672.

20. Catherine Caldwell-Harris, Elizabeth LoTempio, C. Jordan, and N. Ramanayake, "Religious Non-belief Explained by Intellectual Orientation and Childhood Socialization," paper presented at the annual meeting of the American Psychological Association, Boston, MA, 2008.
21. Marjana Lindeman, Annika M. Svedholm-Häkkinen, Tapani Riekki, "Skepticism: Genuine Unbelief or Implicit Beliefs in the Supernatural?" *Consciousness and Cognition*, 2016, 42: 261–228.
22. Peter Boghossian, *A Manual for Creating Atheists* (Durham, NC: Pitchstone Publishing, 2013), 209.
23. David Hemenway, *Private Guns Public Health* (Ann Arbor: University of Michigan Press, 2017); "America's unique gun violence problem, explained in 17 maps and charts," *Vox*, November 8, 2018, www.vox.com/policy-and-politics/2017/10/2/16399418/us-gun-violence-statistics-maps-charts.
24. John Santelli et al., "Abstinence-Only-Until-Marriage: An Updated Review of U.S. Policies and Programs and Their Impact," *Journal of Adolescent Health*, 2017, 61(3): 273–280.
25. Nicole Haberland and Deborah Rogow, "Sexuality Education: Emerging Trends in Evidence and Practice," *Journal of Adolescent Health*, 2015, 56(1): 15–21.
26. Kurt Vonnegut, *Slaughterhouse Five* (New York: Delacorte, 1969).
27. William Adler, *The Man Who Never Died: The Life, Times, and Legacy of Joe Hill, American Labor Icon* (London: Bloomsbury, 2011).
28. J. Dezutter, B. Soenes, K. Luyckx, S. Bruyneel, M. Vantsenkiste, B. Duriez, and D. Hutsebaut, "The Role of Religion in Death Attitudes: Distinguishing Between Religious Belief and Style of Processing Religious Contents," *Death Studies*, 2009, 33: 73–92; M. Pearce, J. Singer, and H. Prigerson, "Religious Coping Among Caregivers of Terminally Ill Cancer Patients: Main Effects and Psychosocial Mediators," *Journal of Health Psychology*, 2006, 11: 743–759.
29. S. Carmel and E. Mutean, "Wishes Regarding the Use of Life-Sustaining Treatments Among Elderly Persons in Israel—an Explanatory Model," *Social Science and Medicine*, 1997, 45: 1715–1727; R. Neimeyer, J. Wittkowski, and R. Moser, "Psychological Research on Death Attitudes: An Overview and Evaluation," *Death Studies*, 2004, 28: 309–340.
30. Yaacov Bachner, Norm O'Rourke, and Sara Carmel, "Fear of Death, Mortality Communication, and Psychological Distress Among Secular and Religiously Observant Family Caregivers of Terminal Cancer Patients," *Death Studies*, 2011, 35(2): 163–187.
31. Andrea Phelps, Paul Maciejewski, Matthew Nillson, and Tracy Balboni, "Association Between Religious Coping and Use of Intensive Life-Prolonging Care Near Death Among Patients with Advanced Cancer," *Journal of the American Medical Association*, 2009, 301(11): 1140–1147.
32. Erlendur Haraldsson, "Popular Psychology, Belief in Life After Death and Reincarnation in the Nordic Countries, Western and Eastern Europe," *Nordic Psychology*, 2006, 58(2): 171–180; George Lakey, *Viking Economics* (Brooklyn, NY: Melville House, 2016); Partanen, *Nordic Theory*.
33. Phil Zuckerman, *Faith No More: Why People Reject Religion* (New York: Oxford University Press, 2012).
34. Phil Zuckerman, *Living the Secular Life* (New York: Penguin, 2014).

35. Haldane, quoted in Ali Rizvi, *The Atheist Muslim* (New York: St. Martin's Press, 2016), 126.
36. Christina Sagioglou and Matthias Forstmann, "Activating Christian Religious Concepts Increases Intolerance of Ambiguity and Judgment Certainty," *Journal of Experimental Social Psychology*, 2013, 49: 933–939.
37. Richard Sorrentino, *The Uncertain Mind: Individual Differences in Facing the Unknown* (Philadelphia: Psychology Press, 2017).
38. Rizvi, *Atheist Muslim*, 125.
39. Sherwin Nuland, *The Doctors' Plague: Germs, Childbed Fever, and the Strange Story of Ignac Semmelweis* (New York: W. W. Norton and Co., 2004).
40. Cragun, *What You Don't Know*, 57–59; Darren Sherkat, "Religion and Scientific Literacy in the United States," *Social Science Quarterly*, 2011, 92(5): 1134–1148.
41. "Scientists and Belief," Pew Research Center, November 5, 2009, www.pewforum.org/2009/11/05/scientists-and-belief.
42. Elaine Howard Ecklund, *Science vs. Religion: What Scientists Really Think* (New York: Oxford University Press, 2012); Ariela Keysar and Barry Kosmin, *Secularism and Science in the 21st Century* (Hartford, CT: ISSSC, 2008).
43. Bill Nye, *Undeniable: Evolution and the Science of Creation* (New York: St. Martin's Griffin, 2015); Christopher DiCarlo, "We Are All African! Can Scientific Proof of Our Commonality Save Us?" *Free Inquiry*, 2010, 30(4): 18–22.
44. Andrew Fiala, *Against Religion, Wars, and States* (Lanham, MD: Rowman and Littlefield, 2013).
45. Paul Kurtz, *Forbidden Fruit: The Ethics of Secularism* (Amherst, NY: Prometheus Press, 2008), 225.
46. Kwame Anthony Appiah, *Cosmopolitanism: Ethics in a World of Strangers* (New York: W. W. Norton, 2006), p. xvi.
47. M. Pepper, T. Jackson, and D. Uzzell, "A Study of Multidimensional Religion Constructs and Values in the United Kingdom," *Journal for the Scientific Study of Religion*, 2010, 49: 127–146; Zuckerman, "Irreligiosity of Du Bois," in Blum and Young, *Souls of W. E. B. Du Bois*; S. Roccas, "Religion and Value Systems," *Journal of Social Issues*, 2005, 61: 747–759; Hood, Hill, and Spilka, *Psychology of Religion*.
48. S. Reiss, "Why People Turn to Religion: A Motivational Analysis," *Journal for the Scientific Study of Religion*, 2000, 39: 47–52; E. McClain, "Personality Differences Between Intrinsically Religious and Non-religious Students: A Factor Analytic Study," *Journal of Personality Assessment*, 1978, 42: 159–166.
49. Benjamin Beit-Hallahmi, "Atheists: A Psychological Profile," in Martin, *Cambridge Companion to Atheism*; Bob Altemeyer, "Why Do Religious Fundamentalists Tend to Be Prejudiced?" *International Journal for the Psychology of Religion*, 2009, 13(1): 17–28; Andrew Greeley and Michael Hout, *The Truth About Conservative Christians: What They Think and What They Believe* (Chicago: University of Chicago Press, 2006); Corwin Smidt, "Religion and American Attitudes Toward Islam and an Invasion of Iraq," *Sociology of Religion*, 2005, 66(3): 243–261; Bruce Hunsberger and Bob Altemeyer, *Atheists: A Groundbreaking Study of America's Nonbelievers* (Amherst, NY: Prometheus Books, 2006).
50. "Christian in Western Europe," Pew Research Center.
51. Tobin Grant, "Patriotism God Gap: Is the U.S. the Greatest Country in the World?" *Chris-*

tianity Today, August 5, 2011, www.christianitytoday.com/news/2011/august/patriotism-god-gap-is-us-greatest-country-in-world.html.

52. Lauren Markoe, "Evangelicals Top Religious Patriotism; Believe in American Exceptionalism, Poll," *Huffington Post*, July 4, 2013, www.huffingtonpost.com/2013/07/04/religious-patriotism-_n_3545537.html.
53. Joseph Chinyong Liow, *Religion and Nationalism in Southeast Asia* (New York: Cambridge University Press, 2016); Rogers Brubaker, "Religion and Nationalism: Four Approaches," *Nations and Nationalism*, 2012, 18(1): 2–20; Peter Van der Veer, *Religious Nationalism: Hindus and Muslims in India* (Berkeley and Los Angeles: University of California Press, 1994); Adrian Hastings, *The Construction of Nationhood: Ethnicity, Religion and Nationalism* (New York: Cambridge University Press, 1997).
54. Genevieve Zubrzycki, "Religion and Nationalism: A Critical Re-Examination," in *The New Blackwell Companion to the Sociology of Religion*, ed. Bryan Turner (Chichester, UK: Wiley-Blackwell, 2010).
55. B. Bushman, E. Ridge, C. Das, and G. Busath, "When God Sanctions Killing: Effect of Scriptural Violence on Aggression," *Psychological Science*, 2007, 18: 204–207; J. Preston and R. Ritter, "Different Effects of Religion and God on Prosociality with the Ingroup and Outgroup," *Personality and Social Psychology Bulletin*, 2013, 39: 1471–1483; Rob Eisinga, Albert Felling, and Jan Peters, "Religious Belief, Church Involvement, and Ethnocentrism in the Netherlands," *Journal for the Scientific Study of Religion*, 1990, 29(1): 54–75; Hood et al., *Psychology of Religion*.
56. Zachary Rothschild, Abdolhossein Abdollahi, and Tom Pyszczynski, "Does Peace Have a Prayer? The Effect of Mortality Salience, Compassionate Values, and Religious Fundamentalism on Hostility Toward Out-Groups," *Journal of Experimental Social Psychology*, 2009, 45: 816–827; David Wulff, *Psychology of Religion: Classic and Contemporary Views* (New York: Wiley, 1991), 219–220.
57. Altemeyer, "Religious Fundamentalists," 18.
58. Hood et al., *Psychology of Religion*, 411.
59. "American Democracy in Crisis: The Challenges of Voter Knowledge, Participation, and Polarization," Public Religion Research Institute, July 17, 2018, www.prri.org/research/american-democracy-in-crisis-voters-midterms-trump-election-2018.
60. D. L. Hall, D. C. Matz, and W. Wood, "Why Don't We Practice What We Preach? A Meta-Analytic Review of Religious Racism," *Personality and Social Psychology Review*, 2010, 14, 126–139; Lynne Jackson and Bruce Hunsberger, "An Intergroup Perspective on Religion and Prejudice," *Journal for the Scientific Study of Religion*, 1999, 38(4): 509–523.
61. Ervin Staub, *The Roots of Evil: The Origins of Genocide and Other Group Violence* (New York: Cambridge University Press, 1992), 214.
62. Martin Hoffman, *Empathy and Moral Development* (New York: Cambridge University Press, 2000), 3.
63. Laura Saslow, Robb Willer, Matthew Feinberg, and Paul Piff, "My Brother's Keeper? Compassion Predicts Generosity More Among Less Religious Individuals," *Social Psychological and Personality Science*, 2013, 4(1): 31–38.
64. Jared Piazza, "If You Love Me Keep My Commandments: Religiosity Increases Preference for Rule-Based Moral Arguments," *International Journal for the Psychology of Religion*, 2012,

22: 285–302; Jared Piazza and J. Landy, "Lean Not on Your Own Understanding: Belief That Morality Is Founded on Divine Authority and Non-utilitarian Moral Judgments," *Judgement and Decision Making*, 2013, 8: 639–661.

65. Cragun, *What You Don't Know*, 87.
66. Andrew Whitehead and Joseph Baker, "Homosexuality, Religion, and Science: Moral Authority and the Persistence of Negative Attitudes," *Sociological Inquiry*, 2012, 82: 487–509; Darren Sherkat, M. Powell-Williams, G. Maddox, and K. de Vries, "Religion, Politics, and Support for Same-Sex Marriage in the United States, 1988–2008," *Social Science Research*, 2011, 40: 167–180; Thomas Linneman and M. Clendenen, "Sexuality and the Sacred," in Zuckerman, *Atheism and Secularity*, 89–112; Jonathan Schwartz and Lori Lindley, "Religious Fundamentalism and Attachment: Prediction of Homophobia," *International Journal for the Psychology of Religion*, 2005, 15(2): 145–157.
67. "Changing Attitudes on Gay Marriage," Pew Research Center, June 26, 2017, www.pewforum.org/fact-sheet/changing-attitudes-on-gay-marriage.
68. P. K. Botvar, "The Moral Thinking of Three Generations in Scandinavia: What Role Does Religion Play?" *Social Compass*, 2005, 52: 185–195; Jared Piazza, "If You Love Me Keep My Commandments: Religiosity Increases Preference for Rule-Based Moral Arguments," *International Journal for the Psychology of Religion*, 2012, 22: 285–302; Jared Piazza and J. Landy, "Lean Not on Your Own Understanding: Belief That Morality Is Founded on Divine Authority and Non-utilitarian Moral Judgments," *Judgement and Decision Making*, 2013, 8: 639–661; M. Van Pachterbeke, C. Freyer, and V. Saroglou, "When Authoritarianism Meets Religion: Sacrificing Others in the Name of Abstract Deontology," *European Journal of Social Psychology*, 2011, 41: 898–903.
69. Catherine Caldwell-Harris, "Understanding Atheism/Non-belief as an Expected Individual-Differences Variable," *Religion, Brain & Behavior*, 2012, 2(1): 4–23.
70. Sam Harris, *The Moral Landscape* (New York: Free Press, 2010).

CHAPTER 9

1. This entire episode comes from Jonathan Pincus, *Base Instincts: What Makes Killers Kill?* (New York: W. W. Norton, 2001), chapter 3.
2. "America's Gun Homicide Rate Is 25 Times Higher Than Other Rich Countries," *Time*, February 3, 2016, www.time.com/4206484/america-violent-death-rate-higher.
3. Pinker, *Better Angels*; Shermer, *The Moral Arc*.
4. "List of Countries by Intentional Homicide Rate," Wikipedia, accessed March 6, 2019, en.wikipedia.org/wiki/List_of_countries_by_intentional_homicide_rate.
5. Simon Baron-Cohen, *The Science of Evil* (New York: Basic Books, 2011), chapter 3.
6. David Evans and Mike Adams, "Salvation or Damnation? Religion and Correctional Ideology," *American Journal of Criminal Justice*, 2003, 28(1): 15–35.
7. Pincus, *Base Instincts*, 49.
8. Pincus, *Base Instincts*, 50.
9. Pincus, *Base Instincts*, 19.
10. Pincus, *Base Instincts*, 29.
11. Cathy Widom, "The Cycle of Violence," *Science*, 1989, 244: 160–166.
12. D. Freedman and D. Hemenway, "Precursors of Lethal Violence: A Death Row Sample,"

Social Science Medicine, 2000, 50: 1757–1770; M. G. Maxfield and C. S. Widom, "The Cycle of Violence Revisited Six Years Later," *Archives of Pediatric and Adolescent Medicine*, 1996, 150: 390–395; Cathy Widom and Michael Maxfield, "An Update on the 'Cycle of Violence,'" National Institute of Justice, February 2001, www.ncjrs.gov/pdffiles1/nij/184894.pdf; E. T. Gershoff, "Corporal Punishment by Parents and Associated Child Behaviors and Experiences: A Meta-Analytic and Theoretical Review," *Psychological Bulletin*, 2002, 128: 539–579.

13. Michael Shermer, *The Science of Good and Evil* (New York: Owl Books, 2004), 68–69.
14. Baron-Cohen, *Science of Evil*, 18.
15. S. Fazel and J. Danesh, "Serious Mental Disorder in 23,000 Prisoners: A Systematic Review of 62 Surveys," *Lancet*, 2002, 359: 545–550.
16. N. Anderson and K. Kiehl, "The Psychopath Magnetized: Insights from Brain Imaging," *Trends in Cognitive Science*, 2012, 16(1): 52–60; J. Blair, D. Mitchell, and K. Blair, *The Psychopath: Emotion and the Brain* (Malden, MA: Blackwell, 2005); M. Brower and B. Price, "Neuropsychiatry of Frontal Lobe Dysfunction in Violent and Criminal Behavior: A Critical Review," *Journal of Neurology, Neurosurgery, and Psychiatry*, 2001, 71(6): 720–726.
17. Arielle De Sousa, Skye McDonald, Jacqueline Rushby, Sophie Li, Aneta Dimoska, and Charlotte James, "Understanding Deficits in Empathy After Traumatic Brain Injury: The Role of Affective Responsivity," *Cortex*, 2011, 47(5): 526.
18. Roger Wood and Claire Williams, "Inability to Empathize Following Traumatic Brain Injury," *Journal of the International Neuropsychological Society*, 2008, 14(2): 289–296.
19. S. G. Shamay-Tsoory, R. Tomer, B. D. Berger, and J. Aharon-Peretz, "Characterization of Empathy Deficits Following Prefrontal Brain Damage: The Role of the Right Ventromedial Prefrontal Cortex," *Journal of Cognitive Neuroscience*, 2003, 15(3): 324–337.
20. Philip Sterzer, Christian Stadler, Fritz Poutzska, and Andreas Kleinschmidt, "A Structural Neural Deficit in Adolescents with Conduct Disorder and Its Association with Lack of Empathy," *NeuroImage*, 2007, 37(1): 335–342.
21. A. Duke, L. Begue, R. Bell, and T. Eisenlohr-Moul, "Revisiting the Serotonin-Aggression Relation in Humans: A Meta-Analysis," *Psychological Bulletin*, 2013, (139)5: 1148–1172.
22. Nigel Barber, *Kindness in a Cruel World* (Amherst, NY: Prometheus Books, 2004), 121.
23. David Moore, *The Dependent Gene: The Fallacy of "Nature vs. Nurture"* (New York: Henry Holt, 2003).
24. D. T. Lykken, *The Antisocial Personalities* (Hillsdale, NJ: Lawrence Erlbaum, 1995).
25. Hrdy, *Mothers and Others*.
26. Hrdy, *Mothers and Others*, 83.
27. Pincus, *Base Instincts*, 70–71.
28. Jude Cassidy and Phillip Shaver, *Handbook of Attachment: Theory, Research, and Clinical Applications* (New York: The Guilford Press, 1999).
29. Machteld Hoeve, Geert Jan Stams, Claudia van der Put, Judith Semon Dubas, Peter van der Laan, and Jasn Gerris, "A Meta-Analysis of Attachment to Parents and Delinquency," *Journal of Abnormal Child Psychology*, 2012, 40(5): 771–785.
30. Sapolsky, *Behave*, chapter 7; D. Buka, T. Stichik, I. Birdthistle, and F. Earls, "Youth Exposure to Violence: Prevalence, Risks, and Consequences," *American Journal of Orthopsychiatry*, 2001, 71(3): 298–310; R. Rhodes, *Why They Kill* (New York: Knopf, 1999); O'Hagan

Selner, Daniel Kindlon, Stephen Buka, Stephen Raudenbush, and Felton Earls, "Assessing Exposure to Violence in Urban Youth," *Journal of Child Psychology and Psychiatry*, 1998, 39(2): 215–224.

31. Widom and Maxfield, "Cycle of Violence."
32. Y. M. Vissing, M. A. Straus, R. J. Gelles, and J. W. Harrop, "Verbal Aggression by Parents and Psychosocial Problems of Children," *Child Abuse and Neglect*, 1991, 15: 223–238.
33. Carolyn Smith and Terence Thornberry, "The Relationship Between Childhood Maltreatment and Adolescent Involvement in Delinquency," *Criminology*, 1995, 33(4): 451–481.
34. D. J. English, C. S. Widom, and C. Brandford, "Childhood Victimization and Delinquency, Adult Criminality, and Violent Criminal Behavior: A Replication and Extension," Final Report to National Institute of Justice, February 2002, www.ncjrs.gov/pdffiles1/nij/grants/192291.pdf.
35. Jennifer Lansford, Shari Miller-Johnson, Lisa Berlin, Kenneth Dodge, John Bates, and Gregory Pettit, "Early Physical Abuse and Later Violent Delinquency: A Prospective Longitudinal Study," *Child Maltreatment*, 2007, 12(3): 233–245; Joshua Mersky and Arthur Reynolds, "Child Maltreatment and Violent Delinquency: Disentangling Main Effects and Subgroup Effects," *Child Maltreatment*, 2007, 12(3): 246–258; Claire Crooks, Katreena Scott, David Wolfe, Debbie Chiodo, and Steve Killip, "Understanding the Link Between Childhood Maltreatment and Violent Delinquency: What Do Schools Have to Add?" *Child Maltreatment*, 2007, 12(3): 269–280.
36. Sunny Shin, Amo Cook, Nancy Morris, Ribyn McDougle, and Lauren Peasley Groves, "The Different Faces of Impulsivity as Links Between Childhood Maltreatment and Young Adult Crime," *Preventive Medicine*, 2016, 88: 201–217.
37. Jaana Haapasalo and Elina Pokela, "Child-Rearing and Child Abuse Antecedents of Criminality," *Aggression and Violent Behavior*, 1999, 4(1): 107–127.
38. James Gilligan, *Preventing Violence* (New York: Thames and Hudson, 2001), 115.
39. J. Bryer, B. Nelson, J. Miller, and O. Korel, "Childhood Sexual and Physical Abuse as Factors in Adult Psychiatric Illness," *American Journal of Psychiatry*, 1987, 144: 1426–1430.
40. Philip Dray, *At the Hands of Persons Unknown: The Lynching of Black America* (New York: The Modern Library, 2002).
41. Dray, *Persons Unknown.*
42. Du Bois, "Lynched by Years, 1885–1914," in Zuckerman, *Social Theory of Du Bois.*
43. Byrne Fone, *Homophobia: A History* (London: Picador, 2001).
44. Fone, *Homophobia.*
45. John Boswell, *Christianity, Social Tolerance, and Homosexuality: Gay People in Western Europe from the Beginning of the Christian Era to the Fourteenth Century* (Chicago: University of Chicago Press, 1981); Fone, *Homophobia.*
46. Jongsoo Lee, *The Allure of Nezahualcoyotl: Pre-Hispanic History, Religion, and Nahua Poetics* (Albuquerque: University of New Mexico Press, 2008).
47. David Crompton, "Homosexuals and the Death Penalty in Colonial America," *Journal of Homosexuality*, 1976, 1(3): 277–293.
48. "LGBT relationships are illegal in 74 countries, research finds," *The Independent*, May 17, 2016, www.independent.co.uk/news/world/gay-lesbian-bisexual-relationships-illegal-in-74-countries-a7033666.html.

49. "Changing Attitudes on Gay Marriage," Pew Research Center, June 26, 2017, www.pewforum.org/fact-sheet/changing-attitudes-on-gay-marriage.
50. Robert Brenneman, *Homies and Hermanos: God and Gangs in Central America* (New York: Oxford University Press, 2012), 87.
51. Arlene Stein, *Shameless: Sexual Dissidence in American Culture* (New York: New York University Press, 2006), 6.
52. Thomas Scheff, *Microsociology: Discourse, Emotion, and Social Structure* (Chicago: University of Chicago Press, 1991).
53. Herbert Thomas, "Experiencing a Shame Response as a Precursor to Violence," *Bulletin American Academy of Psychiatry and Law*, 1995, 23(4): 587–592.
54. Gilligan, *Preventing Violence*, 35.
55. June Tangney, Jeff Stuewig, and Debra Mashek, "Moral Emotions and Moral Behavior," *Annual Review of Psychology*, 2007, 58: 345–372.

CHAPTER 10

1. Peter Balakian, *Black Dog of Fate: A Memoir* (New York: Basic Books, 1997), 214–217.
2. Donald Miller and Lorna Touryan Miller, *Survivors: An Oral History of the Armenian Genocide* (Berkeley: University of California Press, 1993).
3. Miller and Miller, *Survivors*.
4. James Waller, *Becoming Evil: How Ordinary People Commit Genocide and Mass Killing* (New York: Oxford University Press, 2002), 55.
5. Jan Karski, *Story of a Secret State: My Report to the World* (Washington, D.C.: Georgetown University Press, 2010), 329–330.
6. Karski, *Secret State*, 337–338.
7. Daniel Goldhagen, *Hitler's Willing Executioners: Ordinary Germans and the Holocaust* (New York: Vintage, 1996).
8. Waller, *Becoming Evil*, 166–167.
9. Adam Jones, *Genocide: A Comprehensive Introduction* (New York: Routledge, 2006).
10. Alexander Laban Hinton, *Why Did They Kill? Cambodia in the Shadow of Genocide* (Berkeley: University of California Press, 2005), 168.
11. Mark A. Drumbl, "'She Makes Me Ashamed to Be a Woman': The Genocide Conviction of Pauline Nyiramasuhuko, 2011," *Michigan Journal of International Law*, 2012, 34(3), 559–604.
12. Jean Hatzfeld, *Life Laid Bare: The Survivors in Rwanda Speak* (New York: Other Press, 2000), 23–24.
13. David Olusoga, *The Kaiser's Holocaust: Germany's Forgotten Genocide and the Colonial Roots of Nazism* (London: Faber and Faber, 2011).
14. Hinton, *Why Did They Kill*.
15. R. W. Davies and Stephen Wheatcroft, *The Years of Hunger: Soviet Agriculture, 1931–1933* (Basingstoke, UK: Palgrave Macmillan, 2004).
16. Niccolò Pianciola, "The Collectivization Famine in Kazakhstan, 1931–1933," *Harvard Ukrainian Studies*, 2001, 25(3–4): 237–251.
17. Iris Chang, *The Rape of Nanking: The Forgotten Holocaust of World War II* (New York: Penguin, 1998).

18. Leslie Holmes, *Communism: A Very Short Introduction* (New York: Oxford University Press, 2009).
19. Donald Beachler, "The Politics of Genocide Scholarship: The Case of Bangladesh," *Patterns of Prejudice*, 2007, 41(5): 467–492.
20. Steven Burg and Paul Shoup, *Ethnic Conflict and International Intervention: Crisis in Bosnia-Herzegovina, 1990–1993* (New York: Taylor and Francis, 2015).
21. Waller, *Becoming Evil*, 15.
22. McCandless et al., "20th Century Death."
23. Benjamin Beit-Hallahmi, "Morality and Immorality," in Zuckerman, *Atheism and Secularity*; O. Bartov and P. Mack, eds., *In God's Name: Genocide and Religion in the Twentieth Century*, (Oxford and New York: Berghahn Books, 2001); Stephen Law, *The War for Children's Minds* (London: Routledge, 2006); Guenter Lewy, *The Catholic Church and Nazi Germany* (New York: McGraw-Hill, 1964); R. Steigman-Gall, *The Holy Reich: Nazi Conceptions of Christianity, 1919–1945* (New York: Cambridge University Press, 2003); Peter Sperlich, "Atheists, Anti-atheists, and Nazis—Once Again," *Free Inquiry*, 2011, 31(1): 51–52.
24. Jack David Eller, *Cruel Creeds, Virtuous Violence: Religious Violence Across Culture and History* (Amherst, NY: Prometheus Books, 2010).
25. Waller, *Becoming Evil*, 182.
26. Waller, *Becoming Evil*, 153.
27. David Wilson Sloan, *Does Altruism Exist? Culture, Genes, and the Welfare of Others* (New Haven, CT: Yale University Press, 2015).
28. Elliott Sober and David Sloan Wilson, *Unto Others: The Evolution and Psychology of Unselfish Behavior* (Cambridge, MA: Harvard University Press, 1998).
29. Jonathan Haidt, *The Religious Mind*; David Berreby, *Us and Them: Understanding Your Tribal Mind* (New York: Little Brown and Co., 2005); Greene, *Moral Tribes*.
30. R. D. Alexander, *The Biology of Moral Systems* (New York: Aldine de Gruyter, 1987).
31. Sober and Wilson, *Unto Others*, 9.
32. Nigel Barber, *Kindness in a Cruel World* (Amherst, NY: Prometheus Books, 2004), 12.
33. J. F. Dovidio, S. L. Gaertner, and T. Saguy, "Commonality and the Complexity of 'We': Social Attitudes and Social Change," *Personality and Social Psychology Review*, 2009, 13: 3–20.
34. Neha Mahajan and Karen Wynn, "Origins of 'Us' versus 'Them': Prelinguistic Infants Prefer Similar Others," *Cognition*, 2012, 124: 227–233.
35. "The Moral Life of Babies," *New York Times*, May 9, 2010, www.nytimes.com/2010/05/09/magazine/09babies-t.html.
36. Mahajan and Wynn, "Us versus Them."
37. Meagan Patterson and Rebecca Bigler, "Preschool Children's Attention to Environmental Messages About Groups: Social Categorization and the Origins of Intergroup Bias," *Child Development*, 2006, 77(4): 847–860.
38. Muzafer Sherif, O. J. Harvey, B. Jack White, William R. Hood, and Carolyn W. Sherif, *The Robbers Cave Experiment: Intergroup Conflict and Cooperation* (Middletown, CT: Wesleyan University Press, 1961).
39. Henri Tajfel, M. G. Billig, and R. P. Bundy, "Social Categorization and Intergroup Behavior," *European Journal of Social Psychology*, 1971, 1(2): 149–178.
40. Waller, *Becoming Evil*, 176.

41. Lyall Watson, *Dark Nature: A Natural History of Evil* (San Francisco: Harper Perennial, 1997); see also Berreby, *Us and Them.*
42. "The Eight Stages of Genocide," Geocide Watch, 1998, www.genocidewatch.org/about genocide/8stagesofgenocide.html.
43. Thomas Blass, "Psychological Perspectives on the Perpetrators of the Holocaust: The Role of Situational Pressures, Personal Dispositions, and Their Interactions," *Holocaust and Genocide Studies*, 1993, 7: 30–50; Hinton, *Why Did They Kill*; Gerald Prunier, *The Rwanda Crisis: History of a Genocide* (New York: Columbia University Press, 1995).
44. R. J. Rummel, *Death by Government: Genocide and Mass Murder Since 1900* (New York: Routledge, 1997).
45. Staub, *Roots of Evil.*
46. P. Glick, "Choice of scapegoats," in *On the Nature of Prejudice: 50 Years After Allport*, ed. J. F. Dovidio, P. Glick, and L. A. Rudman (Malden, MA: Blackwell Publishing, 2005); P. Glick, "Sacrificial Lambs Dressed in Wolves' Clothing: Envious Prejudice, Ideology, and the Scapegoating of Jews," in *Understanding Genocide: The Social Psychology of the Holocaust*, ed. L. S. Newman and R. Erber (New York: Oxford University Press, 2002); Ervin Staub, *Overcoming Evil: Genocide, Violent Conflict, and Terroris*m (New York: Oxford University Press, 2011).
47. Phillip Goff, Jennifer Eberhardt, Melissa Williams, and Matthew Jackson, "Not Yet Human: Implicit Knowledge, Historical Dehumanization, and Contemporary Consequences," *Journal of Personality and Social Psychology*, 2008, 94(2): 292–306; David Livingstone Smith, *Less Than Human: Why We Demean, Enslave, and Exterminate Others* (New York: St. Martin's Press, 2011).
48. Smith, *Less Than Human*, 71.
49. Benjamin Valentino, "Final Solutions: The Causes of Mass Killing and Genocide," *Security Studies*, 2000, 9(3): 1–59.
50. Jones, *Genocide*, 48–50.
51. Waller, *Becoming Evil*, 264.
52. D. M. Buss, *Evolutionary Psychology: The New Science of the Mind* (Boston: Allyn and Bacon, 2012); David Rowe, Alexander Vazsonyi, and Daniel Flannery, "Sex Differences in Crime: Do Means and Within-Sex Variation Have Similar Causes?" *Journal of Research in Crime and Delinquency*, 1995, 32(1): 84–100; Helena Cronin, *The Ant and the Peacock* (Cambridge, UK: Cambridge University Press, 1991).
53. Peter Singer, *The Expanding Circle: Ethics, Evolution, and Moral Progress* (Princeton, NJ: Princeton University Press, 1981).
54. Singer, *Expanding Circle*, 119.
55. Pinker, *Better Angels.*
56. Scott Straus, *Fundamentals of Genocide and Mass Atrocity Prevention* (Washington, D.C.: United States Holocaust Memorial and Museum, 2016).

CHAPTER II

1. Berreby, *Us and Them*, 174–178.
2. The summaries of the studies in this section rely heavily on the work of Elliott Currie, specifically *Crime and Punishment in America* (New York: Owl Books, 1998).

3. David Olds, Charles R. Henderson, Harriet Kitzman, and Robert Cole, "Effects of Prenatal and Infancy Nurse Home Visitation on Surveillance of Child Maltreatment," *Pediatrics*, 1995, 95(3): 365–372; David Olds, J. Echenrode, C. R. Henderson, H. Kitzman, J. Powers, R. Cole, K. Sidora, P. Morris, L. M. Pettitt, and D. Luckey, "Long-term Effects of Home Visitation on Maternal Life Course and Child Abuse and Neglect: Fifteen-Year Follow-up of a Randomized Trial," *Journal of the American Medical Association*, 1997, 278(8): 637–643; Currie, *Crime and Punishment*, 84–86.
4. Dale Johnson and Todd Walker, "Primary Prevention of Behavior Problems in Mexican-American Children," *American Journal of Community Psychology*, 1987, 15(4): 375–385; Hirokazu Yoshikawa, "Long-Term Effects of Early Childhood Programs on Social Outcomes and Delinquency," *The Future of Children*, 1995, 5(3): 51–75; Elizabeth Drake, Steve Aos, and Marna Niller, "Evidence-Based Public Policy Options to Reduce Crime and Criminal Justice Costs: Implications in Washington State," *Victims and Offenders*, 2009, 4: 170–196.
5. Currie, *Crime and Punishment*, 91–92.
6. Currie, *Crime and Punishment*, 102–103.
7. C. M. Bourduin et al., "Multi-systemic Treatment of Serious Juvenile Offenders: Long-Term Prevention of Criminality and Violence," *Journal of Consulting and Clinical Psychology*, 1995, 63(4): 569–578; Sciott Henggeler et al., "Multisystemic Therapy: An Effective Violence Prevention Approach for Serious Juvenile Offenders," *Journal of Adolescence*, 1996, 19(1): 47–61; Currie, *Crime and Punishment*, 105–106.
8. James Gilligan, *Preventing Violence* (New York: Thames and Hudson, 2001); D. Stanley Eitzen, *Solutions to Social Problems: Lessons from Other Societies* (London: Pearson, 2009); Oscar Newman, *Defensible Space: Crime Prevention Through Urban Design* (New York: Macmillan, 1972).
9. Currie, *Crime and Punishment*, 81; Deborah Prothrow-Stith and Howard Spivak, *Murder Is No Accident: Understanding and Preventing Youth Violence in America* (San Francisco: Jossey-Bass, 2004).
10. Gilligan, *Preventing Violence*, chapter 2.
11. Don Soo Chon, "The Impact of Population Heterogeneity and Income Inequality on Homicide Rates: A Cross-National Assessment," *International Journal of Offender Therapy and Comparative Criminology*, 2012, 56(5): 730–748; Frank Elgar and Nicole Aitken, "Income Inequality, Trust, and Homicide in 33 Countries," *European Journal of Public Health*, 2010, 21(2): 241–246; Dwayne Smith and Margaret Zahn, eds., *Studying and Preventing Homicide: Issues and Challenges* (Thousand Oaks, CA: SAGE, 1999); Barbara Chasin, *Inequality and Violence in the United States* (Amherst, NY: Humanity Books, 1987); James Short, *Poverty, Ethnicity, and Violent Crime* (Boulder, CO: Westview Press, 1997).
12. "Murder rate per million people," NationMaster, accessed March 6, 2019, www.nationmaster.com/country-info/stats/Crime/Violent-crime/Murder-rate-per-million-people.
13. "How Japan's Murder Rate Got to be So Incredibly Low," *Business Insider*, April 11, 2014, www.businessinsider.com/why-japans-murder-rate-is-so-low-2014-4.
14. Ching-Chi Hsieh and M. D. Pugh, "Poverty, Income Inequality, and Violent Crime: A Meta-Analysis of Recent Aggregate Data Studies," *Criminal Justice Review*, 1993, 18(2): 182–202.

15. Pablo Fajnzylber, Daniel Lederman, and Norman Loayza, "Inequality and Violent Crime," *Journal of Law and Economics*, 2002, XLV: 1–40.
16. Richard Wilkinson and Kate Pickett, *The Spirit Level: Why Greater Equality Makes Societies Stronger* (New York: Bloomsbury Press, 2009), 144.
17. "Regional Murder Rates 2001–2017," Death Penalty Information Center, accessed March 6, 2019, www.deathpenaltyinfo.org/murder-rates-nationally-and-state#MRord.
18. Wilkinson and Pickett, *Spirit Level*, 136.
19. James Heckman, *Giving Kids a Fair Chance* (Boston: MIT Press, 2017).
20. Byron Nordstrom, *Scandinavia Since 1500* (Minneapolis: University of Minnesota Press, 2000).
21. George Lakey, *Viking Economics* (Brooklyn, NY: Melville House, 2016).
22. Greg Olsen, *Power and Inequality* (New York: Oxford, 2011); Partanen, *Nordic Theory*.
23. "Global Study on Homicide," United Nations Office on Drugs and Crime, 2013, www.unodc.org/documents/gsh/pdfs/2014_GLOBAL_HOMICIDE_BOOK_web.pdf.
24. "Global Peace Index 2018," Vision of Humanity, accessed March 7, 2019, www.visionofhumanity.org/indexes/global-peace-index.
25. "World Happiness Report 2017," accessed March 7, 2019, worldhappiness.report/ed/2017.
26. Eric Einhorn and John Logue, *Modern Welfare States: Scandinavian Politics and Policy in the Global Age* (Westport, CT: Praeger, 2003).
27. Steven Pinker, *Enlightenment Now: The Case for Reason, Science, Humanism, and Progress* (New York: Viking, 2018).
28. Phil Zuckerman, "Atheism, Secularity, and Well-being: How the Findings of Social Science Counter Negative Stereotypes and Assumptions," *Sociology Compass*, 2009, 3(6): 949–971.
29. Paul Bloom, *Against Empathy: The Case for Rational Compassion* (New York: Ecco/HarperCollins, 2016).
30. J. D. Trout, *The Empathy Gap: Building Bridges to the Good Life and the Good Society* (New York: Viking, 2009), 23.
31. P. Langan and D. Levin, "Recidivism of Prisoners Released in 1994," Bureau of Justice Statistics, U.S. Department of Justice, 2002.
32. "Why Norway's Prison System Is So Successful," Business Insider, December 11, 2014, www.businessinsider.com/why-norways-prison-system-is-so-successful-2014-12.
33. Michelle Pettit and Michael Kroth, "Educational Services in Swedish Prisons: Successful Programs of Academic and Vocational Teaching," *Criminal Justice Studies*, 2011, 24(3): 215–226.
34. P. Smith, "The Effects of Incarceration on Recidivism: A Longitudinal Examination of Program Participation and Institutional Adjustment in Federally Sentenced Adult Male Offenders," unpublished doctoral dissertation, University of New Brunswick, Canada, 2006.
35. Tapio Lappi-Seppala, "Penal Policies in the Nordic Countries 1960–2010," *Journal of Scandinavian Studies in Criminology and Crime Prevention*, 2012, 13(1): 85–111.
36. Gilligan, *Preventing Violence*, 16.
37. Gilligan, *Preventing Violence*, 17.
38. Francis Cullen, Cheryl Jonson, and Daniel Nagin, "Prisons Do Not Reduce Recidivism: The High Cost of Ignoring Science," *Prison Journal*, 2011, 9(3): 485–655; M. K. Chen and

J. M. Shapiro, "Do Harsher Prison Conditions Reduce Recidivism? A Discontinuity-Based Approach," *American Law and Economic Review*, 2007, 9: 1–29; C. L. Jonson, "The Impact of Imprisonment of Reoffending: A Meta-Analysis," unpublished doctoral dissertation, University of Cincinnati, Ohio, 2010.

39. C. Spohn and D. Holleran, "The Effect of Imprisonment on Recidivism Rates of Felony Offenders: A Focus on Drug Offenders," *Criminology*, 2002, 40: 329–347.
40. P. Nieuwbeerta, D. Nagin, and A. Blokland, "The Relationship Between First Imprisonment and Criminal Career Development: A Matched Samples Comparison," *Journal of Qualitative Criminology*, 2009, 25: 227–257.
41. Chen and Shapiro, "Harsher Prison Conditions"; Jonson, "Imprisonment of Reoffending."
42. Stacy Mallicoat, *Crime and Criminal Justice: Concepts and Controversies* (Los Angeles: SAGE, 2017), 297.
43. Einar Thomassen, "Islamic Hell," *Numen: International Review for the History of Religions*, 2009, 56: 401–416.
44. Joseph Baker and Alexis Booth, "Hell to Pay: Religion and Punitive Ideology Among the American Public," *Punishment and Society*, 2016, 18(2): 151–176; A. Cota-McKinley, W. Woody, and P. Bell, "Vengeance: Effects of Gender, Age, and Religious Background," *Aggressive Behavior*, 2001, 27: 343–350.
45. Sherkat, *Changing Faith*, 162.
46. Byron Johnson, *More God, Less Crime: Why Faith Matters and How It Could Matter More* (West Conshohocken, PA: Templeton Press, 2012).
47. "Christians in Australia nearing minority status as religious affiliation declines sharply since 2011," Roy Morgan, April 16, 2014, www.roymorgan.com/findings/5541-fewer-australians-identify-as-christian-december-2013-201404152234; "2016 Community Census Profiles," Australian Bureau of Statistics, accessed March 7, 2019, www.censusdata.abs.gov.au/census_services/getproduct/census/2016/communityprofile/036.
48. "'No religion' tops religion question in Census," News.com.au, June 28, 2017, www.news.com.au/national/no-religion-tops-religion-question-in-census/news-story/a3b45e6b2e35df695932a83535078f51.
49. Baz Dreisinger, *Incarceration Nations* (New York: Other Press, 2016), chapter 6.
50. "List of Countries by Intentional Homicide Rate," Wikipedia, en.wikipedia.org/wiki/List_of_countries_by_intentional_homicide_rate.
51. "Brazil's Deadly Prison System," *New York Times*, January 4, 2017, www.nytimes.com/2017/01/04/opinion/brazils-deadly-prison-system.html; "Prison Conditions Worsen in Brazil," Human Rights Watch, December 8, 2017. www.hrw.org/news/2017/12/08/prison-conditions-worsen-brazil.
52. Dreisinger, *Incarceration Nations*, chapter 5.
53. Stuart Grassian, "Psychiatric Effects of Solitary Confinement," *Washington University Journal of Law and Policy*, 2006, 22: 325–383.
54. Grassian, "Psychiatric Effects," 327.
55. Grassian, "Psychiatric Effects."
56. Craig Haney, "Mental Health Issues in Long-Term Solitary and 'Supermax' Confinement," *Crime and Delinquency*, 2003, 49(1): 124–156.
57. Shira Gordon, "Solitary Confinement, Public Safety, and Recidivism," *University of Mich-*

igan *Journal of Law Reform*, 2014, 47(2): 495–528; "Does Solitary Confinement Make Inmates More Likely to Reoffend?" *Frontline*, PBS, April 18, 2017, www.pbs.org/wgbh/frontline/article/does-solitary-confinement-make-inmates-more-likely-to-reoffend.

58. Pinker, *Better Angels*.
59. Shermer, *The Moral Arc*, 3.
60. Shermer, *The Moral Arc*, 3.
61. Shermer, *The Moral Arc*, 37.

CHAPTER 12

1. Saulo Ferreira Feitosa, Volnei Garrafa, Gabriele Cornelli, Carla Tardivo, and Samuel Jose de Carvalho, "Bioethics, Culture and Infanticide in Brazilian Indigenous Communities: The Zuruahá Case," *Cadernos de Saúde Pública*, 2010, 26(5): 853–878; Gary Granzberg, "Twin Infanticide—A Cross-Cultural Test of a Materialistic Explanation," *Ethos*, 1973, 1(4): 405–412; see also the film "Breaking the Silence" on YouTube, www.youtube.com/watch?v=lKFpcQB-qzo&t=442s.
2. Bernard Mayo, *The Philosophy of Right and Wrong* (London: Routledge and Kegan Paul, 1986), chapter 6; Taylor, "Without the Net," in Antony, *Philosophers Without Gods*.
3. John Ladd, *Ethical Relativism* (Lanham, MD: University Press of America, 1985).
4. Robert Holmes, *Basic Moral Philosophy* (Belmont, CA: Wadsworth, 2007), 150.
5. Neil Levy, *Moral Relativism: A Short Introduction* (Oxford: Oneworld, 2002).
6. "Neonatal and child male circumcision: a global review," World Health Organization/UNAIDS, 2010, www.who.int/hiv/pub/malecircumcision/neonatal_child_MC_UNAIDS.pdf.
7. "Male circumcision: Global trends and determinants of prevalence, safety and acceptability," World Health Organization/UNAIDS, 2007, apps.who.int/iris/bitstream/10665/43749/1/9789241596169_eng.pdf.
8. Maurice Bloch, *From Blessing to Violence: History and Ideology in the Circumcision Ritual of the Merina* (New York: Cambridge University Press, 1986).
9. "Neonatal and child circumcision," World Health Organization/UNAIDS.
10. J. E. Cawte, Nari Djagamara, and M. G. Barrett, "The Meaning of Subincision of the Urethra to Aboriginal Australians," *Psychology and Psychotherapy*, 1966, 39(3): 245–253.
11. Steven Lukes, *Moral Relativism* (New York: Picador, 2008), 29.
12. Melville Herskovits, "Some Further Comments on Cultural Relativism," *American Anthropologist*, 1958, 60(2): 266–273.
13. Mary Midgley, *Can't We Make Moral Judgements?* (New York: St. Martin's Press, 1991), 90.
14. Martha Nussbaum, *Sex and Social Justice* (New York: Oxford University Press, 1999).
15. Lukes, *Moral Relativism*, 119–120.
16. Harris, *Moral Landscape*, 67.
17. Harris, *Moral Landscape*, 62.
18. Aaron Tobian and Ronald Gray, "The Medical Benefits of Male Circumcision," *Journal of the American Medical Association*, 2011, 306(13): 1479–1480.
19. Tobian and Gray, "Medical Benefits."
20. Kai Nielsen, *Naturalism Without Foundations* (Amherst, NY: Prometheus Books, 1996), 27.
21. Harris, *Moral Landscape*, 39.

22. T. M. Scanlon, *What We Owe to Each Other* (Cambridge, MA: Belknap Press, 2000).
23. J. David Velleman, *Foundations for Moral Relativism* (Open Book Publishers, 2013), 69.
24. Midgley, *Can't We Make*, 90.
25. John Kekes, *How Should We Live?* (Chicago: University of Chicago Press, 2014), 95; Shermer, *Science of Good and Evil*, 179–180.
26. Holloway, *Godless Morality*, 130.

CONCLUSION

1. "Global Warming of 1.5°C" Intergovernmental Panel on Climate Change, 2018, www.ipcc.ch/sr15.
2. Joseph Romm, *Climate Change: What Everyone Needs to Know* (Oxford: Oxford University Press, 2015); David Archer, *Global Warming: Understanding the Forecast* (Hoboken, NJ: Wiley, 2011).
3. "Climate Change: How do we know?" NASA, accessed March 7, 2019, climate.nasa.gov/evidence.
4. "It's the Guns," *The Atlantic*, May 18, 2018, www.theatlantic.com/politics/archive/2018/05/its-the-guns/560771.
5. "Gun Violence in America," Everytown for Gun Safety Support Fund, accessed March 7, 2019, www.everytownresearch.org/gun-violence-by-the-numbers.
6. "Fifty Years After the Kerner Commission," Economic Policy Institute, February 26, 2018, www.epi.org/publication/50-years-after-the-kerner-commission.
7. Michelle Alexander, *The New Jim Crow: Mass Incarceration in the Age of Colorblindness* (New York: The New Press, 2012), 98.
8. Noel Cazenave, *Killing African Americans: Police and Vigilante Violence as a Racial Control Mechanism* (New York: Routledge, 2018).
9. Lori Underwood and Dawn Hutchinson, *The Global Status of Women and Girls* (Lanham, MD: Lexington Books, 2017).
10. "AD74: Good neighbours? Africans express high levels of tolerance for many, but not for all," Afrobarometer, March 1, 2016, www.afrobarometer.org/publications/tolerance-in-africa.
11. "New FBI Data Shows Increased Reported Incidents of Anti-LGBTQ Hate Crimes in 2016," The Human Rights Campaign, November 13, 2017, www.hrc.org/blog/new-fbi-data-shows-increased-reported-incidents-of-anti-lgbtq-hate-crimes-i.
12. "2016 was the deadliest year on record for the LGBTQ community," *USA Today*, June 12, 2017, www.usatoday.com/story/news/nation/2017/06/12/2016-deadliest-year-lgbtq-pulse/373840001.
13. Dolores Smith, "Homophobic and Transphobic Violence Against Youth: The Jamaican Context," *International Journal of Adolescence and Youth*, 2017, 23(2): 250–258; "Fear for Life," Human Rights Watch, November 30, 2010, www.hrw.org/report/2010/11/30/fear-life/violence-against-gay-men-and-men-perceived-gay-senegal.
14. "Russia's 'Gay Propaganda' Laws Are Illegal, European Court Rules," *New York Times*, June 20, 2017, www.nytimes.com/2017/06/20/world/europe/russia-gay-propaganda.html.
15. "'They Starve You. They Shock You': Inside the Anti-Gay Pogrom in Chechnya," *New York Times*, April 21, 2017, www.nytimes.com/2017/04/21/world/europe/chechnya-russia-attacks-gays.html.

16. "Where are the most difficult places in the world to be gay or transgender?" *The Guardian*, March 1, 2017, www.theguardian.com/global-development-professionals-network/2017/mar/01/where-are-the-most-difficult-places-in-the-world-to-be-gay-or-transgender-lgbt.
17. "Here are the 10 countries where homosexuality may be punished by death," *Washington Post*, June 13, 2016, www.washingtonpost.com/news/worldviews/wp/2016/06/13/here-are-the-10-countries-where-homosexuality-may-be-punished-by-death-2.
18. "How Iran Solved Its Gay Marriage Problem," *Observer*, May 4, 2015, www.observer.com/2015/05/how-iran-solved-its-gay-marriage-problem.
19. "Myanmar Rohingya: What you need to know about the crisis," BBC News, April 24, 2018, www.bbc.com/news/world-asia-41566561.
20. "For India's Persecuted Muslim Minority, Caution Follows Hindu Party's Victory," *New York Times*, May 17, 2014, www.nytimes.com/2014/05/17/world/asia/india-muslims-modi.html.
21. "United States Commission on International Religious Freedom: 2017 Annual Report," www.uscirf.gov/sites/default/files/2017.USCIRFAnnualReport.pdf; "The top 10 worst countries for Christian persecution," *America: The Jesuit Review*, January 11, 2018, www.americamagazine.org/faith/2018/01/11/top-10-worst-countries-christian-persecution.
22. "Global Issues: Poverty Stats and Facts," Global Issues, January 7, 2013, www.globalissues.org/article/26/poverty-facts-and-stats.
23. "Exodus: Why Americans Are Leaving Religion, and Why They're Unlikely to Come Back," Public Religion Research Institute, September 22, 2016, www.prri.org/wp-content/uploads/2016/09/PRRI-RNS-Unaffiliated-Report.pdf; "Religious 'nones' are gaining ground," *Religion News Service*, November 16, 2017, www.religionnews.com/2017/11/16/religious-nones-are-gaining-ground-in-america-and-theyre-worried-about-the-economy-says-new-study.
24. Joseph Baker and Buster Smith, *American Secularism* (New York: New York University Press, 2015).
25. "Most Americans Still Believe in God," Gallup, June 29, 2016, news.gallup.com/poll/193271/americans-believe-god.aspx.
26. Will Gervais and Maxine Najle, "How Many Atheists Are There?" *Social Psychological and Personality Science*, 2017, 9(1): 3–10.
27. "Canada's Changing Religious Landscape," Pew Research Center, June 27, 2013, www.pewforum.org/2013/06/27/canadas-changing-religious-landscape; "Immigration and Ethnocultural Diversity in Canada," Statistics Canda, 2013, www12.statcan.gc.ca/nhs-enm/2011/as-sa/99-010-x/99-010-x2011001-eng.pdf.
28. "'No Religion' Tops Religion Question in Census," News.com.au, June 28, 2017, www.news.com.au/national/no-religion-tops-religion-question-in-census/news-story/a3b45e6b2e35df695932a83535078f51.
29. Keysar and Navarro-Rivera, "World of Atheism," in Bullivant and Ruse, *Handbook of Atheism*.
30. "2013 Census QuickStats about culture and identity," Stats NZ, April 15, 2014, archive.stats.govt.nz/Census/2013-census/profile-and-summary-reports/quickstats-culture-identity/religion.aspx.

31. Keysar and Navarro-Rivera, "World of Atheism."
32. "Is Latin America Still Catholic?" *Catholic Herald*, January 25, 2018, www.catholicherald.co.uk/issues/january-26th-2018/is-latin-america-still-catholic.
33. "Religion in Latin America," Pew Research Center, November 13, 2014, www.pewforum.org/2014/11/13/religion-in-latin-america; "Is Latin America Still Catholic?"
34. "Religion, Atheism, and Secularism," NationMaster, www.nationmaster.com/country-info/stats/Religion/Secularism-and-atheism/Population-considering-religion-unimportant.
35. "Record number of British people say they have no religion," *The Independent*, September 4, 2017, www.independent.co.uk/news/uk/home-news/british-people-atheist-no-religion-uk-christianity-islam-sikism-judaism-jewish-muslims-a7928896.html.
36. "Atheism Booming in Scotland as Number of Those Without Religion Rises," *The Herald* (Scotland), September 17, 2017, www.heraldscotland.com/news/15540508.Atheism_booming_in_Scotland_as_number_of_those_without_religion_rises.
37. "For first time, majority in Norway don't believe in God," *The Local* (Norway), March 18, 2016, www.thelocal.no/20160318/majority-of-norwegians-dont-believe-in-god.
38. "Sweden opens first atheist cemetery to cater to growing non-religious population," *The Independent*, October 20, 2016, www.independent.co.uk/news/world/europe/sweden-atheist-cemetery-opens-religion-church-of-sweden-a7371006.html; "Christian in Western Europe," Pew Research Center.
39. "Christian in Western Europe," Pew Research Center.
40. "Unlike their Central and Eastern European neighbors, most Czechs don't believe in God," Pew Research Center, June 19, 2017, www.pewresearch.org/fact-tank/2017/06/19/unlike-their-central-and-eastern-european-neighbors-most-czechs-dont-believe-in-god.
41. Keysar and Navarro-Rivera, "World of Atheism."
42. "'Christianity as default is gone': the rise of a non-Christian Europe," *The Guardian*, March 21, 2018, www.theguardian.com/world/2018/mar/21/christianity-non-christian-europe-young-people-survey-religion.
43. Ian Reader, "Secularisation, R.I.P.? Nonsense! The 'Rush Hour Away from the Gods' and the Decline of Religion," *Journal of Religion in Japan*, 2012, 1(1): 7–36.
44. "Why Young South Koreans are Turning Away from Religion" Al Jazeera, May 27, 2017, www.aljazeera.com/indepth/features/2017/05/young-south-koreans-turning-religion-170524144746222.html.
45. Zuckerman, Galen, and Pasquale, *The Nonreligious*.
46. "Invisible Atheists," *The New Republic*, April 23, 2015, www.newrepublic.com/article/121559/rise-arab-atheists; "No God, Not Even Allah," *The Economist*, November 24, 2012, www.economist.com/international/2012/11/24/no-god-not-even-allah.
47. Paul Froese, *The Plot to Kill God* (Berkeley: University of California Press, 2008).
48. "The Age Gap in Religion Around the World," Pew Research Center, June 13, 2018, www.pewforum.org/2018/06/13/the-age-gap-in-religion-around-the-world; Steve Bruce, *Secularization* (Oxford: Oxford University Press, 2011).
49. "The World's Newest Major Religion: No Religion," *National Geographic*, April 22, 2016, news.nationalgeographic.com/2016/04/160422-atheism-agnostic-secular-nones-rising-religion.
50. Stephens, *Imagine There's No Heaven*, 277.

BIBLIOGRAPHY

Adler, William. 2011. *The Man Who Never Died: The Life, Times, and Legacy of Joe Hill, American Labor Icon*. London: Bloomsbury.

Aikin, Scott, and Robert Talisse. 2011. *Reasonable Atheism: A Moral Case for Respectful Disbelief.* Amherst, NY: Prometheus Books.

Alexander, Michelle. 2012. *The New Jim Crow: Mass Incarceration in the Age of Colorblindness*. New York: The New Press.

Alexander, R. D. 1987. *The Biology of Moral Systems*. New York: Aldine de Gruyter.

Altemeyer, Bob. 2004. "Highly Dominating, Highly Authoritarian Personalities." *Journal of Social Psychology* 144(4): 421–447.

Altemeyer, Bob. 2009. "Why Do Religious Fundamentalists Tend to Be Prejudiced?" *The International Journal for the Psychology of Religion* 13(1): 17–28.

Altemeyer, Bob, and Bruce Hunsberger. 1997. *Amazing Conversions: Why Some Turn to Faith and Others Abandon Religion*. Amherst, NY: Prometheus Books.

Aman, Virginia Barnes, and Janice Boddy. 1994. *Aman: The Story of a Somali Girl*. New York: Vintage Books.

Anderson, Elizabeth. 2007. "If God Is Dead, Is Everything Permitted?" in *Philosophers Without Gods*, edited by Louise Antony. New York: Oxford University Press.

Anderson, N., and K. Kiehl. 2012. "The Psychopath Magnetized: Insights from Brain Imaging." *Trends in Cognitive Science* 16(1): 52–60.

Appiah, Kwame Anthony. 2006. *Cosmopolitanism: Ethics in a World of Strangers*. New York: W. W. Norton.

Archer, David. 2011. *Global Warming: Understanding the Forecast*. Hoboken, NJ: Wiley.

Atkinson, Linda. 1985. *In Kindling Flame: The Story of Hannah Senesh, 1921–1944*. New York: Lothrop, Lee, and Shepard Books.

Ayala, Francisco. 2009. "What the Biological Sciences Can and Cannot Contribute to Ethics." In *Contemporary Debates in Philosophy of Biology*, Francisco Ayala and Robert Arp, eds. Oxford: Wiley-Blackwell.

Ayala, Francisco, and Robert Arp, eds. 2009. *Contemporary Debates in Philosophy of Biology*. Oxford: Wiley-Blackwell.

Bachner, Yaacov, Norm O'Rourke, and Sara Carmel. 2011. "Fear of Death, Mortality Communication, and Psychological Distress Among Secular and Religiously Observant Family Caregivers of Terminal Cancer Patients." *Death Studies* 35(2): 163–187.

Baggini, Julian. 2003. *Atheism: A Very Short Introduction*. New York: Oxford University press.

Baker, Joseph, and Alexis Booth. 2016. "Hell to Pay: Religion and Punitive Ideology Among the American Public." *Punishment and Society* 18(2): 151–176.

Baker, Joseph, and Buster Smith. 2015. *American Secularism*. New York: New York University Press.

Balakian, Peter. 1997. *Black Dog of Fate: A Memoir*. New York: Basic Books.

Ball, Philip. 2001. *The Self-Made Tapestry: Pattern Formation in Nature*. New York: Oxford University Press.

Barber, Nigel. 2004. *Kindness in a Cruel World*. Amherst, NY: Prometheus Books.

Barbier, Patrick. 1998. *The World of Castrati*. London: Souvenir Press.

Barker, Dan. 2016. *God: The Most Unpleasant Character in All Fiction*. New York: Sterling.

Baron-Cohen, Simon. 2011. *The Science of Evil*. New York: Basic Books.

Bartov, O., and P. Mack, eds. 2001. *In God's Name: Genocide and Religion in the Twentieth Century*. Oxford and New York: Berghahn Books.

Beachler, Donald. 2007. "The Politics of Genocide Scholarship: The Case of Bangladesh. *Patterns of Prejudice* 41(5): 467–492.

Beit-Hallahmi, Benjamin. 2007. "Atheists: A Psychological Profile." In *The Cambridge Companion to Atheism*, edited by Michael Martin. New York: Cambridge University Press.

Beit-Hallahmi, Benjamin. 2010. "Morality and Immorality Among the Irreligious." *Atheism and Secularity*, vol. 1, edited by Phil Zuckerman. Santa Barbara, CA: Praeger-ABC-CLIO.

Bennion, Janet. 1998. *Women of Principle: Female Networking in Contemporary Mormon Polygyny.* New York: Oxford University Press.

Berger, Peter. 1963. *Invitation to Sociology.* New York: Anchor Books.

Berreby, David. 2005. *Us and Them: Understanding Your Tribal Mind.* New York: Little Brown and Co.

Bibby, Reginald. 2017. *Resilient Gods.* Vancouver, BC: UBC Press.

Bilton, Michael, and Kevin Sim. 1992. *Four Hours in My Lai.* New York: Penguin.

Blackford, Russell. 2016. *The Mystery of Moral Authority.* New York: Palgrave Macmillan.

Blair, J., D. Mitchell, and K. Blair. 2005. *The Psychopath: Emotion and the Brain.* Malden, MA: Blackwell.

Blass, Thomas. 1991. "Understanding Behavior in the Milgram Obedience Experiment: The Role of Personality, Situations, and Their Interactions." *Journal of Personality and Social Psychology* 60: 398–413.

Blass, Thomas. 1993. "Psychological Perspectives on the Perpetrators of the Holocaust: The Role of Situational Pressures, Personal Dispositions, and Their Interactions." *Holocaust and Genocide Studies* 7: 30–50.

Bloch, Maurice. 1986. *From Blessing to Violence: History and Ideology in the Circumcision Ritual of the Merina.* New York: Cambridge University Press.

Bloom, Paul. 2013. *Just Babies: The Origins of Good and Evil.* New York: Broadway Books.

Bloom, Paul. 2016. *Against Empathy: The Case for Rational Compassion.* New York: Ecco/HarperCollins.

Blum, Edward. 2007. *W. E. B. Du Bois: American Prophet.* Philadelphia: University of Pennsylvania Press.

Boehm, Christopher. 2012. *Moral Origins: The Evolution of Virtue, Altruism, and Shame.* New York: Basic Books.

Boghossian, Peter. 2013. *A Manual for Creating Atheists.* Durham, NC: Pitchstone Publishing.

Bolton, Brian. 2019. "Have Christians Accepted the Scientific Conclusion That God Does Not Answer Intercessory Prayer?" *Free Inquiry* Dec. 2018/Jan. 2019, 39(1): 20–24.

Bonger, W. A. 1943. *Race and Crime.* New York, NY: Columbia University Press.

Boswell, John. 1981. *Christianity, Social Tolerance, and Homosexuality: Gay People in Western Europe from the Beginning of the Christian Era to the Fourteenth Century.* Chicago: University of Chicago Press.

Botvar, P. K. 2005. "The Moral Thinking of Three Generations in Scandinavia: What Role Does Religion Play?" *Social Compass* 52: 185–195.

Bourduin, C. M., et al., 1995. "Multi-systemic Treatment of Serious Juvenile Offenders: Long-Term Prevention of Criminality and Violence," *Journal of Consulting and Clinical Psychology* 63(4): 569–578.

Bovin, Mette. 2001. *Nomads Who Cultivate Beauty: Wodaabe Dances and Visual Arts in Niger*. Uppsala, Sweden: Nordic Africa Institute.

Bremmer, Jan. 2007. "Atheism in Antiquity." In *The Cambridge Companion to Atheism*, edited by Michael Martin. New York: Cambridge University Press.

Brenneman, Robert. 2012. *Homies and Hermanos: God and Gangs in Central America*. New York: Oxford University Press.

Brewster, Melanie E. 2014. *Atheists in America*. New York: Columbia University Press.

Brink, David. 2007. "The Autonomy of Ethics." In *The Cambridge Companion to Atheism*, edited by Michael Martin. New York: Cambridge University Press.

Brinkerhoff, M. B., and M. M. Mackie. 1985. "Religion and Gender: A Comparison of Canadian and American Student Attitudes." *Journal of Marriage and the Family* 47: 415–429.

Brinkerhoff, M. B., and M. M. Mackie. 1993. "Casting Off the Bonds of Organized: A Religious-Careers Approach to the Study of Apostasy." *Review of Religious Research* 34: 235–258.

Brooks, Arthur, and James Q. Wilson. 2007. *Who Really Cares: The Surprising Truth About Compassionate Conservatism*. New York: Basic Books.

Brower, M., and B. Price. 2001. "Neuropsychiatry of Frontal Lobe Dysfunction in Violent and Criminal Behavior: A Critical Review." *Journal of Neurology, Neurosurgery, and Psychiatry* 71(6): 720–726.

Brubaker, Rogers. 2012. "Religion and Nationalism: Four Approaches." *Nations and Nationalism* 18(1): 2–20.

Bruce, Steve. 2011. *Secularization*. Oxford: Oxford University Press.

Bryer, J., B. Nelson, J. Miller, and O. Korel. 1987. "Childhood Sexual and Physical Abuse as Factors in Adult Psychiatric Illness." *American Journal of Psychiatry* 144: 1426–1430.

Buka, D., T. Stichik, I. Birdthistle, and F. Earls. 2001. "Youth Exposure to Violence: Prevalence, Risks, and Consequences." *American Journal of Orthopsychiatry* 71(3): 298–310.

Burg, Steven, and Paul Shoup. 2015. *Ethnic Conflict and International Intervention: Crisis in Bosnia-Herzegovina, 1990–1993*. New York: Taylor and Francis.

Bushman, B., E. Ridge, C. Das, and G. Busath. 2007. "When God Sanctions Killing: Effect of Scriptural Violence on Aggression." *Psychological Science* 18: 204–207.

Buss, D. M. 2012. *Evolutionary Psychology: The New Science of the Mind.* Boston: Allyn and Bacon.

Caldwell-Harris, Catherine. 2012. Understanding Atheism/Non-belief as an Expected Individual-Differences Variable. *Religion, Brain & Behavior* 2(1): 4–23.

Caldwell-Harris, Catherine, Elizabeth LoTempio, C. Jordan, and N. Ramanayake. 2008. "Religious Non-belief Explained by Intellectual Orientation and Childhood Socialization." Paper presented at the annual meeting of the American Psychological Association, Boston, MA.

Caldwell-Harris, Catherine, Angela Wilson, Elizabeth LoTempio, and Benjamin Beit-Hallahmi. 2010. "Exploring the Atheist Personality: Well-being, Awe, and Magical Thinking in Atheists, Buddhists, and Christians." *Mental Health, Religion and Culture* 14(7): 659–672.

Carmel, S., and E. Mutean. 1997. "Wishes Regarding the Use of Life-Sustaining Treatments Among Elderly Persons in Israel—an Explanatory Model." *Social Science and Medicine* 45: 1715–1727.

Carrier, Richard. 2005. *Sense and Goodness Without God.* Bloomington, IN: AuthorHouse.

Carville, James. 1996. *We're Right and They're Wrong.* New York: Random House.

Cassidy, Jude, and Phillip Shaver. 1999. *Handbook of Attachment: Theory, Research, and Clinical Applications.* New York: The Guilford Press.

Cawte, J. E., Nari Djagamara, and M. G. Barrett. 1966. "The Meaning of Subincision of the Urethra to Aboriginal Australians." *Psychology and Psychotherapy* 39(3): 245–253.

Cazenave, Noel. 2018. *Killing African Americans: Police and Vigilante Violence as a Racial Control Mechanism.* New York: Routledge.

Chang, Iris. 1998. *The Rape of Nanking: The Forgotten Holocaust of World War II.* New York: Penguin.

Chasin, Barbara. 1987. *Inequality and Violence in the United States.* Amherst, NY: Humanity Books.

Chen, M. K., and J. M. Shapiro. 2007. "Do Harsher Prison Conditions Reduce Recidivism? A Discontinuity-Based Approach." *American Law and Economic Review* 9: 1–29.

Chon, Don Soo. 2012. "The Impact of Population Heterogeneity and Income Inequality on Homicide Rates: A Cross-National Assessment." *International Journal of Offender Therapy and Comparative Criminology* 56(5): 730–748.

Christina, Greta. 2012. "Why Atheism Demands Social Justice." *Free Inquiry* 32(3): 12.

Churchland, Patricia. 2011. *Braintrust.* Princeton, NJ: Princeton University Press.

Clarence-Smith, William Gervase. 2006. *Islam and the Abolition of Slavery*. New York: Oxford University Press.

Clark, Thomas. 2016. "Naturalism and Well-Being." In *Religion: Beyond Religion*, edited by Phil Zuckerman. Farmington Hills, MI: Macmillan.

Cliquet, Robert, and Dragana Abramov. 2018. *Evolution Science and Ethics in the Third Millennium*. Cham, Switzerland: Springer.

Cliteur, Paul. 2010. *The Secular Outlook: In Defense of Moral and Political Secularism*. West Sussex, UK: Wiley-Blackwell.

Comte-Sponville, André. 2006. *The Little Book of Atheist Spirituality*. New York: Viking.

Connors, J. F., R. Leonard, and K. Burnham. 1968. "Religion and Opposition to War Among College Students." *Sociological Analysis* 29: 211–219.

Cornwall, Marie, Camela Courtright, and Laga Van Beek. 1993. "How Common the Principle? Women as Plural Wives in 1860." *Dialogue: A Journal of Mormon Thought* 26 (Summer): 139–153.

Cota-McKinley, A., W. Woody, and P. Bell. 2001. "Vengeance: Effects of Gender, Age, and Religious Background." *Aggressive Behavior* 27: 343–350.

Cragun, Ryan. 2013. *What You Don't Know About Religion (But Should)*. Durham, NC: Pitchstone Publishing.

Cragun, Ryan. 2016. "Defining That Which Is Other to Religion." In *Religion: Beyond Religion*, edited by Phil Zuckerman. Farmington Hills, MI: Macmillan.

Craig, William Lane. 1984. *Apologetics: An Introduction*. Chicago: Moody Press.

Crompton, David. 1976. "Homosexuals and the Death Penalty in Colonial America." *Journal of Homosexuality* 1(3): 277–293.

Cronin, Helena. 1991. *The Ant and the Peacock*. Cambridge, UK: Cambridge University Press.

Crooks, Claire, Katreena Scott, David Wolfe, Debbie Chiodo, and Steve Killip. 2007. "Understanding the Link Between Childhood Maltreatment and Violent Delinquency: What Do Schools Have to Add?" *Child Maltreatment* 12(3): 269–280.

Cullen, Francis, Cheryl Jonson, and Daniel Nagin. 2011. "Prisons Do Not Reduce Recidivism: The High Cost of Ignoring Science." *The Prison Journal* 9(3): 485–655.

Curley, Edwin. 2007. "On Becoming a Heretic." In *Philosophers Without Gods*, edited by Louise Antony. New York: Oxford University Press.

Currie, Elliott. 1968. "Crimes Without Criminals: Witchcraft and Its Control in Renaissance Europe," *Law and Society Review* 3(1): 7–32.

Currie, Elliott. 1998. *Crime and Punishment in America*. New York: Owl Books.

Davidov, Maayan, Carolyn Zahn-Waxler, Ronit Roth-Hanania, and Ariel Knafo. 2013. "Concern for Others in the First Year of Life: Theory, Evidence, and Avenues for Research." *Child Development Perspectives* 7(2): 126–131.

Davies, R. W., and Stephen Whearcroft. 2004. *The Years of Hunger: Soviet Agriculture, 1931–1933*. Basingstoke, UK: Palgrave Macmillan.

Davis, Angela. 2003. *Are Prisons Obsolete?* New York: Seven Stories Press.

Dawkins, Richard. 2006. *The God Delusion*. New York: Houghton Mifflin.

Dawkins, Richard. 2015. *The Blind Watchmaker*. New York: W. W. Norton and Company.

Decety, J., and M. Svetlova. 2012. "Putting Together Phylogenetic and Ontogenetic Perspectives on Empathy." *Developmental Cognitive Neuroscience* 2: 1–24.

De Dreu, Carsten, Lindred Greer, Michale Handgraaf, Shaul Shalvi, Gerben Van Kleef, Matthijs Baas, Femke Ten Velden, Eric Van Dijk, and Sander Feith. 2010. "The Neuropeptide Oxytocin Regulates Parochial Altruism in Intergroup Conflict Among Humans." *Science* 328(5984): 1408–1411.

Delaney, Carol. 1998. *Abraham on Trial: The Social Legacy of Biblical Myth*. Princeton, NJ: Princeton University Press.

DeLeeuw, J., L. Galen, C. Aebersold, and V. Stanton. 2007. "Support for Animal Rights as a Function of Belief in Evolution and Religious Fundamentalism." *Animals and Society* 15: 353–363.

Dennett, Daniel. 2007. "Atheism and Evolution." In *The Cambridge Companion to Atheism*, edited by Michael Martin. New York: Cambridge University Press.

De Sousa, Arielle, Skye McDonald, Jacqueline Rushby, Sophie Li, Aneta Dimoska, and Charlotte James. 2011. "Understanding Deficits in Empathy After Traumatic Brain Injury: The Role of Affective Responsivity." *Cortex* 47(5): 526.

De Waal, Frans. 2011. "Prehuman Foundations of Morality." In *The Joy of Secularism*, edited by George Levine. Princeton, NJ: Princeton University Press.

De Waal, Frans. 2013. *The Bonobo and the Atheist*. New York: W. W. Norton.

Dezutter, J., B. Soenes, K. Luyckx, S. Bruyneel, M. Vantsenkiste, B. Duriez, and D. Hutsebaut. 2009. "The Role of Religion in Death Attitudes: Distinguishing Between Religious Belief and Style of Processing Religious Contents." *Death Studies* 33: 73–92.

DiCarlo, Christopher. 2010. "We Are All African! Can Scientific Proof of Our Commonality Save Us?" *Free Inquiry* 30(4): 18–22.

Didyoung, J., E. Charles, and N. J. Rowland. 2013. "Non-Theists Are No Less Moral Than Theists: Some Preliminary Results." *Secularism and Nonreligion* 2: 1–20.

Domes, Gregor. 2007. "Oxytocin Improves 'Mind-Reading' in Humans." *Biological Psychiatry* 61(6): 731–733.

Dovidio, J. F., S. L. Gaertner, and T. Saguy. 2009. "Commonality and the Complexity of 'We': Social Attitudes and Social Change." *Personality and Social Psychology Review* 13: 3–20.

Drake, Elizabeth, Steve Aos, and Marna Niller. 2009. "Evidence-Based Public Policy Options to Reduce Crime and Criminal Justice Costs: Implications in Washington State." *Victims and Offenders* 4: 170–196.

Dray, Philip. 2002. *At the Hands of Persons Unknown: The Lynching of Black America*. New York: The Modern Library.

Dreier, James. 2006. "Moral Relativism and Moral Nihilism." In *The Oxford Handbook of Ethical Theory*, edited by David Copp. New York: Oxford University Press.

Dreisinger, Baz. 2016. *Incarceration Nations*. New York: Other Press.

Drumbl, Mark A. 2012. "'She Makes Me Ashamed to Be a Woman': The Genocide Conviction of Pauline Nyiramasuhuko, 2011." *Michigan Journal of International Law* 34(3): 559–604.

D'Souza, Dinesh. 2007. *What's So Great About Christianity?* Washington, D.C.: Regnery.

Du Bois, W. E. B. 1907. "The Value of Agitation." *The Voice of the Negro*, vol. IV: 109–110. In Phil Zuckerman, editor, *The Social Theory of W. E. B. Du Bois*, edited by Phil Zuckerman. 2004. Thousand Oaks, CA: Pine Forge.

Duke, A., L. Begue, R. Bell, and T. Eisenlohr-Moul. 2013. "Revisiting the Serotonin-Aggression Relation in Humans: A Meta-Analysis." *Psychological Bulletin* (139)5: 1148–1172.

Durkheim, Émile. 1982 [1895]. *The Rules of Sociological Method*. New York: Free Press.

Durkheim, Émile. 1984 [1893]. *The Division of Labor in Society*. New York: Free Press.

Dworkin, Ronald. 1996. "Objectivity and Truth: You'd Better Believe It." *Philosophy and Public Affairs* 25(2): 87–139.

Ebstein, R., S. Israel, E. Lerer, F. Uzefosky, I. Shalev, I. Gritsenko, M. Riebold, S. Salomon, and N. Yirmiya. 2009. "Arginine, Vasopressin, and Oxytocin Modulate Human Social Behavior." *Annals of the New York Academy of Sciences* 1167: 87–102.

Ecklund, Elaine Howard. 2012. *Science vs. Religion: What Scientists Really Think*. New York: Oxford University Press.

Einhorn, Eric, and John Logue. 2003. *Modern Welfare States: Scandinavian Politics and Policy in the Global Age*. Westport, CT: Praeger.

Eisinga, Rob, Albert Felling, and Jan Peters. 1990. "Religious Belief, Church Involvement, and Ethnocentrism in the Netherlands." *Journal for the Scientific Study of Religion* 29(1): 54–75.

Eitzen, D. Stanley. 2009. *Solutions to Social Problems: Lessons from Other Societies.* London: Pearson.

Elgar, Frank, and Nicole Aitken. 2010. "Income Inequality, Trust, and Homicide in 33 Countries." *European Journal of Public Health* 21(2): 241–246.

Eller, David. 2004. *Natural Atheism.* Cranford, NJ: American Atheist Press.

Eller, Jack David. 2010. *Cruel Creeds, Virtuous Violence: Religious Violence Across Culture and History.* Amherst, NY: Prometheus Books.

Eller, Jack David. 2010. "What Is Atheism?" In *Atheism and Secularity*, edited by Phil Zuckerman. Santa Barbara, CA: Praeger.

Ellis, Lee. 2002. "Denominational Differences in Self-Reported Delinquency." *Journal of Offender Rehabilitation* 35: 179–192.

Ellison, Christopher, and Darren Sherkat. 1993. "Obedience and Autonomy: Religion and Parental Values Reconsidered." *Journal for the Scientific Study of Religion* 32: 313–329.

Emde, R. N., Z. Biringen, R. Clyman, and D. Oppenheim. 1991. "The Moral Self of Infancy: Affective Core and Procedural Knowledge." *Developmental Review* 11: 251–270.

Emerson, Michael, and Christian Smith. 2000. *Divided by Faith.* New York: Oxford University Press.

English, D. J., C. S. Widom, and C. Brandford. 2002. "Childhood Victimization and Delinquency, Adult Criminality, and Violent Criminal Behavior: A Replication and Extension." Final Report to NIJ: www.ncjrs.gov/pdffiles1/nij/grants/192291.pdf.

Epley, Nicholas, Benjamin A. Converse, Alexa Delbosc, George A. Monteleone, and John T. Cacioppo. 2009. "Believers' Estimates of God's Beliefs Are More Egocentric Than Estimates of Other People's Beliefs." *Proceedings of the National Academy of Sciences of the United States of America* 106(51): 21533–21538.

Evans, David, and Mike Adams. 2003. "Salvation or Damnation? Religion and Correctional Ideology." *American Journal of Criminal Justice* 28(1): 15–35.

Fajnzylber, Pablo, Daniel Lederman, and Norman Loayza. 2002. "Inequality and Violent Crime." *Journal of Law and Economics* XLV: 1–40.

Falcioni, Ryan. 2016. "Secularism and Morality." In *Religion: Beyond Religion*, edited by Phil Zuckerman. Farmington Hills, MI: Macmillan Reference USA.

Fazel, S., and J. Danesh. "Serious Mental Disorder in 23,000 Prisoners: A Systematic Review of 62 Surveys." *Lancet* 359: 545–550.

Feitosa, Saulo Ferreira, Volnei Garrafa, Gabriele Cornelli, Carla Tardivo, and Samuel Jose de Carvalho. 2010. "Bioethics, Culture and Infanticide in Brazilian Indigenous Communities: The Zuruahá Case." *Cadernos de Saúde Pública* 26(5): 853–878.

Feuerbach, Ludwig. 1989 [1841]. *The Essence of Christianity*. Amherst, NY: Prometheus Books.

Fiala, Andrew. 2007. *What Would Jesus Really Do?* Lanham, MD: Rowman and Littlefield.

Fiala, Andrew. 2013. *Against Religion, Wars, and States*. Lanham, Maryland: Rowman and Littlefield.

Firat, Rengin, and Chad Michael McPherson. 2013. "Toward an Integrated Science of Morality: Linking Mind, Society, and Culture." In *Handbook of the Sociology of Morality*, edited by Steven Hitlin and Stephen Vaisey. New York: Springer.

Flake, Kathleen. 2004. *The Politics of American Religious Identity*. Chapel Hill, NC: University of North Carolina Press.

Flanagan, Owen. 2017. *The Geography of Morals*. New York: Oxford University Press.

Fone, Byrne. 2001. *Homophobia: A History*. New York: Picador.

Foster, Lawrence. 1984. *Religion and Sexuality*. Urbana: University of Illinois Press.

Frazier, Jessica. 2013. "Hinduism." In *The Oxford Handbook of Atheism*, edited by Stephen Bullivant and Michael Ruse. Oxford: Oxford University Press.

Freedman, D., and D. Hemenway. 2000. "Precursors of Lethal Violence: A Death Row Sample." *Social Science Medicine* 50: 1757–1770.

Froese, Paul. 2008. *The Plot to Kill God*. Berkeley, CA: University of California Press.

Froese, Paul, Christopher Bader, and Buster Smith. 2008. "Political Tolerance and God's Wrath in the United States." *Sociology of Religion* 69(1): 29–44.

Gale, Richard. 2007. "The Failure of Classical Theistic Arguments." In *The Cambridge Companion to Atheism*, edited by Michael Martin. New York: Cambridge University Press.

Galen, Luke. 2015. "Atheism, Wellbeing, and the Wager: Why Not Believing in God (with Others) Is Good for You." *Science, Religion and Culture* 2(3): 54–69.

Galen, Luke, and J. Kloet. 2011. "Mental Well-being in the Religious and the Non-religious: Evidence for a Curvilinear Relationship." *Mental Health, Religion, and Culture* 14: 673–689.

Garcia, R., and N. King, eds. 2009. *Is Goodness Without God Good Enough?* New York: Rowman and Littlefield.

Gay, D., and C. Ellison. 1993. "Religious Subcultures and Political Tolerance: Do Denominations Still Matter?" *Review of Religious Research* 34: 311–332.

Geach, Peter. 1969. *God and the Soul*. London: Routledge & Kegan Paul.

Gershoff, Elizabeth. 2010. "More Harm Than Good: A Summary of Scientific Research on the Intended and Unintended Effects of Corporal Punishment on Children." *Law and Contemporary Problems* 73(2): 31–56.

Gershoff, E. T. 2002. "Corporal Punishment by Parents and Associated Child Behaviors and Experiences: A Meta-Analytic and Theoretical Review." *Psychological Bulletin* 128: 539–579.

Gert, Bernard. 2004. *Common Morality: Deciding What to Do*. New York: Oxford University Press.

Gervais, Will, and Maxine Najle. 2017. "How Many Atheists Are There?" *Social Psychological and Personality Science* 9(1): 3–10.

Gervais, W. M., A. F. Shariff, and A. Norenzayan. 2011. "Do You Believe in Atheists? Distrust Is Central to Anti-Atheist Prejudice." *Journal of Personality and Social Psychology* 101(6): 1189–1206.

Getz, I. 1984. "Moral Judgment and Religion: A Review of the Literature." *Counseling and Values* 28: 94–116.

Gilligan, James. 2001. *Preventing Violence*. New York: Thames and Hudson.

Ginsburg, Faye. 1989. *Contested Live: The Abortion Debate in an American Community*. Berkeley, CA: University of California Press.

Glick, P. 2002. "Sacrificial Lambs Dressed in Wolves' Clothing: Envious Prejudice, Ideology, and the Scapegoating of Jews." In *Understanding Genocide: The Social Psychology of the Holocaust*, edited by L. S. Newman and R. Erber. New York: Oxford University Press.

Glick, P. 2005. "Choice of Scapegoats." In *On the Nature of Prejudice: 50 Years After Allport*, edited by J. F. Dovidio, P. Glick, & L. A. Rudman. Malden, MA: Blackwell Publishing.

Goff, Phillip, Jennifer Eberhardt, Melissa Williams, and Matthew Jackson. 2008. "Not Yet Human: Implicit Knowledge, Historical Dehumanization, and Contemporary Consequences." *Journal of Personality and Social Psychology* 94(2): 292–306.

Goldhagen, Daniel. 1996. *Hitler's Willing Executioners: Ordinary Germans and the Holocaust*. New York: Vintage.

Goldman, Emma. 1916. "The Philosophy of Atheism." In *The Portable Atheist*, edited by Christopher Hitchens. 2007. Cambridge, MA: Da Capo Press.

Gordon, Sarah Berringer. 2002. *The Mormon Question: Polygamy and Constitutional Conflict in Nineteenth-Century America*. Chapel Hill, NC: University of North Carolina Press.

Gordon, Shira. 2014. "Solitary Confinement, Public Safety, and Recidivism." *University of Michigan Journal of Law Reform* 47(2): 495–528.

Graham, J., and J. Haidt. 2010. "Beyond Beliefs: Religions Bind Individuals into Moral Communities." *Personality and Social Psychology Review* 14(1): 140–150.

Grant, Tobin. 2011. "Patriotism God Gap: Is the U.S. the Greatest Country in the World?" www.christianitytoday.com/news/2011/august/patriotism-god-gap-is-us-greatest-country-in-world.html.

Granzberg, Gary. 1973. "Twin Infanticide—A Cross-Cultural Test of a Materialistic Explanation." *Ethos* 1(4): 405–412.

Grassian, Stuart. 2006. "Psychiatric Effects of Solitary Confinement." *Washington University Journal of Law and Policy* 22: 325–383.

Grayling, A. C. 2013. "Critiques of Theistic Arguments." In *The Oxford Handbook of Atheism*, edited by Stephen Bullivant and Michael Ruse. Oxford: Oxford University Press.

Grayling, A. C. 2013. *The God Argument*. New York: Bloomsbury.

Greeley, Andrew, and Michael Hout. 2006. *The Truth About Conservative Christians: What They Think and What They Believe*. Chicago: University of Chicago Press.

Greene, Joshua. 2013. *Moral Tribes: Emotion, Reason, and the Gap Between Us and Them*. New York: Penguin Press.

Grim, Patrick. 2007. "Impossibility Arguments." In *The Cambridge Companion to Atheism*, edited by Michael Martin. New York: Cambridge University Press.

Guth, James, John Green, Lyman Kellstedt, and Corwin Smidt. 2005. "Faith and Foreign Policy: A View from the Pews." *Review of Faith and International Affairs* 3: 3–9.

Haapasalo, Jaana, and Elina Pokela. 1999. "Child-Rearing and Child Abuse Antecedents of Criminality." *Aggression and Violent Behavior* 4(1): 107–127.

Haberland, Nicole, and Deborah Rogow. 2015. "Sexuality Education: Emerging Trends in Evidence and Practice." *Journal of Adolescent Health* 56(1): 15–21.

Haidt, Jonathan. 2012. *The Righteous Mind: Why Good People are Divided by Politics and Religion*. New York: Vintage.

Hall, D. L., D. C. Matz, and W. Wood. 2010. "Why Don't We Practice What We Preach? A Meta-Analytic Review of Religious Racism." *Personality and Social Psychology Review* 14, 126–139.

Hamil-Luker, Jenifer, and Christian Smith. 1998. "Religious Authority and Public Opinion on the Right to Die." *Sociology of Religion* 59(4): 373–391.

Hamilton, R. F. 1968. "A Research Note on the Mass Support for 'Tough' Military Initiatives." *American Sociological Review* 33: 439–445.

Hamlin, J. Kiley, Karen Wynn, Paul Bloom, and Neja Mahajan. 2011. "How Infants and Toddlers React to Antisocial Others." *PNAS* 108(50): www.pnas.org/content/108/50/19931.

Haney, Craig. 2003. "Mental Health Issues in Long-Term Solitary and 'Supermax' Confinement." *Crime and Delinquency* 49(1): 124–156.

Haraldsson, Erlendur. 2006. "Popular Psychology, Belief in Life After Death and Reincarnation in the Nordic Countries, Western and Eastern Europe." *Nordic Psychology* 58(2): 171–180.

Harris, Sam. 2006. *Letter to a Christian Nation*. New York: Knopf.

Harris, Sam. 2010. *The Moral Landscape*. New York: Free Press.

Harrison, Guy P. 2008. *50 Reasons People Give for Believing in God*. Amherst, NY: Prometheus Books.

Hassig, Ross. 1988. *Aztec Warfare: Imperial Expansion and Political Control*. Norman: University of Oklahoma Press.

Hastings, Adrian. 1997. *The Construction of Nationhood: Ethnicity, Religion and Nationalism*. New York: Cambridge University Press.

Hatzfeld, Jean. 2000. *Life Laid Bare: The Survivors in Rwanda Speak*. New York: Other Press.

Hauser, Marc. 2006. *Moral Minds: The Nature of Right and Wrong*. New York: Harper Perennial.

Hayes, Bernadette. 1995. "Religious Identification and Moral Attitudes: The British Case." *British Journal of Sociology* 46: 457–474.

Hecht, Jennifer Michael. 2003. *Doubt: A History*. San Francisco: Harper Perennial.

Heckman, James. 2017. *Giving Kids a Fair Chance*. Boston: MIT Press.

Hedges, Chris. 2006. *American Fascists: The Christian Right and the War on America*. New York: Free Press.

Hemenway, David. 2006. *Private Guns, Public Health*. Ann Arbor, MI: University of Michigan Press.

Henggeler, Sciott, et al. 1996. "Multisystemic Therapy: An Effective Violence Prevention Approach for Serious Juvenile Offenders." *Journal of Adolescence* 19(1): 47–61.

Herskovits, Melville. 1958. "Some Further Comments on Cultural Relativism." *American Anthropologist* 60(2): 266–273.

Hinton, Alexander Laban. 2005. *Why Did They Kill? Cambodia in the Shadow of Genocide*. Berkeley, CA: University of California Press.

Hinton, Alexander. 1998. "Why Did You Kill? The Cambodian Genocide and the Dark Side of Face and Honor." *Journal of Asian Studies* 57: 93–122.

Hinton, Alexander Laban, ed. 2013. *Hidden Genocides: Power, Knowledge, and Memory*. Newark, NJ: Rutgers University Press.

Hitchens, Christopher, ed. 2007. *The Portable Atheist: Essential Readings for the Nonbeliever*. Cambridge, MA: Da Capo Press.

Hitchens, Christopher. 2012. *The Missionary Position: Mother Teresa in Theory and Practice*. New York: Twelve.

Hitlin, Steven. 2008. *Moral Selves, Evil Selves: The Social Psychology of Conscience*. New York: Palgrave Macmillan.

Hoeve, Machteld, Geert Jan Stams, Claudia van der Put, Judith Semon Dubas, Peter van der Laan, and Jasn Gerris. 2012. "A Meta-Analysis of Attachment to Parents and Delinquency." *Journal of Abnormal Child Psychology* 40 (5): 771–785.

Hoffman, J., and A. Miller. 1997. "Social and Political Attitudes Among Religious Groups: Convergence and Divergence Over Time." *Journal for the Scientific Study of Religion* 36: 52–70.

Hoffman, Martin. 2000. *Empathy and Moral Development*. New York: Cambridge University Press.

Holloway, Richard. 1999. *Godless Morality: Keeping Religion Out of Ethics*. Edinburgh, UK: Canongate.

Holmes, Leslie. 2009. *Communism: A Very Short Introduction*. New York: Oxford University Press.

Holmes, Robert. 2007. *Basic Moral Philosophy*. Belmont, CA: Wadsworth.

Hood, Ralph, Peter Hill, and Bernard Spilka. 2009. *The Psychology of Religion: An Empirical Approach*. New York: The Guilford Press.

Horwitz, Tony. 2011. *Midnight Rising: John Brown and the Raid That Sparked the Civil War*. New York: Picador, Henry Holt and Co.

Hrdy, Sarah Blaffer. 2009. *Mothers and Others: The Evolutionary Origins of Mutual Understanding*. Cambridge, MA: Belknap Harvard Press.

Hsieh, Ching-Chi, and M. D. Pugh. 1993. "Poverty, Income Inequality, and Violent Crime: A Meta-Analysis of Recent Aggregate Data Studies." *Criminal Justice Review* 18(2): 182–202.

Hume, David. 1985 [1738]. *A Treatise of Human Nature*. New York: Penguin Books.

Hunsberger, Bruce, and Bob Altemeyer. 2006. *Atheists: A Groundbreaking Study of America's Nonbelievers*. Amherst, NY: Prometheus Books.

Hunsberger, Bruce, B. McKenzie, and M. Pratt. 1993. "Religious Doubt: A Social Psychological Analysis." *Research in the Social Scientific Study of Religion* 5: 27–51.

Hyman, Gavin. 2010. *A Short History of Atheism*. London: Tauris.

Jackson, Elton, et al. 1995. "Volunteering and Charitable Giving: Do Religious and Associational Ties Promote Helping Behavior?" *Nonprofit and Voluntary Sector Quarterly* 24(1; Spring).

Jackson, Lynne, and Bruce Hunsberger. 1999. "An Intergroup Perspective on Religion and Prejudice." *Journal for the Scientific Study of Religion* 38(4): 509–523.

Jacoby, Susan. 2004. *Freethinkers: A History of American Secularism*. New York: Henry Holt.

Jensen, Gary. 2006. "Religious Cosmologies and Homicide Rates Among Nations: A Closer Look." *Journal of Religion and Society* 8: 1–14.

Johnson, B. C. 1981. *The Atheist Debater's Handbook*. Amherst, NY: Prometheus Books.

Johnson, Brian. 2008. *W. E. B. Du Bois: Toward Agnosticism, 1868–1934*. Lanham, Maryland: Rowman and Littlefield.

Johnson, Byron. 2012. *More God, Less Crime: Why Faith Matters and How It Could Matter More*. West Conshohocken, PA: Templeton Press.

Johnson, Dale, and Todd Walker. 1987. "Primary Prevention of Behavior Problems in Mexican-American Children." *American Journal of Community Psychology* 15(4): 375–385.

Jones, Adam. 2006. *Genocide: A Comprehensive Introduction*. New York: Routledge.

Jonson, C. L. 2010. "The Impact of Imprisonment of Reoffending: A Meta-Analysis." Unpublished doctoral dissertation, University of Cincinnati, Ohio.

Joshi, S. T. 2000. *Atheism: A Reader*. Amherst, NY: Prometheus Books.

Joyce, Richard. 2006. *The Evolution of Morality*. Cambridge, MA: MIT Press.

Kapoor, Suneera, and Shrawan Singh. 2005. "Gandhi and Nehru on Religion." *The Indian Journal of Political Science* 66(3): 503–514.

Karski, Jan. 2010. *Story of a Secret State: My Report to the World*. Washington, D.C.: Georgetown University Press.

Keen, Suzanne. 2007. *Empathy and the Novel*. New York: Oxford University Press.

Kekes, John. 2014. *How Should We Live?* Chicago: University of Chicago Press.

Keysar, Ariela, and Barry Kosmin. 2008. *Secularism and Science in the 21st Century*. Hartford, CT: ISSSC.

Keysar, Ariela, and Juhem Navarro-Rivera. 2013. "A World of Atheism: Global Demographics." In *The Oxford Handbook of Atheism*, edited by Stephen Bullivant and Michael Ruse. Oxford: Oxford University Press.

Kierkegaard, Søren. 1986 [1843]. *Fear and Trembling*. New York: Penguin Classics.

King, Iain. 2008. *How to Make Good Decisions and Be Right All the Time: Solving the Riddle of Right and Wrong*. London: Continuum.

King, Martin Luther, Jr. 1963. *Strength to Love*. New York: Harper and Row.

Klug, Petra. 2018. "Anti-Atheism in the United States." Doctoral dissertation, University of Bremen, Germany.

Knafo, A., C. Zahn-Waxler, C. Van Hulle, J. Robinson, and S. Rhee. 2008. "The Developmental Origins of a Disposition Toward Empathy: Genetic and Environmental Contributions." *Emotions* 7: 737–752.

Ko, Dorothy. 2005. *Cinderella's Sisters: A Revisionist History of Footbinding*. Berkeley: University of California Press.

Kochanska, Grazyna. 2002. "Mutually Responsive Orientation Between Mothers and Their Young Children: A Context for the Early Development of Conscience." *Current Directions in Psychological Science* 11(6): 191–195.

Koenig, H. 1995. "Religion and Older Men in Prison." *International Journal of Geriatric Psychiatry* 10: 219–230.

Kosfeld, Michael, M. Heinrichs, P. J. Zak, U. Fischbacher, and E. Fehr. "Oxytocin Increases Trust in Humans." *Nature* 435(7042): 673–676.

Kottak, Conrad Philip. 2000. *Anthropology: The Exploration of Human Diversity*. Boston: McGraw Hill.

Kurtz, Paul. 2008. *Forbidden Fruit: The Ethics of Secularism*. Amherst, NY: Prometheus Press.

Ladd, John. 1985. *Ethical Relativism*. Lanham, Maryland: University Press of America.

Laible, D. J., and R. Thompson. 2000. "Mother-Child Discourse Attachment Security, Shared Positive Affect, and Early Conscience Development." *Child Development* 71: 1424–1440.

Lakey, George. 2016. *Viking Economics*. Brooklyn: Melville House.

Langan, P., and D. Levin. 2002. "Recidivism of Prisoners Released in 1994." Washington, D.C.: Bureau of Justice Statistics, U.S. Department of Justice.

Lansford, Jennifer, Shari Miller-Johnson, Lisa Berlin, Kenneth Dodge, John Bates, and Gregory Pettit. 2007. "Early Physical Abuse and Later Violent Delinquency: A Prospective Longitudinal Study." *Child Maltreatment* 12(3): 233–245.

Lappi-Seppala, Tapio. 2012. "Penal Policies in the Nordic Countries 1960–2010." *Journal of Scandinavian Studies in Criminology and Crime Prevention* 13(1): 85–111.

Law, Stephen. 2006. *The War for Children's Minds*. London: Routledge.

Law, Stephen. 2013. "What Is Humanism?" In *The Oxford Handbook of Atheism*, edited by Stephen Bullivant and Michael Ruse. Oxford: Oxford University Press.

Lee, Jongsoo. 2008. *The Allure of Nezahualcoyotl: Pre-Hispanic History, Religion, and Nahua Poetics*. Albuquerque, NM: University of New Mexico Press.

Le Poidevin, Robin. 2010. *Agnosticism: A Very Short Introduction*. New York: Oxford University Press.

Levy, Neil. 2002. *Moral Relativism: A Short Introduction*. Oxford: Oneworld.

Lewy, Guenter. 1964. *The Catholic Church and Nazi Germany*. New York: McGraw-Hill.

Lewy, Guenter. 2008. *If God Is Dead, Everything Is Permitted?* New Brunswick, NJ: Transaction.

Lindeman, Marjana, Annika M. Svedholm-Häkkinen, and Tapani Riekki. 2016. "Skepticism: Genuine Unbelief or Implicit Beliefs in the Supernatural?" *Consciousness and Cognition* 42: 261–228.

Lindenbaum, Shirley. 1979. *Kuru Sorcery: Disease and Danger in the New Guinea Highlands*. Palo Alto, CA: Mayfield Publishing.

Linneman, Thomas, and M. Clendenen. 2010. "Sexuality and the Sacred." In *Atheism and Secularity*, edited by Phil Zuckerman, vol. 1, 89–112. Santa Barbara, CA: Prager ABC-CLIO.

Liow, Joseph Chinyong. 2016. *Religion and Nationalism in Southeast Asia*. New York: Cambridge University Press.

Loftus, John. 2008. *Why I Became an Atheist*. Amherst, NY: Prometheus Books.

Loveland, Matthew, Alexander Capella, and India Maisonet. 2017. "Prosocial Skeptics: Skepticism and Generalized Trust." *Critical Research on Religion* 5(3): 251–265.

Lukes, Steven. 2008. *Moral Relativism*. New York: Picador.

Lukes, Steven. 2013. "The Social Construction of Morality?" *Handbook of the Sociology of Morality*, edited by Steven Hitlin and Stephen Vaisey. New York: Springer.

Lykken, D. T. 1995. *The Antisocial Personalities*. Hillsdale, NJ: Lawrence Erlbaum.

Maccoby, E. E. 1999. "The Uniqueness of the Parent-Child Relationship." In *Minnesota Symposia on Child Psychology*, vol. 30, *Relationships as Developmental Contexts*, edited by W. A. Collins and B. Laursen, 157–175. Hillsdale, NJ: Erlbaum.

MacIntyre, Alasdair. 1998 [1966]. *A Short History of Ethics*. London: Routledge.

Mackie, J. L. 1977. *Ethics: Inventing Right and Wrong*. New York: Penguin.

Mackie, J. L. 1983. *The Miracle of Theism: Arguments For and Against the Existence of God*. New York: Oxford University Press.

MacKinnon, Barbara, and Andrew Fiala. 2015. *Ethics: Theory and Contemporary Issues*. Stamford, CT: Cengage.

Mahajan, Neha, and Karen Wynn. 2012. "Origins of 'Us' versus 'Them': Prelinguistic Infants Prefer Similar Others." *Cognition* 124: 227–233.

Malik, Kenan. 2014. *The Quest for a Moral Compass: A Global History of Ethics*. Brooklyn: Melville House.

Mallicoat, Stacy. 2017. *Crime and Criminal Justice: Concepts and Controversies*. Los Angeles: SAGE.

Marino, Gordon, ed. 2010. *Ethics: The Essential Writings*. New York: Modern Library.

Markoe, Lauren. 2013. "Evangelicals Top Religious Patriotism; Believe in American Exceptionalism, Poll." www.huffingtonpost.com/2013/07/04/religious-patriotism-_n_3545537.html.

Martin, Michael. 1990. *Atheism: A Philosophical Justification*. Philadelphia: Temple University Press.

Martin, Michael. 1991. *The Case Against Christianity*. Philadelphia: Temple University Press.

Martin, Michael. 2002. *Atheism, Morality, and Meaning*. Amherst, NY: Prometheus.

Marx, Karl. 1994 [1852]. *The Eighteenth Brumaire of Louis Bonaparte*. New York: International Publishers.

Mason, Patrick. 2011. *The Mormon Menace: Violence and Anti-Mormonism in the Postbellum South*. New York: Oxford University Press.

Maxfield, M. G., and C. S. Widom. 1996. "The Cycle of Violence Revisited Six Years Later." *Archives of Pediatric and Adolescent Medicine* 150: 390–395.

Mayo, Bernard. 1986. *The Philosophy of Right and Wrong*. London: Routledge and Kegan Paul.

McCaffree, Kevin. 2015. *What Morality Means: An Interdisciplinary Synthesis for the Social Sciences*. New York: Palgrave Macmillan.

McClain, E. 1978. "Personality Differences Between Intrinsically Religious and Non-religious Students: A Factor Analytic Study." *Journal of Personality Assessment* 42: 159–166.

Mehta, Hemant. 2013. "What Percentage of Prisoners Are Atheists? It's a Lot Smaller Than We Ever Imagined." www.patheos.com/blogs/friendlyatheist/2013/07/16/what-percentage-of-prisoners-are-atheists-its-a-lot-smaller-than-we-ever-imagined.

Mehta, Hemant. 2015. "Atheists Now Make Up 0.1% of the Federal Prison Population." www.patheos.com/blogs/friendlyatheist/2015/08/21/atheists-now-make-up-0-1-of-the-federal-prison-population.

Mersky, Joshua, and Arthur Reynolds. 2007. "Child Maltreatment and Violent Delinquency: Disentangling Main Effects and Subgroup Effects." *Child Maltreatment* 12(3): 246–258.

Midgley, Mary. 1991. *Can't We Make Moral Judgements?* New York: St. Martin's Press.

Milgram, Stanley. 2009. *Obedience to Authority: An Experimental View.* New York: Harper Perennial Modern Classics.

Miller, Donald, and Lorna Touryan Miller. 1993. *Survivors: An Oral History of the Armenian Genocide.* Berkeley, CA: University of California Press.

Moore, David. 2003. *The Dependent Gene: The Fallacy of "Nature vs. Nurture."* New York: Henry Holt.

Moreland, J. and William Lane Craig. 2003. *Philosophical Foundations for a Christian Worldview.* Downers Grove, IL: InterVarsity Press.

Morhenn, V., J. Park, E. Piper, and P. Zak. 2008. "Monetary Sacrifice Among Strangers Is Mediated by Endogenous Oxytocin Release After Physical Contact." *Evolution and Human Behavior* 29: 375–383.

Morris, Celia. 1984. *Fanny Wright: Rebel in America*. Cambridge, MA: Harvard University Press.

Nagel, Thomas. 1987. *What Does It All Mean?* New York: Oxford University Press.

Najle, Maxine, and Will Gervais. 2016. "Dislike of and Discrimination Against Atheists and Secular People." In *Religion: Beyond Religion*, edited by Phil Zuckerman. Farmington Hills, MI: Gale-Cengage-Macmillan.

Nall, Jeff. 2012. "Disparate Destinations, Parallel Paths: An Analysis of Contemporary Atheist and Christian Parenting Literature." In *Religion and the New Atheism*, edited by Amarnath Amarasignam. Chicago: Haymarket Books.

Narvaez, D., I. Getz, J, Rest, and S. Thoma. 1999. "Individual Moral Judgment and Cultural Ideologies." *Developmental Psychology* 35: 478–488.

Nehru, Jawaharlal. 1941. *Toward Freedom: The Autobiography of Jawaharlal Nehru.* New York: The John Day Company.

Neimeyer, R., J. Wittkowski, and R. Moser. 2004. "Psychological Research on Death Attitudes: An Overview and Evaluation." *Death Studies* 28: 309–340.

Newman, Oscar. 1972. *Defensible Space: Crime Prevention Through Urban Design.* New York: Macmillan.

Nielsen, Kai. 1990. *Ethics Without God.* Amherst, NY: Prometheus Books.

Nielsen, Kai. 1996. *Naturalism Without Foundations.* Amherst, NY: Prometheus Books.

Nieuwbeerta, P., D. Nagin, and A. Blokland. 2009. "The Relationship Between First Imprisonment and Criminal Career Development: A Matched Samples Comparison." *Journal of Qualitative Criminology* 25: 227–257.

Noddings, Nel. 2013. *Caring*. Berkeley: University of California Press.

Nordstrom, Byron. 2000. *Scandinavia Since 1500*. Minneapolis: University of Minnesota Press.

Nuland, Sherwin. 2004. *The Doctors' Plague: Germs, Childbed Fever, and the Strange Story of Ignac Semmelweis*. New York: W. W. Norton and Co.

Nussbaum, Martha. 1999. *Sex and Social Justice*. New York: Oxford University Press.

Nye, Bill. 2015. *Undeniable: Evolution and the Science of Creation*. New York: St. Martin's Griffin.

Olds, David, J. Echenrode, C. R. Henderson, H. Kitzman, J. Powers, R. Cole, K. Sidora, P. Morris, L. M. Pettitt, and D. Luckey. 1997. "Long-term Effects of Home Visitation on Maternal Life Course and Child Abuse and Neglect: Fifteen-Year Follow-up of a Randomized Trial." *Journal of the American Medical Association* 278(8): 637–643.

Olds, David, Charles R. Henderson, Harriet Kitzman, and Robert Cole. 1995. "Effects of Prenatal and Infancy Nurse Home Visitation on Surveillance of Child Maltreatment." *Pediatrics* 95(3): 365–372.

Olsen, Greg. 2011. *Power and Inequality*. New York: Oxford.

Olusoga, David. 2011. *The Kaiser's Holocaust: Germany's Forgotten Genocide and the Colonial Roots of Nazism*. London: Faber and Faber.

Oppy, Graham. 2013. "Arguments for Atheism." In *The Oxford Handbook of Atheism*, edited by Stephen Bullivant and Michael Ruse. New York: Oxford University Press.

Orenstein, David, and Linda Ford Blaikie. 2015. *Godless Grace: How Nonbelievers are Making the World Safer, Richer, and Kinder*. Washington, D.C.: Humanist Press.

Parenti, Michael. 2010. *God and His Demons*. Amherst, NY: Prometheus Books.

Parfit, Derek. 1984. *Reasons and Persons*. New York: Oxford University Press.

Partanen, Anu. 2016. *The Nordic Theory of Everything: In Search of a Better Life*. New York: HarperCollins.

Patterson, Meagan, and Rebecca Bigler. 2006. "Preschool Children's Attention to Environmental Messages About Groups: Social Categorization and the Origins of Intergroup Bias." *Child Development* 77(4): 847–860.

Paul, Gregory. 2005. "Cross-National Correlations of Quantifiable Societal Health with Popular Religiosity and Secularism in the Prosperous Democracies." *Journal of Religion and Society* 7: 1–17.

Pearce, M., J. Singer, and H. Prigerson. 2006. "Religious Coping Among Caregivers of Terminally Ill Cancer Patients: Main Effects and Psychosocial Mediators." *Journal of Health Psychology* 11: 743–759.

Pepper, M., T. Jackson, and D. Uzzell. 2010. "A Study of Multidimensional Religion Constructs and Values in the United Kingdom," *Journal for the Scientific Study of Religion* 49: 127–146.

Petersen, L., and G. V. Donnenworth. 1998. "Religion and Declining Support for Traditional Beliefs About Gender Roles and Homosexual Rights." *Sociology of Religion* 59: 353–371.

Pettit, Michelle, and Michael Kroth. 2011. "Educational Services in Swedish Prisons: Successful Programs of Academic and Vocational Teaching." *Criminal Justice Studies* 24(3): 215–226.

Pfaff, Donald. 2015. *The Altruistic Brain: How We Are Naturally Good.* New York: Oxford University Press.

Phelps, Andrea, Paul Maciejewski, Matthew Nillson, and Tracy Balboni. 2009. "Association Between Religious Coping and Use of Intensive Life-Prolonging Care Near Death Among Patients with Advanced Cancer." *JAMA* 301(11): 1140–1147.

Pianciola, Niccolò. 2001. "The Collectivization Famine in Kazakhstan, 1931–1933." *Harvard Ukrainian Studies* 25(3–4): 237–251.

Piazza, Jared. 2012. "If You Love Me Keep My Commandments: Religiosity Increases Preference for Rule-Based Moral Arguments." *International Journal for the Psychology of Religion* 22: 285–302.

Piazza, Jared, and J. Landy. 2013. "Lean Not on Your Own Understanding: Belief That Morality Is Founded on Divine Authority and Non-utilitarian Moral Judgments." *Judgement and Decision Making* 8: 639–661.

Pincus, Jonathan. 2001. *Base Instincts: What Makes Killers Kill?* New York: W. W. Norton.

Pinker, Steven. 2011. *The Better Angels of Our Nature: Why Violence Has Declined.* New York: Penguin.

Pinker, Steven. 2018. *Enlightenment Now: The Case for Reason, Science, Humanism, and Progress.* New York: Viking.

Plantinga, Alvin. 2011. "Comments on 'Satanic Verses: Moral Chaos in Holy Writ.'" In *Divine Evil? The Moral Character of the God of Abraham*, edited by Michael Bergmann, Michael J. Murray, and Michael C. Rea, 109–114. Oxford: Oxford University Press.

Pojman, Louis. 2004. *The Moral Life.* Oxford: Oxford University Press.

Prichard, H. A., and Jim MacAdam. 2002. *Moral Writings.* Clarendon Press.

Preston, J., and R. Ritter. 2013. "Different Effects of Religion and God on Prosociality with the Ingroup and Outgroup." *Personality and Social Psychology Bulletin* 39: 1471–1483.

Prothrow-Stith, Deborah, and Howard Spivak. 2004. *Murder Is No Accident: Understanding and Preventing Youth Violence in America*. San Francisco, CA: Jossey-Bass.

Prunier, Gerald. 1995. *The Rwanda Crisis: History of a Genocide*. New York: Columbia University Press.

Putnam, Robert, and David Campbell. 2010. *American Grace: How Religion Divides and Unites Us*. New York: Simon and Schuster.

Quinn, Philip. 2006. "Theological Volunteerism." In *The Oxford Handbook of Ethical Theory*, edited by David Copp. New York: Oxford University Press.

Rabaka, Reiland. 2008. *Du Bois's Dialectics*. Lanham, MD: Lexington Books.

Rapetti, Pierre, ed. 1850. *Li Livres de Jostice et de plet*. Paris: Firmen Didot Frères.

Reader, Ian. 2012. "Secularisation, R.I.P.? Nonsense! The 'Rush Hour Away from the Gods' and the Decline of Religion." *Journal of Religion in Japan* 1(1): 7–36.

Reiss, S. 2000. "Why People Turn to Religion: A Motivational Analysis." *Journal for the Scientific Study of Religion* 39: 47–52.

Rey, Georges. 2007. "Meta-Atheism: Religious Avowal and Self-Deception." In *Philosophers Without Gods*, edited by Louise Antony. New York: Oxford University Press.

Rhodes, R. 1999. *Why They Kill*. New York: Knopf.

Riddley, Matt. 1996. *The Origins of Virtue: Human Instincts and the Evolution of Cooperation*. New York: Penguin.

Rivera, B., and C. S. Widom. 1990. "Childhood Victimization and Violent Offending." *Violence Victims* 5: 19–35.

Rizvi, Ali. 2016. *The Atheist Muslim*. New York: St. Martin's Press.

Robinson, Richard. 1964. *An Atheist's Values*. Oxford: Clarendon Press.

Roccas, S. 2005. "Religion and Value Systems." *Journal of Social Issues* 61: 747–759.

Rodrigues, Luis. 2010. *Open Questions: Diverse Thinkers Discuss God, Religion, and Faith*. Santa Barbara, CA: Praeger.

Romm, Joseph. 2015. *Climate Change: What Everyone Needs to Know*. Oxford: Oxford University Press.

Roth-Hanania, Ronit, Maayan Davidov, and Carolyn Zahn-Waxler. 2011. "Empathy Development from 8 to 16 Months: Early Signs of Concern for Others." *Infant Behavior and Development* 34: 447–458.

Rothschild, Zachary, Abdolhossein Abdollahi, and Tom Pyszczynski. 2009. "Does Peace Have a Prayer? The Effect of Mortality Salience, Compassionate Values, and Religious Fundamentalism on Hostility Toward Out-Groups." *Journal of Experimental Social Psychology* 45: 816–827.

Rowe, David, Alexander Vazsonyi, and Daniel Flannery. 1995. "Sex Differences in Crime: Do Means and Within-Sex Variation Have Similar Causes?" *Journal of Research in Crime and Delinquency* 32(1): 84–100.

Royle, Edward. 1974. *Victorian Infidels: The Origins of the British Secularist Movement, 1791–1866*. Manchester, UK: Rowman and Littlefield.

Royle, Edward. 1980. *Radicals, Secularists and Republicans: Popular Freethought in Britain, 1866–1915*. Manchester, UK: Rowman and Littlefield.

Rummel, R. J. 1997. *Death by Government: Genocide and Mass Murder Since 1900*. New York: Routledge.

Ruse, Michael. 2015. *Atheism: What Everyone Needs to Know*. New York: Oxford University Press.

Russell, Bertrand. 1927. *Why I Am Not a Christian*. New York: Touchstone.

Sagan, Carl, and Ann Druyan. 2007. *The Varieties of Scientific Experience: A Personal View of the Search for God*. New York: Penguin.

Sagioglou, Christina, and Matthias Forstmann. 2013. "Activating Christian Religious Concepts Increases Intolerance of Ambiguity and Judgment Certainty." *Journal of Experimental Social Psychology* 49: 933–939.

Santelli, John, et al. 2017. "Abstinence-Only-Until-Marriage: An Updated Review of U.S. Policies and Programs and Their Impact." *Journal of Adolescent Health* 61(3): 273–280.

Sapolsky, Robert. 2017. *Behave: The Biology of Humans at Our Best and Worst*. New York: Penguin Press.

Saroglou, V. 2002. "Religion and the Five Factors of Personality: A Meta-analytic Review." *Personality and Individual Difference* 32: 15–25.

Sartre, Jean-Paul. 1993 [1943]. *Being and Nothingness*. New York: Washington Square Press.

Sartre, Jean-Paul. 2007 [1945]. *Existentialism Is a Humanism*. New Haven, CT: Yale University Press.

Saslow, Laura, Robb Willer, Matthew Feinberg, and Paul Piff. 2013. "My Brother's Keeper? Compassion Predicts Generosity More Among Less Religious Individuals." *Social Psychological and Personality Science* 4(1): 31–38.

Scanlon, T. M. 2000. *What We Owe to Each Other*. Cambridge, MA: Belknap Press.

Scheff, Thomas. 1991. Microsociology: *Discourse, Emotion, and Social Structure*. Chicago: University of Chicago Press.

Schwartz, Jonathan, and Lori Lindley. 2005. "Religious Fundamentalism and Attachment: Prediction of Homophobia." *The International Journal for the Psychology of Religion* 15(2): 145–157.

Schwartz, Laura. 2015. *Infidel Feminism: Secularism, Religion and Women's Emancipation, England 1830–1914.* Manchester, UK: Manchester University Press.

Selner, O'Hagan, Daniel Kindlon, Stephen Buka, Stephen Raudenbush, and Felton Earls. 1998. "Assessing Exposure to Violence in Urban Youth." *Journal of Child Psychology and Psychiatry* 39(2): 215–224.

Senesh, Hannah. 2007 [1941]. *Her Life and Diary.* Nashville, TN: Jewish Lights.

Shamay-Tsoory, S. G., R. Tomer, B. D. Berger, and J. Aharon-Peretz. 2003. "Characterization of Empathy Deficits Following Prefrontal Brain Damage: The Role of the Right Ventromedial Prefrontal Cortex." *Journal of Cognitive Neuroscience* 15(3): 324–337.

Shapiro, Stewart. 2007. "Faith and Reason, the Perpetual War: Ruminations of a Fool." In *Philosophers Without Gods,* edited by Louise Antony. New York: Oxford University Press.

Sherif, Muzafer, O. J. Harvey, B. Jack White, William R. Hood, Carolyn W. Sherif. 1961. *The Robbers Cave Experiment: Intergroup Conflict and Cooperation.* Middletown, CT: Wesleyan University Press.

Sherkat, Darren. 2011. "Religion and Scientific Literacy in the United States." *Social Science Quarterly* 92(5): 1134–1148.

Sherkat, Darren. 2014. *Changing Faith: The Dynamics and Consequences of Americans' Shifting Religious Identities.* New York: New York University Press.

Sherkat, Darren, M. Powell-Williams, G. Maddox, and K. de Vries. 2011. "Religion, Politics, and Support for Same-Sex Marriage in the United States, 1988–2008." *Social Science Research* 40: 167–180.

Shermer, Michael. 2004. *The Science of Good and Evil.* New York: Owl Books.

Shermer, Michael. 2015. *The Moral Arc.* New York: Henry Holt.

Shin, Sunny, Amo Cook, Nancy Morris, Ribyn McDougle, and Lauren Peasley Groves. 2016. "The Different Faces of Impulsivity as Links Between Childhood Maltreatment and Young Adult Crime." *Preventive Medicine* 88: 201–217.

Short, James. 1997. *Poverty, Ethnicity, and Violent Crime.* Boulder, CO: Westview Press.

Singer, Peter. 1981. *The Expanding Circle: Ethics, Evolution, and Moral Progress.* Princeton, NJ: Princeton University Press.

Singer, Peter. 2009 [1975]. *Animal Liberation.* San Francisco: HarperCollins.

Singer, Peter. 2016. *Ethics in the Real World.* Princeton, NJ: Princeton University Press.

Sinnott-Armstrong, Walter. 2009. *Morality Without God?* New York: Oxford University Press.

Sloan, R., E. Bagiella, and T. Powell. 1999. "Religion, Spirituality, and Medicine." *Lancet* 353: 664–667.

Slote, Michael. 2006. "Moral Sentimentalism and Moral Psychology." In *The Oxford Handbook of Ethical Theory*, edited by David Copp. New York: Oxford University Press.

Smidt, Corwin. 2005. "Religion and American Attitudes Toward Islam and an Invasion of Iraq." *Sociology of Religion* 66(3): 243–261.

Smith, Carolyn, and Terence Thornberry. 1995. "The Relationship Between Childhood Maltreatment and Adolescent Involvement in Delinquency." *Criminology* 33(4): 451–481.

Smith, David Livingstone. 2011. *Less Than Human: Why We Demean, Enslave, and Exterminate Others*. New York: St. Martin's Press.

Smith, Dolores. 2017. "Homophobic and Transphobic Violence Against Youth: The Jamaican Context." *International Journal of Adolescence and Youth* 23(2): 250–258.

Smith, Dwayne, and Margaret Zahn, eds. 1999. *Studying and Preventing Homicide: Issues and Challenges*. Thousand Oaks, CA: SAGE.

Smith, George. 1989. *Atheism: The Case Against God*. Amherst, NY: Prometheus Books.

Smith, Ken. 1995. *Ken's Guide to the Bible*. New York: Blast Books.

Smith, P. 2006. "The Effects of Incarceration on Recidivism: A Longitudinal Examination of Program Participation and Institutional Adjustment in Federally Sentenced Adult Male Offenders." Unpublished doctoral dissertation, University of New Brunswick, Canada.

Snarey, John. 1996. "The Natural Environment's Impact upon Religious Ethics: A Cross-Cultural Study." *Journal for the Scientific Study of Religion* 35(2): 85–96.

Sober, Elliott, and David Sloan Wilson. 1998. *Unto Others: The Evolution and Psychology of Unselfish Behavior*. Cambridge, MA: Harvard University Press.

Sorrentino, Richard. 2017. *The Uncertain Mind: Individual Differences in Facing the Unknown*. Philadelphia: Psychology Press.

Sperlich, Peter. 2011. "Atheists, Anti-atheists, and Nazis—Once Again." *Free Inquiry* 31(1): 51–52.

Spiegel, James. 2012. *The Making of an Atheist: How Immorality Leads to Unbelief*. Chicago: Moody Publishers.

Spohn, C., and D. Holleran. 2002. "The Effect of Imprisonment on Recidivism Rates of Felony Offenders: A Focus on Drug Offenders." *Criminology* 40: 329–347.

Starks, Brian, and Robert Robinson. 2005. "Who Values the Obedient Child

Now? The Religious Factor in Adult Values for Children, 1986–2002." *Social Forces* 84(1): 343–359.

Staub, Ervin. 1989. *The Roots of Evil: The Origins of Genocide and Other Group Violence*. New York: Cambridge University Press.

Staub, Ervin. 2011. *Overcoming Evil: Genocide, Violent Conflict, and Terrorism*. New York: Oxford University Press.

Steigman-Gall, R. 2003. *The Holy Reich: Nazi Conceptions of Christianity, 1919–1945*. New York: Cambridge University Press.

Stein, Arlene. 2006. *Shameless: Sexual Dissidence in American Culture*. New York: New York University Press.

Stein, Rebecca, and Philip Stein. 2010. *The Anthropology of Religion, Magic, and Witchcraft*. New York: Routledge.

Steitz, Victoria. 1990. "Intervention Programs for Impoverished Children: A Comparison of Educational and Family Support Models." *Annals of Child Development* 7: 84–87.

Stenger, Victor. 2006. "Do Our Values Come from God? The Evidence Says No." *Free Inquiry* 26(5): 42–45.

Stenger, Victor. 2008. *God: The Failed Hypothesis*. Amherst, NY: Prometheus Books.

Stephens, Mitchell. 2014. *Imagine There's No Heaven: How Atheism Helped Create the Modern World*. New York: Palgrave Macmillan.

Sterzer, Philip, Christian Stadler, Fritz Poutzska, and Andreas Kleinschmidt. 2007. "A Structural Neural Deficit in Adolescents with Conduct Disorder and Its Association with Lack of Empathy." *NeuroImage* 37(1): 335–342.

Stevenson, Charles. 1963. "The Emotive Meaning of Ethical Terms." *Mind* 46(181): 14–31.

Stewart, Matthew. 2014. *Nature's God: The Heretical Origins of the American Republic*. New York: W. W. Norton.

Stone, Alison. 2013. "Existentialism." In the *Oxford Handbook of Atheism*, edited by Stephen Bullivant and Michael Ruse. Oxford: Oxford University Press.

Straus, Scott. 2016. *Fundamentals of Genocide and Mass Atrocity Prevention*. Washington, D.C.: United States Holocaust Memorial and Museum.

Streib, H., R. Hood, B. Keller, R. Csöff, and C. Silver. 2009. *Deconversion: Qualitative and Quantitative Results from Cross-Cultural Research in Germany and the United States of America*. Göttingen, Germany: Vandenhoek and Ruprecht.

Tajfel, Henri, M. G. Billig, and R. P. Bundy. 1971. "Social Categorization and Intergroup Behavior." *European Journal of Social Psychology* 1(2): 149–178.

Tan, Sor-Hoon. 2007. "Secular Ethics, East and West." In *The Oxford Handbook of Secularism*, edited by Phil Zuckerman and John Shook. New York: Oxford University Press.

Tangney, June, Jeff Stuewig, and Debra Mashek. 2007. "Moral Emotions and Moral Behavior." *Annual Review of Psychology* 58: 345–372.

Tännsjö, Torbjörn. 2013. *Understanding Ethics*. Edinburgh, UK: Edinburgh University Press.

Taylor, Kenneth. 2007. "Without the Net of Providence: Atheism and the Human Adventure." In *Philosophers Without Gods*, edited by Louise Antony. New York: Oxford University Press.

Teehan, John. 2017. "Ethics, Secular and Religious: An Evolved-Cognitive Analysis." In *The Oxford Handbook of Secularism*, edited by Phil Zuckerman and John Shook. New York: Oxford University Press.

Thomas, Herbert. 1995. "Experiencing a Shame Response as a Precursor to Violence." *Bulletin American Academy of Psychiatry and Law* 23(4): 587–592.

Thomas, William, and Dorothy Thomas. 1928. *The Child in America: Behavior Problems and Programs*. New York: Knopf.

Thomassen, Einar. 2009. "Islamic Hell." *Numen: International Review for the History of Religions* 56: 401–416.

Thrower, James. 2000. *Western Atheism: A Short History*. Amherst, NY: Prometheus Books.

Tillich, Paul. 1948. *The Shaking of the Foundations*. New York: Charles Scribner's Sons.

Tillich, Paul. 1951. *Systematic Theology*, vol. 1. Chicago: University of Chicago Press.

Tobian, Aaron, and Ronald Gray. 2011. "The Medical Benefits of Male Circumcision." *JAMA* 306(13): 1479–1480.

Trout, J. D. 2009. *The Empathy Gap: Building Bridges to the Good Life and the Good Society*. New York: Viking.

Turner, Jonathan. 2013. "Natural Selection and the Evolution of Morality in Human Societies." *Handbook of the Sociology of Morality*, edited by Steven Hitlin and Stephen Vaisey. New York: Springer.

Underwood, Lori, and Dawn Hutchinson. 2017. *The Global Status of Women and Girls*. Lanham, Maryland: Lexington Books.

Valentino, Benjamin. 2000. "Final Solutions: The Causes of Mass Killing and Genocide." *Security Studies* 9(3): 1–59.

Van der Veer, Peter. 1994. *Religious Nationalism: Hindus and Muslims in India*. Berkeley and Los Angeles: University of California Press.

Van Pachterbeke, M., C. Freyer, and V. Saroglou. 2011. "When Authoritarianism

Meets Religion: Sacrificing Others in the Name of Abstract Deontology." *European Journal of Social Psychology* 41: 898–903.

Velleman, J. David. 2013. *Foundations for Moral Relativism*. Cambridge: Open Book Publishers.

Verma, Vidhu. 2017. "Secularism in India." In *The Oxford Handbook of Secularism*, edited by Phil Zuckerman and John Shook. New York: Oxford University Press.

Vissing, Y. M., M. A. Straus, R. J. Gelles, and J. W. Harrop. 1991. "Verbal Aggression by Parents and Psychosocial Problems of Children." *Child Abuse and Neglect* 15: 223–238.

Vonnegut, Kurt. 1969. *Slaughterhouse Five*. New York: Delacorte.

Wakefield, Eva Ingersoll, ed. 1951. *The Letters of Robert Ingersoll*. New York: Philosophical Library.

Waller, James. 2002. *Becoming Evil: How Ordinary People Commit Genocide and Mass Killing*. New York: Oxford University Press.

Walters, Kerry. 2010. *Atheism: A Guide for the Perplexed*. London: Continuum.

Waraken, Felix, and Michael Tomasello. 2006. "Altruistic Helping in Human Infants and Young Chimpanzees." *Science* 311(5765): 1301–1303.

Watson, Lyall. 1997. *Dark Nature: A Natural History of Evil*. San Francisco: Harper Perennial.

Watson, P. J., Z. Chen, N. Ghorbani, and M. Vartanian. 2015. "Religious Openness Hypothesis: I. Religious Reflection, Schemas, and Orientations Within Religious Fundamentalist and Biblical Foundationalist Ideological Surrounds." *Journal of Psychology and Christianity* 34(2): 99–113.

Watson, P. J., Z. Chen, R. Morris, and E. Stephensen. 2015. "Religious Openness Hypothesis: III. Defense Against Secularism Within Fundamentalist and Biblical Foundationalist Ideological Surrounds." *Journal of Psychology and Christianity* 34(2): 125–140.

Watson, P. J., Z. Chen, and R. W. Hood. 2011. "Biblical Foundationalism and Religious Reflection: Polarization of Faith and Intellect Oriented Epistemologies Within a Christian Ideological Surround." *Journal of Psychology and Theology* 39(2): 111–121.

Watson, P. J., Z. Chen, and R. Morris. 2014. "Varieties of Quest and the Religious Openness Hypothesis Within Religious Fundamentalist and Biblical Foundationalist Ideological Surrounds." *Religions* 5: 1–20.

Wattles, Jeffrey. 1996. *The Golden Rule*. New York: Oxford University Press.

Weisberger, Andrea. 2007. "The Argument from Evil." In *The Cambridge Companion to Atheism*, edited by Michael Martin. New York: Cambridge University Press.

White, Ronald. 2013. "Notes to Self." *Harper's Magazine* 336: 49–52.

Whitehead, Alfred North. 1978. *Process and Reality*. New York: The Free Press.

Whitehead, Andrew, and Joseph Baker. 2012. "Homosexuality, Religion, and Science: Moral Authority and the Persistence of Negative Attitudes." *Sociological Inquiry* 82: 487–509.

Whitehead, Andrew, Samuel Perry, and Joseph Baker. 2018. "Make America Christian Again: Christian Nationalism and Voting for Donald Trump in the 2016 Presidential Election." *Sociology of Religion* 79(2): 147–171.

Whitmarsh, Tim. 2015. *Battling the Gods: Atheism in the Ancient World*. New York: Alfred Knopf.

Widom, Cathy. 1989. "Child Abuse, Neglect, and Violent Criminal Behavior." *Criminology* 27(2): 251–271.

Widom, Cathy. 1989. "The Cycle of Violence," *Science* 244: 160–166.

Widom, Cathy, and Michael Maxfield. 2001. "An Update on the 'Cycle of Violence.'" Washington, D.C.: National Institute of Justice.

Wielenberg, Erik. 2014. *Robust Ethics: The Metaphysics and Epistemology of Godless Normative Realism*. New York: Oxford University Press.

Wilkinson, Richard, and Kate Pickett. 2009. *The Spirit Level: Why Greater Equality Makes Societies Stronger*. New York: Bloomsbury Press.

Wilson, David Sloan. 2015. *Does Altruism Exist? Culture, Genes, and the Welfare of Others*. New Haven, CT: Yale University Press.

Wolf, Susan. 1982. "Moral Saints." *Journal of Philosophy* 79: 419–439.

Wong, David. 2006. *Natural Moralities: A Defense of Pluralistic Relativism*. New York: Oxford University Press.

Wood, Forrest. 1990. *The Arrogance of Faith: Christianity and Race in America from the Colonial Era to the Twentieth Century*. New York: Knopf.

Wood, Roger, and Claire Williams. 2008. "Inability to Empathize Following Traumatic Brain Injury." *Journal of the International Neuropsychological Society* 14(2): 289–296.

Wulff, David. 1991. *Psychology of Religion: Classic and Contemporary Views*. New York: Wiley.

Yerkes, R. M. 1925. *Almost Human*. New York: Century.

Yoshikawa, Hirokazu. 1995. "Long-Term Effects of Early Childhood Programs on Social Outcomes and Delinquency." *The Future of Children* 5(3): 51–75.

Zak, Paul. 2011. "The Physiology of Moral Sentiments." *Journal of Economic Behavior and Organization* 77: 53–65.

Zak, Paul. 2012. *The Moral Molecule: How Trust Works*. New York: Penguin.

Zubrzycki, Genevieve. 2010. "Religion and Nationalism: A Critical Re-

Examination." In *The New Blackwell Companion to the Sociology of Religion*, edited by Bryan Turner. West Sussex, UK: Blackwell Publishing.

Zuckerman, Phil, ed. 2004. *The Social Theory of W. E. B. Du Bois*. Thousand Oaks, CA: Pine Forge.

Zuckerman, Phil. 2008. *Society Without God: What the Least Religious Nations Can Teach Us About Contentment.* New York: New York University Press.

Zuckerman, Phil. 2009. "Atheism, Secularity, and Well-being: How the Findings of Social Science Counter Negative Stereotypes and Assumptions." *Sociology Compass* 3(6): 949–971.

Zuckerman, Phil. 2009. "The Irreligiosity of W. E. B. Du Bois." In *The Souls of W. E. B. Du Bois*, edited by Edward Blum and Jason Young. Macon, GA: Mercer University Press.

Zuckerman, Phil. 2012. *Faith No More: Why People Reject Religion*. New York: Oxford University Press.

Zuckerman, Phil. 2013. "Atheism and Societal Health." In *The Oxford Handbook of Atheism*, edited by Stephen Bullivant and Michael Ruse. Oxford: Oxford University Press.

Zuckerman, Phil. 2014. *Living the Secular Life*. New York: Penguin.

Zuckerman, Phil, Luke Galen, and Frank Pasquale. 2016. *The Nonreligious: Understanding Secular People and Secular Societies*. New York: Oxford University Press.

© Scott Phillips

PHIL ZUCKERMAN is the author of several books, including *The Nonreligious*, *Living the Secular Life*, and *Society Without God*. He is a professor of sociology at Pitzer College and the founding chair of the nation's first secular studies program. He lives in Claremont, California, with his wife and three children.